OXFORD MONOGRAPHS

BORN FOR THE MUSES

DATE DUE

Frontispiece: Portrait of Jacob Obrecht, by an unknown Flemish master (1496)

BORN FOR THE MUSES

THE LIFE AND MASSES OF JACOB OBRECHT

Rob C. Wegman

CLARENDON PRESS · OXFORD

OX2 6DP

am
Delhi Florence Hong Kong Istanbul Karachi
Kuala Lumpur Madras Madrid Melbourne
Mexico City Nairobi Paris Singapore
Taipei Tokyo Toronto
and associated companies in
Berlin Ibadan

Oxford is a trade mark of Oxford University Press

Published in the United States by
Oxford University Press Inc., New York

© Rob C. Wegman 1994

First published 1994
Paperback edition 1996

British Library Cataloguing in Publication Data
Data available

Library of Congress Cataloging in Publication Data
Data available
ISBN 0–19–816650–8

10 9 8 7 6 5 4 3 2 1

Printed in Great Britain by
Biddles Ltd, Guildford and King's Lynn

PRELUDE

¹Let us now praise famous men, and our fathers that begat us. ²The Lord hath wrought great glory by them through his great power from the beginning. ³Such as did bear rule in their kingdoms, men renowned for their power, giving counsel by their understanding, and declaring prophecies: ⁴Leaders of the people by their counsels, and by their knowledge of learning meet for the people, wise and eloquent in their instructions: ⁵Such as found out musical tunes, and recited verses in writing: ⁶Rich men furnished with ability, living peaceably in their habitations: ⁷All these were honoured in their generations, and were the glory of their times. (Ecclus. 44: 1–7.)

In his *Complexus effectuum musices* of *c.*1480 Johannes Tinctoris cited the fifth and seventh of these verses to demonstrate the nineteenth effect of music: *musica peritos in ea glorificat*, it glorifies those skilled in it. To exemplify the point he went on, after citing several classical examples, to list ten composers who were known for having won musical glory in his time—beginning with Dunstable, Dufay, and Binchois, continuing with Ockeghem, Busnoys, and their contemporaries, and ending finally with a man mentioned nowhere else in his writings: Iacobus Obrechts (Ch. 3).

Tinctoris's recognition of Obrecht comes at such a remarkably early date—the composer was in his early twenties at the time—that one almost overlooks how he missed the point of the passage cited. For it is not so much about glory (whether achieved through musical skills or through leadership) as about *remembrance*. And in this respect Tinctoris does indeed seem to have missed the point. 'If I may refer to what I have heard and seen,' he wrote in the preface to his *Liber de arte contrapuncti* (1477), 'I have formerly held in my hands several old songs of unknown authorship called apocrypha, so absurdly, so awkwardly composed that they much sooner offended the ears than pleased them.' Undoubtedly the composers of these works had once been the glory of their times, yet Tinctoris, like everyone else in his time, could not bring himself to remember their names and recount their glories, let alone to take their music seriously.

This, obviously, is the reverse side of his remarkable readiness to hail the young Obrecht as the latest musical prodigy. 'For Time', as Shakespeare made Ulysses say in *Troilus and Cressida*, 'is like a fashionable host,

That slightly shakes his parting guest by th'hand; And with his arms out-stretch'd, as he would fly, Grasps in the comer' (III. iii. 165–8). The truth of this would eventually catch up with Obrecht, too. For whatever musical glory he had won by the late 1470s (apart from the survival of *Lacen adieu* in a source dating *c.*1480, Tinctoris remains our only testimony), scarcely three decades later he had himself become the parting guest, Josquin the comer.

Yet Tinctoris was unable to imagine that Obrecht, or any of the other nine composers listed in the *Complexus*, could ever become the parting guests of time. For him they had not just won glory 'in our time', but by their exceptional virtue had gained 'immortal fame'. In so confidently predicting their future reception, the theorist envisaged the future of music simply as an unchanging prolongation of his present. How could future generations possibly look upon his time as he looked upon the composers of the 'apocrypha'? How could they possibly perceive Obrecht's music in any other way than he himself perceived it: as exhaling the utmost sweetness (*summa dulcedo*) and being worthy of the highest praises (*summae laudes*)? How could any generation ever come to think of itself as having progressed beyond this summit of musical perfection? In this inability to historicize his present, Tinctoris directly parallels the poet Martin le Franc, who in 1440–2 had invoked the current state of perfection in music (the 'nouvelle pratique' of Dufay and Binchois) to demonstrate that the End of Time was imminent.

It is precisely Ben Sira's call for remembrance that might have led Tinctoris to take a more historical interest in mensural polyphony, to recover and study the 'apocrypha' with the same zeal that led humanists around him in Naples to recover and study ancient texts. When the theorist did write something that might be called a general history of music, in the preface to his *Proportionale musices* (1472–3), his narrative was structured, in typical medieval fashion, on the three key events of the Creation, Christ's Incarnation ('that greatest musician . . . who made [God and man] one in duple proportion'), and the Second Coming. Within this thoroughly medieval conception of history Tinctoris revealed his humanistic bias when speaking of ancient Greek musicians: 'Nevertheless, we know hardly anything about how they might have performed or composed in writing, although it is most probable that they did this in the most elegant manner.' The same benefit of the doubt was not subsequently given to composers of a more recent musical past, all of whom were ignored up to Dunstable—despite the wealth of primary source material (including the 'apocrypha') to which the theorist must have had access.

Yet this is not the whole picture. In a different sense the fifteenth century showed itself extremely sensitive to the words of Ben Sira. In the verses following those cited at the beginning, the author pauses for one brief moment to contemplate what lies beyond remembrance: the fathomless void of oblivion.

⁸There be of them, that have left a name behind them, that their praises might be reported. ⁹And some there be, which have no memorial; who are perished, as though they had never been; and are become as though they had never been born; and their children after them.

These seem the words of a man who has despaired (and perhaps still does) at the human powerlessness to halt the perpetual slipping away of memories, the memories that give meaning to our lives, into nothingness. Yet the fifteenth century did not despair. It found consolation in the 'blanket commemoration' of all souls, for whom even the little choirboys in Ghent said their prayers every day (Ch. 2). And those with sufficient means could afford to have their names, and those of their loved ones, kept in perpetual memory in endowed prayers and Masses for the dead. Perpetual, that is, until the Day of Judgement, when even those who had perished 'as though they had never been' would rise from their graves, and find the burden of their sins diminished by the commemorations of those who had come after them. Then they would find ultimate consolation: 'And God shall wipe away all tears from their eyes; and there shall be no more death, neither sorrow, nor crying, neither shall there be any more pain: for the former things are passed away' (Rev. 21: 4). Countless foundations, endowments, bequests, donations, and trusts—inspired by this very vision—led to a massive commemoration 'industry', of which the flowering of liturgical polyphony was a direct outgrowth. Within this elaborate system Jacob Obrecht could act as a benefactor (as in *Mille quingentis*, for instance, to ensure the commemoration of his father Willem; Chs. 1 and 5), yet his whole livelihood as a priest and musician depended on his implementing the musical wishes of other benefactors, in the cities of Bergen op Zoom, Cambrai, Bruges, and Antwerp.

That system has almost entirely collapsed, and with it the consolation it offered to those who supported it. (From Tinctoris's point of view, ironically, it would have been we who had missed Ben Sira's point, in having no commemoration culture remotely on the scale of that in his time.) And yet, no century in the modern period has been more painfully aware than ours that the least we can do—must do—for those who are perished 'as though they had never been' is to remember them, to recover and renew their meanings, to keep their history alive in human consciousness. For although the course of time has separated them from the community of the living, the writing of history may allow us to see *ourselves* as part of a wider community, one in which past and present are simultaneously incorporated, and nothing is in principle regarded as lost for all time. The German philosopher of history Hermann Lotze conceived this idea in words that seem almost a direct response to Ben Sira:

The premonition that we will not be lost for the future, that those who have come before us may well have departed from our earthly existence but not from all reality, and that, in however mysterious a manner, the progress of history also takes place for them, this belief alone allows us to speak as we do of a humanity and its history. (Quoted after B. Thomas, *The New Historicism and Other Old-Fashioned Topics* (Princeton, 1991), 110.)

It is in this enlarged sense of the human community that we might wish to read the words of Ben Sira in our secular age. We write music history not just to *commemorate* the famous men 'who found out musical tunes, and recited verses in writing', but to affirm that as members of a wider human community they, and their contemporaries, are still with us. We make Jacob Obrecht and his time 'our own', by walking a precarious middle path between aggressive appropriation of the past and over-conscientious detachment from it (see the Introduction). Only in this sense can Jacob Obrecht and his music become more than names or titles in our history books, and our history books more than obituaries. They live, if we can bring them into our experience, and will constantly renew themselves as they enter more deeply into that experience. That is the adventure of music history: those are the stakes.

ACKNOWLEDGEMENTS

THIS book is a somewhat expanded version of my dissertation *Obrecht in Missa*, which was submitted for the doctoral degree at the University of Amsterdam in January 1993. I have added an Introduction to clarify my methods and working assumptions, and in Chapters 1, 2, and 3 I have incorporated new archival evidence discovered in Ghent since the completion of the thesis in July 1992.

My greatest debt is to my teacher, Chris Maas, for suggesting the topic, securing the funding, helping me to overcome bureaucratic obstacles, providing me with stacks of unpublished material, painstakingly reading the thesis in all its versions, and administering criticism and encouragement in judicious combination. My debt to him is immeasurable, and his influence is evident throughout this book.

The research presented in this study has benefited much from recent work in literary criticism. I have felt a particular affinity with the new historicism, whose stated aim is to grasp simultaneously 'the historicity of texts and the textuality of history'. (For the musicologist this is basically a poststructuralist expansion of Carl Dahlhaus's principle that one should try to see the place of an individual musical work in history by revealing the history contained within the work itself.) The understanding of history and of historical situations as 'textualities' whose meanings we can explore is an extremely powerful one—even if it ultimately undermines my working assumption of musical autonomy (see the Introduction and Ch. 10). Yet that working assumption, so far as I can see, is the only remedy to one of the central problems of the new historicism: that its insistence on synchronic interpretation (or 'thick description') leads to an image of the past in which nothing really happens. Some measure of autonomy must be assumed if we wish to do justice to the diachronic dimension of music history (which is much more pronounced here than it is in literary history), that of change and development. Another important issue is that the concepts, values, and assumptions that we bring to bear on the past are themselves subject to historical change (both today and in the fifteenth century), and should therefore be historicized as much as possible. All these points are elaborated in the Introduction. A second affinity is with the study of narrative as a mode of historical representation. The idea that historical understanding can be conveyed not only through formal types of 'story-telling' (for instance, plot elements on various levels), but through the very structure of the narrative, has been an extremely inspiring one. This point, too, is elaborated in the Introduction. Although my debts are not stated explicitly in the main text, I owe much to the writings of Hayden White, Brook Thomas, and several authors in the collection of essays edited by Aram Veeser.

David Fallows and Reinhard Strohm have read and commented on this book in all stages of its preparation; my interest in music criticism goes back to a happy year spent at Manchester in 1988–9 as an M.Phil. student of David Fallows. Margaret Bent's astonishingly profound insights into the nature and workings of mensural polyphony, which she has shared with me in numerous inspiring discussions at Oxford, have greatly enriched my understanding of Obrecht's music. Bonnie Blackburn and Leofranc Holford-Strevens have selflessly and enthusiastically given me the benefit of their seemingly boundless knowledge and expertise on countless occasions. Daniël Lievois's help in the archives of Ghent has been invaluable; long and fruitful discussions with him have substantially benefited the sections on Willem Obrecht's life in Ghent. Others to whom I am grateful for their comments on chapters of this book include Jaap van Benthem, Willem Elders, Barbara Haggh, Barton Hudson, Keith Polk, and Marcel Zijlstra. In matters of Latin idiom and interpretation I received valuable help from Leofranc Holford-Strevens, Mark Edwards, and Eddie Vetter. Important items of information and references were given to me by Lewis Baratz, Marc Boone, Jeffrey Dean, Polly Fallows, Iain Fenlon, Paula Higgins, Andrew Kirkman, Frans Rikhof, Eugeen Schreurs, Richard Sherr, and Rembrandt Wolpert. Jennifer Bloxam and Barbara Haggh have kindly shared material with me in advance of its publication. The maps and graphs in this book were designed by my brother Ruut Wegman. I am deeply indebted to Bruce Phillips and David Blackwell of Oxford University Press for the efficiency and understanding with which they have guided this book through the printing process.

I also owe thanks to friends and colleagues who brought Obrecht's music to life. The experience of singing *Missa Malheur me bat* with Julie Bray and the Manchester Music Department Choir in 1989 was unforgettable; I still cherish my recording of the concert. During the final stages of the thesis I had the privilege of working together with Gary Cooper and The Dufay Consort in reviving fifteenth-century polyphony and producing a compact disc of Obrecht's *Missa Ave regina celorum*. This experience has proved invaluable, and has benefited this study enormously.

The research for this book was carried out with a research fellowship funded by the Netherlands Organisation for Scientific Research (NWO) in The Hague. During the four years of this fellowship (1987–91), I was hosted by the Music Department at the University of Amsterdam. A British Council Fellowship, and additional financial support from the University of Amsterdam, enabled me to do research at the University of Manchester in 1988–9. I finished the thesis in 1991–2 as a Junior Research Fellow at New College, Oxford (where, by some coincidence, I was scheduled to read the lesson from Ecclus. 44 during an Evensong in October 1992). The Vereniging voor Nederlandse Muziekgeschiedenis kindly allowed me to quote musical examples from the *New Obrecht Edition*; permission to use copyright materials in Pls. 7, 11, 12, and 14 was generously granted by the British Library, the Österreichische National-bibliothek, Vienna, the National Gallery of Art, Washington, DC, and the Gemeentelijke Archiefdienst, Bergen op Zoom, respectively. I also extend my warmest thanks to the City Archive in Ghent, for all their help during my research and for allowing various documents to be reproduced in this book. A *Music & Letters* Award in 1992 enabled me to spend four extremely profitable weeks in the archives in Ghent. Publication of the book was supported by a generous subvention from the Netherlands Organisation for Scientific Research (NWO) in The Hague. I am indebted to all these institutions and organizations for their support.

My wife Heleen van Rossum has helped me on numerous occasions to overcome the chief enemy of this study, writer's block. I wish to dedicate *Born for the Muses* to my parents, Kees and Diny Wegman.

ROB C. WEGMAN

New College, Oxford
29 July 1993

CONTENTS

List of Illustrations

Portrait of Jacob Obrecht, by an unknown Flemish master
(1496)   *frontispiece*

LIST OF FIGURES

LIST OF TABLES

LIST OF MUSIC EXAMPLES

ABBREVIATIONS

CMM   Corpus mensurabilis musicae

MGG   *Die Musik in Geschichte und Gegenwart*

NOE   *New Obrecht Edition*, gen. ed. C. J. Maas (Utrecht, 1983–)

Archives

BAR   Brussels, Algemeen Rijksarchief

CBV   Cambrai, Bibliothèque de la Ville

HAR   The Hague, Algemeen Rijksarchief

LAN   Lille, Archives du Nord

RAG   Ghent, Rijksarchief

SAG   Ghent, Stadsarchief

SJG   Ghent, Archief Sint-Jacob

UBG   Ghent, Universiteitsbibliotheek

Sigla of Manuscripts

AostaS D19   Aosta, Biblioteca del Seminario Maggiore, MS A¹ D 19

BerlS 40021   Berlin, Staatsbibliothek — Preußischer Kulturbesitz, MS Mus. 40021 (*olim* Z 21)

BrusBR 215–16   Brussels, Koninklijke Bibliotheek, MSS 215–16

BrusBR II 270   Brussels, Koninklijke Bibliotheek, MS II 270

EtonC 178   Eton, College Library, MS 178

FlorC 2439   Florence, Biblioteca del Conservatorio di Musica Luigi Cherubini, MS Basevi 2439

JenaU 22   Jena, Universitätsbibliothek, MS 22

LeipU 51	Leipzig, Universitätsbibliothek, MS Thomaskirche 51
LeipU 1494	Leipzig, Universitätsbibliothek, MS 1494
ModE M.1.2	Modena, Biblioteca Estense e Universitaria, MS α. M. 1. 2 (Lat. 457; *olim* VI. H. 1)
MunBS 3154	Munich, Bayerische Staatsbibliothek, Musiksammlung, Musica MS 3154
NapBN 40	Naples, Biblioteca Nazionale, MS VI E 40
RomeC 2856	Rome, Biblioteca Casanatense, MS 2856 (*olim* O. V. 208)
SegC s.s.	Segovia, Archivio Capitular de la Catedral, MS s. s.
SienBC K.1.2	Siena, Biblioteca Comunale degli Intronati, MS K. 1. 2
TrentC 87	Trent, Museo Provinciale d'Arte, Castello del Buon Consiglio, MS 1374 (*olim* 87)
TrentC 91	Trent, Museo Provinciale d'Arte, Castello del Buon Consiglio, MS 1378 (*olim* 91)
TrentC 92	Trent, Museo Provinciale d'Arte, Castello del Buon Consiglio, MS 1379 (*olim* 92)
VatS 15	Vatican City, Biblioteca Apostolica Vaticana, MS Cappella Sistina 15
VatS 35	Vatican City, Biblioteca Apostolica Vaticana, MS Cappella Sistina 35
VatS 51	Vatican City, Biblioteca Apostolica Vaticana, MS Cappella Sistina 51
VatS 160	Vatican City, Biblioteca Apostolica Vaticana, MS Cappella Sistina 160
VatSM 26	Vatican City, Biblioteca Apostolica Vaticana, MS Santa Maria Maggiore 26 (*olim* JJ. III. 4)
VerBC 755	Verona, Biblioteca Capitolare, MS DCCLV
VienNB Mus. 15495	Vienna, Österreichische Nationalbibliothek, Musiksammlung, MS Mus. 15495

NOTE ON CURRENCIES

DOCUMENTS from fifteenth-century Flanders and Brabant mention a confusing array of currencies and coins: Flemish money *groot*, Flemish money *parisis*, Brabant money *groot* (each with its pounds, shillings, and groats or deniers), and various coins like the *Rijnsgulden*, *Davidsgulden*, *stuiver*, *braspenning*, *oortken*, and others. Fortunately, however, all exchange rates in the Burgundian Netherlands were fixed (since 1433). For that reason it makes no particular difference which currency is used in any given document: a treasurer might pay or receive money in one currency, for instance, but he would administer it in another if the latter happened to be the currency chosen for accounting purposes. The choice of accounting currency could vary even between different administrations in the same city. Since the exchange rates were fixed, however, no conceivable purpose is served by preserving such arbitrary variations of accounting in the narrative. Accordingly, amounts cited in the main text (including all translations of documents) have been converted to a common denominator as much as possible.

The common denominator chosen is not a currency but a coin, the Flemish groat (*groot*; gr.). There are 12 groats to the *scelling* (sc.), and 20 *scellingen* to the *pond* (lb.). An amount written as 'ij lb. xj sc. iiij gr.' in the original document will be given as '616 groats' in the translation. Other currencies in the Burgundian Netherlands are similarly converted, according to the fixed exchange rates that had been in use since 1433. In the case of Brabant cities like Bergen op Zoom and Antwerp, where Flemish groats were not used, it will be duly emphasized in the text that amounts cited are only equivalents of the amounts mentioned in the documents. Currencies outside the Burgundian Netherlands, whose exchange rates with the Flemish groat were not fixed, will not be converted, although in most cases some indication will be given of the approximate value in Flemish groats, according to the rate current at the time.

The word 'groot' and its abbreviation 'gr.' were used not only for the coin, but also for the currency as such, usually to distinguish it from Flemish money *parisis*. That is to say, 'sc. gr.' or 'lb. gr.' means shilling or pound in money *groot*, in the same way that 'sc. par.' or 'lb. par.' means shilling or pound in money *parisis*. Potential confusion between Flemish and Brabant money *groot* was usually prevented by using the abbreviations 'vl.' and 'brab.'. The exchange rates were as follows:

1 gr. brab. = 2/3 gr. vl.   1 sc. gr. brab. = 8 gr. vl.   1 lb. gr. brab. = 160 gr. vl.
1 den. par. = 1/12 gr.   1 sc. par. = 1 gr.   1 lb. par. = 20 gr.

It is not possible to give even the most approximate indication of the relative value of medieval money in a modern currency. An important advantage of converting amounts to a common denominator, however, is that one may get a clearer sense of what amounts mean in their own context. Generally speaking, a single adult living in a city like Bruges or Ghent in the late fifteenth century could survive (just) on an income of about one groat per day. Present-day estimates of musicians' incomes are, if anything, likely to be too low, not only because there often was payment *in natura* (loaves, for instance, whose value depended on the wildly fluctuating grain prices, or housing), but also because the total income was usually the accumulation of payments received from several different financial administrations, not all of whose records are likely to have survived. Jacob Obrecht's average working day in Bruges, Antwerp, or Bergen op Zoom, for instance, included a range of duties paid from different accounts (the choristers' foundation, the trust responsible for services in the nave, the church fabric, confraternities, and several smaller trusts). Similarly, Willem Obrecht and his colleagues were almost certainly part-time city trumpeters: their services for the city might not have been needed, on average, on more than one in six days (see Ch. 2).

NOTE ON TITLES AND PROPER NAMES

Her or *heer* is the Flemish counterpart of *dominus* in Latin, *messire* in French, and *don* in Italian, and is the title used for priests. *Meester* similarly is the counterpart of *magister* in Latin, *maistre* in French, and *maestro* in Italian, and indicates the title of master of arts. Both these titles will be left untranslated in the text. However, whenever *heer* is used in the sense of *seigneur* (that is, for a ruler), it will be translated as 'lord'. Similarly, *sanck meester* (literally, song master) will be translated as 'choirmaster', since it denotes a position rather than a title.

Flemish legal sources often add 'filius/filia' plus father's name (in the genitive, with '-s') to the name of an individual: Jacop Hoebrecht *filius* Willems, Marien Laps *filia* Jacops. This is a variant of the more common patronymic form 'Willemssone' or 'Jacopsdochtere', and will also be left untranslated.

Original spellings of names are retained in the translations, but regularized in the narrative. For the spelling of the composer's name I have followed modern convention. Jacob Obrecht wrote his first name as 'Jacobus' in Latin and formal contexts, and might have written it as 'Jacop', 'Jacobe', or 'Jacoppe' in Middle Dutch. (The spelling 'Jacob' was actually quite rare in the Netherlands.) The composer wrote his surname as 'Hobrecht' (the initial 'h' might not have been pronounced), but many other spellings are found in Flemish documents that mention him or his father: Obrecht, Obrechts, Oebrecht, Hoebrecht, Oobrecht, Hoobrecht, Hoobrechts. It would be anachronistic to suppose that the composer would have perceived any of these spellings as somehow less 'correct'. The idea of one authoritative spelling did not exist in the fifteenth century, and modern rules of uniformity in editing and birth registration should not lead us into a misguided purism about names—not even if perceived numerological schemes are at stake.

INTRODUCTION

THIS book is a case-study in late fifteenth-century music history. Its underlying theme is part of a broader one, the transformation of the cyclic mass in the so-called Josquin period, roughly 1480–1520. In textbook terms this is the transition from 'cantus firmus' to 'parody' mass, yet the complex of changes was much broader, and affected a range of interconnected features: techniques of imitation, functional relationships between voices, the modal conception of counterpoint, relative ranges, mensural usage and theory, the matching of music and text, and, least tangible, that intersubjectively perceived quality which we call musical style. The transition, in short, amounted to a complete transformation of the received musical language.

Jacob Obrecht played a key role in the earlier stages of this process—a role probably more important than he has been seen to have in comparison with his near-contemporary Josquin des Prez. Grounds for this suggestion emerge, paradoxically, from a comparison with Josquin. In Obrecht's mass *œuvre* we find conventional Busnoys- and Ockeghem-type cycles, settings that continue existing trends in modified form, as well as works that seem to break with received traditions altogether. Several of these masses have now been dated with confidence, and this allows us to document the break (if such it was) before the early 1490s. As it happens, this is just before the earliest surviving sources for Josquin's masses were copied, and well before the latter's masses begin to survive in any number. That may be coincidence—even granted that the heavy Italian bias of the surviving manuscripts should have favoured Josquin (who was permanently active in Italy) at the expense of Obrecht (who was not). If so, it is probably not the only such coincidence. Before 1500 there are virtually no contemporary statements mentioning Josquin as a composer of any eminence, whereas we have plenty for Obrecht, going back as far as *c.*1480, and, as chance would have it, all but one from Italy.

For the history of mass composition during Obrecht's lifetime this raises an immediate and troubling question. Why is it that Josquin's perceived leadership during the 1480s and 1490s has to be sustained by postulating vagaries of transmission which, it would appear, conspired to obliterate clear evidence of it? How well do we understand the period if we have singled out as its chief protagonist a man who does not clearly stand out as such? One answer quickly suggests itself: the Josquin of the sixteenth century acts as an almost irresistible magnetic force on our understanding of the later fifteenth. After 1500, and particularly after his death in 1521, Josquin became the object of universal veneration as the supreme musical genius of his time. Musicology, from its very beginnings, has tended to perpetuate that tradition rather than investigate it as a historical phenomenon that is part of sixteenth-century reception history. More problematically still, it has extrapolated the tradition back into the fifteenth century, where Josquin's perceived pre-eminence has by now become a mere cliché.

The present study is not the place to review this historiographical article of faith; suffice it to say (and it needs saying) that there has emerged no need to invoke it. To assess Obrecht 'on his own terms' is to disregard the sixteen years that Josquin outlived and eclipsed him, and to suspend all direct comparisons until we know whether they can be made on the same historical terms or not. In view of what has been said above, this unavoidably opens the possibility that Obrecht was, and was widely perceived to be, the more prominent mass composer during his lifetime. The reversal of that situation after his death does not necessarily diminish that possibility, if only because Obrecht himself may have contributed to creating the conditions for that reversal. By the early 1490s he had fundamentally reviewed nearly every aspect of mass style, and the wide distribution of his 'new' masses during the rest of the decade suggests an impact on musical tastes that might at least partly have set the stage for Josquin's breakthrough in the next decade. A suggestive documentary example is provided by the court of Ferrara, where Obrecht's masses had been much sought after in the 1480s and 1490s, and had even been collected in a manuscript anthology, ModE M.1.2, yet whose chapel was 'crowned' (in the words of one ducal agent) with the appointment of Josquin in 1503—a man in whom court sources reveal no interest before 1501.

The nature and subject of the present study should be understood against this background. If we take a 'wide-angle' view of the history of the cyclic mass, it may be perfectly legitimate to speak of 'the Josquin generation', yet if we focus on the period itself, the concept becomes dangerously unhistorical. The 'solar system' notion of one-supreme-master-plus-lesser-contemporaries (which shapes the narrative of most textbooks on Renaissance music history) implies comparisons that may not even be valid for the entire period in question. Obrecht, if categorized as an orbiting member of the generation, emerges as a conservative by virtue of having died sixteen years before Josquin. He might equally well emerge as a progressive by virtue of having died eight years after Ockeghem, and thirteen after Busnoys. To look at the Josquin period with historical eyes, then, is to expose the problematic nature of such comparisons, and to draw new attention to composers for whom the comparison has been particularly inappropriate. That is why this book, being a historical study, focuses on Obrecht, not because there is a need to cover yet another self-contained niche beside Josquin, but because Obrecht was one of the most significant protagonists of his *own* time.

Historical studies typically highlight the continuity and cohesion of events, and this often results in seamless narratives that almost cover up the conceptual problems inherent in their approach. We may object to the 'solar system' model of the Josquin period, yet the musicologist needs other models of interpretation if he wishes to extract historical knowledge from what would otherwise be a mere accumulation of facts. ('Continuity' and 'cohesion' are in fact two such models.) Stated positively, these are the vision that underlies his work; stated negatively, they are his prejudices. Either way, they need to be brought out into the open and subjected to scrutiny.

This is necessary even for the underlying theme of this book, the transformation of the cyclic mass. From the 'wide-angle' view of history one might easily take this for granted as something that just happened, that requires no explanation. Yet for the historian who prefers not to believe in laws of historical inevitability it is a problem. Why did the developments take the course they did? Was that course dictated by the exigencies of the musical material, by aesthetic premises, by musical culture and reception, by society at large, or perhaps by the invention of one individual? How did the fifteenth century value musical change and innovation, as opposed to continuity and tradition? What, in fact, were the aesthetic premises of the time? To what extent are we justified in viewing and comparing masses as autonomous musical creations, and to what extent do we have to consider them in their biographical, social, political, intellectual, and cultural contexts?

In the masses of Jacob Obrecht we have an opportunity to explore these questions. Yet even before the enquiry begins some provisional answers need to be formulated.

A Past without a Music History

Fifteenth-century polyphony, unlike that of the sixteenth, had no perceived history until modern musicology wrote it. The only historical relief to the repertory in circulation, at any given time, was the fading memory of the most recently discarded repertory. Musical style was in this sense intimately historical: the notion of a musical 'essence' that might transcend the bounds of style, and stand apart from history, was foreign to the time. The fifteenth century was unable or uninclined to consider an intrinsic aesthetic value in old compositions whose 'ancient' styles precluded musical value to begin with. To this extent it is true to say that 'modernity' was regarded as an *aesthetic* criterion. Yet unlike its nineteenth-century counterpart, this criterion was not associated with concepts like innovation or originality, which imply a perceived necessity for progress to continue into the future. In the fifteenth century, musical progress was always seen as having already reached its peak in the present, where to be 'novel' or 'modern' was to be seen to confirm the newest tastes. Reflections on the musical past, if they were made at all, were intended to highlight the state of perfection of the present, not to consider the possibility (let alone the historical necessity) of further progress. There were no annals, no chronicles, no histories of mensural polyphony: it is we who perceive the need for them.

How do we view innovation in this context? Fifteenth-century mass composers, so far as we can tell, had no vision of the future of the cyclic mass, and did not innovate with the intention of 'making history'. At most their concern could have been to write a better work for the present than it yet possessed. And they would have considered it better in terms of already existing tastes, not of tastes anticipated in the future. For this reason, innovation could arise only 'unawares' from efforts to capitalize on the state of perfection of the present—which could just as well be the genuinely inspired realization of existing potential as the mindless repetition of a cliché in the hands of a mannerist. It was not a mark of value by itself. However, its antithesis, stagnation, was condemned, at least if it became very obvious that a composer was out of step with the present.

Our models of interpretation must take account of these conditions if we wish to avoid anachronism. Given that change was perceived and valued in the fifteenth century, albeit only after the event, it seems justifiable for us to value it as historically significant. Since change was not pursued for its own sake, however, we have to find other explanations why it did (or did not) come about. Since historical awareness was limited at the time, those explanations, in so far as they assume conscious creative decisions, must be sought in the composer's immediate present and past. We cannot value innovation positively unless we know why it was made, and, more to the point, whether it represented a genuine artistic contribution in terms of the tastes and fashions then current.

Yet anachronism cannot be avoided altogether. We do need recourse to the 'wide-angle' view of music history—particularly to the hindsight that it gives us—for methodological reasons. That is a step fraught with difficulties: hindsight inevitably colours our interpretation of the past, guides our selection of evidence, and shapes our theories. Indeed in many cases (including, as we have seen, that of Josquin's role in the 1480s and 1490s) it might be better for us to do without it. Yet our attitude to hindsight knowledge will always remain an ambivalent one, in the sense that we need it as much as we need to get rid of it. The transformation of the cyclic mass, for instance, is a theme that can be recognized in Obrecht's mass *œuvre* in hindsight, yet the composer himself is unlikely to have perceived any such theme at any time. For that reason, as said above, our attempt must be to recapture and understand the immediate present and past of each creative moment, to reopen its future—in short, to forgo the advantage of hindsight.

That is more easily said than done, however. The masses of most fifteenth-century composers are largely undated, and this means that there are in fact very few fixed moments that one might recapture and understand. It is only with the benefit of hindsight that we can make a considered guess what the other moments are. That is to say, our 'wide-angle' knowledge of long-term developments enables us to identify retrospectively the early and late features in each mass, and these features may in turn suggest a relative chronological position, perhaps within an existing framework of secure dates. This is the standard approach to dating fifteenth-century masses, and it has led to substantial scholarly consensus in a number of cases, notably those of Dufay, Ockeghem, and Josquin. Ludwig Finscher followed the approach for Obrecht's masses, in his concise but brilliant *MGG* article, and in its basic outlines his chronology still stands as the most comprehensive and considered view on the composer's musical development.

So we need hindsight to 'locate' masses provisionally in time, where we then try to understand them without it. That may appear to be a some-what self-contradictory approach, yet I believe it can work to our strength. 'With hindsight' one can differentiate between early and late masses, yet the main limitation of that approach is that it orders chronologically rather than explains historically. 'Without hindsight', however, one can put that order to the test, by examining how well it enables us to explain each mass in terms only of its immediate present and past. (I must leave aside for the moment *what* is to be explained, and *how*.) A purely descriptive model, in other words, is tested for its explanatory potential. In a close and dialectical relationship the two approaches may allow us to put forward, not just a chronological order, but an explanatory theory of musical change.

That is what this study aims to do for the masses of Jacob Obrecht. It tries to recapture and understand creative 'moments' in the composer's life, and in doing so works out, mass by mass, an overall conception of his musical development. Since the masses are discussed in what I take to be their most plausible chronological order, that conception is embodied in the narrative structure of the book rather than argued explicitly. For that very reason it cannot be motivated or justified in terms of full hindsight until the book is finished. Before that point it has to undergo a more severe test: how well it enables us to explain and understand musical change. If it passes that test, unaided by hindsight, this book has succeeded in its chief aim: to arrive at a historical understanding of Obrecht's musical language.

In order to do this it has been necessary to postulate approximate dates for a number of masses. The methodological status of these datings requires some comment. It goes without saying that datings are not the goal of this book. The historical understanding elaborated here presupposes certain dates, but is not a means towards arriving at them. (To say that one is dating on stylistic grounds is, in a sense, to place the wrong heuristic emphasis, for a date, by itself, is less informative than the stylistic grounds for proposing it.) I do believe, however, that one should try to make such presuppositions as concrete as possible, for that exposes the understanding to objective testing, at least potentially, as new external dating evidence is uncovered in years to come. If the argument is to be of any value, it must be concrete enough to be disproved or modified where it is wrong. Dates and what they mean are in this way inseparably linked—or at least they ought to be. If dates have to be revised on external grounds, then our musical and historical understanding has to be revised accordingly. And if our understanding is revised on internal grounds (as I propose to do in this study), we have a responsibility to keep it subject to external testing, by working out its dating implications as far as we reasonably can.

The Historicity of Musical Texts

The idea of a *theory* of musical change should not be taken too rigidly. It is precisely by considering the creative 'moment' that we can assess in what way long-term continuity of change is a valid notion for Obrecht at all. As will become apparent in this study, continuity can seem more conspicuous at some points than at others, and at times it may even appear to be non-existent (Ch. 6). That does not preclude the possibility of underlying continuity. Yet the format of this book, as explained above, is such that this cannot become apparent until the later chapters, where the threads of continuity can be pulled tighter and tighter together.

Briefly stated, that underlying continuity lies chiefly in Obrecht's attempts to formulate a musically meaningful relationship between the cantus firmus and the surrounding counterpoint. A mass tenor, especially if treated schematically, is a *fait accompli* in the creative process, yet in writing counterpoint around it the composer has an opportunity to make it appear musically motivated. Obrecht's concern to do so could cause his contrapuntal style to change (Ch. 4), but if his style changed for other reasons (Ch. 8) the existing relationship between tenor and counterpoint could be 'upset', and would have needed reformulation. Since this in turn could cause the style to change further, we may picture the reality as a complex of interacting 'causes' whose effects Obrecht tried to balance in the musical discourse. In the end, however, stylistic changes could lead to a point where the very possibility of a meaningful tenor–counterpoint relationship might become open to question (Ch. 10). If there is a tragic element to Obrecht's creative career, it is that his death prevented him from answering that question, which in hindsight turns out to have been one of critical historical importance.

This brief outline already incorporates several of the working assumptions underlying this book. First of all, the approach has a strong formalist element. That is to say, the starting-point of our enquiry is not an innate, timeless musical quality or meaning—an aesthetic essence that speaks to us directly through time-bound features—but the musical morphology itself: phrases, units, themes, motifs, devices, elements, shapes. Each of these properties has musical content, of course, but none is treated in such a way as to put its stamp decisively on a mass as a whole. To state it by exaggeration, it would be impossible to produce a commercial item called

'Theme from *Missa Malheur me bat*'. Certainly nothing in the contra-puntal tissue would qualify, and the cantus firmus itself is not only bor-rowed, but dismembered into segments, each of which is stretched out and mensurally disfigured on the structural rack. Thus the model, by being consciously 'alienated', becomes the very opposite of a recognizable binding theme. Yet if the victim can be dissected, its remains can also be restored to new life, by implantation in a fertile contrapuntal tissue. The result is so tightly interwoven that to take it apart would be to take the very life out of the mass (Ch. 8). On the other hand, the 'alienation' of the cantus firmus is not complete: since it is stated in the top voice, and is taken from the top voice of the song, one can hardly listen to the song again without hearing momentary flashes from Obrecht's mass all the time. Somewhere along the line, new musical *meaning* has been engen-dered.

As this account suggests, there is also a linguistic element to the ap-proach. The relationship between model and mass is not unilaterally causal or genetic, but intertextual. The model, by giving up its old life within the mass, receives new life in return, just as a text quotation, by being placed in a new context, can acquire new meaning. This type of relationship can be seen to characterize Obrecht's style as a whole. A central assumption in this book is that formal properties are musically meaningful not just on account of their individual form and content, but because of the differing ways in which they interact in networks of musical relationships. The aim of the enquiry is therefore not to catalogue and describe isolated features, but to explore their musical relationships, and to explain features and their relationships as functions of each other. A second assumption is that this network of relationships extends beyond the individual mass itself. That is to say, a particular device, and particu-larly the way it is treated, can acquire musical meaning against a back-ground of other masses that employ the same device.

One might argue that in an early mass like *Petrus apostolus* the head-motif is an isolatable 'theme' at least in the sense of being an audible reminder: it is a self-contained unit, stated five times in the course of the mass, and prominently placed at the beginning of each movement (Ch. 4). Oddly enough, however, it is precisely this self-contained quality, this susceptibility to isolation, that appears to have troubled Obrecht. In the next few masses his concern seems to have been to give new meaning to the device, by making it a longer and more fully integrated part of the musical discourse. In other words, he deliberately 'de-thematized' the head-motif. Ultimately this led to a point where the designation 'head-motif', although strictly speaking still applicable, no longer captures what seems truly meaningful about its new function and relationships (as in *Sicut spina rosam*, Ch. 4). Not surprisingly, perhaps, Obrecht abandoned the device not long after, by maintaining its new function and relationships while abandoning the principle of recurrence. (The whole process, which is intimately linked with the changing musical functions of the cantus firmus, is summarized from hindsight in Ch. 8.)

Language is a powerful metaphor for describing such changes in musical meaning, yet it also raises a potentially paralysing awareness: that the very isolation and designation of formal properties is ultimately an arbitrary matter. To call something a head-motif, a phrase, a melody, an imitation, a cadence, is to make a categorization that is in effect no more than a vague assumption, since none of these words can be defined with any precision. Where do we draw the line between a head-motif and an integral stretch of the musical discourse? Between a head-motif and a non-recurring but similarly structured opening? Between a long motif and a short phrase? Between a cadence and a suggestively conclusive chord progression? Between an imitation and a superficial resemblance between parts? And all this from one mass to the next? The decision in every single case depends as much on the perceived inherent qualities of a feature as on its treatment and context. And in fact even the inherent qualities are conditioned by a context, namely, countless previous decisions, not all of which may be equally straightforward. The words cannot be nailed down: they are used in an 'understood' sense, and this understanding arises from a history of previous decisions. As we apply the words in more and more situations, that understanding inevitably changes: it may erode, but it may also deepen.

Yet it is precisely for this reason that language is a powerful *tool* as well as metaphor. For how would, say, an average choirboy have learnt the musical language of his time? How would he have come to share the current sense of what was 'stylish' in music? Presumably by discerning formal conventions that had little meaning to him at first, but whose accepted musical sense he gradually came to appreciate as he sang more repertory. This process can be paralleled directly in the present book, since we aim to learn Obrecht's musical language in very much the same way. In the first mass, *Petrus apostolus* (Ch. 4), there is little option but to categorize features that, in the virtual absence of comparison, can be explained only as borrowed conventions (and this is true of our designations as well): 'cantus firmus', 'head-motif', 'motivic device', 'imitation', and so on. As the narrative proceeds, however, intertextual meaning begins to accumulate in each of these features (as well as in our designations), since they are treated in a variety of contexts, in a variety of ways, to a variety of apparent ends.

Against this background it becomes less and less easy simply to categorize an individual feature by calling it, say, 'imitation'. For to do so is then to beg a range of questions: imitation of what material? in which context? in what way? with what apparent musical end—articulative, structural, ornamental, or none at all? (To return to a question pretermitted earlier on, this is *what* is to be explained, and *how*.) At some points we may find that a particular feature has changed almost beyond recognition, and that our designation no longer serves us well (as is true of 'head-motif' in *Sicut spina rosam*, Ch. 4). At other points we may find that a known designation is strictly speaking applicable (as is true of 'parody' in *Je ne demande*, Ch. 8), but does not become truly meaningful and informative until later (as in *Si dedero*, Ch. 10). It is in this sense, I assume, that a musical language undergoes change: the same feature no longer seems to have the same musical meaning; the same designation no longer expresses quite the same thing.

So the narrative discourse of this study directly mirrors its subject, the transformation of Obrecht's musical language, as well as the process by which we are learning that language in the first place. Broadly speaking, the earlier chapters are more formalist in approach, and need more words and more music examples to 'get into' the language. In later chapters the picture gradually becomes more intertextual, the discourse tighter and more self-referential, and fewer music examples are needed. Recurring keywords and key phrases that refer back to previous situations give and acquire meaning in new situations, and tauten the narrative. Somewhere along the line new musical meaning is generated.

Somewhere along the line, too, 'old' musical meaning evaporates. To appreciate a new musical language is to become less and less able to appreciate older musical languages on the same terms. What makes imitation highly effective and targeted in *Fortuna desperata* (Ch. 8) necessarily makes imitation seem less motivated and more mannerist in, say, Faugues's *Missa Le serviteur* (*c*.1460). If the device derives its new effectiveness partly from the network of relationships in which it is activated, then the same network in Faugues will seem more conspicuously archaic (as it evidently was by the 1490s, since Faugues turns up in no source from or after that decade). But even within Obrecht's *œuvre* that process can be traced. By the end of Chapter 8 it is possible to recognize that his early and mature masses speak quite different languages, and cannot be compared and evaluated on the same terms. And after his death it was the cantus firmus (a constructive element, ironically, which Obrecht's own musical language had done so much to undermine) that quickly came to stand out as the most conspicuously conservative element in his masses (Ch. 10). The fifteenth century, as said before, could muster little understanding for its recent musical past. It perceived no musical essence or innate aesthetic value that might transcend style, and move beyond the reaches of history. The explanation offered in this study is that musical meaning and value were seen to reside in formal properties and their interrelationships, in the musical *language*, and were time-bound for that very reason.

For fifteenth-century music that seems a valid assumption to make. Where we have specific statements on the kinds of qualities that a piece of composed music should possess, they often stress two criteria, *ars* and *ingenium*. Both criteria were understood in a tangible, formal sense. *Ars* was basically synonymous with 'learning', and was by definition a musical quality susceptible to reason, to intellectual contemplation. *Ingenium* was partly synonymous with *ars*, but stressed in addition the specific aspect of artifice, and particularly the necessity of handling it with variety and good taste. It is typical that composers could be praised for displaying these qualities at one time, and criticized (or forgotten) for lacking them one or two generations later. Evidently, while it was never questioned that *ars* and *ingenium* defined good composition, and while it seemed reasonably self-evident at any particular time what this meant, that meaning itself did not remain constant over time. Other aesthetic criteria are hard to come by. The notion of music giving sensuous pleasure, being agreeable to the ears, could be used at most to distinguish between technically competent counterpoint and musical discord, or between a good performance and a bad performance—not between, say, Obrecht and Faugues. A theorist might speculate about beauty in the metaphysical sense, but that beauty could not be concretely immanent in a composition unless it became thereby susceptible to reason as well (for instance, in number and proportion). To speak of a beauty transcending the tangible properties of a musical work, escaping its time-bound features, and standing apart from history, was to speak of God Himself, not of human handiwork.

The overall picture, then, is one of extreme relativism: one formal feature relative to another, one network of musical relationships relative to another, one musical language relative to another, and ultimately, everything relative to time. This is what has always been so seemingly disorienting about fifteenth-century music: there are no absolutes, no essences, no fixities, where we tend to presuppose them—in meaning, value, understanding, denotation, and even in pitch, duration, and tempo (see App. II). With the approach outlined above we may stand a good chance of capturing this as a historical condition.

The Textuality of Music History

Yet the approach does have its limitations. By taking fifteenth-century masses as objects of enquiry, I necessarily assume that they possess a certain autonomy and self-sufficiency as musical creations, to the virtual exclusion of historical context. And that is tacitly to pass over the question: 'musical' relative to what?

This question needs to be carefully understood, for it is a much more fundamental critique of my approach than may appear at first sight. It is not simply a call for considering music in its historical context, for that is already to presuppose that 'music' and 'its context' are separable entities. It suggests instead that the historical surroundings—rather than being external to (or even detracting from) a perceived musical autonomy—might in fact have provided the indispensable conditions for Obrecht's masses to be understood as music in the first place.

To give just one example, it would have been inconceivable to the fifteenth century that there could be a genuine understanding of music separate from Christian doctrine. Rather than being external to music, Christianity, as understood at the time, was essential to its definition as an art and science. That is, to speak of Music was to take for granted its essential Christian nature, just as we might take for granted its essentially autonomous nature. To speak of Christian faith was to take for granted its defining role in such spheres of human activity as music or mathematics, just as we might take for granted its essential separation from those spheres. Some sense of that all-pervasive unity can be recognized, for instance, in *Mille quingentis* (Chs. 1 and 5). The text of this motet (which was written to commemorate Obrecht's father Willem) 'distances' itself in the last two lines from the music, and comments upon its specific role: 'therefore sweetly sing this song, gentle choir of succentors, so that his soul may be carried to Heaven and be given the palm.' That is to say, to produce the sound of the motet is to intercede for Willem Obrecht. Intercession is not an 'extra-musical' function, for the physical sound enacts the intercession: the more sweetly that sound is realized as music, the more effective it will be as intercession. It follows that the less we understand the motet as intercession, the less we are able to grasp how

Obrecht understood it as music. That is the historical condition hinted at in the question above.

There are points in this study where this problem rises to the surface. My discussion of *Maria zart*, for instance, breaks off just when the possibility of intellectual content becomes very real—so that there is at least the suggestion that we may be paying a price for the perceived musical autonomy (Ch. 10). An even clearer example is *Sub tuum presidium* (in the same chapter). This singular work simply will not yield itself to the kind of musical and historical understanding that I have tried to elaborate. Significantly, of all Obrecht's masses this is perhaps the one richest in what we would call 'extra-musical' content. In its numerology and cantus firmus selection it is firmly anchored in a world excluded here as external to the autonomous musical work. For that reason it is this mass that shows most clearly that 'musical', 'extra-musical', or 'contextual' are themselves mere categorizations, vague assumptions, which are ultimately no better than 'motif', 'phrase', or 'cadence'. They serve us while they can, but there may come a point at which their underlying assumptions begin to become problematic.

In the context of this book that is a price we have to pay. Not to assume, for the purposes of enquiry, that a working distinction between 'musical' and 'extra-musical' may be useful would require us to write a different kind of study altogether. (Such a study would be well worth writing.) What we can do, however, is to remain conscious of the price we are paying. It is here that Obrecht's biography comes in. Initially the biography was intended merely to add historical 'colour' to the musical picture: the idea of alternating musical and biographical chapters was as preconceived as a segmented cantus firmus. As research proceeded, however, the 'context' began to undermine the autonomy of the musical picture, and became a historical 'intertext', particularly in those chapters that are based on new archival evidence (Chs. 1, 2, and 3).

My main concern in these chapters has been to obtain some sense of how Obrecht might have viewed his existence, and his professional musicianship as part of that existence. That was to draw in a large number of historical dimensions—social, religious, political, cultural, and economic. Yet the reader will readily notice that the distinctions between these dimensions fade away as archival documents, by bearing upon each other, begin to suggest a wider picture. In the fifteenth century, the thought of something being socially or politically significant without having a defining religious dimension was inconceivable. Religion, in so far as it could be translated into human activity (worship, prayer, pilgrimage, charity, music), could be translated into financial terms as well, without being any less religious for it. Human activity in general—whether craft, trade, labour, education, or devotion—needed a corporate social organization (guild, confraternity), which could be given concrete religious expression if financial resources allowed: chapels, altar-pieces, statues, polyphonic masses. Those expressions may be recognized today as pertaining to the history of architecture, art, or music, without therefore losing their religious, social, economic, and political dimensions.

One thing that comes out very clearly is that it is difficult to speak of third-estate individuals without speaking of their communities: the family, the parish, the city, the guild, the confraternity, the craft, the church. The sense of individual identity, in other words, was inseparably bound up with the sense of communal identity: an individual without a community was a nobody. That is why, in the first three chapters, it is necessary to view Jacob Obrecht and his parents in terms of their wider affiliations. Numerous relatives, colleagues, and fellow citizens tell us who they were, define their identities, in a complex network of social relationships: Roeland and Lodewijk Ghijs, Ghiselbrecht and Arend de Keyser, Jan Obrecht, Andries Gheeraerts and Marien Laps, Pieter Bordon, and many others. This was a network, a 'textuality', far less responsive to historical change than Obrecht's musical language. When he entered the priesthood and became a professional musician, it largely ceased to define him.

In the later biographical chapters, which are based mostly on secondary literature, Obrecht emerges more as an individual in the modern sense (Chs. 5, 9, and 11). I do not believe that this is due entirely to the selective nature of the evidence, or to Romantic preconceptions about the heroic artist 'in charge of his own destiny'. The kind of musicianship to which Obrecht devoted his life lacked a social organization (Ch. 2), and he failed to realize that all-important medieval sense of belonging in other spheres (in the way that, for instance, Dufay or Josquin settled down in what we call their 'retirement'). The unsettled life of Obrecht's last seven years— Bergen op Zoom, Bruges, Antwerp, Innsbruck, and Ferrara (Chs. 9 and 11)—is one that even a professional musicologist in the 'age of the individual' would scarcely enjoy. Against the stable and secure background of his Ghent childhood, sketched in Chapters 1, 2, and 3, Obrecht's death at Ferrara acquires a deep poignancy: no living relatives, no known friends, no professional position—an uprooted *individual* in a foreign community (Ch. 11). In medieval terms it seems almost inconceivable that a man born in a protected bourgeois environment in a powerful metropolis should have willingly brought himself into such a forsaken position, for the sake of his musicianship. That is the deeper meaning I perceive in Obrecht's words 'born for the Muses', even if he himself did not intend it.

A Music History without a Present?

To perceive unintended meaning in five-hundred-year-old words: that, in a way, sums up the fundamental dilemma of our field. We are maintaining a line of communication with a musical culture long dead, and it cannot be a lifeline unless we accept that most obvious anachronism of all: that it leads into a modern culture completely foreign to that on the other end. By decoding messages not encoded for us we inevitably transform them. For all the fear of anachronism expressed in this introduction, the present study is in fact riddled with anachronisms: music examples in modern notation, modern technical vocabulary, conventions of scholarly writing, narrativity, statistics. Indeed, even in 'restoring' Obrecht's music to its historical context we can never do more than take a bit of 'context' out of context as well. For the context in which we see and value Obrecht is inescapably ours.

The Obrecht that we like to see today—that I try to sketch in this book—is original, authentic, 'as he really was', as his contemporaries understood him. All these expressions are bywords for one thing: what we like to see today. And what we like to see in particular is the removal of the Romantic assumptions and prejudices of older generations of musicologists. What we end up seeing, however, is the product of our own assumptions and prejudices—which would have been equally objectionable to those older generations as theirs are to us. Late nineteenth-century scholarship prided itself in recognizing more than a primitive stage in the evolution of musical technique in the works of Obrecht and Josquin, a recognition that presupposes the typically Romantic distinction between 'mere' craftsmanship and a timeless aesthetic quality. After centuries of virtual neglect this essentialist assumption was not exactly a harmful one—much though we recognize in 'essence' a byword for what the Romantic period liked to see. Obrecht 'as he really was' was the man of genius whom previous centuries, and perhaps even his own time, had failed to recognize. Small wonder, then, that documents were considered more significant if they supported this Great Man interpretation of music history. For Josquin in particular this included all posthumous statements that elevated him to the rank of musical genius—at the expense of archival documents that showed both him and Obrecht involved in the base necessities of everyday life, in an apparently unappreciative society.

The present study almost reverses the picture, simply because it makes a different assumption about what is historically significant. It relegates sixteenth-century statements to posthumous reception history (see above for Josquin, and, for Obrecht, Ch. 8), and basically regards these as products of a culture that needed musical heroes as much as did early musicology. Obrecht 'as he really was' is now the Obrecht whom his own time understood better than early musicology did. Small wonder, then, that I have given such interpretive scrutiny to archival documents known but largely neglected for more than half a century (Chs. 5, 9, and 11), in an attempt to show that Jacob Obrecht, the Great Man of All Time, was really a man of his own time. It cannot be denied that he was, of course, but the view that this is significant can only be my assumption (or if you like my prejudice). I make it consciously, but future scholars may well wish to remove it in order to see Obrecht as he really, *really* was.

In its own historical context this book is obviously shaped by the view that essentialism is to be avoided as a nineteenth-century anachronism. Its central concern is not to show that Obrecht's music speaks to all time, for that would imply the presumption that we are its diviners for all time. (And Romantic interpretations of Renaissance music show what a dangerous presumption that is to make.) After centuries of neglect the fact that Obrecht's music speaks to our time can only be seen as a unique historical phenomenon. Yet it is, emphatically, a *historical* phenomenon: we have no way of telling what it says about our time and what about the music. We may use words like 'original' or 'authentic' where the nineteenth century used 'essence', and the fifteenth 'ars' and 'ingenium', but all we are highlighting are qualities to which we happen to be receptive. The context in which those qualities seem meaningful is inescapably ours.

That may seem a bleak and self-destructive note on which to end this introduction. Yet the fundamental dilemma is, in fact, what makes Renaissance musicology such an exciting field. The answer to the dilemma must be this: that there is no point in denying that *we* maintain the line of communication; that our assumptions, values, and prejudices make us who we are; that we need them to say anything meaningful about the composer at all. We cannot create an image of Obrecht unless we partly create him in our image. We cannot 'revive' his life and music unless we breathe our life into them. Dogmatic 'old' historicism and 'authenticism' (as Richard Taruskin aptly identified it) can only lead us down into escapism, self-denial, and ultimately to a paralytic fear of touching Obrecht at all.

Rather than denying ourselves and our time, we should take them into the enquiry without fear, transforming the message, yes, but allowing it to transform us, too. The most glaring anachronism in this book lies perhaps in my inability to suppress a deep sense of wonder: at the seeming incompatibility between the ordinary man-of-his-time that I created and the astonishing force with which his music shines into our time. The more I believed to understand his musical language 'on its own terms', the more forcefully it seemed to speak on my terms. That two-sided communication may be a historical phenomenon, of which I am only a part. Yet whatever its historical and cultural delimitations, it is a communication I should not wish to stop, and to which, in this book, I am inviting others.

PART ONE
1457/8–1485

1 THE ORPHIC JACOB

EIGHT lines of Latin poetry hold the key to Jacob Obrecht's origins. They were written by the composer himself, and have survived together with the music to which he set them: the motet *Mille quingentis*. The poem gives two crucial items of biographical information: Obrecht's father was called Guillermus, and he died in 1488. This was enough for the Belgian historian Berten De Keyzer, in 1953, to identify the man in documents from the city archive in Ghent.[1] Civic pay records establish that a Willem Obrecht worked as a trumpeter in that city from 1452 until his death in 1488. To confirm the identification, the only offspring mentioned in documents concerning his estate is 'meester Jacop Hobrecht priestre'.

A recently discovered portrait by an unknown Flemish master holds the key to another question, the composer's date of birth.[2] Dated 1496, it identifies the sitter, a cleric, as 'Ja. Hobrecht', and gives his age as 38 (see the Frontispiece). Jacob was born in Ghent in 1457–8.

A poem and a painting would seem unlikely starting-points for the biography of a fifteenth-century composer. Yet nothing else in Jacob Obrecht's documented career tells us where he came from, or what his background was. Musical centres record his professional activity only from April 1480, by which time he is already a choirmaster with a university education, trained for the priesthood, which he receives shortly afterwards. Thereafter the movements of the composer can be traced almost year by year until his death in 1505. Yet the first twenty-two or so years of his life remain obscure: for this period we depend entirely on the clues

---

[1] B. De Keyzer, 'Jacob Obrecht en zijn vader Willem: De Gentse relaties', *Mens en Melodie*, 8 (1953), 317–19.

[2] D. De Vos, 'Een belangrijk portret van Jacob Obrecht ontdekt: Een werk uit de nalatenschap van het atelier van Hans Memling?', *Jaarboek 1989–90 Stad Brugge, Stedelijke Musea* (Bruges, 1991), 192–209; R. C. Wegman, 'Het "Jacob Hobrecht" portret: Enkele biografische observaties', *Musica Antiqua*, 8 (1991), 152–4; *Important Old Master Paintings: New York, Friday, January 15, 1993*, auction catalogue, Sotheby's (New York, 1993), lot 139. The painting was bought by the Kimbell Museum, Fort Worth, Texas, on 15 Jan. 1993.

given by the poem and the painting. These, then, must be our points of departure, and by following up the clues we may attempt to bridge the gap between Obrecht's unknown past and his documented professional career.

Mille quingentis

Obrecht's motet *Mille quingentis* was not known with its original text until 1936. In that year Higini Anglès published his inventory of the Segovia choirbook SegC s.s., which included a fully texted concordance for a piece known until then only under the incipit 'Requiem eternam'.[3] In the newly discovered source this text was provided only under the tenor, which quotes the Introit for the Mass of the Dead, *Requiem aeternam*. The other voices were underlaid with a non-liturgical text that relates the death of Guillermus Hobrecht, father of Jacobus, expressing the wish that sweet singing of the motet might speed his soul to heaven.

The Segovia manuscript is a remarkably accurate textual source for Obrecht's work.[4] Although written in Spain, the orthography of his Middle Dutch songs is immaculate, a feature that sets it apart from most other Mediterranean sources. The choirbook, moreover, transmits the full texts of Obrecht's two occasional motets—works whose significance can only have escaped singers outside the composer's circle. One of these is his musical 'letter of application' *Inter preclarissimas virtutes* (see Ch. 9), the other *Mille quingentis*. The text of the latter work is not without its problems, and has often been emended, but the three voices transmitting it agree on almost every detail.[5] A full account of the textual problems is given below.[6] Suffice it to say at this point that the reading involving the

[3] H. Anglès, 'Un manuscrit inconnu avec polyphonie du XVᵉ siècle, conservé à la cathédrale de Ségovie', *Acta musicologica*, 8 (1936), 6–17. The only known copy until 1936 was in Petrucci's *Motetti C* (RISM 1504¹), which gives the incipit 'Requiem eternam' in all voices. In the third source, FlorC 2439, the top voice alone has the incipit 'Requiem'.

[4] On the possible connections between this source and the musical culture of Bruges, see R. Strohm, *Music in Late Medieval Bruges* (Oxford, 1985), 142–4.

[5] Some of the few disagreements are probably attributable to Obrecht himself, and may thus confirm the authority of the Segovia manuscript. For instance, the insertion of tenor text in the top voice, line 7 ('et lux perpetua'), coincides with a musical quotation from the tenor. Textual-musical quotations of this type can be found in reliable copies of several Obrecht masses, e.g. *O lumen ecclesie* and *Sicut spina rosam* (see Ch. 4).

[6] See App. I, Doc. 43. I am greatly indebted to Dr Leofranc Holford-Strevens for sharing his thoughts on the text of *Mille quingentis*. For previous discussions of that text, see A. Smijers, 'Twee onbekende motetteksten van Jacob Hobrecht', *Tijdschrift der Vereeniging voor Nederlandsche Muziekgeschiedenis*, 16 (1941), 133–4; R. C. Wegman, 'Music and Musicians at the Guild of Our Lady at Bergen op Zoom, c.1470–1510', *Early Music History*, 9 (1989), 199–201; and R. Strohm, *The Rise of European Music, 1380–1500* (Cambridge, 1993) 487–8. The manuscript reading *oram* (shore; l. 6) was emended to *coram* (before) by Smijers and Wegman, and to *os* by Strohm.

least editorial intervention is also the one that agrees most closely with what is known of Willem Obrecht's life. This reading can be translated as follows:

After fifteen hundred less twice six years had lapsed since the birth of Christ, Son of the Virgin, the Sicilian Muses wept as the Fates took away, on the feast of St Cecilia, Guillermus Hobrecht, adorned with great probity, who travelled through the Sicilian shore;

It is he, also, who begot the Orphic Jacob for the Muses: therefore sweetly sing this song, gentle choir of succentors, so that his soul may be carried to Heaven and be given the palm.

The weeping of the Sicilian Muses is described as a past event, taking place in a year which the composer is at some pains to specify ('mille quingentis verum bis sex minus annis'). The obvious implication seems that the poem was not written in the same year: it was more probably intended for annual commemoration services on the day of Willem's death, beginning in 1489. It may well be for this reason that the actual date of death is also specified, and that the motet expresses the hope that when all obit services will finally cease, on the Day of Judgement, Willem's soul may be spared Purgatory, and enter Heaven directly.

Willem died on the feast of St Cecilia, 22 November. This is broadly confirmed by archival evidence: two references in Ghent documents indicate that he certainly died after 1 October 1488, and most probably in the last two weeks of November (see Ch. 5). The Sicilian Muses wept for him, and they had good reason to do so, for we read that Willem had once travelled through the island—spelt here as 'Cecilia'. This was apparently an important event in his life, to which the death-date, St Cecilia's day, refers.[7] No documentation on a journey to the Mediterranean Sea undertaken by Willem Obrecht has as yet come to light.

The composer invites the choir of succentors to sing sweetly because it was Willem who begot him. He does not reveal more about himself, evidently because further autobiographical details are not relevant to the central concern of the motet, the salvation of Willem's soul. Yet the composer does not appear to be lacking in self-esteem. He calls himself Orpheus-like (which may mean anything from 'musical' to 'exceptionally gifted'),[8] and adds that he was born for the Muses, that is, to serve them. And Jacob is evidently grateful to Willem for having begotten him. It is

[7] The received interpretation is that Willem crossed Sicily at the time of his son's birth, but Dr Holford-Strevens points out that this conclusion is not warranted by the grammar; see his commentary to Doc. 43.

[8] It is unlikely that connotations with the notorious Orphic rites of ancient Greece would have been perceived in the 15th c.

for this reason ('ergo') that he addresses his poem finally to the singers, wishing his father's soul to reach Heaven and to be given the palm. What might bring that about is the sound of the motet ('melos'), and its execution ('dulce'). Jacob's prominence in the text may indicate that he endowed the commemoration service on behalf of his father. His motet could then be the musical equivalent of an endowment contract, its basic message being that Jacob, son of Willem Obrecht, orders a motet in polyphony to be sung in perpetuity on the day of his father's death, 22 November.

Mille quingentis is an extremely important document. It tells us not only about the love Jacob bore his father, but also about his perception of both Willem and himself as historical figures. It seems significant, for instance, that he chose to write a tenor motet with liturgical cantus firmus at all: traditionally this form was associated with memorable events involving princes, prelates, states, or cities. A parallel case is Johannes de Sarto's *Romanorum rex*, a work that uses the same tenor as Obrecht's motet, and treats it in similar fashion, in a lament for Albrecht II, King of the Romans, who died in 1439.[9] Willem Obrecht's death was obviously not quite as historic an event, yet the musical and textual differences between the two laments are negligible. Here is a city trumpeter remembered in rhymed Latin verse complete with allusions to classical poetry, his soul to be given the palm, symbol of victory, honour, and glory.[10] This seems language befitting a hero or a saint.

Who then was Willem Obrecht? The clues given by the poem lead to the archives of Ghent, where Willem's fascinating life has left a long trail of documentary references—long enough, in fact, to write a monograph about him alone. Proper assessment of that documentation is beyond the scope of this study. We must therefore limit ourselves to those aspects that provide a context for the early years of his son: social background, civic status, religious life, professional contacts. Of course, without detailed documentation on Jacob, a certain amount of speculation is inevitable. On the other hand, such documentation as one might expect to find—references to him as a choirboy and a student—would merely confirm the self-

[9] In this motet, too, it is the singers who are addressed, with a request to pray to Christ and Mary for the departed king's soul. For the motet's authorship and further literature, see B. J. Blackburn, E. E. Lowinsky, and C. A. Miller, *A Correspondence of Renaissance Musicians* (Oxford, 1991), 663–4. A parallel to Obrecht's transposition of the F Lydian Introit to E Phrygian can be found in Josquin's *Nymphes des bois*.

[10] Obrecht undoubtedly had in mind the Adoration of the Lamb, as prophesied in Rev. 7: 9: 'After this I beheld, and, lo, a great multitude, which no man could number, of all nations, and kindreds, and people, and tongues, stood before the throne, and before the Lamb, clothed with their white robes, and palms in their hands.'

evident. That Jacob had been a choirboy at some establishment, and a student at a university, is no more than to be expected, given the course of his later career. Yet that expectation is the product of hindsight. In the context of Willem Obrecht's life the picture is reversed: given Jacob's background, neither training, nor indeed the course of his later career, could have been self-evident or expected. That is why his biography must start from the other end: in the hectic everyday life of a medieval metropolis, where one ordinary boy, amidst tens of thousands of other citizens, grew up to beat the odds and immortalize his name.

Willem Obrecht

In November 1452, Ghent seethed with war and revolution.[11] Eleven months earlier, after years of worsening relationships with Philip the Good, duke of Burgundy, the people had seized control of the town. The civic constitution and existing government had been overturned. Three elected captains now ruled the city. Lengthy dossiers were compiled on the crimes and misrule of those who had governed Ghent in the past fifteen years. Those suspected of supporting the duke of Burgundy were rounded up and beheaded in the market-place. Duke Philip responded by decreeing a blockade of the town and ordering the arrest of all Ghenters who could be apprehended. By the autumn of 1452 the two parties were involved in open warfare, their armies raiding and pillaging towns and fortifications across eastern Flanders.

It is at this time, on 24 November 1452, that the Ghent authorities made the following resolution, which has survived in the yearbooks of the magistrates of the by-law (Doc. 4; see Pl. 1):[12]

We, the aldermen and the council of Ghent, make known to whomever shall see or hear these present letters that—for the honour, welfare, and interests of the said city, and in order that the same shall from now on be virtuously maintained, for which [reason] it needs capable men playing the trumpet—[we] have

---

[11] For the Ghent war of 1449–53, see V. Fris, *Histoire de Gand* (Brussels, 1913), 125–36; R. Vaughan, *Philip the Good: The Apogee of Burgundy* (London, 1970), 302–33; J. Decavele (ed.), *Gent: Apologie van een rebelse stad* (Antwerp, 1989), 99–103.

[12] Previously published in F. De Potter, *Gent, van den oudsten tijd tot heden*, i (Ghent, 1882), 556, and De Keyzer, 'Jacob Obrecht en zijn vader Willem', 318. The magistrates of the by-law (*scepenen vander kuere*) registered financial and legal transactions between Ghent citizens, foundations and endowments, decisions made by the city magistrates, and passed and recorded verdicts in civil lawsuits. Their massive yearbooks, on which this study heavily draws, are kept as series 301 in the city archive of Ghent (SAG). Similarly voluminous yearbooks were produced by the magistrates of inheritance (*scepenen van gedele*); these are kept as series 330 in the city archive (for an explanation of their purpose and nature, see the paragraph on Lysbette Gheeraerts below). The third major source used in this study are the accounts of the city of Ghent (SAG, series 400).

Pl. I. Willem Obrecht's appointment as city trumpeter at Ghent in 1452 (Doc. 4)

appointed, at the command of the three Members of the said city, Ghisel de Keysere, Theeus Nijs, Roel Ghijs, Willem Oebrecht, Loykin Ghijs, and Jan Toysbaert, trumpeters, in the service of the said city for as long as they shall live. And we have fixed, in the name of the same city, the annual remuneration of these men at 720 Flemish groats each, and two liveries to be provided by the city, that is, a striped and a plain one, for which salaries and liveries [they shall be obliged] to serve the said city, and to remain [loyal] to its lords, as is proper [for them to do]. In certification of the truth, we, the aldermen and council, have sealed this present [letter] as above [24 November 1452], etc.

This document, the earliest to mention Willem Obrecht, is of considerable historical interest, for the appointment is the first of its kind in the Low Countries. Yet the motivation behind it was probably political rather than musical. The city could easily meet its musical needs by hiring freelance trumpeters on an *ad hoc* basis, as it had always done in the past. By appointing six men for life it undertook a new, and not inconsiderable, financial obligation. At a time of war such a decision would have needed justification in the most pragmatic terms. Evidently the advantages perceived in having a permanent band of trumpeters were considerable, and these were most keenly felt in times of crisis. No doubt the trumpeters were expected to serve an important political and diplomatic goal: the public manifestation of Ghent's sovereignty and power. This was worth some long-term investment.

The document confirms this. Its statement that the six trumpeters were appointed 'for the honour, welfare, and interests of the said city, and in order that the same shall from now on be virtuously maintained' is probably to be taken at face value. In fact the command to appoint them had come from the three Members, who shared the political power of Ghent between them: the burgesses, the guild of woolweavers, and all other craft guilds. Even the stipulation that the trumpeters were 'to serve the said city and remain loyal to its lords' must have been intended quite literally: at this time the merest suspicion of siding with Burgundy was enough to risk execution.

Who were the six trumpeters? Very little documentation on them survives prior to 1452, but there is every reason to assume that they were born and bred Ghenters who fully supported the city's cause. We learn from a closely contemporary document that the trumpeters of Ghent were organized in the Guild of St Andrew. This trumpeters' guild had its own seal and officially approved ordinance 'since old times', and was ruled by a dean with four sworn councillors, or *proviserers*.[13] All Ghent guilds

[13] Doc. 3: a case brought before the magistrates of the by-law, between the trumpeters' Guild of St Andrew, represented by Gheeraert vanden Velde and Arende Yman *alias* Van der Meer, and

keenly guarded their professional interests, restricting membership to fellow townsmen, and barring all outsiders from practising their trade in the city. For this reason alone the appointment of the six trumpeters in such an enviable position would have been unthinkable if they had had no previous association with the trumpeters' guild: they must already have enjoyed its protection before 1452.

In a broader political context this picture is confirmed. In 1452 Ghent stood virtually alone in its conflict with Philip the Good: with the exception of Ninove all Flemish towns sided with Burgundy. At such a difficult juncture, any trumpeter undertaking to serve the city for the rest of his life would have to be closely associated with its cause, and be a Ghenter himself. Documentary evidence for this assumption is circumstantial, but telling. Of the six men, two were also active as woolweavers: the brothers Roeland and Lodewijk Ghijs.[14] As such they must have been members of the guild of woolweavers; in fact we know that Roeland was a sworn member by 1457. Now the woolweavers' guild was among the most powerful political forces in Ghent. It was one of the three governing Members of the town—the very body that gave the command to appoint Willem Obrecht and his companions in 1452. The staunchly anti-Burgundian guild of woolweavers was also the prime mover behind the uprising of 1451–3. This adds a further dimension to the appointment of the trumpeters. Two of the six men came from the very circles that led the revolt and that, having seized power, appointed them in permanent service. Their guild associations, and their choice to serve the city at such a difficult time, indicate that they were trusted members of the Ghent artisan class, fully dedicated to its political interests.

The combination of weaving and trumpeting may seem an odd one. In the case of the Ghijs brothers it almost certainly means that they were entrepreneurs who left the actual labour to journeymen, and who spent most of their time managing their business and earning a full income as trumpeters. Given the hereditary and protected nature of the two profes-

---

Janne Muelenijser, member of the same guild. Only the opening sentence survives; the space left open to record the actual nature of the dispute and the eventual verdict was never filled. On trumpeters' guilds in general, see K. Polk, 'Flemish Wind Bands in the Late Middle Ages: A Study of Improvisatory Instrumental Practices' (Ph.D. diss., University of California, Berkeley, 1968), 74–6; C. Lingbeek-Schalekamp, *Overheid en muziek in Holland tot 1672* (Poortugaal, 1985), 108–16; Strohm, *Music in Late Medieval Bruges*, 89–90; K. Polk, *German Instrumental Music of the Late Middle Ages: Players, Patrons and Performance Practice* (Cambridge, 1992), 123–6.

[14] Roeland Ghijs is mentioned as a sworn member of the woolweavers' guild by 1457, living in 't Zand (now Lange Violettenstraat; see SAG 195.1, fo. 5[r], where he is listed next to his father-in-law, Arend vanden Bounbeke). 'Louwijc Ghijs, tromper ende wullewever' is mentioned as living in the same street in 1477 and 1484/5 (SAG 20.1, fo. 15[r], and RAG K3957, fo. 1[v]).

sions, both must already have been in the family. It was not uncommon for children to inherit presumptive rights in different guilds from several ancestors—although the usual pattern was that one son (normally the eldest) followed his father in the trade, different provision being made for the other sons. The latter is unlikely to have happened with the Ghijs brothers, however, for they were the oldest of the three children left by the Ghent citizen Lauwereinse Ghijs after his death some time before 1449; the third son was Andries Ghijs, who was also to become a city trumpeter.[15] Evidently the three brothers had inherited their professions and guild associations from Lauwereinse or another ancestor.

In Willem Obrecht's case, on the other hand, it seems more likely that his parents had bought him into the trumpeters' guild at a young age. The Obrecht family in Ghent probably originated from Lokeren (see Fig. 1), and must have settled in the city sometime before 1400. It was a small family of middle-class entrepreneurs; during the early decades of the century virtually all its known members were involved in the shipping trade, but related professions were soon adopted by younger members of the clan. One of Willem's closest relatives must have been Jan Obrecht *filius* Jans,[16] a wealthy shipper and spice-trader who became one of Ghent's most prominent and influential citizens in the second half of the fifteenth century.[17] Jan Obrecht may have been instrumental in arranging

[15] Lauwereinse Ghijs left a widow, Lysbette sKempen, and three sons, Roeland, Lodewijk, and Andries; the latter was still a minor in 1450 (SAG 330.24, 1449/50[1], fo. 4[r], and 1450/1, fos. 26[v] and 28[r]).

[16] Jan's earliest traceable ancestors are the wealthy shipper Heinric Obrecht and his wife Kateline van Overmeere *filia* Jans. Kateline must have died shortly before 8 Mar. 1407 (SAG 301.19, 1406/7, fo. 31[v]), leaving Heinric with two sons and two daughters. The elder son was Jacob Obrecht (see below, n. 18). The second son was Jan Obrecht *filius* Heinricx, who became emancipated after marriage on 17 Sept. 1424 (SAG 330.18, 1424/5, fo. 6[r]), and must have become the father of Jan Obrecht *filius* Jans within the next few years. The two daughters are Kateline Obrecht, who survived her two successive husbands Janne vander Sporct and Janne Wauters (SAG 330.18, 1425/6, fo. 32[v]; 330.24, 1448/9, fo. 14[r]), and Margriete Obrecht, who died in Mar. or Apr. 1441, leaving a son Jooskin from her marriage with Willem Wandelaert (SAG 330.18, 1425/6, fo. 35[v]; 330.22, 1440/1, fo. 83[r]; Jooskin had died by 9 Oct. 1448, see 330.24, 1448/9, fo. 14[r]). Heinric Obrecht himself had remarried Kateline Snoers by 4 June 1431 (SAG 330.20, 1430/1, fo. 61[r]). He died on 27 Jan. 1442 (NS), and was buried in the chapel of the Conception of Our Lady in the monastery of the calced Carmelites at Ghent (Lange Steenstraat). His tombstone no longer survives, but the inscription with the death-date is recorded in UBG G11766, fo. 209[r] (document kindly brought to my attention by Daniël Lievois). Heinric had bought his tomb by 13 Sept. 1431, when he ordered a perpetual obit on his death-date, and a one-year cycle of memorial Masses, to be held in the chapel after his death (330.20, 1431/2, fo. 7[r]).

[17] Jan Obrecht *filius* Jans is the only known son of Jan *filius* Heinricx, although Willem Obrecht (who was probably about five years his junior) may well have been a brother of his. Jan first turns up as a surety for his father on 10 Feb. 1447 (SAG 330.24, 1446/7, fo. 64[r]), was married to Petronelle Goethals by 21 Jan. 1452 (SAG 330.25, 1451/2, fo. 32[v]), with whom he held possessions in Lokeren (SAG 330.28, 1459/60, fo. 103[v]). Without their patronymics the two Jan Obrechts are difficult to tell apart, although the father is mentioned only as a shipper, whereas the son is referred to as a spice-trader ('crudenier') as well as shipper. The last known document to mention the father

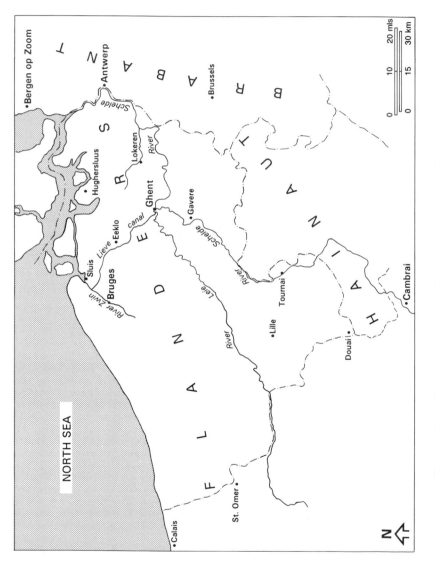

Fig. 1. Map of the southern Low Countries in the late fifteenth century

the young trumpeter's first marriage, some time between 1453 and 1457, and after the death of Willem's wife, in 1460, he was to act temporarily as legal guardian of his son Jacob (see below). The possibility of a direct family relationship between Willem and Jan is strengthened by the fact that the latter had an uncle Jacob Obrecht, also a shipper, who can be traced in Ghent during the years 1427–59.[18] Willem was probably a younger brother of Jan, or possibly (if he was the son of the shipper Jacob Obrecht) a cousin. Less likely, though not impossible, is his descent from the brewer Willem Hoebrecht *filius* Willems, who was born *c.*1395.[19]

The most likely scenario seems that the father of Willem Obrecht was

unambiguously as '*filius* Heinricx' dates from 21 Feb. 1452 (SAG 301.44, 1451/2, fo. 69ᵛ), but he may well have lived on until shortly before 21 Nov. 1459, when his son rewarded Lysbette vander Sporct for having served his parents (SAG 301.45, 1459/60, fo. 27ʳ; domestic servants usually remained unpaid during the lifetimes of their masters, and received their accumulated wages only from their effects, even though they were normally overlooked in their masters' wills; this evidently happened to Lysbette, but also, for instance, to Dufay's domestic servants in 1474).

[18] Heinric Obrecht's son Jacob is mentioned as a brother of Jan *filius* Heinricx on 17 Apr. 1429 (SAG 330.19, 1428/9, fo. 46ᵛ), and in various later documents. He can be traced borrowing money and buying ships from 1427 to 1459 (see, e.g., SAG 330.19, 1427/8, fo. 4ʳ; 330.20, 1432/3, fos. 36ᵛ and 104ʳ; 330.22, 1441/2, fo. 493ʳ; 301.39, 1446/7, fo. 19ᵛ; 330.24, 1447/8, fo. 53ʳ; 301.45, 1459/60, fo. 14ʳ; 330.28, 1459/60, fo. 19ʳ). His two known children are Lysbette Obrecht and the shipper Vincent Obrecht, both of whom had become emancipated by 12 May 1440, and must therefore have been born in the years around 1420 (330.22, 1439/40, fo. 80ʳ). Vincent is regularly found buying ships and acting as a surety for his father during the 1440s and early 1450s, but he disappears thereafter (e.g., SAG 330.22, 1441/2, fo. 493ʳ; 301.39, 1446/7, fo. 12ʳ; 301.41, 1450/1, fo. 123ʳ). It is not impossible that Willem Obrecht might have been a younger brother of Vincent—in which case the composer would have been named after his grandfather. What argues against this, however, is the disparity in age between Vincent, Lysbette, and Willem (the latter would have been at least ten years their junior), and the virtual absence of any evidence suggesting that members of the Obrecht family were named after their grandparents.

[19] Willem Hoebrecht *filius* Willems was enrolled as a 'bruwers kint' in the guild of brewers in 1401/2, probably at the age of about six or seven (SAG 160.6, fo. 30ᵛ); his father Willem Hoebrecht had become a member of the same guild in 1394/5 (ibid. fo. 27ʳ; I am grateful to Mr Dieudonné Marijns for pointing out these references to me). Among other prominent Obrechts at Ghent is the Jan Obrecht who bought a ship on 7 Sept. 1409 (SAG 301.20, 1409/10, fo. 2ʳ). After his death in 1419, he left a widow Lysbette van Houtem *filia* Simoens, and one child, Hannekin, for whom his brother Bertelmeeus Obrecht acted as legal guardian (the report of property, dated 4 May 1419, lists various possessions, mainly in the region of Steeland; SAG 330.17, 1419/20, fo. 33ᵛ; a second report of property, after the death of Lysbette van Houtem in 1432, is in 330.20, 1431/2, fo. 43ʳ). After his emancipation and marriage in 1439, Hannekin acquitted his uncle Bertelmeeus of his guardianship (SAG 330.22, 1438/9, fo. 73ʳ). Bertelmeeus Obrecht himself died some time before 13 May 1449, leaving a widow Lysbette van Doenessele, and one child from a previous marriage, Margriete Obrecht, now the wife of Pieter Boudins *filius* Jacops (SAG 301.40, 1448/9, fo. 153ʳ). A Pieter Obrecht borrowed money on 5 Oct. 1403 (SAG 301.19, 1403/4, fo. 9ʳ); he must be the father of Laureins Obrecht *filius* Pieters, who died some time before 1456, and whose brother Lievin Obrecht acted as legal guardian for his children (SAG 301.43, 1455/6, fo. 102ᵛ). Finally, a Gillis Obrecht died some time before 13 Dec. 1438, leaving a widow Lysbette sCroecx, and two daughters, Margriete Obrecht, wife of Joosse ser Obrechts *alias* Vander Walle, and Martine Obrecht, wife of Arend vander Moers (330.22, 1438/9, fo. 64ʳ⁻ᵛ; Lysbette sCroecx died in 1470/1, see 400.22, fo. 153ʳ).

a member of an established trade guild, perhaps that of the shippers or brewers, and had his son enrolled at a young age in order to secure his rights to carry on the family business. As Willem grew older, however, his interest and aptitude must have drawn him to trumpeting, for which his father likewise arranged guild entry. Unlike in the case of the enterprising Ghijs brothers, there is no evidence of any commercial side-activities on the part of Willem during the thirty-six years of his documented career.

Willem Obrecht must have spent most of the 1440s as a trumpeter's apprentice with an established master. Boys, even as apprentices, were expected to work for their support. They reached legal majority at the age of 15, and achieved emancipation as fully independent citizens as soon as they had given sufficient proof of financial and legal competence, normally at the age of about 20.[20] Willem Obrecht's appointment as city trumpeter in 1452 must have marked his emancipation; he was born presumably in the early 1430s. Prior to the appointment, however, Willem must have lived and worked with a master trumpeter, who collected his revenues and provided for his training. This would have been the normal pattern.

The master-trumpeter in question may well have been Ghiselbrecht de Keyser, who was nearly a generation older than the other trumpeters appointed in 1452. Ghiselbrecht was probably the son of the trumpeter Pieter de Keyser, whose professional activities in Ghent stretch back to 1409,[21] and who stands at the head of a long dynasty of De Keysers, who remained in the trade until at least 1736.[22] In 1428/9 Pieter de Keyser played at Dendermonde together with an unnamed son, probably Ghiselbrecht; later in the same year 'the son of Pieter de Keyser, and his companions' were paid for playing at the procession in Dendermonde.[23] The payment comes much too early to suggest that any of the 'companions' might have been identical with Willem Obrecht, Roeland and

---

[20] Roeland Ghijs had become emancipated by 9 Sept. 1449, when he acquitted his mother Lysbette sKempen of her guardianship (SAG 330.24, 1449/50¹, fo. 4ʳ). His brother Lodewijk had achieved emancipation by 28 Mar. 1452 at the latest (SAG 330.25, 1451/2, fo. 68ʳ). Significantly, his name is given as 'Loykin' in Doc. 4: the suffix '-kin' normally indicates minority in Ghent legal documents (see below, n. 41). Both brothers must have been born in the early to mid 1430s. Jan Toysbaert must have become emancipated through his marriage with Lievyne sCosters, before 1451 (SAG 330.25, 1450/1, fo. 58ᵛ). For Willem Obrecht and Mattheus Nijs the appointment in Nov. 1452 is the earliest known evidence of emancipation.

[21] SAG, city accounts 1409/10, fos. 221ʳ, 221ᵛ, and 234ʳ (kindly brought to my attention by Keith Polk). For other documents, see also Polk, 'Flemish Wind Bands', 21–4 and 73.

[22] De Potter, *Gent, van den oudsten tijd*, i. 556.

[23] 'Pietren den Keyser ende sinen sone' and 'Pietre Keysers zone ende sijnen ghesellen'; see BAR 38004, 1428/9, pp. [1], [3], and [12] (information kindly supplied by Keith Polk).

Lodewijk Ghijs, Mattheus Nijs, or Jan Toysbaert: these could have been hardly more than toddlers at the time.[24]

The earliest known document to mention Ghiselbrecht de Keyser in a professional capacity dates from 1441/2, when the city of Ghent rewards his freelance services as a trumpeter.[25] This is the earliest payment to any of the six men, by a margin of more than ten years. Several other indications confirm that Ghiselbrecht was the oldest member of the group. His son, the trumpeter Arend de Keyser, acted as an emancipated citizen by 1457,[26] and was to join the six trumpeters on several important occasions and journeys in the next years. (By comparison, none of the other trumpeters' sons turns up before about 1480.) Moreover, charters and official documents listing the six trumpeters' names usually mention Ghiselbrecht first.[27] It seems likely that Ghiselbrecht de Keyser had formed the group from the most promising trumpeters' apprentices in Ghent, several of whom may have been his own pupils, and that it was he who had trained and perfected their ensemble playing.

A picture thus begins to emerge of Willem Obrecht's social and professional background. Although he is not documented before 1452, we may take it that he had lived long enough in the city for the authorities to trust him to remain loyal at a time of crisis. As a city trumpeter, and a member of the Guild of St Andrew, Willem belonged to the powerful and well-organized class of urban professionals—a proud community of craftsmen confident enough to take on even the duke of Burgundy. It is thus probably no coincidence that his documented career starts during the Ghent revolt of 1451–3.

The uprising itself ended in bloody disaster. On 23 July 1453 more than 16,000 Ghenters lost their lives on the battlefield near Gavere—a staggering number even by today's standards.[28] The victorious Burgundian

[24] The men probably did play at Dendermonde in 1455, when the accounts of that city mention 'six trumpeters of Ghent' (Polk, German Instrumental Music, 224 n. 15).

[25] SAG 400.16, 1441/2, fo. 55ᵛ; see also 1444/5, fo. 224ʳ, where Ghiselbrecht de Keyser is mentioned together with a Lieven de Rode, also trumpeter. (I thank Keith Polk for pointing out these references to me.) The earliest known document to mention Ghiselbrecht as an emancipated citizen dates from 18 June 1440 (SAG 330.22, 1439/40, fo. 110ᵛ); he had died by 30 Aug. 1473 (SAG 301.52, 1473/4, fo. 37ᵛ).

[26] In 1457 Arend, son of Ghiselbrecht de Keyser and the late Margriete Teerlincx, first appears before the magistrates of the by-law and inheritance in Ghent. This presupposes legal majority plus emancipation, and would suggest that Arend was in his late teens at the very least. See SAG 301.44, 1456/7, fo. 61ᵛ (8 Mar. 1457) and 330.27, 1456/7, fo. 145ᵛ (29 July 1457).

[27] See Docs. 4, 14, and 17.

[28] Among the casualties at Gavere on the day before the battle was a trumpeter about whom the chronicler Jehan de Waurin tells the following story: 'A celle heure estoit layans une trompette qui avoit autresfois servy aulcun seigneur de lost du duc [of Burgundy], quy se fut rendu Gantois, lequel se prinst a tromper le plus haultement quil peult et du plus hault lieu du chastel [of Gavere]; puis se prinst a dire plusieurs parolles injurieuses du duc et lappelant tyrant et en le mannechant que bien

forces stopped short of occupying or plundering the city, but the duke imposed a peace treaty demanding humiliating concessions and astronomical reparations. The civic constitution was changed to reduce the power of the guilds. Ducal supporters were planted in places of high office, where they dictated a firmly pro-Burgundian policy for the next few years. Three weeks after the battle of Gavere, the six city trumpeters took up their work,[29] serving a city that was now rapidly changing its political complexion. Yet they remained loyal to its lords, as they had undertaken to do, staying in their service for the rest of their lives.

Ghent's policy in the years after Gavere was to regain its former political strength by winning back Philip the Good's favour. This was a slow process that took most of the 1450s and culminated in the duke's *joyeuse rentrée* on 23 April 1458—an event so magnificent that it seemed, according to one local chronicler, 'as though God had descended from heaven'.[30] The band of trumpeters, ironically, was an important asset in the new policy. The ensemble playing of the six men must have been of a very high standard, unmatched in the Low Countries—a fact soon appreciated in Burgundian circles. Over a period of at least sixteen years (1454–70), Charles of Charolais, son of Philip the Good, regularly borrowed the trumpeters on important occasions or missions. And when the powerful Burgundian peer John, Duke of Cleves, went on an official embassy to Mantua in 1459, he wished Willem Obrecht and his companions to be the

---

brief les Gantois luy abaisseroient son orgueil, de laquele chose le bon duc ne fist que rire, tournant tout en la folye de celle trompette' (*Recueil des croniques et anchiennes istories de la Grant Bretaigne, a present nomme Engleterre*, ed. W. Hardy, v (London, 1891), 227–8). After the castle had been surrendered, Philip the Good ordered all men inside it, 'et aussi la trompette quy avoit le duc injurie', to be hanged and strangled (ibid. 228). The last man to be hanged, according to another chronicler, was a Ghent trumpeter by the name of Haloguet. He was already climbing the ladder to his death when news arrived that a massive army was approaching Gavere from Ghent. During the tumult that followed, Haloguet evidently realized that he might still save his skin if he could somehow win time until the arrival of his fellow Ghenters. He beseeched the lords in charge to ask Philip the Good to have mercy on him, promising that he would serve the duke as a trumpeter from that day onward. When they responded that he should be giving thought to his soul since he would die presently, Haloguet, in a last desperate attempt, requested that 'au moins devant sa mort, il euist grâce et poüst sonner ung cop [de] la trompette'. Just at that point shouts and cries went up everywhere to get ready for battle, and this caused such general commotion in the camp that Haloguet was left standing on his ladder 'autant que il peut vivre' (anon., *Chronique des Pays-Bas, de France, d'Angleterre et de Tournai* [1294–1467], in J.-J. De Smet (ed.), *Corpus chronicorum Flandriae*, iii (Brussels, 1856), 518).

[29] The city account from the financial year 1453/4, starting on 15 Aug. 1453 (SAG 400.17), is the first to mention the new trumpeters by name (except for Jan Toysbaert, who was apparently replaced by Jan Aelterman and may well have died at Gavere), to record the payment of their annual salary (fo. 411ʳ), and to make a careful distinction between 'the six trumpeters of this city' (e.g., fos. 386ʳ, 413ʳ, 419ʳ) and, more generally, 'the trumpeters and pipers of this city' (fo. 412ʳ). By comparison, the city account from the previous year uses the latter formulation only (SAG 400.17, fos. 320ʳ, 321ʳ, 328ᵛ, 330ᵛ), which implies that the appointment had not yet taken effect.

[30] Fris, *Histoire de Gand*, 137.

trumpeters in his retinue. The city of Ghent not only allowed its band of trumpeters to be lent out but, despite its strained finances, actively subsidized their journeys—no doubt as a gesture of goodwill towards the Burgundian powers that be.

The connections between the Ghent trumpeters and Burgundy may well date back to February 1454, when Philip the Good organized the Feast of the Pheasant in Lille. Ghent sent its own delegates to the shooting games accompanying the feast, and the six trumpeters were paid for joining them.[31] It was probably on this occasion that they first met the then 19-year-old Charles the Bold, Count of Charolais. Charles was evidently impressed by their musical skills, for only eight months later the trumpeters returned to Lille to play at his wedding with Isabelle of Bourbon (30 October).[32] Of course this may still have been part of their duty to represent the city of Ghent on important occasions. But two years later, in July 1456, they joined the retinue of Count Charles, accompanying him on his travels through the county of Holland as governor and lieutenant-general of the Netherlands.[33] Seven months after that, in February 1457, they went to Brussels to play at the baptism of Charles's daughter, Mary of Burgundy.[34] In April and May of the same year they were in Charles's retinue again, this time at the jousts in Bruges.[35]

---

[31] Doc. 5 (1453/4): 'Item, given at the command of the aldermen to the six trumpeters of this city, for having gone with the deputy of this city to the aforesaid place [Lille] at the shooting games, 288 Flemish groats.'

[32] Doc. 6: 'Item, given on 8 November [1454], at the command of the aldermen, to Willem Hoebrecht for himself and his five companion trumpeters of this city, to help them with their expenses in travelling to Lille to our redoubtable lord the Count of Charolais at the feasts and jousts held there, 480 Flemish groats.'

[33] Doc. 7: 'Item, given at the command of the aldermen to the six trumpeters of this city, when they travelled to Holland to our redoubtable lord and prince, on 13 July [14]56, 240 Flemish groats.' Charles of Charolais had been appointed governor and lieutenant-general of the Netherlands in 1454; see Vaughan, Philip the Good, 341–2.

[34] Mary of Burgundy was born on 13 Feb. 1457, and was baptized four days later, on 17 Feb. See Doc. 8: 'Item, given at the same command as above to the six trumpeters of this city, to help them in their expenses when they travelled to Brussels because of the happy tidings of the noble birth of the daughter of our redoubtable lord, my lord the Count of Charolais, as is declared in the warrant, on 7 Mar. [14]57, 48 Flemish groats.' The single surviving account from the household of Charles of Charolais, over the calendar year 1457, contains a corresponding payment (Doc. 9).

[35] Charles was in Bruges from 17 Apr. to early May 1457. See Doc. 10: 'Item, given at the command of the aldermen to the six trumpeters of this city, when they went to Bruges with the Germans, with the consent of the aforesaid aldermen as declared in the warrant, for the rent of their horses, 72 Flemish groats.' Again there is a corresponding payment in the account of Charles of Charolais's household (Doc. 11). It is worth noting that a 'sire Wague Feutrier, prebstre, demourant a Tournay' also received payment at the jousts (LAN B3661, fo. 38ʳ). He is not mentioned here as a musician, yet is undoubtedly identical with the singer Waghe Feustrier who worked at the French royal court in 1464–72. See L. L. Perkins, 'Musical Patronage at the Royal Court of France under Charles VII and Louis XI (1422–83)', Journal of the American Musicological Society, 37 (1984), 554.

Lysbette Gheeraerts

By now, in the summer of 1457, Willem Obrecht was a married man: within the next year or so his wife Lysbette Gheeraerts was to give birth to his son Jacob. The birthdate can be established approximately with the help of Jacob Obrecht's portrait, which tells us that he was 38 years old by 1496. This means that his thirty-eighth birthday fell in either 1495 or 1496, pointing to 1457 or 1458 as the year of birth. No marriage contract between Willem Obrecht and Lysbette Gheeraerts has survived: such expensive legal acts were drawn up only for the richest families of the town. Yet we are not completely in the dark as to the background of the marriage: the Obrecht and Gheeraerts families must already have known each other well by the 1440s.

This is apparent from a number of early documents on Jacob Obrecht's maternal grandfather, his mother, and himself, written by the magistrates of inheritance at Ghent. The peculiar nature of these documents requires some explanation. The chief task of the magistrates of inheritance was to protect the heritage of under-age orphans. Upon the death of the father or mother (or both), they immediately assumed chief guardianship over the children, depriving the remaining parent temporarily of all parental responsibility. The magistrates then appointed an acting guardian, normally a close relative who had no rights of inheritance himself. The guardian was given forty days to negotiate the orphans' inheritance with the other inheritors (usually the remaining parent and all adult children); after the matter was resolved to everyone's satisfaction, the guardian returned to the magistrates and submitted a full report on the inheritance of the children. This report was then read out in the presence of all other inheritors, and, upon their approval, was entered in the yearbook of the magistrates. (These yearbooks have survived virtually complete for the period 1349–1795, and are a fascinating source of information on domestic life in medieval Ghent.[36]) Finally, the guardian was discharged of his responsibility, and the remaining parent or someone else was given permanent guardianship. The magistrates of inheritance did not normally intervene in matters of inheritance in which no children were involved:[37] it is

---

[36] SAG, series 330; see the excellent study by David Nicholas, *The Domestic Life of a Medieval City: Women, Children, and the Family in Fourteenth-Century Ghent* (Lincoln, Nebr., and London, 1985).

[37] They did, however, register testaments, quitclaims (cf. Doc. 47), renunciations or claims to the estates of deceased citizens (cf. Doc. 20), investments of money on behalf of the orphans who had

due to the untimely deaths of Jacob Obrecht's maternal grandfather and mother that we possess some unique documents on the wealth and social background of his mother's family.

The first two documents were written after the death of Obrecht's grandfather Andries Gheeraerts, in mid-April 1450. Andries left a widow, Marien Laps, and five children, three of whom were under age. His death therefore had to be reported to the magistrates of inheritance. These decided, on 17 April, to appoint the wealthy shipper and spice-trader Jan Obrecht *filius* Jans as guardian over the three orphans, and recorded their decision in the yearbook as follows: 'Jan Hobrecht became guardian over Ghijselin, Gheleynen, and Betkin, children of Andries Gheeraerds, [who have] inherited *de patre*. Done on 17 April 1450' (Doc. 1). The last-named of the three children, Betkin ('Betty') is Willem Obrecht's future wife Lysbette—as yet legally under age and unmarried (since she would otherwise have been represented by her husband). This is the earliest surviving document to mention Jacob Obrecht's mother; it confirms what we can now infer from the portrait, that the composer was born well after 1450. Girls reached legal majority at the age of 12; the age of consent was 15.[38] Since Lysbette was less than 12 in 1450 but over 15 in 1457–8 (Jacob's date of birth), she must have been born between 1438 and 1442.

More significant, however, is the magistrates' decision to appoint Jan Obrecht as guardian, a responsibility normally assumed by a brother or other direct relative of the deceased. This can only mean that the Obrecht and Gheeraerts families were on intimate terms well before 1450: no relative being available, a close friend or business partner of the deceased was asked to protect the inheritance of his youngest children. Evidently the marriage of Willem and Lysbette was to seal a family relationship that stretched back into their childhoods.

Jan Obrecht needed less than a month to settle the inheritance of the three orphans. On 11 May 1450 he returned to the magistrates of inheritance and submitted a detailed account of their share in Andries Gheeraerts's estate (Doc. 2). The inheritance turns out to have been rich but problematic. Andries Gheeraerts and Marien Laps held substantial possessions in land in northern Flanders, mainly around their native

inherited that money (usually in the form of hereditary rents or loans), problems with the repayment of debts, and their resolution, and all legal conflicts that might ensue from these matters.

[38] Even without the portrait, then, it can be established from Docs. 1 and 2 that Lysbette Gheeraerts could not have reached the age of consent until 1453, and consequently that her son was unlikely to have been born before 1454.

village of Hughersluus (about half-way between Ghent and Bergen op Zoom; see Fig. 1). The total of about 16 ha. may seem comparatively little today, but in the densely populated county of Flanders, with its heavy dependence on agriculture and pasture, it was a source of considerable income, certainly enough for a large family to live from comfortably.[39] In addition Andries and Marien owned two houses in Hughersluus, and one in Ghent—further sources of regular income. Yet there were also debts, 'owed to many diverse persons', amounting to the astronomical figure of nearly 35,000 groats. Whatever his trade, Andries Gheeraerts plainly had been a man who made substantial business investments with borrowed money, probably repaying each of his creditors on a regular basis. This is quite a normal pattern for entrepreneurs in the fifteenth century (as indeed in our own), and is unlikely to suggest financial recklessness. It just was Andries's misfortune that he died in the midst of building up or expanding his business, leaving his wife and children with a particularly complex legacy.

As a guardian Jan Obrecht did not have to square the account:[40] it was his responsibility merely to record fairly what the three orphans had inherited, in assets as well as liabilities. In the long run more than half the possessions would have to be sold, but Lysbette's inheritance nevertheless remained substantial. Her dowry was fixed at 2,400 groats, a huge sum, and she was to retain her fair share of what was left of the lands and houses in and around Hughersluus. Lysbette was a good match for the young trumpeter Willem, as Jan Obrecht was perhaps in the best position to know: if anyone suggested and negotiated their marriage it must have been Jan. We do not know at what point between 1453 and 1457 the marriage was concluded, but there is indeed evidence of a continued and close association between Jan Obrecht and the young couple.

This evidence is provided by two further documents, which were drawn up by the magistrates of inheritance ten years after Andries Gheeraerts's death, on 30 July 1460. These documents are formally identical to the two previous ones: the first is the appointment of a guardian, and the second a report on the inheritance of an orphan. The guardian, once again, is Jan Obrecht. The deceased is Lysbette Gheeraerts, wife of

---

[39] In contemporary units of measurement Andries Gheeraerts possessed 36 *gemeten*, each *gemet* being approximately 0.4456 ha. (1.1011 acres), and yielding 30 groats per annum. The total income from these lands alone, then, amounted to 1,080 groats, that is, one and a half times Willem Obrecht's annual salary as city trumpeter.

[40] It was not too late, however, to cancel Andries's recent purchase of a parcel of land in the region of Steeland, and thus to reduce the debt by 1,728 groats. See SAG 330.24, 1449/50, fo. 24ʳ, 11 May 1450 (it is this document, incidentally, that mentions the guardian Jan Obrecht as 'filius Jans', thus confirming his identity with the shipper and spice-trader).

Willem Obrecht. The orphan is her little boy Jacob, who now, at the age of 2, enters recorded history: 'Jan Hobrecht became guardian of Willem Hoebrecht's child from Lysbette Gheeraerts [who has] inherited *de matre*. Done on 30 July 1460' (Doc. 15; see Pl. 2).

Lysbette died prematurely: she was certainly less than about 22 (since she had still been under age in 1450), but over 18 (since she must have reached the age of consent by 1457). Moreover, she left only one child; the average urban family in late medieval Flanders counted three to four children. Jan Obrecht settled the inheritance on behalf of Lysbette's son, and he did so very quickly. On the same day, 30 July, he submitted the 'report of property' of the boy, and the magistrates of inheritance drew up the earliest surviving document to mention the composer by his name: Copkin, that is, 'little Jacop' (Pl. 3).[41] The text is too lengthy to be cited here in translation; the opening sets the tone in typically verbose legal phraseology:

Be it known, etc., that this is the report of property pertaining to Copkin Hoebrecht *filius* Willems with Lysbette Gheeraerts, who was his lawful wife, received and inherited, etc., by the aforenamed orphan upon the death of the aforesaid Lysbette, his late mother, which property was submitted by Jan Oebrecht as guardian of the aforenamed orphan, just as it had been shared, squared, and settled against Willem, his aforenamed father, in the home of the aforenamed Lysbette, his late mother, in the presence of kindred and friends [close relatives], etc., for the best possible profit and interest of the same orphan . . . (Doc. 16.)

Jan Obrecht then went on to list the possessions that Jacob had inherited from his mother. This *staet van goed* can be summarized as follows:

1. Possessions acquired by the deceased before marriage. Under Ghent law these became the property of the children; the surviving parent could not inherit any of this, but was entitled to half the usufruct for the rest of his or her life. Lysbette had brought her share in Andries Gheeraerts's

---

[41] The diminutive Copkin sounds attractively endearing in Dutch, yet in Ghent legal documents it was simply standard practice to add the suffix '-kin' to the first names of children who had not yet reached legal majority. Children who had reached that age but were not as yet emancipated were usually named without the suffix. For instance, Lysbette Gheeraerts is consistently called Betkin in Docs. 1 and 2, but her brothers Ghiselin and (with one exception) Ghelain are called by their adult names. All three children needed a guardian, but Lysbette was evidently under age (under 12), whereas Ghiselin and Ghelain had reached the age of legal majority for boys (15) but were not as yet emancipated. Yet Ghiselin was older than Ghelain, for he was already allowed to conduct his own affairs (albeit under the loose supervision of his guardian) 'since he is advanced in years and wisdom'. Ghelain was not yet allowed to do this, and his name is given once as Ghelainkin. Evidently he was little over 15, whereas Ghiselin was probably approaching 20. Very rarely an individual might retain the suffix throughout his life, perhaps as an affectionate sobriquet. This is true of Josquin, but also, for instance, of the composer Roelkin ('little Roeland') in SegC s.s.

Pl. 2. Appointment of Jan Obrecht as guardian of Jacob Obrecht in 1460 (Doc. 15)

PL. 3. Report of the property inherited by Jacob Obrecht from his deceased mother Lysbette Gheeraerts (Doc. 16)

estate into the marriage, now greatly reduced, but free of debts: 4 *gemeten* (1.78 ha.) of land in Steeland near Hughersluus, altogether yielding 120 groats per annum. Since Jacob's grandmother Marien Laps was still alive, she was entitled to half these revenues; Willem Obrecht, in turn, was entitled to half the rest. During their lifetime, then, Jacob would receive only 30 groats per annum.

2. Common property, bought by the couple after marriage. The surviving parent always inherited half of this, and was entitled to half the usufruct of the remainder (which would be divided equally among the children). Willem and Lysbette had bought a total of 5 *gemeten* (2.23 ha.) of land in Steeland and Hughersluus, altogether yielding 420 groats per annum. Jacob was entitled to 105 groats during his father's lifetime, Willem to 315 groats.

3. Cash, chattels, and other various household possessions. These were valued at 720 groats, after deduction of the expenses for the execution of the testament, the funeral service, and the burial. From this sum Willem undertook 'to support his aforesaid orphan with food, drink, clothes, stockings, shoes, etc.' For this he would normally be allowed, despite the Church's prohibitions against usury, to use the interest (usually ten per cent, that is, 72 groats per annum), but not to diminish the sum itself. Willem's sureties were Victoer Symoens and the tailor Pieter Clays.[42]

4. The dowry, 2,400 groats. Under Ghent law, every daughter who received a dowry on her wedding was to return the sum upon the death of either or both of her parents; thereafter she could share equally in their inheritance. Alternatively, it was possible to keep the dowry but to surrender all rights of inheritance (as Willem Obrecht seems to have done on behalf of his second wife; see Doc. 20). Jacob Obrecht inherited his mother's dowry, but would have to return the sum after the death of his grandmother Marien Laps; thereafter he could share her inheritance equally with his aunts and uncles. During Marien's lifetime, however, the dowry might have been invested on his behalf as a hereditary rent, normally at 5 or 6.25 per cent interest, yielding 120 to 150 groats per annum.

Having thus acquitted himself of his task, Jan Obrecht was discharged of the guardianship, and Willem Obrecht resumed legal responsibility

---

[42] Since sureties were usually direct relatives, one would expect Willem Obrecht to have named here at least one brother or parent. His failure to do so might possibly suggest that he was the only adult member of his parents' household who was alive (or resident in Ghent) in the late 1450s. This would be consistent with the fact that throughout the period examined for this study (1438–92), the magistrates of inheritance never once record Willem's appearance in connection with his own family, even though he was to appear several times on behalf of his second wife Beatrijse Jacops (see below).

over his son. He was to keep looking after the inheritance even after Jacob had reached legal majority (in 1472–3) and was emancipated (April 1480 at the latest, on receiving the priesthood). On 29 March 1484, for instance, the composer empowered his father to collect 480 groats in revenues from his lands in Hughersluus, to be paid by the widow of his uncle Ghelain Gheeraerts (Doc. 30). And Willem kept in his possession, until his death in 1488, an unspecified sum of cash that Jacob had inherited from Lysbette, presumably the dowry (Doc. 47; see Ch. 5). Yet as far as the magistrates of inheritance were concerned, the matter was now settled. And so, with the standard conclusion 'Actum xxxᵃ julij aº lx' they ended the last known document to mention the composer for twenty years.

Jan Obrecht was not to return in the documented life of the composer. However, the position of trust he enjoyed with Willem Obrecht, Lysbette Gheeraerts, and her parents indicates that he was and remained an important figure to the family. His position as guardian of Jacob strongly suggests previous involvement in the household, perhaps as a witness or a godfather. Subsequent involvement cannot be ruled out either. During the 1470s and 1480s Jan Obrecht became one of Ghent's most prominent and powerful citizens, a man of substantial wealth who seems to have been on excellent terms with the Burgundian rulers. It is tempting to speculate what strings he might have pulled to further the education and career of his erstwhile charge.

Willem Obrecht could not afford to stay a single parent for long: as a professional trumpeter he earned most of his living out of doors, and his connections with the court of Charles of Charolais would continue to provide occasions for lucrative travels away from Ghent. Jacob was hardly 3 years old, and his needs alone dictated that Willem remarry as soon as possible. Thus we need not be surprised that a second wife, Beatrijse Jacops, is mentioned as early as September 1464. By then she may well have been Jacob Obrecht's stepmother for several years.

Beatrijse Jacops, like Lysbette Gheeraerts, came from a wealthy rural family that had moved into Ghent while retaining income from possessions in their native region.[43] Upon the death of Beatrijse's father Pieter Jacops, in September 1464, she and Willem formally surrendered

---

[43] Beatrijse's parents are mentioned as a couple in Ghent documents as early as Sept. 1441 (SAG 330.22, 1441/2, fo. 10ᵛ). As pointed out earlier, it is probable that the Obrecht family, too, originated from outside Ghent. A strong possibility is Lokeren: references to property in this town can be cited for the shipper Heinric Obrecht (SAG 301.9, 1406/7, fo. 31ᵛ), and for Jan Obrecht *filius* Jans (SAG 330.28, 1459/60, fo. 103ᵛ, and SAG 301.45, 1459/60, fo. 106ᵛ). This would make sense, given the shipping background of the Obrecht family, for Lokeren was one of the most important shipping towns between Ghent and Antwerp along the main connecting waterways.

all rights of inheritance, possibly, as suggested above, because they preferred to keep her dowry (Doc. 20). They did, however, inherit lands and
hereditary rents from her mother Lysbette Smeets and her great-uncle
Lievin Jacops, all in the area around Eeklo (about half-way between Ghent
and Bruges).[44] Willem and Beatrijse do not appear to have had any children in the more than twenty-four years of their marriage.

[44] On 29 Apr. 1465 Willem Obrecht formally acquitted Lysbette Matthijs, the widow of Beatrijse's former guardian, her uncle Jacop de Smet, in connection with the inheritance from her
mother Lysbette Smeets (SAG 330.30, 1464/5, fo. 51ᵛ). Four days previously Willem and Beatrijse
had sold the inheritance to Lievin vanden Speye (Doc. 21). The inheritance from Beatrijse's great-
uncle Lievin Jacops *filius* Lievins was sold to Lievin vanden Speye on 24 Feb. 1478 (SAG 301.54,
1477/8, fo. 74ᵛ). Jacob Obrecht is mentioned implicitly in the latter two documents as 'haerlieder
hoyr' ('their heir', nom. sing.). All possessions were situated in the parishes of Eeklo, Wakken,
Waarschoot, and Lembeek, north-west of Ghent.

2 BORN FOR THE MUSES

AT the age of 2, Jacob Obrecht had a secure future virtually mapped out for him. The inheritance of his mother alone would eventually guarantee him a regular income of 540 groats per year—at a time when one groat per day represented an acceptable living standard. And although no documentation survives on the financial situation of his father, surely he was to leave him a similar legacy: Willem Obrecht could not have married two daughters of well-to-do citizens if he himself brought no commensurate capital to the marriage.

Then there was the professional and social legacy. Willem Obrecht was a burgess of Ghent and a member of the trumpeters' guild of St Andrew, two privileged positions that were hereditary. Everything in Jacob's background predicted that he would become a trumpeter: his education and subsequent livelihood were secured and protected by the trumpeters' guild, his legal and financial rights by the city of Ghent. There is ample documentary evidence to confirm that this was the obvious career pattern. In the later decades of the fifteenth century several sons of Willem Obrecht's colleagues are mentioned as trumpeters in Ghent: Arend de Keyser *filius* Ghiselbrechts, Jooris Nijs *filius* Mattheus, and Joos Ghijs *filius* Lodewijks. And although Roeland Ghijs died childless in January 1489, he had been the legal guardian of his nephews, the trumpeters Arend and Christoffel Ghijs *filii* Lievins, in 1454–62.[1]

It is not at all obvious that anyone should wish to exchange such a stable and socially accepted future in a rich Flemish town for that of a singer. Singers were musical mercenaries, migrating from town to town, rarely enjoying citizen's privileges. Their profession was nowhere protected: if

---

[1] SAG 330.26, 1453/4, rolle fo. 23^v (19 July 1454); 330.29, 1461/2, rolle fo. 5^r (13 Jan. 1462); 330.38, 1488/9, rolle fo. 8^r (9 Jan. 1489). In the last-cited document Lodewijk Ghijs registered his claim to the inheritance of the recently deceased Roeland, which can only mean that the latter had left no children. Jan Aelterman seems to have fathered only daughters (SAG 330.36, 1482/3, fo. 84^v).

there was a conflict with an employer or with a colleague, there was no guild to take the case to court. Nor was there any protection against outside competition, any organized control of the labour market and salaries: singers basically stood on their own, negotiating their terms of employment individually—which may be one reason why they generally earned less than trumpeters.[2] No individual derived any social status merely from being a singer: where we have documentation it is clear that employers sometimes faced the greatest difficulty in disciplining the behaviour of their musicians—which could range from neglect of duty, insults, and indecency to street fights and seductions. (Here again, guilds would have enforced a measure of self-discipline.) Nor was composition a profession in its own right, let alone a protected one: a composer was simply a singer who wrote music in his own time.

Yet the priesthood was an attractive option. In the church there were no limitations to upward mobility, except in terms of one's own intellectual ability and political skills. If, some time in the mid 1460s, it was decided that Jacob be trained for the priesthood, this was surely not with the intention that he should eventually lead the life that he did, but that he should rise above the social position of his father. In this respect Obrecht was to fail: compared with other trumpeters' sons, his existence was insecure, unstable, and unprotected. Major crises in his life exposed his social vulnerability: frictions with his employers, dismissal, illness. Yet he was a man of exceptional musical ability, and perhaps we may entertain the romantic notion that Jacob Obrecht sacrificed a promised rise in the hierarchy of the church for a passionate love of music—just as many later composers could not bring themselves to pursue a career in law. He was the Orphic Jacob, born for the Muses.

Genuine piety in the Obrecht household undoubtedly played a part, but then piety, too, had a social dimension. We know that Willem Obrecht was a member of the Guild of Our Lady in the church of St John at Ghent (Doc. 42). Yet this probably tells us more about his status as a parishioner than about the intensity of his faith. Veneration of the Virgin was commonplace; what is significant is the fact that the guild had relatively restricted membership. A more 'open' guild like the Confraternity at 's-Hertogenbosch (which had a particularly energetic recruitment policy) annually inscribed new members by the dozens. In *Mille quingentis*

---

[2] This seems to have been the general pattern throughout Europe; see, for instance, L. Lockwood, *Music in Renaissance Ferrara, 1400–1505* (Oxford, 1984), 177–84, especially 184: 'even the least of the trumpeters are paid more than twice as much as the singers, while the average is more like three times as much for trumpeters'.

Willem Obrecht is described as 'adorned with great probity', yet it is difficult for us to know what the fifteenth century might have chosen to describe as honest: often it is no more than a synonym for 'Christian'.[3] Nor should we read too much into the statement, made at Ferrara in 1510, that Jacob Obrecht had been 'persona pia' (Doc. 50). The composer had shown his piety with a legacy made in his dying days—when intense piety is to be expected even in the worst sinner.

Obrecht's later ideas of music and musicianship were undoubtedly shaped by his early upbringing as the son of a master trumpeter. This was the world he left behind, but musically it was never far removed from his own. Not only civic and political life were punctuated by trumpeting at every occasion—weddings, receptions, proclamations, feasts, and processions—but vocal and instrumental forces frequently joined in the parish churches of Ghent. And Willem Obrecht already knew what it meant to serve in court circles. The composers of *De tous biens playne* and *N'aray-je jamais* (to name but two models for later masses by Jacob) were not distant figures: Willem himself had travelled and worked together with Hayne van Ghizeghem and Robert Morton. It is this trumpeters' world that nurtured the precocious talent of Copkin Hoebrecht *filius* Willems. The vast archival riches of Ghent allow us to sketch that world in some detail, and suggest numerous musical experiences that must have left lasting impressions in the boy's mind.

Corporate Musicianship in Ghent

With Philip the Good's magnificent reception in April 1458 the city of Ghent had finally succeeded in its conciliatory policy towards the duke. The six trumpeters were still free to serve in Burgundian circles, yet the city no longer paid them for doing so. Thus our main source of information on Willem Obrecht's Burgundian activities, the Ghent city accounts, dries up altogether after 1458.

---

[3] Johannes Ockeghem, for instance, was universally praised as a 'good man', yet it is clear from Guillaume Cretin's lament on the composer's death that his virtues were simply those that were expected of any prosperous man; see *Déploration de Guillaume Cretin sur le trépas de Jean Okeghem*, ed. Er. Thoinan (Paris, 1864). Ockeghem's 'honesty' had strong overtones of social status and administrative prudence ('il a vescu si très honnestement, et haultement son estat maintenu, riens n'a gasté par fol gouvernement', ibid. 38). Most of the other relevant statements by Cretin reveal more about the composer's last will than about his character. He goes on at some length about Ockeghem's generosity towards the poor and his 'many foundations', which are of course paralleled by the endowments of countless benefactors in the Christian world. Indeed Cretin explicitly urges his readers to follow Ockeghem's example in their own wills ('vous qui vivez prenez de bien tester' to avoid 'la lascheté des faulx exécuteurs', ibid. 39). All we can read from his description, then, is that Ockeghem had died as a good Christian, having done what befitted a man of his wealth and status.

Yet there is plenty of other evidence to confirm that the contacts continued. On 26 June 1459, for instance, the magistrates of the by-law recorded the decision that the six trumpeters were to receive an advance payment of three months' salary, or 240 groats, each. This sum, the magistrates stated, would enable them to enter the service of John I, Duke of Cleves, who was about to depart for Mantua. During the journey, Lysbette Gheeraerts and the other trumpeters' wives would still receive their husbands' monthly salaries:[4]

The magistrates of the bye-law have agreed, at the most urgent plea and request from the high and mighty prince, my lord the duke of Cleves, that Pieter Beys, receiver and treasurer of the city's finances, shall lend to the six trumpeters and clarion-players who are to travel in the service of my aforesaid lord of Cleves on the journey that he has undertaken to make in the name of our valiant and redoubtable lord and prince [Philip the Good] to [the Congress of] our Holy Father the Pope of Rome, summoned at Mantua in Lombardy, the sum of 1,440 groats, to enter the same service, which sum shall not be deducted from their salaries during their absence; their wives shall receive the salary every month, so that these and their children can support themselves during the said journey. But when the same trumpeters and clarion-players shall have returned from the aforesaid service, the city will deduct the said sum from their salaries, which deduction is to escheat to the city. The aforesaid trumpeters and clarion-players have each individually consented to this. (Doc. 12.)

The purpose of John's journey was to represent Duke Philip the Good at the Congress of Mantua, which had been summoned by Pope Pius II to launch a new crusade against the Turks.[5] None of the invited European rulers showed much enthusiasm for the initiative, and 'Philip [the Good], involved in worsening relations with France, could only offer to contribute a contingent and hope to receive papal favours in return for not abandoning the crusade altogether.'[6] John of Cleves was sent as an ambassador to convey the duke's token support, and his role was an important one. For although Philip did not expect to win much political capital at the congress, the summit nevertheless offered a public stage on which it was vital for Burgundy to be seen as one of Europe's key players. On occasions like this, no ruler, not even one who sent a deputy, could afford to have his public image tarnished for lack of palpable magnificence. Here, as on similar events, political power was manifested loud and bright, in sounds

---

[4] Previously published in G. Pietzsch, *Archivalische Forschungen zur Geschichte der Musik an den Höfen der Grafen und Herzöge von Kleve-Jülich-Berg (Ravensberg) bis zum Erlöschen der Linie Jülich-Kleve im Jahre 1609* (Beiträge zur rheinischen Musikgeschichte, 88; Cologne, 1971), 120-1.

[5] For the Congress of Mantua and Philip the Good's response, see J. D. Hintzen, *De kruistocht-plannen van Philips den Goede* (Rotterdam, 1918), 139-46, and Vaughan, *Philip the Good*, 216 and 368-9.   [6] Vaughan, *Philip the Good*, 368.

and colours, flags and banners, shining armour, weaponry, trumpets and clarions, and an impressive train of followers and servants, from knights down to barbers and cooks. Not surprisingly, John of Cleves's retinue numbered over 400 men, and we learn from the Ghent document that he 'most urgently' wished to add the six trumpeters to their number. That the choice fell on Willem Obrecht and his colleagues is telling but perhaps not surprising. Charles of Charolais had repeatedly hired them over the previous five years, and surely he would not have continued making use of their services if they were not the most impressive trumpeters available in the Burgundian Netherlands.

The city of Ghent duly made its advance payment to the six men: the city accounts of 1459/60 mention that they each received 240 groats 'to help them with the purchase of their horses when they travelled to Mantua' (Doc. 13). John of Cleves and his 400-strong retinue were at Mantua from mid August until September. The trumpeters have been traced in Wesel on 20 October 1459, by which time they were no doubt on their way back to Ghent.[7] We can only guess what kinds of exchanges had taken place between the Ghent trumpeters and their colleagues from other national delegations. Chronicles are characteristically vague, but Pamela Starr has discovered several papal payments to foreign 'trombetti e piffari', in connection with the anniversary of Pius II's coronation, which was celebrated in the ducal palace of Mantua on 20 August.[8] No trumpeters except those of the Duke of Ancona are specified by household, but we may take it that Burgundy made a strong presence.

This must explain at least in part the existence of a papal bull, drawn up shortly after the congress, in which the six trumpeters were granted certain indulgences in connection with the foundation and maintenance of their guild chapel, in the parish church of St John at Ghent:[9]

Pius etc., greetings to all the faithful of Christ who shall read this present letter. The glorious and most high Lord, who illuminates the world with His inexpressible brightness, moves and inspires all the faithful of Christ to do good, in order that by their good works they may be able and deserve to win the rewards, prizes, and gifts of eternal bliss. Since, therefore, as We have learned, [Our] beloved sons Gisbertus Cesaris alias de Keyser, Rolandi Gijs, Mattheus Nijs, Ludovicus Gijs,

---

[7] G. Pietzsch, *Fürsten und fürstliche Musiker im mittelalterlichen Köln* (Beiträge zur rheinischen Musikgeschichte, 66; Cologne, 1966), 142–3 n. 87. See also J. Marix, *Histoire de la musique et des musiciens de la cour de Bourgogne sous le règne de Philippe le Bon (1420–1467)* (Strasburg, 1939), 77. John II of Glymes, Jacob Obrecht's later employer in Bergen op Zoom, also joined the mission to Mantua. See C. Slootmans, *Jan metten Lippen: Zijn familie en zijn stad; een geschiedenis der Bergen-op-Zoomsche heeren van Glymes* (Rotterdam, 1945), 33.   [8] Kind communication, 28 Dec. 1992.

[9] See H. Dubrulle, *Bullaire de la province de Reims sous le pontificat de Pie II* (Lille, 1905), 72. This exceedingly important document was first noted by Pietzsch, *Archivalische Forschungen*, 119.

Villhelmus Obrecht, Johannes van Alterer, and Arnoldus de Keyser, laymen of the town of Ghent in the diocese of Tournai, trumpeters of [Our] beloved son, the noble Johannes, Duke of Cleves, desiring to convert in a worthwile exchange things terrestrial into things celestial, and things transitory into things eternal, for the well-being of their souls and those of their ancestors and friends, have from the good things bestowed on them by God caused a certain chapel to be constructed and built for the honour and veneration and under the name of St Andrew in the church of St John in the said town, and situated in the crypt of the same church, and [since] this same chaplaincy is in need of a chaplain or chaplains serving therein in divine worship, of enhancement, and also of chalices, books, and other ecclesiastical ornaments, and [since] the resources of the chaplaincy do not suffice, and therefore the support of Christ's faithful is most seasonable:

We, wishing the said chaplaincy to be attended with suitable honours, and properly sustained with ecclesiastical ornaments, and duly maintained in its buildings, and that therein laudable service be rendered in divine worship, and that the faithful themselves flock thither all the more willingly out of devotion, and all the more readily stretch forth helping hands for such maintenance and increase thereof, so that through this gift of heavenly grace in the same place they may see themselves the more lavishly restored by the mercy of Almighty God and of the blessed Peter and Paul, apostles:

Mercifully grant, in reliance upon His authority, to all those being truly penitent and having made confession, who shall have devoutly visited the said chaplaincy annually on the feasts of St Andrew, St Lazarus, the Nativity of St John the Baptist, and St John the Evangelist, as well as Pentecost, and throughout the octaves of the same feasts, and on the first Friday in Lent, and on the Tuesday after Easter, and who shall have stretched forth the aforesaid helping hands for the maintenance and increase [of the chapel], on each of the aforesaid feasts from first Vespers to second Vespers, and on the Friday and the Tuesday, remission of three years and as many forty-day periods of penances enjoined upon them, the present grant to last for future times in perpetuity. Given at Mantua in the year of the Incarnation of Our Lord 1459, on 13 November, in the second year of Our pontificate. (Doc. 14.)

From a distance of five centuries this may at first sight seem a somewhat unusual document. The guild of the Ghent city trumpeters was a professional association, whose primary function was to protect the livelihoods of its several dozen members. The foundation of a chapel placed their profession in a spiritual context: the privilege of remission was sought from no one less than the Pope himself. Strikingly, given that we are dealing with one of Ghent's smaller guilds, the indulgence was granted, and in no small measure either.

Yet it is clear from many other documents that this was not an unusual course of action for a self-respecting guild—in fact not even the extraordinary success of the six trumpeters seems exceptional. A close parallel is provided by another musicians' guild in Ghent, that of the city carillonneurs or *beyaerders*. This association, dedicated to St Margaret, and based in the parish church of St Nicholas, had been founded on 19 August 1473.[10] A lengthy charter of that date recounts how, 'not long ago', a heavy thunderstorm had raged over the city. Three carillonneurs climbed the tower of St Nicholas's to ring the church bells against the storm, yet lightning struck, killed two of the men, and left the third severely injured on his head and back. Thereupon the carillonneurs of the city, hoping that the intercession of St Margaret might prevent such tragedies from happening in the future, decided to found a guild in her honour, in one of the side-chapels of St Nicholas's. Nearly six years later, on 7 January 1479, the same guild endowed two annual Masses 'with deacon and subdeacon, discant, organs, and trumpets, and also including carillon playing' on the feasts of the 11,000 Virgins and 10,000 Martyrs (21 October and 22 June, respectively). These Masses were to be carried out in the same manner 'as the aforesaid guild is already accustomed to have done . . . every year on St Margaret's Day'.[11] The endowment was motivated by the fact that a certain *her* Pieter de Rue, priest,

has had the chapel of St Margaret in the aforesaid church of St Nicholas ornately and beautifully repaired, at his expense and charge, and similarly has obtained at his expense a certain bull from twelve cardinals concerning the confirmation of the same guild, and certain indulgences, all done, obtained, and executed by the same *her* Pieter.

It is unlikely that *her* Pieter de Rue was the composer Pierre de La Rue. Although the latter has in fact left a polyphonic mass for St Margaret, he could hardly have had the wealth and the influence at this time to obtain such favours for the carillonneurs. More importantly, there are references to Ghent citizens called De Rue throughout the fifteenth century, whereas the composer is known with certainty to have come from Tournai. Be that as it may, there can be no doubt that the bull obtained by *her* Pieter was very similar in content to the one issued for the trumpeters in 1459.[12]

[10] SAG 301.52, 1473/4, fo. 13[r].

[11] SAG 301.55, 1478/9, fo. 117[v]: 'eene ghezonghene messe met dyaken, subdyaken, discante, organen ende trompetten, ooc mede te doene beyaerden alzo wel sdaeghs te vooren als up de voorscreven twee principael daghen, ende hendelic al in zulcker voormen ende mannieren als zij ghehouden hebben ende houden de feeste van Sente Margrieten voornoemt'. (The document of 19 Aug. 1473 had called only for 'a sung Mass with deacon, subdeacon, and organ' on St Margaret's Day.)

[12] There is a highly suggestive (though admittedly circumstantial) context to this document. One of the sworn councillors of the carillonneurs' guild in 1479 is a Jan Hauttrappe. He is undoubtedly identical with the trumpeter Jan Hauttrappe who had fulfilled the same function in the trumpeters'

Although similar documentation has not so far been uncovered for other Ghent guilds, we may take it that the request by Willem Obrecht and his colleagues was not excessively immodest, and the favourable reply not completely out of the ordinary.

Did the plans for a chapel of St Andrew come to fruition? The archives of the trumpeters' guild are lost, but a legal document from 1468 confirms that the association was based in the church of St John (Doc. 23). And a similar document from 1472 gives more information (Doc. 27). This text concerns a civil case between the trumpeters' guild and one of its members.[13] We learn that the association is now called the Guild of St Andrew and St Lazarus (the veneration of the latter saint may explain his prominence in the papal bull of 1459). The guild is ruled by a dean with four sworn councillors.[14] It is based in the crypt of the church of St John, where its members 'honour [the two saints] with the art of trumpeting and piping'. A weekly Mass is celebrated in the chapel on Sundays.

The chapel of St Andrew can be identified: it is the first of the radiating chapels on the north side of the crypt (Pl. 4).[15] The architectural structure of this part of the building was in existence long before the trumpeters had founded their chapel: the Gothic crypt of St John had been built around

guild in 1472 (Doc. 27), and who sold a hereditary rent to that guild in 1479 (Doc. 29). His documented activities as a carillonneur stretch back to 5 Apr.–24 June 1470, when the church of St James paid him for *beyaerdene* during the newly established weekly polyphonic Mass of the Holy Ghost, endowed by Philips uter Zwane (SJG 1201, 1469/70, fo. [5ʳ]). Interestingly, in 1486 Jan Hauttrappe sold a house to a Janne de Rue, possibly a relative of *her* Pieter (SAG 301.58, 1485/6, fo. 90ᵛ).

[13] Doc. 27: a case brought before the Ghent by-law between the Guild of St Andrew and St Lazarus, and one of its members, Christoffel Ghijs (a nephew of Roeland and Lodewijk Ghijs). Some time earlier Christoffel had played in the city of Thielt together with a trumpeter who was not a member of the guild. This earned him a fine of 12 Flemish groats. Christoffel did not accept this fine, called the guild's decision a 'malicious verdict', and thus incurred yet another fine, of 60 groats. After his continued refusal to pay, the guild brought the case before the magistrates of the by-law. These, having heard both parties, and considering 'the youth and small understanding' of Christoffel, sentenced him 'to come to the crypt of St John's on the next Sunday, at the Mass of the aforesaid guild brothers, and to pray each, dean and councillors, on one knee to forgive him the aforesaid words for the love of God', by which the second fine would be struck off, and to pay the first.

[14] The normal practice for Ghent guilds was to celebrate the feast of the patron saint with a solemn Mass, followed by a meal during which each of the councillors elected his successor for the next year. The new councillors would subsequently elect the new dean. Documentation from the trumpeters' guild itself is lacking, but we know from legal documents that in 1468 Lodewijk Ghijs was dean and Mattheus Nijs and Jan Aelterman councillors (Doc. 23), and that Willem Obrecht and Arend Ghijs were councillors in 1479 (Doc. 29).

[15] The chapel can be identified on the basis of RAG K10467, a notarial act from 17 May 1736 concerning a tombstone inscription 'in St Andrew's chapel in the crypt of the cathedral church of St Bavo'. For this and other inscriptions in the chapel, see K. De Volkaersbeke, *Les Églises de Gand*, i (Ghent, 1857), 207–9. For a detailed report on excavations and restorations, see F. De Smidt, *Krypte en koor van de voormalige Sint-Janskerk te Gent* (Ghent, 1959). The guild still used its chapel in 1539–41; see De Potter, *Gent, van den oudsten tijd*, i. 559–60.

PL. 4. The trumpeters' chapel of St Andrew and St Lazarus, in the church of St John, Ghent (now the Cathedral of St Bavo)

the older, Romanesque one in the late fourteenth century. The trumpeters' chapel was situated exactly opposite the chantry chapel of Joos Vijdt and Elizabeth Borluuts (in the church proper), where the well-known Ghent altarpiece by Jan and Hubert van Eyck had been admired by all visitors since its completion in 1432. And it was less than 15 m. removed from the tomb of Jan Obrecht, who had been the guardian of Jacob Obrecht and his mother. Jan's little tombstone still survives: it carries a shield with a mortar and two pestles, the banderole reading 'Here lies Jan Hobrecht, spice-trader'.[16] His tomb in the crypt lies exactly beneath the chapel of the Guild of Our Lady, which counted Willem Obrecht among its members. The life of the Obrecht family, it seems, revolved around the church of St John—professionally, socially, and devotionally.[17] Indeed we know for a fact that Willem Obrecht was a parishioner of St John's during at least the last three years of his life (see Ch. 5).

[16] 'Hier licht Jan Hobrecht crudenier'. The stone has meanwhile been moved from Jan Obrecht's tomb to the chapel next to that of the trumpeters, where it is now mounted in the wall.

[17] De Potter (*Gent, van den oudsten tijd*, v. 414) cites two important documents on early polyphonic practice in the church of St John. An endowment made by Lieven van Leins in 1446 called

But more striking than this are the surviving artistic remains of the trumpeters' devotion. Pre-war restorations in the chapel have revealed fifteenth-century ceiling paintings glorifying the art of trumpeting (Pl. 5). Seven man-size angels in colourful robes are depicted playing the trumpet and shawm, against a background decorated with various wind instruments and rattles. Every Christian would have been reminded here of what is written in Rev. 8: 2, 6, after the breaking of the seventh seal: 'And I saw the seven angels which stood before God; and to them were given seven trumpets . . . And the seven angels which had the seven trumpets prepared themselves to sound.' Not only the angels and their robes but also the instruments themselves are painted with meticulous realism— down to finger-holes, reeds, and, one assumes, their relative size. The iconographic evidence of these paintings can be supplemented with documentary evidence. When Roeland Ghijs redrafted his testament on 14 May 1465, his wife Kathelijne vanden Bounbeke was promised 'one of my silver trumpets, namely the best one, weighing approximately 34 *onsen*' (1.046 kg.) as a reward for executing his will.[18] Even more specific on weight was a contract of 30 April 1470 in which Willem Obrecht sold one of his silver trumpets to Pieter tHaerne, trader in second-hand goods (Doc. 25). Since Willem was paid per ounce of silver, the contract specified the exact weight: 29.625 *onsen* (911 g.).[19] Together, the artistic and documentary evidence from Ghent may bring us a step closer to determining the physical properties of fifteenth-century trumpets.

However this may be, a guild that could afford to have its chapel ornamented in this way either was wealthy or enjoyed the patronage of

for a motet to be sung annually on the eve of St Michael before the altar of that saint (SAG 301.38, 1445/6, fo. 169ʳ). The motet was to be performed by the *cotidiane* of the church 'just as is currently done every year for St Agatha', suggesting that polyphonic practice was by then well established. A rather more lavish endowment, by Laureins de Maegh and his wife Loyse van den Hove in 1460, called for daily Masses to be performed 'by seven priests of the *cotidiane* singing discant' (SAG 301.46, 1460/1, fo. 49ʳ). Unfortunately, only one *cotidiane* account of St John's has survived, for the financial year 1484/5 (RAG K3957). Beside the quarterly lists of priests and singers, it mentions, on fo. 9ʳ, a payment to the tenorist *heer* Gillis Haezart, for copying two 'messen in discant'.

[18] 'Te wetene den vorscreven Katelijne, mijnen wive, een van mijnen zelveren trompetten, te wetene tbeste, weghende xxxiiij onsen, lettel min ofte meer' (SAG 330.30, 1464/5, fo. 50ʳ). The unit of measurement was the *ons* (30.76 g.) of 20 *inghelsen*. The other executor, Joes vanden Audenhove, was to receive Roeland's harness. Roeland and Kathelijne had previously drafted a joint testament on 23 June 1463 (SAG 330.29, 1462/3, fo. 131ʳ). Unfortunately, no similar documents have survived for the other Ghent trumpeters.

[19] The trumpet was described as weighing 29 *onsen* 12.5 *inghelsen* (911.27 g.). Willem Obrecht was paid 50 groats per *ons*, yet the agreed total sum, puzzlingly, was not 29.625 × 50 = 1,481.25 groats, but only 1,464 groats. It is interesting to note that the guild of traders in second-hand goods (*oudecleercopers*) had a monthly Mass for St Nicholas celebrated with singers and trumpeters in their guild chapel in the church of St James. See F. Verstraeten, *De Gentse Sint-Jacobsparochie* (Ghent, 1976), i. 106.

PL. 5. Fifteenth-century ceiling paintings in the trumpeters' chapel of St Andrew and St Lazarus, Ghent

a benefactor like *her* Pieter de Rue. Contributions of the faithful were a major source of income, and quite possibly the papal bull of 1459 indirectly enabled the guild to commission the ceiling paintings, from one of the members of the Ghent guild of painters. (The best-known member of that guild, after 1467, was Hugo van der Goes.) The lack of further documentation is frustrating, yet the odd legal document from the magistrates of the by-law does occasionally throw light on the guild's financial situation. In 1479, for instance (when Willem Obrecht happened to be a sworn councillor), the guild of St Andrew and St Lazarus bought a hereditary rent from its member Jan Hauttrappe, for the substantial sum of 2,640 groats (Doc. 29). This was effectively an investment of surplus capital: the annual interest was 132 groats, or 5 per cent. Nor did the guild lack resources to take its case to the city magistrates when members had violated the guild ordinance and refused to pay the fine: this happened to Janne Muelenijser in 1451, Ghiselbrecht de Keyser in 1468, and Christoffel Ghijs in 1472.[20]

The guild of St Andrew provided an existential framework to musicianship in a way unknown to singers. It was within this framework that a trumpeter could feel respected socially, proud professionally, and endorsed spiritually. Within that framework a Ghent citizen could contemplate addressing a request to the Pope, and evidently it was within that framework that the request was granted. For that reason alone, and no doubt for musical and 'touristic' reasons as well, the journey to Mantua must have been a high point in Willem Obrecht's career—and it would be surprising, in an age that delighted in elaborate travel accounts, if none of this was to be recounted at length to Jacob in years to come.

A Different Course

Yet there were other travels, and these opened up musical contacts outside the neatly organized world of trumpeting—contacts that may well have proved decisive for the early musical development of Jacob Obrecht. Although none of the travels was subsidized by the city of Ghent, and we consequently lack direct information, there is enough circumstantial evidence to show that the activities in Charles of Charolais's retinue continued. In some cases this is merely the payment of a *pourboire* whenever the Ghent trumpeters happened to pass through a centre whose documentation has been studied. Examples are the following payments, made in 1462

[20] See Docs. 3, 23, and 26.

and 1464 at the court of Frank van Borselen, Count of Oostervant, at Brielle near Rotterdam:[21]

Item, given on 20 August [1462] . . . to seven[22] trumpeters who were with my Lord [Frank van Borselen] at Brielle, and who belonged to my gracious lord [Charles] of Charolais and the city of Ghent, 8 *postulatus* guilders . . . (Doc. 18.)

Item, given on 8 August [1464] . . . to six trumpeters who had no badges[23] and said that they wanted to go to my lord of Charolais, who was in Gorinchem at that time, 3 *postulatus* guilders . . . (Doc. 19.)

On both occasions the Ghent trumpeters must have accompanied Charles of Charolais in his capacity as governor and lieutenant-general of the Netherlands. It is impossible to say how many other journeys they may have made without leaving a documentary trace at Brielle. Since Charles does not appear to have employed a permanent band, any trumpeters found in his company during these years are likely to have been Willem Obrecht and his colleagues.[24]

The travels through the Netherlands, for Charles of Charolais, were mere routine visits that did not demand elaborate ceremony. If he required the presence of the Ghent trumpeters even on these journeys, there is every reason to assume that they would have been in his service on more important occasions as well. One particularly tantalizing possibility is the coronation of Louis XI at Reims, on 15 August 1461—like Mantua two years earlier a virtual stage for the public display of political power. Here, if anywhere, the future duke of Burgundy would have needed the presence of outstanding trumpeters, and the six Ghenters would have been his

[21] Incomplete transcription in Lingbeek-Schalekamp, *Overheid en muziek*, 205. The Ghent trumpeters probably visited Utrecht in the same year; see M. Beukers, '"For the Honour of the City": Utrecht City Minstrels between 1377 and 1528', *Tijdschrift van de Vereniging voor Nederlandse Muziekgeschiedenis*, 41 (1991), 17.

[22] The seventh trumpeter was undoubtedly Arend de Keyser, son of Ghiselbrecht, who had joined the six trumpeters on their journey to Mantua as well (see Doc. 14).

[23] Count Frank's officials were evidently somewhat suspicious of the six men, as they could provide no proof of association with an institution, household, or guild. A payment of 22 Mar. 1465 tells us that all the acknowledged trumpeters' badges were listed in a reference book: 'Item, on 22 March [1465], given to three trumpeters who carried the badges of Lord Philip of Wassenaar, which could not be found in the book, 6 sc. 9 gr.' (Lingbeek-Schalekamp, *Overheid en muziek*, 205). There is ample evidence that 15th-c. trumpeters often lost or forgot to wear their badges (ibid. 92–4). A silver badge of a Ghent trumpeter or shawm-player, dated 1483, is kept in the Bijloke Museum, Ghent (see the colour plate in Decavele (ed.), *Gent: Apologie van een rebelse stad*, 93).

[24] See, for instance, M. A. Vente (ed.), *Bouwstenen voor een geschiedenis der toonkunst in de Nederlanden*, iii (Amsterdam, 1980), 151, for a payment in 1460 by the city of Haarlem, to 'the pipers' of Count Charles of Charolais. On the other hand, there is a payment at the court of Frank van Borselen, on 12 May of the same year, to 'four trumpeters and five pipers of my gracious lord of Burgundy, who were with my gracious lord of Charolais at Brielle' (Lingbeek-Schalekamp, *Overheid en muziek*, 204). At this time Charles was decidedly out of favour at the Burgundian court, yet this did not, apparently, prevent him from occasionally hiring his father's musicians.

obvious choice. Direct evidence is lacking, but that is only to be expected, for the trumpeters would not have been subsidized by the city, and Charles's household accounts for these years are in any case lost.[25] Yet it seems suggestive that only ten days before the coronation, on 5 August, Willem Obrecht and his five colleagues, as a group, bought six new trumpets from the Ghent goldsmith Michiel Baert (Doc. 17). This was a substantial investment (6,616 groats), and the sum was to be repaid in seven three-monthly instalments, starting nearly twelve weeks after the event, on 4 November. One hardly needs to stretch the evidence to suggest that the purchase was made in connection with Louis XI's imminent coronation, and that the six men went to Reims in the retinue of Charles of Charolais. (Charles left the southern Netherlands for Reims on 10 August.) If they did, Willem Obrecht would undoubtedly have played there in the direct presence of two fellow musicians who were to have a profound influence on his son: Johannes Ockeghem, first chaplain of the French royal chapel, and Antoine Busnoys, cleric of Tours cathedral, who had written his *Resjois-toi, terre de France* specially for the occasion. And even if no opportunities for direct contact arose during the several days of celebration, which seems unlikely, Charles of Charolais, himself by now an amateur composer,[26] would not have missed the opportunity personally to enjoy and reward the musical excellence gathered in the city.

Yet whether Willem was there or not, the very fact that a credible case can be made shows that Jacob Obrecht could hardly have been born in a more favourable musical milieu. Even before his talent might have revealed itself, his father must have destined him for a musical career, and have had him inscribed as a member of the trumpeters' guild. Such a move would not have reflected the wishful thinking of an ambitious father, but rather the prudent foresight of any parent working in a fiercely protected profession—Willem would have done the same had he been a brewer or shipper, irrespective of Jacob's aptitude or talent. After the enrolment, however, any emerging musicianship in Jacob could only have

---

[25] That Charles of Charolais had trumpeters with him at the coronation is, however, implied in the chronicle of Jehan de Waurin (*Recueil des croniques*, 402): on 31 Aug. 1461, Louis XI, Philip the Good, and Charles of Charolais entered Paris with their followers, including 'les trompettes nombrees a chinquante quatre *de toutes partyes*' (my italics). After Paris, Charles travelled on to Tours with a retinue of over 350 men on horseback (ibid. 409).

[26] D. Fallows, *Dufay* (London, 1982), 73–4. See also the statement by the Burgundian court official Philips Wielant: 'He also took pleasure in music and was himself a musician. He could compose and sing willingly though he by no means had a good voice' (R. Vaughan, *Charles the Bold: The Last Valois Duke of Burgundy* (London, 1973), 162). Wielant was in a position to judge, for he himself patronized music in Ghent: in 1474 he augmented Philips uter Zwane's endowment of a weekly polyphonic Mass of the Holy Ghost in St James's, with 96 groats annually (SJG 1206, 1474/5, fo. [3ᵛ]; see also above, n. 12).

been encouraged. For the obvious next step, after the boy had reached the age of about 7, was to have him trained by a master trumpeter, under whose tutorship he would acquire all necessary skills before legal majority. (Ghent boys, as a rule, were not apprenticed to their own fathers.)

Yet before it ever came to that step Willem Obrecht must have decided otherwise. Early in the 1460s, he exchanged the protection of the trumpeters' guild for that of the church. The direct reasons for his decision are difficult to establish. It is likely that Jacob, even as an infant, had shown signs of exceptional musical talent—a good voice, comparative ease in reading and memorizing tunes, a flair for improvisation. Yet this was almost certainly not the only reason, perhaps not even the most important one. For, unlike entry into the trumpeters' guild, the move to the church was a step that would definitely have reflected the social ambitions of a middle-class father. In this context Jacob's intellectual abilities may well have been more decisive than his musical talent (which could equally well have justified keeping him in the trumpeters' profession).

Then there is the financial part of the equation. It is true that churches were responsible for the maintenance and education of their choirboys—which made it very attractive for impoverished parents to send their boys to a choir school.[27] Yet Jacob Obrecht, even as a little boy, was already entitled to a personal annual income of 207 groats from his share in Lysbette Gheeraerts's estate. Willem had to administer these finances for him, yet he was answerable to the magistrates of inheritance, and was under law obliged to keep annual accounts—to be produced whenever the magistrates might suspect improper use. Jacob's income had to be used in his best possible interests.

As far as his son's future was concerned, this placed Willem in a comfortable situation. Many musical centres in the Low Countries considered Ghent (Pl. 6) an ideal hunting-ground for potential choristers; no

---

[27] There can be no doubt, however, that many middle-class parents, even those living in comparative poverty, considered it very important that their children be trained in chant and polyphony, even if they could not secure a free place for them in a chorister's foundation. A concrete example is provided by the appointment contract of *meester* Jacobus Tick as choirmaster at St Peter's, Leiden, of 16 Oct. 1454 (C. C. Vlam and M. A. Vente, *Bouwstenen*, i (Utrecht, 1965), 171–3). Among the eventualities covered in the contract was the following: 'Further, *meester* Jacop has promised that he will properly, and to the best of his ability, teach chant and *discant* to every schoolchild whose parents desire and request him to train their children in *discant* . . . And if someone came to the aforesaid *meester* Jacop, desired to have his children taught in *discant*, and were so poor that he could not give weekly wages to the aforesaid *meester* Jacop, then the aforesaid *meester* Jacop would cordially and in a friendly manner accept his children, and train them in *discant* and chant just as well as he teaches the other children who give him weekly wages.' After the poor children would have finished their musical education with Tick, the city magistrates of Leiden would appoint an income-related fee to be paid by their parents, 'and *meester* Jacop shall amicably and graciously be content with this'. Tick was later active in Bruges (Strohm, *Music in Late Medieval Bruges*, 123 and 159).

PL. 6. Panoramic view of Ghent (1534). Ghent, Bijlokemuseum (Copyright A.C.L.-Bruxelles)

doubt it would have required little effort to get a musically gifted boy placed somewhere. For instance, in September 1462 (when Jacob was nearly old enough to be trained as a chorister), a Willem de Grone, sexton of Sint-Maartensdijk near Rotterdam, went to Ghent and various other places in search of suitable boys.[28] Yet Willem Obrecht could hardly have been so desperate as to send his son to a musical and intellectual outpost like Sint-Maartensdijk. As a professional trumpeter he was well connected, both within and outside Ghent, and he could reasonably expect to make much more advantageous arrangements. Wherever Jacob was to receive his early training, he plainly was going to enjoy the very best of two worlds. His upbringing in an active musical milieu gave him a head start as a choirboy, and this in turn made it easier to pursue a career in vocal polyphony. His creative development in particular must have benefited from the emphasis on improvised counterpoint in the trumpeters' world: from improvisation it was only a small step to composition.[29]

In Ghent itself the only foundation for choristers in the mid-fifteenth century, and the most eminent educational centre, was in the prestigious collegiate church of St Veerhilde or Veerle (Faraïlde), opposite the castle of the counts of Flanders and a few hundred metres from St John's. The four main parish churches of Ghent—St Nicholas, St James, St Michael, and St John—employed only adult *cotidianisten*, who were responsible for the daily observance of the liturgy before the main altar, and who could be called upon to sing private services in the side chapels as well. The primary duty of *cotidianisten* was to sing plainchant, but isolated pieces of evidence indicate that regular polyphonic services were added piecemeal in the course of the fifteenth century. If such services called for choristers, these were normally borrowed from the church of St Veerhilde. (Exchanges of musical personnel between churches were common in Ghent.)

Within Ghent, then, the choir school of St Veerhilde's would have been the obvious place for Jacob Obrecht to receive his early training. Next to nothing is known about musicians active at this church, but Reinhard Strohm has discovered a document from 1423 that describes the arrangements for the choristers in some detail.[30] Boys were not taken into the care of the church unless they were perfectly healthy: they should not be

---

[28] Lingbeek-Schalekamp, *Overheid en muziek*, 205. It may have been on this journey that the Ghent boys Hencke and Adryaen were gained for the chapel of Sint-Maartensdijk: six years later, on 29 Mar. 1468, their voices had broken, and they were given money 'to travel to a school' (ibid. 208).

[29] Polk, 'Flemish Wind Bands', 76–9 and 82–8, and *German Instrumental Music*, 163–213.

[30] RAG S228, fos. [ix], x, and xvij (1423). I am most indebted to Reinhard Strohm for sharing his microfilm of this important document.

disabled, have injuries, sores, or contagious diseases, should not have 'a bad breath or short breath', nor be unable 'to retain their water'. As usual in medieval foundations, the choristers had to pray every day for the founder, Symoen van Hale, and for all souls. They lived with a master who was responsible for their instruction, governance, and sustenance. They had to sing a *Christe qui lux es et dies* in the evening, a *De profundis* before going to sleep ('at a reasonable and proper hour'), and a *Jam lucis orto sidere* after their master had woken them up in the morning. He would then send the boys to school, for which he gave each his instruction material; they had to be back by lunch-time.

The original foundation does not appear to have included provisions for polyphony, but it was apparently augmented later in the century: further regulations concerning the musical instruction and duties of the choirboys were added by a later hand.[31] The boys were now in the care of a school-master (*scolastre*). It was his responsibility to find a suitable *cantere*, who would 'teach and instruct the children well and faithfully in discant, plainchant, and otherwise, and in good, virtuous morals and manners'.[32] Further instruction in music and liturgy was given by the so-called *sub-monituers* of St Michael's and St James's, where the boys would regularly sing Masses, Offices, and processions under their supervision. By 1447 at the latest they also worked in St John's, where the Guild of Our Lady paid them for singing in the Lady Vespers and Masses every Friday and Saturday.[33] Altogether the choristers of St Veerhilde's must have had a busy life, divided between school, rehearsals, and a continuing round of services in the various churches of Ghent. Perhaps we may picture Jacob Obrecht among them, as Chaucer's 'litel clergeon, seven yeer of age, that day by day to scole was his wone', who learned there 'to syngen and to rede, as smale children doon in hire childhede'.

A different type of arrangement, for which Jacob would not strictly speaking have qualified as a middle-class boy, was education in an aristo-cratic household. Willem Obrecht and his five colleagues had close con-nections with the court of Charles of Charolais: they were effectively (if irregularly) 'his' trumpeters—a fact that would have been made visually apparent by distinctive uniforms and banners, as in the city of Ghent. Despite the almost total loss of the count's household accounts, the single surviving one of 1457 reveals that musically gifted boys could indeed

---

[31] RAG S228, fos. viij, xviij, and xix (after 1423).

[32] 'Item, so es de scolastre ghehouden hem te versiene van eenen cantere die abele ende souffisant sij, omme de kinderen wel ende ghetrouwelic te leerene ende te instrueerene in discante, in simple musiiken, ende andersins in goeden duechdeliken zeden ende mannieren, alsoo daer toe behoort' (RAG S228, fo. viijʳ).   [33] RAG K roll 29, 1447/8; see also K5224, 1475/6, fo. 3ʳ.

receive a court education. For, as is well known, there are two payments covering fourteen months of maintenance of a 'jeusne filz appellé Hayne van Ghizeghem'.[34] And ten years later this same Hayne, by then internationally famous as the author of *De tous biens plaine*, is mentioned as a Burgundian singer and *valet de chambre*, which confirms that he had received a formal court education. Given the total lack of documentation for the early 1460s, it may be better not to speculate whether a similarly talented boy called Copkin Hoebrecht might have enjoyed such an apprenticeship. The least we can say is that it would not have been unprecedented if Willem had presented his son occasionally as a musical prodigy to the count. During the 1450s and 1460s the Holland composer *meester* Jacobus Tick (himself a bailiff of the duke of Burgundy) regularly sang his latest songs and 'masses in discant' with his sons and daughters at the court of Oostervant at Briclle.[35] And the example of Hayne van Ghizeghem shows that Charles of Charolais, at the very least, would have appreciated musical talent in a boy.

Speculation aside, the Burgundian plot clearly thickens later in the 1460s. In the first months of 1467, when Philip the Good is ill and Charles of Charolais has effectively assumed ducal power, the court accounts immediately confirm what circumstantial evidence had suggested all along. The Ghent trumpeters worked so regularly for Charles that they could in fact be described as the 'trompettes de guerre de mondit seigneur de Charrolois':

To Ghysbrecht de Keysere, Matheus Nijs, Loys Ghijs, Jehan Aelteman, Willem Obrecht, and Adrian de Keysere,[36] war trumpeters of my said Lord of Charolais, the sum of four pounds and one shilling of the said currency, which my said lord had given them on the day of his departure from the said city of Ghent . . . on 23 February 1467. (Doc. 22.)

At this very time, Charles of Charolais had another man in his service who was to become a major influence on Willem's son Jacob: Antoine Busnoys. Only nineteen days after the above payment was made, on 14 March 1467, Busnoys received the sum of 8 pounds for daily activity over an unspecified period, presumably about six weeks.[37] In his motet *In hydraulis*,

[34] LAN B3661, fos. 28ʳ and 89ᵛ (covering the periods 1 Nov. 1456 to 30 Apr. 1457, and 1 May to 31 Dec.).

[35] Lingbeek-Schalekamp, *Overheid en muziek*, 203–8. No works are mentioned by title except a mass of St Martin (20 Dec. 1458, ibid. 204). No music has survived under Jacobus Tick's name.

[36] Roeland Ghijs is not mentioned in this payment, but he had in fact received payment on 28 Feb. 1467, for having worked continuously in Charles's service since 23 Nov. of the previous year (LAN B2064, fos. 64ᵛ–65ʳ).

[37] P. Higgins, '*In hydraulis* Revisited: New Light on the Career of Antoine Busnois', *Journal of the American Musicological Society*, 39 (1986), 36–86, esp. 41–53.

written around this time, the composer styles himself 'unworthy musician of the illustrious Count of Charolais'.[38] The surviving documentation indicates that he was indeed little more than that: like Willem Obrecht he was employed by the count on an irregular basis, receiving gifts rather than wages.

Here, then, are two musicians, mentioned as servants of 'mondit seigneur' at the same time and in the same place: Ghent in February–March 1467. Willem's connections with Charles the Bold stretch back at least thirteen years, Busnoys's less than one. Willem is one of the most brilliant trumpeters in the Burgundian Netherlands, and a man of modest wealth. Busnoys is among the lowest-paid servants of the duke, as yet neither priest nor master of arts,[39] although he can claim some experience as a choirmaster. But plainly he is now one of the three most famous composers of the Christian world, and he has worked for at least five years with another of the three, Johannes Ockeghem. Indeed Busnoys's star is rising to international heights in exactly these years: by 1472–3, when he has written his most famous work, the *Missa L'homme armé*, Johannes Tinctoris ranks him among the leading composers of Europe.[40] Willem has an exceptionally gifted son, now about 10 years old and, we may take it, experienced in singing and understanding mensural polyphony. Clearly it would have been in Copkin's interests to bring him to the attention of Busnoys, who, in between his journeys with Charles the Bold, must have lived and worked somewhere in the region.

The duke's travels were to bring Busnoys back to Ghent several times in the next years—and each time was perhaps another occasion for Copkin to be introduced to Busnoys. After Charles had become duke of Burgundy, in June 1467, several irregular payments to Busnoys surface; the

[38] See the transcription and translation in L. Perkins, 'The L'Homme Armé Masses of Busnoys and Okeghem: A Comparison', *Journal of Musicology*, 3 (1984), 364, and Antoine Busnoys, *Collected Works, Part 2: The Latin-Texted Works*, ed. R. Taruskin (Masters and Monuments of the Renaissance, 5/2; New York, 1990).

[39] Busnoys must have celebrated his first Mass between Sept. 1468 (when Charles the Bold's accounts describe him still as 'Anthoine de Busne *dit* Busnoys') and Oct. 1470 ('*Messire* Anthoine de Busne'; cf. Higgins, '*In hydraulis* Revisited', 84). This would suggest a date of birth of *c*.1438–45. The composer had been elevated to the order of subdeacon in Tours on 7 Apr. 1465, for which the minimum age was 18; this suggests a birthdate before 1447 (ibid. 70–6). Busnoys is styled *maistre* in Charles the Bold's accounts from 1473 onwards (ibid. 51 and 84).

[40] In the *Proportionale musices*; cf. Tinctoris, *Opera theoretica*, ed. A. Seay (Corpus scriptorum de musica, 22; American Institute of Musicology, 1978), iia. 10, 49, and 55. Another sacred work by Busnoys predating 1472–3 is *Gaude celestis domina* (ibid. 52; cf. R. C. Wegman, Letter to the Editor, *Music & Letters*, 71 (1990), 635). The earliest documentary evidence of sacred music composed by Busnoys dates from 1471: it concerns the lost setting of *Asperges me Domine* by 'Bunoys', copied in a choirbook for the French royal chapel (Perkins, 'Musical Patronage at the Royal Court of France', 535). Busnoys's activities as a poet and chanson composer must stretch back to the late 1450s; it was in this field that he acquired his first fame as a composer.

rate of payment is approximately 16 pounds per three months, hardly more than the salary earned by a court domestic.[41] At this rate, the surviving payments would cover approximately the periods February to mid-March 1467, and late May 1467 until October or November 1468.[42] During these periods Antoine Busnoys and Willem Obrecht must have had several opportunities to meet each other as colleagues in the same household, for Willem, too, was to serve the duke again: he reappears with his five fellow trumpeters in January 1470 (Doc. 24).[43] Any encounter in these years, whether it took the form of education or music-making, is likely to have left a lasting impression on the boy. Musical reflections on such possible encounters can be found in several of Obrecht's masses, most clearly in what seems to be his earliest surviving setting, *Missa Petrus apostolus* (see Ch. 4).

The likelihood of personal encounters between Willem Obrecht and Antoine Busnoys diminished after 1470, when the latter became permanently appointed as a singer at the Burgundian court. In this capacity he followed the duke's household on all travels and campaigns, now mainly through the southern territories of the Burgundian state.[44] Not that we should rule out further contacts altogether. Chance evidence suggests that numerous activities simply may have left no trace in the obvious documentary sources. A payment conflict of 2 October 1477, for instance, reveals that Roeland Ghijs had served as a trumpeter with Lord Jacques of Harchies, one of Charles the Bold's army captains, 'during the war'— no doubt the campaign that had ended disastrously on the battlefield near Nancy on 5 January (Doc. 28). Roeland claimed 2,880 groats' arrears of

---

[41] Higgins, '*In hydraulis* Revisited', 46–7.

[42] The payment of 8 pounds on 14 Mar. 1467 probably covered service for six weeks, beginning around 1 Feb. The 16 pounds paid to Busnoys on 26 Aug. 1467 could have covered three months from late May. The next payment, of 20 pounds in Oct. 1467, might have been partly an advance payment, covering the last four months of the year. Paula Higgins has established that Busnoys was in continuous service from Dec. 1467 until June 1468. The payment of 24 pounds in Sept. 1468 probably covered a period of 4½ months, starting around 1 July. For the payments, see Higgins, '*In hydraulis* Revisited', 46 and 83–4. During the periods of Busnoys's presumed Burgundian activity, Charles the Bold was mostly in Brabant and Flanders. This, together with the irregular nature of the composer's employment, suggests that he was living somewhere in this area. All evidence suggests that Busnoys was a native of either southern Flanders or Artois: his benefices were situated concentrically around Ghent: Brussels, Condé (?), Mons, Veurne (or Oost-Voorne), Tholen, and Lier. For Busnoys's prebends, see Higgins, '*In hydraulis* Revisited', 51–2, and the literature cited there, and B. Haggh, 'New Documents from the Low Countries', paper read at the meeting of the Capital Chapter of the American Musicological Society, Washington, DC, 20 Jan. 1990.

[43] Cf. Marix, *Histoire de la musique*, 122. I have not had the opportunity to study the Burgundian court accounts systematically, and consequently it remains possible that several less specific payments (for instance, mentioning only 'six trumpeters of Ghent') have so far escaped notice. I am grateful to Paula Higgins for sharing with me her transcription of Doc. 24.

[44] Higgins, '*In hydraulis* Revisited', 53–61. Charles the Bold returned to Ghent on 6–11 May 1472 (see below), 23–8 Jan. and 12–13 Apr. 1473, and 10–11 July 1475.

salary, suggesting that he had served for perhaps as much as a year; yet there is no other evidence concerning his activities as a trumpeter in the Burgundian army, and had it not been for the conflict we should probably never have known about them altogether. What this might suggest for Willem Obrecht, and by implication for his son Jacob, it is impossible to say.

The problem is not that we have too few documents on Willem's professional activities: in the 1470s and 1480s there are scores of payments to him in the Ghent city accounts.[45] The reasons are obvious: in an age without newspapers or television sets, urgent news had to be announced in every major street and market square to the sound of trumpets—the latest victory (or defeat) of the Burgundian duke, the conclusion of a peace treaty, the announcement of a general procession to celebrate the same,[46] the imminent arrival of a prince or prelate, orders from the magistrates to clear the streets of snow, ice, or litter, and even, in the early 1470s, to find the white parrot of Duchess Margaret of Burgundy, which repeatedly escaped from her castle in Ghent.[47] Yet payments for such proclamations and numerous other petty jobs are of importance mainly to the history of trumpeting, and reveal little that is of potential biographical interest.

Among the few exceptions are two payments to Willem Obrecht in November 1471, which are interesting not so much for what they say as for what they suggest by association:

Item, paid to Willem Hoebrecht for riding with the trumpet behind [the magistrates of] the city and for announcing the happy tidings of the alliance of King Frenant and our aforenamed valiant and redoubtable lord and prince [Charles the Bold], on 11 November 1471, 12 groats. Item, Willem Hoebrecht for riding with the trumpet behind [the magistrates of] the city, and announcing the general procession to be held in this city because of the aforesaid happy tidings of King

---

[45] In spite of what had been decided in 1452, the six trumpeters no longer received a fixed annual salary from 1468 onwards. Instead the city paid them for one-day services, normally at a rate of 12 groats. Since the grounds for each payment were stated at length, for reasons of accountability, the city accounts provide a complete picture of the typical duties of a Ghent city trumpeter. That picture obviously cannot be explored here, yet it is important to note that each trumpeter would have needed to work for the city only sixty days a year to accumulate the amount of 720 groats previously received as a fixed salary. This suggests that the bulk of the trumpeters' activities lay elsewhere—in the churches and chapels of Ghent, in the homes and gardens of private individuals, in the households of aristocratic rulers, and (for Roeland and Lodewijk Ghijs) in the woolweaving industry.

[46] A payment from 1465 indicates that such celebrations could involve services with polyphony: on 12 Nov. of that year, the city paid 60 groats to 'the priests and companions who sang the service and the discant after the general procession that was held because of the peace' (SAG 400.21, 1465/6, fo. 23ᵛ).

[47] SAG 400.23, 1471/2, fo. 89ʳ, and 1472/3, fo. 141ʳ (announced by Mattheus Nijs and Roeland Ghijs, respectively).

Frenant of Sicily and our aforenamed redoubtable lord. Done on 15 November 1471. 12 groats. (Doc. 26.)

What we have here, on a very superficial reading, is the only known document apart from *Mille quingentis* to mention Willem Obrecht's name in one breath with 'Cecylien', the Kingdom of Sicily. Of course that is of no consequence in itself, since the text does not remotely suggest that Willem might have travelled through 'the Sicilian shore'. On the other hand, it is clear from the evidence gathered above that all extended journeys undertaken by the Ghent trumpeters—to Holland, Mantua, Nancy, and possibly Reims—were made in the service of Burgundy. If we assume this to have been true also of the (undocumented) journey to Sicily, then the two payments do appear to suggest, quite fortuitously, some promising lines of thought.

The alliance between Charles the Bold and Ferrante of Naples (solemnly announced on 1 November 1471 at Saint-Omer) was the cause of public rejoicing in Ghent—or that, at least, was the official line. The city accounts tell us that the festivities included a nightly ceremony before the council of the by-law (for which 200 torches were bought on 12 November), a general procession (announced by Willem Obrecht on 15 November), and various games (prizes were presented on 18 November by the *presentmeester*, accompanied by Willem Obrecht and Jan Aelterman).[48] When Charles the Bold visited Ghent six months later, on 6–11 May 1472, the city magistrates went out of their way to present him a festive welcome. Hugo van der Goes was commissioned to make several paintings of the coats of arms of the duke and duchess, which were to be placed on the Torrepoorte and various other buildings along the route prepared for the Burgundian train.[49] The six trumpeters welcomed the duke on the Waelpoorte, and other 'companions' played for him on the sites for which Hugo van der Goes had made his paintings; after Charles the Bold had reached the council of the by-law, the six trumpeters played for him during the *esbatementen* held there.

This magnificent reception inaugurated more than yet another possible occasion for Jacob Obrecht to see Antoine Busnoys. For, given the recently concluded alliance with Naples, it is surely no coincidence that within a month of the Burgundian visit, a certain '*her* Gregorius Bourgois, tenorist of the King of Naples' appeared before the magistrates of the by-law at Ghent.[50] Bourgois's name has not surfaced in the woefully

---

[48] SAG 400.23, 1471/2, fo. 91^{r-v}.
[49] SAG 400.23, 1471/2, fo. 109^v. For the next sentence, see ibid. fo. 98^v.
[50] SAG 301.51, 1471/2, fo. 116^r (10 June 1472): 'Scepenen vander kuere etc., ghehoort de

fragmentary documentation from the court of Naples.[51] We owe the totally unexpected reference to him here to a Ghent citizen called Arend vanden Couden, who was plainly not a man one would buy a used car from. He had sold Bourgois a horse that proved so intractable that it had injured several of his companions. Since Vanden Couden had apparently kept silent about the horse's 'condition', Bourgois demanded that he take back the animal, return the money, and pay for the injuries. His suit proved unsuccessful, but at least it has left firm evidence that the Burgundian–Neapolitan alliance led to immediate musical exchanges, for which Ghent had evidently offered a venue in May and June 1472. As a documentary tip of the proverbial iceberg it confirms that the European musical world could be very small for those who lived in the right place and operated in the right circles. This was true of Willem Obrecht, and it might have benefited his son's musical career in numerous untold ways.

Political ties between Burgundy and Naples were strengthened in the years following the alliance, and in this context the possibility of Willem Obrecht's involvement as a trumpeter becomes increasingly plausible— even without the knowledge that he had once crossed 'the Sicilian shore'. In May 1473 King Ferrante was elected to the Order of the Golden Fleece, and in July 1474 Charles the Bold ordered his first chamberlain, 'le grand bastard' Antoine of Burgundy, to convey the news of the election to Ferrante, and to take the king's oath upon the statutes. Antoine and his followers were in Naples in April–June 1475; no detailed documentation on the journey has as yet been unearthed.[52] Yet it need not be doubted that the official embassy conferring membership in an extremely prestigious order on an extremely valued ally would have called for similar musical forces as the Burgundian embassy to Mantua in 1459. Nor need it be doubted that when Jacob Obrecht wrote *Mille quingentis*, thirteen years later, he might truthfully have described Naples, the residence of the

ansprake die vor hemlieden dede her Gregorius Bourgois, tenoriste sConincx van Napels, jeghen Arend vanden Coude, porter van deser stede, om hem bedwonghen thebbene weder tanveerdene j paert als hij jeghen den selven Arent ghecocht hadde, wederkeerende tgelt dat hij daer af ont-fanghen hadde, ende voort hem up te rechtene sin interest vanden quetse die tselve paert sins den date vanden selven coope eenighe siner lieden ghedaen hadde . . .'.

[51] It is quite possible, however, that he is identical with the priest Gregorio who sang as a tenorist at St Peter's, Rome, in 1461–6; see F. X. Haberl, 'Die römische "schola cantorum" und die päpstlichen Kapellsänger bis zur Mitte des 16. Jahrhunderts', *Vierteljahrsschrift für Musikwissenschaft*, 3 (1887), 236–7.

[52] E. Pontieri, 'Sulle mancate nozze tra Federico d'Aragona e Maria di Borgogna (1474–1476)', *Per la storia del regno di Ferrante I d'Aragona re di Napoli* (2nd edn.; Naples, 1969), 197–8. Pontieri, who originally published his essay in 1938, refers to several Neapolitan court payments and gifts to Antoine and his followers; the relevant accounts were destroyed in 1943. See also R. Woodley, 'Tinctoris's Italian Translation of the Golden Fleece Statutes: A Text and a (Possible) Context', *Early Music History*, 8 (1988), 173–244.

king of Sicily, as 'the Sicilian shore'. It is, moreover, clear from the
evidence presented above that Willem Obrecht's employers, the Ghent
city magistrates, were extremely supportive of the political union. If this
might not have made them favourably disposed to lending out their best
trumpeters, then surely it would have been their cordial relationship with
Antoine of Burgundy: on 22 October 1472 they gave him 10,476 groats
worth of gilded silver jugs 'because of certain services that he has done for
the city at various times'.[53] Compared to such a lavish gesture, lending out
trumpeters for an embassy to Naples would have been a trifle.

The scenario cannot be proved, of course,[54] but in this case plausibility
is perhaps more important than proof. It would be reassuring if we could
demonstrate that Willem Obrecht 'Ceciliam peragravit oram' in 1475, but
in the end this would yield no more than a biographical titbit. What is
more significant historically is the fact that a plausible case can be made at
all: it would have been *typical* of Willem's life and career if he had
travelled with Antoine of Burgundy to Naples. And this typical pattern, of
his professional status and political allegiance, suggests a multitude of
other, undocumented possibilities and opportunities, not only for him but
also for his son.

[53] SAG 400.23, 1472/3, fo. 160ʳ. As first chamberlain of Charles the Bold, in charge of the
Burgundian court, Antoine would certainly have known the Ghent trumpeters.

[54] There is no evidence to disprove the scenario either: the city accounts for 1474/5 (SAG
400.24) do not mention Willem Obrecht between Feb. and July 1475 (not even implicitly as one of
'de zesse trompetten'). However, Jan Aelterman and Mattheus Nijs are mentioned on 22 Mar. and
18 May, respectively (fos. 99ᵛ and 101ᵛ), and consequently the possibility of their presence in Naples
can be ruled out.

3 FORMATIVE YEARS

JACOB OBRECHT had turned 15 by 1473. Legally this age marked his majority, but effectively he was to remain under the loose supervision of his legal guardian, Willem Obrecht, until he had shown himself competent to conduct his own affairs. This was also about the age when his voice would have broken, and hence the moment to leave the choristers' foundation (wherever it was) where he must have received his musical training.

The next seven years are a period of total documentary silence, yet the broad outline of this period can nevertheless be sketched with reasonable confidence. For the first document to break the silence, written at Bergen op Zoom in April 1480 (see below), immediately reveals that Obrecht had become master of arts and, very recently, had received the priesthood. Of these two attainments only the priesthood comes unusually early; at the age of 22 or 23 it would certainly have required dispensation, which would be granted if it could be shown to be useful or necessary to the church. As for the master's degree, it would have been no more than normal if Jacob acquired it at the age of 20 or 21, and consequently that he had been enrolled as a student some time around 1473.

Early Career: Patterns and Parallels

This broad outline can be filled in somewhat thanks to the parallel biography of another Ghent composer, and a close contemporary of Obrecht, Pieter Bordon (c.1450–after 1484). He was the son of the Ghent citizens Valeriaen Bordon and Margriete van Wijniersch; since his father had died while he was still under-age, the magistrates of inheritance were responsible for ensuring his legal rights during minority. In this connection we find the earliest documents on the composer in the yearbooks of inheritance; the last document to mention him there, dating 11 September 1465, describes him as 'Pieterkin Bordon', indicating that he was almost certainly under 15 at the time.[1] That he could have been scarcely much younger than 15 is indicated by the fact that he was professionally active as a singer by the next year: in 1466–9 'Pieter Bordoen' is listed among the *cotidianisten* of St James's.[2] By then he must already have been in minor orders, for on 2 December 1472 his mother gave him a life annuity of 480 groats, 'since Pieter Bordon Valeriaenszone is intending shortly to join, by the grace of God, the state of the priesthood'.[3] Since Bordon could have been at most 22 in 1472, his ordination offers a plausible precedent to that of Jacob Obrecht in 1480.

Bordon is last mentioned in Ghent in 1478, when he served briefly as a *cotidianist* in St Michael's.[4] Within the next year his career took him to Italy: he was a singer at Treviso cathedral in 1479–80.[5] Bordon almost certainly went to Italy to pursue university studies, possibly at Siena: in August and September 1484 he is styled 'maestro Pietro Bordone chonpositore de chanto figurato' in accounts of Siena cathedral.[6] He is then paid 'for the composition of motets, Credos, and other figural songs for this church'. None of these pieces has survived under his name, although there must be several candidates among the anonymous masses and motets in the Sienese choirbook SienBC K.I.2. Today, Bordon is known only as a composer of song arrangements: a four-part *L'homme armé* arrangement in RomeC 2856 is ascribed to 'Borton', and a three-part *De tous biens plaine* setting in Petrucci's *Odhecaton A* to 'Pe. Bourdon'.[7]

---

[1] SAG 330.30, 1465/6, fo. 4ᵛ.

[2] Between 24 June 1466 and 24 June 1469; SJG 1198–1200 (1466/7–1468/9). Bordon worked again at St James's between 1 Oct. 1470 and 24 June 1472 (SJG 1202–3, 1470/1–1471/2). His father is listed as a *cotidiane* singer in the same church during the period 24 June 1440–24 June 1452 ('Valeriaen Bourdoen'; SJG 1174–1183, 1440/1–1451/2)..

[3] 'uute dien dat Pieter Bordon Valeriaenszone in meeninghen es bij de gracie Gods hem curtlinghs te voughene ten state vanden priesterschepe', SAG 301.52, 1472/3, fo. 46ᵛ. The ordination is reflected in the *cotidiane* accounts of St Michael's, where Bordon worked between 25 Dec. 1471 and 25 Mar. 1474: from 1473 onwards the composer is listed as 'dominus Petrus Burdoen' (RAG 524, 1471/2–1473/4). The composer is also styled 'her Pieter Bordon presbytre' on 10 May 1475, when he sold a house in Ghent to Janne Aenbec for 1,440 groats (SAG 301.53, 1474/5, fo. 108ʳ).

[4] Between 24 June and 23 Sept. (RAG 524, 1478/9).

[5] Between Aug. 1479 and Feb. 1480; see G. D'Alessi, 'Maestri e cantori fiamminghi nella Cappella Musicale del Duomo di Treviso, 1411–1531', *Tijdschrift der Vereeniging voor Nederlandsche Muziekgeschiedenis*, 15 (1939), 157 ('Petrus Bordonus de Flandria').

[6] F. A. D'Accone, 'A Late 15th-Century Sienese Sacred Repertory: MS K.I.2 of the Biblioteca Comunale, Siena', *Musica disciplina*, 37 (1983), 131–2. In one of the payments 'messer' is crossed out and replaced by 'maestro'.

[7] The latter piece survives with an attribution to Agricola in SegC s.s., fo. 173ᵛ. The spelling 'Borton' is occasionally found in Ghent documents; see, for instance, the Cornelis Borton in SAG 400.28, 1484/5, fo. 387ʳ. The *L'homme armé* arrangement ascribed to 'Borton' adds a fourth part to an anonymous three-part combinative chanson texted *Il sera pour vous/L'homme armé*. On the basis of the ascription of the former, most authors have assumed that the latter is by Robert Morton, although Richard Taruskin has recently suggested Antoine Busnoys's authorship (see his 'Antoine

Pieter Bordon's career somewhat resembles that of Antoine Busnoys, in that he was active as a musician for about fifteen years before pursuing university studies in his early thirties. In this context it is worth pointing out that there were no specifically musical incentives for studying at the university: the main reason why a priest, or someone in minor orders, would wish to become master of arts was that it opened the way for an administrative career in the church.[8] This required a substantial financial investment (the minimum required annual budget was about 500–800 groats), unless a student enjoyed the patronage of a college foundation. Failing that, even poor students (*pauperes*) could still cover the costs by working as scribes, secretaries, servants, or singers. Yet relatively well-to-do bourgeois children like Jacob Obrecht and Pieter Bordon would certainly have been classed among the *divites*—those who always and everywhere paid the fees and honoraria demanded. Bordon's life annuity alone ensured that he would never have to worry about his financial situation. The same is true of Obrecht, particularly since his annual income from Lysbette Gheeraerts's estate would have accumulated to a substantial capital during his eight or so years as a 'self-supporting' chorister.

Compared with the careers of Bordon and Busnoys, Obrecht's is more typical of the late-medieval student: given that he had obtained his master's degree by the age of 22, he must have sworn the oath of matriculation at the age of about 15—as did the vast majority of new entrants. It is not known at which university Obrecht was educated. Clearly in his case there were no financial obstacles to studying anywhere in Europe, nor linguistic ones, since Latin was spoken at every university. But there were political obstacles—particularly in view of his father's close association with the Burgundian court. In 1470 King Louis XI had expelled 400 students from Paris because they were subjects of Charles the Bold, and this can only mean that the first choice for Jacob Obrecht, the son of a 'trompette de

Busnoys and the *L'Homme armé* Tradition', *Journal of the American Musicological Society*, 39 (1986), 271–3 and 290–2, where further literature is cited).

[8] This is particularly clear in the case of Guillaume Dufay, who obtained the degree of bachelor in canon law, presumably before 1436 (Fallows, *Dufay*, 31). The well-known illumination from Martin le Franc's *Le Champion des dames* (Arras, 1451; ibid., pl. 7) depicts him as 'Maistre Guillaume Dufay' with his academic insignia: a purple tabard with a scarlet shoulder-piece, and a scarlet biretta. The text of Dufay's *Iuvenis qui puellam* must have been written as part of his examination for the bachelor's degree. It is cast in the typical academic form of the *disputatio*, which candidates for the degree had to uphold on a question drawn by lot in the morning (here a legal case from the mid-12th c.). Dufay duly enunciates the relevant general principles of law (*argumenta* or *generalia*) and gives comparisons of possible decisions for and against (*solutiones contrarietatum*). His solution of the case has not survived, but he obtained the degree. See for this W. Elders, 'Guillaume Dufay's Concept of Faux-Bourdon', *Revue belge de musicologie*, 43 (1989), 179–83.

guerre de mondit seigneur', would have had to be a university in either the Empire or Italy. His name has not so far been found in the matriculation records of the four or five universities nearest to Ghent. The Jacobus Obrecht who was enrolled at Louvain on 17 August 1470 was definitely not the composer: his father was called Jacob rather than Willem, he came from the diocese of Liège rather than Tournai, and he needed no adult to swear his matriculation oath for him, as the 13-year-old Jacob would have.[9] But then it would certainly be wrong to assume that he would necessarily have tried to stay close to Ghent.

The parallel case of Bordon, who must have studied in Italy in the early 1480s, is instructive here, for it illustrates the mobility of fifteenth-century Flemish students: they are found in significant numbers at all the main Italian universities, Bologna, Padua, Ferrara, Pavia, and others. The actual choice for Jacob may well have depended on contacts and connections, and it is not at all implausible that Willem Obrecht would have capitalized on his connections at the Burgundian court—if not with the duke himself, then perhaps one of the court officials. One possibility, which is as exciting as it seems unobvious at first sight, is Naples. At the very least this might explain why the earliest recognition of Jacob Obrecht as a composer comes from Naples around 1480—indeed why he is then already ranked among the leading composers of the century, along with Dunstable, Dufay, Binchois, Ockeghem, and Busnoys:[10]

In our time we have experienced how very many musicians have been affected by glory. For who has not known Iohannes Dunstaple, Guillelmus Dufay, Egidius

---

[9] J. Wils, *Matricule de l'Université de Louvain*, ii (Brussels, 1946), 238. On the same page Wils mentions a Jacob Obrecht, *magister in artibus*, who was admitted to the council of the university on 14 Mar. 1477; he was presumably the same man. Another Jacob Obrecht, from the diocese of Utrecht, became a student of law at Cologne University on 10 Oct. 1452 (H. Keussen, *Die Matrikel der Universität Köln*, i (Bonn, 1928), 554). Bain Murray has also examined the matriculation records of Paris, Heidelberg, and Basle, without finding any trace of the composer ('New Light on Jacob Obrecht's Development—A Biographical Study', *Musical Quarterly*, 43 (1957), 502).

[10] Tinctoris, *Complexus effectuum musices*; translated after Woodley, 'Tinctoris's Italian Translation', 192; the date of *c*.1480 for this passage was proposed by Woodley, ibid. 193–4. The passage survives in only one source, UBG 70 (fo. 77ᵛ), which was completed in 1504 for the library of Raphael de Marcatellis, abbot of St Bavo's, Ghent. The possibility that Obrecht's name, along with those of Carlier and Morton, might have been added by the scribe of this source has to be admitted, yet is obviously weakened by the fact that similar 'additions' were not made to the list of composers in the Preface to the *Proportionale* (later on in the same manuscript), which list is otherwise identical with that in the *Complexus*. While it is true that the *Complexus* was originally written before 1475 (when Obrecht was plainly too young to have acquired international fame as a composer), there is clear evidence that Tinctoris revised and expanded the treatise around 1481–3 (see Woodley, 'Tinctoris's Italian Translation', 191–4, for a summary of the dating problems). The Ghent version of the *Complexus* predates this major revision and expansion, but, as Woodley argues, may well contain additions made around 1480, when Tinctoris was already considering the eventual re-working. Certainly this must be assumed in the case of Morton, for instance, whose name is unlikely to have been incorporated after the early 1480s, and must therefore go back to Tinctoris himself.

Binchois, Iohannes Okeghem, Anthonius Busnois, Iohannes Regis, Firminus Caron, Iacobus Carlerii, Robertus Morton, Iacobus Obrechts? Who does not accord them the highest praises, whose compositions, distributed throughout the whole world, fill God's churches, the palaces of kings, the houses of private individuals, with the utmost sweetness?

The statement comes from Johannes Tinctoris, of course, whose recent knowledge of 'the whole world' is likely to have been limited to Italy, the Low Countries, and northern France. It is not improbable that the odd composition by Obrecht might have reached Naples from the North before about 1480.[11] Yet Tinctoris is saying much more than that: at the age of 22, the young man enjoyed universal fame as a composer, at least from a Neapolitan perspective. Such a testimony would be difficult to explain if Obrecht had been a distant figure who had just completed his university studies somewhere in the North.

Evidence of reciprocal esteem comes from a two-part *Regina celi* by Obrecht, a piece that was evidently designed to demonstrate the peculiarly Tinctorian theory of cumulative proportions.[12] Within the space of sixty *tempora* Obrecht introduces no fewer than thirteen different proportions, in such a way that each relates directly to the previous one, which in turn relates to the one before, and so on. As a result the proportional relationship between the notes in any passage and those under the initial signature is the accumulation of all intervening relationships. This cumulative conception of proportions is thought to have been introduced by Johannes Tinctoris in his *Proportionale musices* (*c*.1472–3); it was to be adopted and expanded by his erstwhile colleague in Naples, Franchinus Gaffurius.[13]

What is no less significant about *Regina celi* is the fact that it far exceeds anything that Obrecht would have had to teach even the most advanced choirboy: it presupposes grounding in Boethian mathematics, as taught (before music) in the curriculum of liberal arts. That the setting was intended to teach or to demonstrate is apparent from its 'text underlay', which consists of the Latin designations of all the relevant proportions. At

---

[11] David Fallows, for instance, has noted a concordance for Obrecht's *Lacen adieu* in the Glogauer Liederbuch of *c*.1480 (review of M. Picker, *Johannes Ockeghem and Jacob Obrecht: A Guide to Research* (Garland Composer Research Manuals, 13; New York and London, 1988), in *Music & Letters*, 79 (1989), 249), and I propose a date in the late 1470s for *Missa Petrus apostolus* (see below, Ch. 4).

[12] H. Hewitt, 'A Study in Proportions', in *Essays on Music in Honor of Archibald Thompson Davison* (Cambridge, Mass., 1957), 69–81.

[13] A. M. Busse Berger, 'The Origin and Early History of Proportion Signs', *Journal of the American Musicological Society*, 41 (1988), 403–33, and the same author's *Mensuration and Proportion Signs: Origins and Evolution* (Oxford, 1993), 164–226.

the very least, then, *Regina celi* is a reflection of Obrecht's university education, perhaps of his teaching as a bachelor or master of arts. The strongly Tinctorian bent in the piece suggests not only thorough acquaintance with the *Proportionale*, but unqualified acceptance of its most innovatory teachings. In this context it is worth observing that those teachings bear every sign of having been disseminated initially within a university context.[14] Indeed there are compelling grounds for believing that Tinctoris was attracted to Naples partly because of his qualifications to teach law, mathematics, and music at the university.[15]

What is most important, however, is the fact that the tightening of political relations in 1471–3 brought Naples firmly within Obrecht's purview. This must have been true also of Tinctoris himself. From what is known of his early career—birth in Braine-l'Alleud, singer at Cambrai, student at Orléans, choirmaster at Orléans and Chartres—one could not possibly have predicted his move to Naples around 1472: for Tinctoris it is as unobvious as it would have been for Obrecht. Yet this merely underlines the fact that actual events, if we are fortunate enough to know about them, tend to defy the most self-evident scenarios, and to exceed the most

[14] Several of the titles by which the theorist styles himself in his treatises—'inter legum artiumque mathematicarum professores', 'in legibus licentiatus', 'legum artiumque professor', and so on—would have had little meaning in a courtly context: all refer to his qualification to teach law and the liberal arts at a school or university. Indeed in the *Proportionale* Tinctoris states explicity that his treatise was written for 'youths wishing to learn this liberal and honest art'—by which he could have meant only students of an arts faculty (*Opera theoretica*, iia. 11). This explains what is by far the most distinctive trait of Tinctoris's writings: his persistent endeavour to formulate music theory as an internally consistent system of rational thought, fully consonant with the overarching system to which it belongs, that of the liberal arts. Numerous nuances and overtones in his formulations and reasonings would have escaped readers who had no acquaintance with mathematics or geometry. This is what Tinctoris must have meant when he wrote, in the *Liber de arte contrapuncti* (1477), that true musicians, 'after a certain general knowledge of pitches, notes, quantities, and concords' (as acquired by every choirboy), reach perfection in their art 'having relied upon the arithmetical rather than the musical instruction of Boethius' (as taught in the curriculum of liberal arts; *Liber de arte contrapuncti*, in *Opera theoretica*, ii. 156).

[15] Tinctoris's court position, and his several dedications to King Ferrante of Naples, do not weaken this point, but rather strengthen it. The University of Naples enjoyed royal patronage and protection, for obvious reasons. Its primary function was to be a training centre for civil servants, and in this respect it competed directly against Bologna in the education of jurists. 'Like rulers elsewhere, the fifteenth-century Italian princes and republican oligarchies were ambitious to possess *studia* renowned for the quality of their teaching and able to train a ruling class and a professional elite . . . All the *studia* that flourished in Italy in the late Middle Ages vied with each other in recruiting masters at high salaries and offering students better living conditions.' (P. Nardi, 'Relations with Authority', in H. de Ridder-Symoens (ed.), *A History of the University in Europe*, i (Cambridge, 1992), 105–6.) In this connection it seems likely that Tinctoris, a man 'in legibus licentiatus', was attracted to Naples for more than musical reasons: he had been educated at Orléans, traditionally a strong law university. Nor is it difficult to see why Tinctoris should have compiled 'nonnulla opuscula' on music within the first ten years of his appointment. Naples was one of the eleven medieval universities that employed the *pecia* system: teaching texts, corrected and approved by the professors, were deposited with the university stationers, who sold copies to students, or lent them against payment to be copied by others.

wildly speculative ones. From the infinitesimal sample of events that happen to be documented it is often impossible to guess the ones that really matter. But then history, even biography, is not about establishing events, but about making sense of them. Even if we possessed a wealth of documents on Obrecht's university years it would be our task to move beyond them, and to sketch the kind of explanatory background that is hinted at by the documents we have. To raise Naples as a possibility is no more than to sketch such a background for something as yet unknown, and to argue that it would be much more difficult to do the same if Obrecht turned out to have studied somewhere else, say, Vienna, Rome, or Cracow.

The degree of master, which Jacob Obrecht may have acquired as early as 1477 or 1478, was more than an intellectual qualification. It gave him genuine social dignity, access to the world of the privileged, indeed to that of the nobility, in ways well beyond the reach of his parents. Combined with the relative prosperity of his background, and his approaching ordination to the priesthood, this could make for a rapid rise in the hierarchy of the church—if that is what Obrecht wanted most. The obvious starting-point for such a career, in his case, would have been a musical teaching position; this is what he was most qualified to do. In due course such work could be combined with more responsible administrative duties in the church, to be rewarded eventually with chaplaincies and canonries.

The only evidence we have on Jacob Obrecht's early teaching activities dates from more than three decades after his death: it is provided by Henricus Glareanus in his *Dodekachordon*, published in 1547:[16]

the composer Iacob Hobrechth . . . [was] second to none with regard to prolificacy and to majesty of song in the opinion of our teacher, *Dominus* Erasmus of Rotterdam, and also in our opinion. And he was the teacher in music of the boy Erasmus, as we ourselves heard many years ago from Erasmus's own lips.

Jacob Hobrechth . . . who in fact was the teacher of *Dominus* Erasmus of Rotterdam, whose opinion of [Obrecht] we have reported [earlier].

There is little reason to doubt Glareanus' testimony. He had met Erasmus during the latter's first Basle stay (August 1514 to March 1515), corresponded with him in the subsequent years, and became a close friend and pupil in 1521–9, when Erasmus was resident in Basle.[17] Since the

---

[16] H. Glareanus, *Dodekachordon* (Basle, 1547; facs. edn., New York, 1969), 256 and 456. Translations taken from *Dodecachordon*, trans. C. A. Miller (Musicological Studies and Documents, 6; American Institute of Musicology, 1965), ii. 252 and 277.

[17] In Glareanus' own words: 'Truly, I have been on very friendly terms with Erasmus for many years, not in the same house, but so near that, whenever it was convenient, we visited one another for daily discussion of literary matters and works' (*Dodecachordon*, trans. Miller, i. 129).

Dutch humanist had received his musical training as a boy, and since he was born in 1469, we may take it that Obrecht had taught him before about 1484.

Beyond that very little can be established with certainty. Erasmus himself never refers to his years as a chorister in his autobiographical writings. All we know is that he was a pupil at the Latin School of Deventer by 1475 (when he was 6 years old) and finished the curriculum in about eight years.[18] This latter time-span indicates extraordinarily slow progress, since the six grades Erasmus had completed by 1484 would normally have covered six years. Yet there is evidence that he was an exceptionally bright student: 'not only did he know the whole of Terence by heart before he left Deventer, but when he removed to 's-Hertogenbosch [in 1484] he was conscious of greater intellectual capacity than some of his own teachers possessed'.[19] For this reason it has been argued that he could well have spent an interim period as a chorister: 'He probably remained two or three years at Deventer, whereupon his father and mother decided to have him sing . . . Should his voice prove satisfactory, he would secure free education . . . and afterward a prebend in the church.'[20] For Erasmus to have passed six grades at Deventer by 1484, the presumed choristership should have lasted no longer than about two years. If that was the case, his musical apprenticeship is unlikely to have been very successful: for some reason Erasmus must have been sent back to Deventer, where he completed the curriculum. This could explain the absence of any reference to the period in Erasmus' writings and correspondence.

It is not only Glareanus' testimony that compels us to assume that Erasmus had been a choirboy around 1480. Beatus Rhenanus, an equally close friend of the Dutch humanist (he met Erasmus at Basle in the same year as Glareanus), wrote a biographical preface to the first authorized Erasmus edition of 1540, in which we read:[21]

The next praise [for having hosted Erasmus] is claimed by Deventer, which received him to be educated, having taken him when still a little boy chorister— from the holy church of Utrecht, where he, usually undertaking small singing duties, also on account of his *vox tenuissima*, served the choirmasters in the manner of cathedral churches.

[18] A. Hyma, *The Youth of Erasmus* (Ann Arbor, Mich., 1930), 72.
[19] Ibid. 73.   [20] Ibid.
[21] Erasmus, *Omnia opera*, i (Basle, 1540), fo. A²; modern edition in *Opus Epistolarum Des. Erasmi Roterodami*, ed. P. S. Allen, i (Oxford, 1906), 56–71. The passage reads: 'Proximam sibi laudem vendicat Dauentria, quae puellum adhuc ex aede sacra Traiectensi cantorculum deductum, vbi praecentiunculas obire solitus phonascis etiam tenuissimae vocis gratia pro more templorum cathedralium inseruierat, instituendum suscepit' (ibid. 56–7).

Rhenanus' Latin is extremely dense, and there are several ambiguities that make it difficult to draw firm conclusions concerning Obrecht's biography. It seems puzzling, for instance, that after Rotterdam, Deventer is the next town entitled to praise for having hosted Erasmus, not Utrecht. This might confirm our previous impression that Erasmus' time as a chorister was an unpleasant episode. Does Deventer perhaps deserve praise for having released the boy from his unhappy life ('deductum')? Again the text is ambiguous. 'Tenuissima vox' could mean 'a most refined voice' (in which case Erasmus enjoyed the special distinction of being allowed to serve the choirmasters), a 'very feeble' one (in which the choirmasters simply charged him with tedious jobs, having no use for him in the choir), or perhaps simply a 'very high' voice.[22] Although the chronology of events in Rhenanus (Utrecht–Deventer) differs from the one suggested above (Deventer–Utrecht–Deventer), his text could be seen as consistent with that scenario: Rhenanus may have omitted to mention Erasmus' early years in Deventer, and concentrated on the boy's return to that city from Utrecht.

A further statement on Obrecht and Erasmus comes from a much later source, Pieter Opmeer's *Opus chronographicum*, printed in 1611, but written before 1595, the year of the author's death.[23] It must be stressed, however, that this book has no independent authority. Glareanus and Rhenanus had known Erasmus personally; Opmeer, who did not, simply seems to have conflated their two statements:[24]

Various composers then started to become famous, one of whom was Jacobus Obrechtus, who dominated that period, and who had been the teacher in music of the boy Erasmus of Rotterdam, at Utrecht, where the latter served as a choirboy on account of the *exilitas* [thinness] of his *vox acuta* [high voice].

The choice of words is virtually identical with that of Glareanus; the statement on Erasmus' voice seems to be a rephrasing of Rhenanus' cryptic comments. Since Opmeer cannot therefore be regarded as an independent source, all we may conclude from the passage is that according to a late sixteenth-century tradition, Obrecht had worked in Utrecht.

[22] For a discussion of the 'vox tenuissima' question, see J.-C. Margolin, *Érasme et la musique* (Paris, 1965), 36–7.

[23] P. Opmeer, *Opus chronographicum orbis universi a mundi exordio usque ad Annum M.DC.XI. continens historiam, icones et elogia summorum pontificium, imperatorum, regum ac virorum illustrium, in duos tomos divisum* (Antwerp, 1611).

[24] Ibid. 426: 'Coeperunt tunc innotescere varii symphonetes, inter quos hac aetate vel primus fuit Jacobus Obrechtus, qui Erasmo Roterodamo puero praeceptor fuit in musicis Ultrajecti, ubi ob exilitatem acutae vocis Erasmus choraulem agebat.'

There is no independent documentary evidence to confirm or disprove the accounts of Glareanus and Rhenanus. Singer lists are extant for several minor churches in Utrecht, but none of these contains the names of Jacob Obrecht and Erasmus of Rotterdam.[25] Utrecht Cathedral can be firmly ruled out, thanks to the recent archival research of Frans Rikhof.[26] This leaves the possibility that Obrecht worked in the private chapel of Bishop David of Burgundy, like 'le grand bastard' Antoine a half-brother of Charles the Bold. In view of Willem Obrecht's Burgundian connections, this is perhaps the hypothesis that makes most sense, but again there is no documentation to confirm or disprove it.[27]

Bergen op Zoom and Cambrai, 1480–1485

It is only in 1480 that we finally reach firm documentary ground. The surviving accounts of the Guild of Our Lady at Bergen op Zoom tell us that a *meester* Jacop was choirmaster there from at least 1480/1 to 1483/4.[28] Although his surname is never mentioned in the documents, this man is certainly to be identified with the composer. On 28 July 1484 he was appointed master of the choristers at Cambrai Cathedral, and the chapter minutes of that institution describe him then as '*magister* Jacobus Obreth de Bergis'.[29]

The Guild of Our Lady at Bergen op Zoom was a relatively new institution when Obrecht became its choirmaster: it had been founded in the late 1460s by the Lord of Bergen op Zoom, John II of Glymes, and the

[25] See Vlam and Vente, *Bouwstenen*, i. 212–307; ii (Amsterdam, 1971), 157–235; Vente, *Bouwstenen*, iii. 225–55.

[26] Frans Rikhof is preparing a dissertation on the lesser clergy at Utrecht Cathedral in the late Middle Ages, and has kindly checked for me whether Obrecht's name appears in any of the relevant documents for the period *c.*1470–80. Among the various singers and choirmasters listed during this period, none could conceivably be identical with the composer. The possibility that he worked in the cathedral can therefore safely be ruled out.

[27] There is little published information on the private chapel of the bishop of Utrecht, David of Burgundy. In 1473, he received papal permission for his chaplains and singers to hold their benefices *in absentia* (G. Brom, *Archivalia in Italië belangrijk voor de geschiedenis van Nederland*, i/2 (The Hague, 1909), 604). An important Utrecht composer was Anthonius de Vinea (van den Wijngaerde), who was active as a choirmaster in Antwerp by 1471, and has been traced in Utrecht in 1479–1508 (J. A. Bank, 'Uit het verleden van de Nederlandse kerkmuziek', *Sint Gregoriusblad*, 1939, 4–5). In 1480, Jean Keysere and Pasquier Blideman were called 'les meilleurs chantres' of the bishop's chapel (A. Pinchart, *Archives des arts, sciences et lettres: Documents inédits*, i/3 (Ghent, 1881), 163–4). Some information on music at the bishop's court is given in the description of Arnoldus Heymricius, but his authority is diminished by the excessively flattering tone of the account (cf. S. B. J. Zilverberg, *David van Bourgondië: Bisschop van Terwaan en van Utrecht (± 1427–1496)* (Groningen, 1951), 109–14).   [28] For this and what follows, see Wegman, 'Bergen op Zoom'.

[29] A. Pirro, 'Obrecht à Cambrai', *Tijdschrift van de Vereeniging voor Nederlandsche Muziekgeschiedenis*, 12 (1927), 78.

burgomaster and aldermen of the city. The association was based in the Chapel of the Blessed Virgin, which had just been built in the church of St Gertrude. Although its initial budget for polyphonic music was quite modest, the guild's revenues grew rapidly after John of Glymes endowed it with the incomes from the twice-yearly Bergen op Zoom fairs, in an ordinance dated 31 December 1474. The dean and jurors of the guild were obliged to submit each year on the Feast of the Assumption (15 August) a detailed account of their receipts and expenditure, which was then to be approved by the lord and the city government.

Jacob Obrecht is mentioned in the earliest surviving account, that of 1480/1, but we know that he was active in Bergen op Zoom already in the previous financial year, 1479/80. Two references to 'meester Jacobe den sangmeester' dating from before 15 August 1480 are found in the accounts of the steward of Oudenbosch and its environs. These are accounts of the household of John of Glymes at Oudenbosch (about 20 km. north-east of Bergen op Zoom), where the Lord of Bergen op Zoom spent much of his time, presumably because his mistress Mayken Sanders lived there. The composer is first mentioned in a payment of 23 April 1480: 'On the twenty-third of the same month, paid at the command etc., to *meestere* Jacobe the choirmaster on his first Mass, 240 Brabant groats [180 Flemish groats].' Four weeks later Obrecht received another payment: 'Paid to *meester* Jacop the choirmaster for having sung four Masses in Whitsuntide, 144 Brabant groats [96 Flemish groats].' Brief though these references are, they confirm Obrecht's activity as a choirmaster and priest in Bergen op Zoom before 15 August 1480. During his years in Bergen op Zoom, Jacob Obrecht had at least one opportunity to meet Antoine Busnoys again. On 2 September 1481, Busnoys passed through Bergen op Zoom in the retinue of Archduke Maximilian I of Austria.[30] It is likely that the two composers met on that occasion, albeit very briefly.

Information concerning Obrecht's activities during the period 15 August 1480 to 15 August 1484 derives entirely from the accounts of the Guild of Our Lady. These deal primarily with financial matters, of course, but they also contain a few biographical details. We learn that the composer received an annual salary equivalent to 480 Flemish groats in 1480/1 and 1481/2—quite a lot more than the salary that had been reserved for his predecessor Willem de Brouwer in 1470. On 24 June 1482

---

[30] This can be deduced from information given in Higgins, '*In hydraulis* Revisited', 66, and H. Vander Linden, *Itinéraires de Marie de Bourgogne et de Maximilien d'Autriche (1477–1482)* (Brussels, 1934), 107.

the rulers of the guild decided that Obrecht could take part, like his fellow singers, in the distribution of the *loten* (tokens). Henceforth he would receive a *loot* for every service in which he participated; these could later be exchanged for cash. Obrecht's *loten* equalled 2 Flemish groats, less than the 2.5 groats earned by the two best-paid singers of the guild. Effectively this change from an annual salary to a more flexible way of payment could amount to an increase in the composer's income of about 75 per cent if he attended all services. Apparently the guild was quite satisfied with the performance of his duties. In 1483/4 Jacob Obrecht lived together with Reynier 'with the hump' (Reynier *metten bulten*) who also sang in the services of the Guild of Our Lady and was paid, like Obrecht, *loten* worth the equivalent of 2 Flemish groats. Together, Jacob and Reynier earned 637 *loten* in 1483/4, pointing to an average attendance for both singers of around 75 per cent of the services.

During his tenure in 1480–4 Jacob Obrecht was in charge of the copying of polyphonic music in new gatherings and choirbooks with a total size of at least 575 sheets (= 1,150 leaves, or 2,300 pages). In 1481/2, some 480 sheets of writing paper were purchased 'for a songbook of Our Lady'. Two years later Obrecht was paid the equivalent of 12 Flemish groats 'for paper for his songbooks' (covering approximately 96 sheets) and a sum equalling 2 Flemish groats 'for compiling an index'. Several similar payments (some of them quite substantial) were made to the composer later in his life, and these indicate that he was prolific not only as a composer but also as a scribe. It is natural to assume that much of the music he copied was of his own making. If that assumption is correct, Obrecht must have been actively involved in the distribution of his music throughout his life. Several patterns in the transmission of Obrecht's masses suggest that autographs were in some way involved; one scribe stated explicitly that he copied a mass 'ab exemplari eiusdem [Obrecht]'. This is a matter that will be explored in more detail below.

Obrecht's scribal activity may help to explain the early transmission of his mass music to Italy. On 6 July 1481, the Sienese singer Matheus Gay received a payment for copying a new choirbook for Siena Cathedral. If this choirbook has survived as SienBC K.I.2, as has recently been argued,[31] then the *Missa Beata viscera*, which is found on fos. 156ᵛ–168ʳ of that source, was available in Italy as early as 1481. More concrete evidence is offered by the correspondence of Duke Ercole d'Este of Ferrara: in

---

[31] D'Accone, 'A Late 15th-Century Sienese Sacred Repertory' (see, however, the reservations expressed below, Ch. 4).

August 1484 he thanked his singer Cornelio di Lorenzo for sending him a mass by Obrecht:[32]

The mass of Jacob Obrecht that you sent has been gratefully received, and we have seen and received it most willingly and thus we thank you for it and commend you.

Obrecht's international reputation was evidently rising rapidly in these years. So it is perhaps not surprising that he succeeded, in 1484, in obtaining a position at one of the most prestigious musical centres in Europe, Cambrai Cathedral. This extremely wealthy church was the administrative centre of an enormous diocese stretching from Antwerp to Arras, and comprising one of the most prosperous and densely urbanized areas in Europe. From the fourteenth century onwards, the cathedral had cultivated polyphony with a vigour not surpassed by any other church in the Low Countries. Obrecht's appointment at this centre was a major promotion, and provides clear evidence of his growing international recognition.

But other factors probably played a part as well. The bishop of Cambrai, Henry of Glymes (1449–1502), was a son of John II, Lord of Bergen op Zoom. The composer seems to have been on good terms with John of Glymes, who had paid a substantial sum for his first Mass in 1480. Moreover, the Guild of Our Lady—of which John of Glymes was the ruler—must have been satisfied with Obrecht's services, since he received a large pay rise in 1482. It seems possible, therefore, that the application for the position in Cambrai was supported by favourable recommendations from Bergen op Zoom, which reached the cathedral chapter through powerful political channels.

Favourable recommendations he would certainly have needed, for it is difficult to imagine that Obrecht would have obtained the position without external influence. To begin with, there was no vacancy. In order to appoint Obrecht, the chapter had to dismiss its master of the choristers, Jean Hemart (Doc. 31):[33]

28 July [14]84 . . . The lords of the chapter have today retained *dominus* Jacobus Obreth of Bergen [op Zoom] as master of the children or choristers, in place of Johannes Hemart, the previous master of the choristers.

Hemart was an experienced musician with a long record of service at the

---

[32] Lockwood, *Ferrara*, 162–3. The reference is striking in that it precedes the first mention of Josquin in the surviving ducal correspondence by nearly two decades.
[33] See the reproduction in Pirro, 'Obrecht à Cambrai', 78.

cathedral.[34] He had been master of the choristers for fifteen years, and the chapter acts record no irregularities that might have justified his dismissal. Obrecht, on the other hand, was an outsider. He had had no previous association with the cathedral, and he came from a musical centre that was more than 160 kilometres removed from Cambrai. The sudden decision to push out Hemart in favour of Obrecht cannot be explained by the latter's reputation alone, however impressive it may have been. The chapter would certainly have wanted some assurance of Obrecht's administrative and didactic skills, and quite possibly—given the notoriously loose morals of clerical singers—of his virtuous behaviour as well. Even if such assurances could be provided (as was evidently the case) it must have taken some persuasion to convince the chapter of the need to replace a man who had done his job satisfactorily for fifteen years. The succinct record of the chapter's decision of 28 July 1484 may therefore well conceal intensive manœuvring behind the scenes.

Unless Hemart was perhaps promoted, there is the possibility that Obrecht had secured the support of the Bishop of Cambrai through the Lord of Bergen op Zoom, and submitted an unsolicited application to the chapter of Cambrai Cathedral. This would obviously not have been a manœuvre of the highest ethical standard: it involved the dismissal of a competent and trusted Cambrai singer. On the other hand, Paula Higgins has recently discovered that Antoine Busnoys and Philippe Basiron used these very tactics to obtain similar positions in Poitiers and Bourges in the late 1460s.[35] However this may be, Obrecht took up his position at Cambrai Cathedral on 6 September 1484; as it happens this was three weeks after the financial year at the Guild of Our Lady in Bergen op Zoom had ended.

It seems likely that the composer travelled to Cambrai in the second half of August. The quickest way to Cambrai was along the River Schelde, one of the major trade routes in the Low Countries.[36] This would have given Jacob the opportunity to see his father in Ghent, and perhaps to meet fellow singers at Antwerp and Lille. While travelling through Flanders in August 1484, Obrecht was undoubtedly aware that the greatest living composer of the time, Johannes Ockeghem, was visiting the area.

[34] Hemart is listed in Loyset Compère's so-called singers' prayer, the motet *Omnium bonorum plena* of *c.*1470.

[35] See P. Higgins, 'Tracing the Careers of Late Medieval Composers: The Case of Philippe Basiron of Bourges', *Acta musicologica*, 62 (1990), 7–8, and 'Musical Politics in Late Medieval Poitiers: A Tale of Two Choirmasters', paper read at the Eighteenth Medieval and Renaissance Music Conference, Royal Holloway and Bedford New College, 6–9 July 1990.

[36] See W. Prevenier and W. Blockmans, *The Burgundian Netherlands* (Cambridge, 1986), 16–22.

The city accounts of Damme record a payment for six jugs of wine presented to 'my lord the provost of Tours, first chaplain of the king of France, and his company' on 8 August.[37] On 25 August, a similar payment is recorded in the chapter acts of St Donatian's:[38]

My lords [of the chapter] consent with the payment made by the treasury for six jugs of wine, for the support of the *socii de musica* [singer-clerks of St Donatian's] in a dinner held some time ago [on 15 August] for the Lord Treasurer of Tours, *Dominus* Johannes Okeghem, first chaplain of the king of France [and] most excellent musician, and his companions.

It seems likely that Obrecht had received news in advance of Ockeghem's imminent visit to Bruges. Only half a year later, in February 1485, we learn that he had a 'friend' at St Donatian's, probably the internationally famous singer Jean Cordier.[39] Certainly he would have spared no effort to meet Ockeghem while he was travelling through Flanders on his way to Cambrai. Never again would their paths bring them so close to one another: one could travel from Ghent to Bruges in one day. It is thus tempting to assume that the two composers met in August 1484. This might even have inspired Obrecht to write a counterpart to Busnoys's *In hydraulis*, to welcome Ockeghem 'in patria'. If he did, the composition in question could well have been the mass *Sicut spina rosam*, which quotes the entire bass line of the Kyrie of Ockeghem's *Missa Mi–mi* in its Agnus Dei. Ockeghem's *Missa Mi–mi* was well known in Flanders and Brabant: it was copied in Bruges in 1475/6,[40] and part of its second Agnus Dei survives in a set of fragments discovered by Jaap van Benthem in Antwerp. According to Edgar Sparks, Obrecht's mass 'seems to be conceived as a gesture of respect to the older master'.[41] The date of the *Missa Sicut spina rosam* is still uncertain, however,[42] so it is difficult to pursue this speculation without comparative stylistic analysis (see Ch. 4).

On 9 September 1484, three days after he had started his work at

[37] See, for a full transcription, the exhibition catalogue *Johannes Ockeghem en zijn tijd* (Dendermonde, 1970), 119.

[38] For transcription, explanation, and further literature, see *Johannes Ockeghem en zijn tijd*, 115–16. It is generally assumed that Ockeghem came to Flanders on a diplomatic mission, but his dinner with the *socii de musica* of St Donatian's was an exclusively musical occasion. Ockeghem had probably travelled to Flanders by ship, in which case he obviously disembarked at Damme on (or shortly before) 8 Aug., and then travelled with his company to Bruges.

[39] Strohm, *Music in Late Medieval Bruges*, 37–8.

[40] See the excerpts from the fabric accounts of St Donatian's in *Johannes Ockeghem en zijn tijd*, 117–19.

[41] E. H. Sparks, *Cantus Firmus in Mass and Motet, 1420–1520* (Berkeley and Los Angeles, 1963), 276.

[42] See most recently B. Hudson, 'Obrecht's Tribute to Ockeghem', *Tijdschrift van de Vereniging voor Nederlandse Muziekgeschiedenis*, 37 (1987), 3–13.

Cambrai Cathedral, the chapter of that church decided to give Obrecht a copy of the ordinance prescribing his duties (Doc. 32):

9 September [1484]. In the general chapter [meeting] on the day following the Nativity of the Blessed Virgin Mary [8 September], the ordinance was read that was made on the spiritual and temporal welfare of the choirboys, and which is written out in the chapter acts of 22 September 1458. By the resolution and command of the chapter, the human authority of government was given to the recently installed master of the choirboys, in order that he (following what is declared in that ordinance) shall diligently guide and instruct those boys, etc., and render account of the proceeds from gifts and gratuities made to those boys, and this every year, unfailingly.

This is the last we hear about Obrecht for at least five months, and we must therefore assume that everything went well. At the beginning of 1485, then, Jacob Obrecht, now in his late twenties, could look back on a most promising start of a clerical and musical career. His masses were copied and performed in Italy and probably in other countries as well. He had obtained a position at Cambrai through a combination of musical talent, prolificity, diligence, and (possibly) clever political manœuvring. These same qualities could now make for a spectacular rise within the hierarchy of the church, something that would obviously have been more difficult, if not impossible, had he stayed in Bergen op Zoom. Even a lucrative position at one of the great court chapels in Europe could soon become within reach.

But Obrecht appears to have decided otherwise, for reasons that will probably never be recovered. The five-month silence in his biography is broken, not by documents of Cambrai Cathedral, but of St Donatian's at Bruges. In February 1485 Obrecht informs the canons of St Donatian's 'that he very much desires to serve this church in the office of succentor'.

4 Beyond Busnoys

THE masses *Petrus apostolus*, *Beata viscera*, *O lumen ecclesie*, and *Sicut spina rosam* form a separate group in Obrecht's mass œuvre; they share a range of features not found in other works. At the same time there are differences of emphasis between them suggesting that they represent successive stages in a continued stylistic development. That development, which will be the main subject of this chapter, must have taken place in the years around 1480. The style of *Petrus apostolus* points to a date in the mid- to late 1470s, *Beata viscera* is believed to have been copied in 1481, and *O lumen ecclesie* and *Sicut spina rosam* bridge the stylistic distance between these works and *Missa De Sancto Martino* of 1486.

The four masses are all based on one or more freely elaborated versions of a plainchant cantus firmus. The elaboration used in the Kyrie is invariably treated as the primary version: in each cycle it is restated literally in one or more movements following the Kyrie, and features in the head-motif. *Beata viscera* has eight different elaborations; the primary one appears in the Kyrie and Agnus Dei. *Sicut spina rosam* employs seven elaborations, of which the Kyrie version is restated in the Gloria and Sanctus. *Petrus apostolus* has three elaborations, each of which is repeated one or more times in the course of the mass. In *O lumen ecclesie* the chant melody assumes only one rhythmized form. In the last two cycles the greater degree of uniformity is counteracted by mensural changes in restatements, which cause rhythmic variation in performance. Strict restatement of a chant elaboration with rhythmic differentiation through mensural changes is a practice that betrays the influence of Antoine Busnoys.[1]

That influence is also suggested by the style of *Petrus apostolus*, which immediately recalls the idiom of Busnoys's masses *L'homme armé* and

---

[1] Two other features that set these four works apart from Obrecht's other masses include the use of strict canon (usually at the fifth) in tenorless sections, and the total absence of cantus-firmus material in the same sections.

O crux lignum triumphale. None of Obrecht's masses links up more directly with stylistic trends current in the 1470s than *Petrus apostolus*. The masses *Beata viscera* and *O lumen ecclesie* basically adhere to the idiom of *Petrus apostolus*, but show a progressive development towards textural variety and freedom. *Sicut spina rosam* brings that development to an extreme point, which was to be maintained only in modified form in *De Sancto Martino*. Isolated features of *O lumen ecclesie* and *Sicut spina rosam* recur not only in this work, but also in other masses from the late 1480s, notably *Salve diva parens* and *Ave regina celorum* (see Chs. 6 and 7).

Beyond Busnoys, Jacob Obrecht increasingly 'discovered' Ockeghem. In *Sicut spina rosam* the early Busnoys-inspired features had been expanded and variegated so far beyond their starting-point that there was room to pay stylistic tribute to another musical personality, whose identity is given away by quotations from Ockeghem's *Missa Mi–mi*. In this respect *Sicut spina rosam* once again lays the bridge to masses composed in the late 1480s, particularly *De Sancto Martino* and *De Sancto Donatiano* (see Ch. 6).

It would appear that the early 1480s were years of experimentation for Obrecht. The basic line of development represented by the four masses was towards a redefinition, within the received framework, of the contrapuntal function of the cantus firmus. Obrecht's preoccupation with the structural voice, its shape, identity, and interaction with the surrounding counterpoint, characterizes all his masses to some extent. In the early 1480s that preoccupation brought about a rapid transformation of the working methods he had inherited from Busnoys.

Missa Petrus apostolus

Little in the *Missa Petrus apostolus* suggests that such a transformation was to take place.[2] Despite the late date of its main source, Grapheus' *Missae tredecim quatuor vocum* (printed at Nuremberg in 1539), it must be among Obrecht's earliest works.[3] In virtually every respect the cycle looks to the

[2] For this mass, see B. Meier, *Studien zur Meßkomposition Jacob Obrechts* (Inaug.-Diss., Albert-Ludwigs-Universität, Freiburg im Breisgau, 1952), 12–14; M. Kyriazis, *Die Cantus firmus-Technik in den Messen Obrechts* (Inaug.-Diss., Universität Bern, 1952), 28–9 and 32; A. Salop, 'The Masses of Jacob Obrecht (1450–1505): Structure and Style' (Ph.D. diss., Indiana University, 1959), 15–21, 134, and 235–7; Sparks, *Cantus Firmus*, 269–72; R. Larry Todd, 'Retrograde, Inversion, Retrograde-Inversion, and Related Techniques in the Masses of Jacobus Obrecht', *Musical Quarterly*, 64 (1978), 63–4. The cantus firmus is the Magnificat antiphon for first and second Vespers for the Octave Day of Saints Peter and Paul, Apostles (*NOE* 8, pp. xxvii–xxviii).

[3] Ludwig Finscher placed *Petrus apostolus* in the earliest of the three chronological groups he distinguished in Obrecht's mass *œuvre* ('Obrecht, Jacob', *MGG* 9, col. 1820). Barton Hudson

past. It aspires to aesthetic goals that Obrecht was to abandon in the early 1480s. But *Petrus apostolus* is not a crude or immature work—quite the contrary: in this work the young Obrecht demonstrates his full command of the smooth and balanced mass idiom of the 1470s. The rapid developments in his subsequent works are not so much signs of growing skill and experience, but rather reflect the gradual elaboration of new aesthetic principles. The background to the style of *Petrus apostolus* must therefore not be sought in Obrecht's own *œuvre*. It lies in the repertory of an earlier generation.

The Et in terra illustrates this point well (Ex. 1). The section starts with an extended introductory duo for top voice and contratenor (bars 1–12). The first self-contained unit of that duo, which closes with a cadence on G in bar 5, is the head-motif of the mass. The top voice here quotes the beginning of the cantus firmus, thus anticipating the entry of the tenor in bar 13. In shorter movements like the Kyrie, Sanctus, and Agnus Dei, the cantus firmus enters immediately after the brief two-voice motto, so that the top voice relates to the tenor as a pre-imitation. But in the Et in terra the introductory duo is extended by two further imitative units, in which the top two voices explore their modal ranges (bars 5–9 and 9–12). The entry of the tenor in bar 13 marks a shift to four-part writing: imitation all but ceases, and the periodicity of the introductory duo gives way to an unbroken flow of counterpoint.[4] As soon as the tenor has finished its first statement, in bar 29, Obrecht reverts to the imitative style of the introductory duo. The interlude in bars 30–7, which bridges the period between the first and second statements of the cantus firmus, is woven almost entirely out of imitative motifs and phrases. The re-entry of the tenor in bar 38 brings a return to the non-imitative four-part counterpoint.

All this recalls the practices of mass composers in the 1460s and 1470s. The contrast between full and reduced scoring is exploited here to articulate the presence and absence of the cantus firmus. That contrast is

dubbed the style of the work 'relatively primitive', but nevertheless proposed a date in 1485–7, in view of the possibility that the mass might have been written for the chapel dedicated to SS Peter and Paul at St Donatian's, Bruges ('Obrecht's Tribute to Ockeghem', 11 n. 17).

[4] A noteworthy feature is chant-text underlay in the tenor (*NOE* 8, pp. xxxii–xxxiii), a feature that characterizes many of Obrecht's chant-based masses (*O lumen ecclesie, Sicut spina rosam, De Sancto Martino* and *Donatiano, Ave regina celorum, Sub tuum presidium*, and, if it is chant-based, *Salve diva parens*). The only apparent exceptions are *Beata viscera* and *Libenter gloriabor*, but this is probably to be attributed to corrupt transmission. Chant-text underlay in mass tenors seems to have been a typical Netherlandish feature; see A. E. Planchart, 'Parts with Words and without Words: The Evidence for Multiple Texts in Fifteenth-Century Masses', in S. Boorman (ed.), *Studies in the Performance of Late Mediaeval Music* (Cambridge, 1983), 227–51, and B. Hudson, 'On the Texting of Obrecht's Masses', *Musica disciplina*, 42 (1988), 122–5. Scribes outside the Low Countries (particularly in Italy) tended to replace chant texts by the appropriate texts from the Ordinary.

heightened through stylistic differentiation: the tenorless passages are highly imitative, whereas the full passages avoid imitation. In masses like *Beata viscera* and particularly *O lumen ecclesie* Obrecht is increasingly concerned to break away from this dichotomy, to bring the two styles closer together, and to treat passages with and without tenor as counterparts rather than opposites. These are significant developments that will throw important light on the development of Obrecht's early style.

Returning to the four-voice passage in bars 13–30, there are several conservative stylistic features here. The stream of counterpoint flows forward at a steady pace, and avoids anything that might interrupt or alter that pace or imply a structural division. This can be seen, for instance, in the treatment of cadences. The basic two-voice framework of the cadence in fifteenth-century theory was the progression from an imperfect to perfect consonance (third to unison, sixth to octave), usually with a suspended dissonance.[5] This type of progression can be found repeatedly in bars 13–30, but in all cases the cadential effect is softened by the other voices. In bar 15, for example, there is a clear cadence on C in the three lower voices, but the top voice is in the midst of a three-bar phrase that still awaits its conclusion. As a consequence, the cadence is perceived merely as a transient progression in the broader contrapuntal flow, not as a conclusion. Each of the following three bars ends with a cadential progression on G, but again the sense of continuity prevails over that of musical periodization. In bars 16–17, the bass moves to the sixth degree on the final chord of the cadential progression, thus creating the effect of a 'deceptive' cadence. The contratenor does the same in bars 17–18. In these and similar ways all subsequent cadences (in bars 19, 21, 22, 25, 26, 27, and 30) are smoothened.

What is significant here is not only the consistent practice of smoothening itself, but the fact that cadential progressions dominate the counterpoint to such an unusual extent. They are an essential ingredient of the style. In later masses Obrecht was to use far fewer cadences; those that he did introduce generally received much stronger emphasis. Also significant is the *variety* of the cadences. Each time the basic two-part framework is

---

[5] For discussions of 15th-c. 'cadence' theory, see H. Besseler, *Bourdon und Fauxbourdon: Studien zum Ursprung der niederländischen Musik* (2nd rev. edn., Leipzig, 1974), 29–44; B. Meier, *Die Tonarten der klassischen Vokalpolyphonie* (Utrecht, 1974), 75–102; and K. Berger, *Musica Ficta: Theories of Accidental Inflections in Vocal Polyphony from Marchetto da Padova to Gioseffo Zarlino* (Cambridge, 1987), 122–39. For cadences and their textural role in Obrecht's music, see A. Leszczyńska, 'Kadencja w Fakturze Motetów Jacoba Obrechta', *Muzyka*, 33/2 (1988), 41–51. In the present study, references to cadences in musical examples always cite the bar that contains the final perfect consonance of the two-voice framework, even if the preceding imperfect consonance (whether with or without suspended dissonance) is in a different bar.

Ex. 1. Obrecht, *Missa Petrus apostolus*, Et in terra

stated by a different pair of voices. In bars 15–30, for instance, that
framework is found successively in the following parts: C–B, C–T, C–B,
S–T, C–B, S–T, C–B, S–T. On average a cadential progression occurs
between *some* pair of voices every one or two bars, while the remaining
parts persistently conceal or soften that progression. On the whole, then,
the contrapuntal writing has what might be called a 'cadential' quality:
chords tend, as it were, to 'fall' into another, as falling dominoes in
a series. Cadences are used, paradoxically, to create a sense of momentum
and continuity, not of periodization.

The contrapuntal writing is smooth: leaps and sharply profiled motifs
are avoided. The top voice (and to a lesser extent the other voices) has
a tendency to move within a restricted range, usually no more than
a fourth or fifth (see, for instance, the extended top-voice line in bars 24–
30). This contrasts with the extreme melodic agility and exuberance found
in so many of Obrecht's later masses. Melodic motion is generally stepwise and fluent, and there is a tendency to subtle rhythmic differentiation.
In all voices, dotted or off-beat rhythms alternate freely with simple semibreve or minim motion. The combined texture is thus characterized by

a delicate interplay of overlapping, coinciding, and interlocking rhythms, in which the semibreve beats receive varying degrees of emphasis. Again this contrasts with the more figurative contrapuntal writing in Obrecht's mature masses. In these works the melodic lines tend to outline triads, and are generally built from incisive rhythmic patterns (see Ch. 8). It is also in these pieces that we find closer rhythmic co-operation between the voices, causing the basic pulses to receive regular, emphatic stresses.

Before attempting to trace the origins of the style of *Petrus apostolus* in the 1470s, it is worth sketching briefly the historical background against which the mass needs to be assessed.[6] The third quarter of the fifteenth century had been a period of energetic stylistic exploration and expansion. In the course of that period the relatively uniform mass style of the 1450s ramified in a variety of local traditions and individual styles. By the time Jacob Obrecht entered the compositional stage, there was still a broad, commonly accepted musical idiom, but within that general framework a wide range of compositional options was available. As regards cantus-firmus treatment, for instance, anything between extreme ornamentation and literal quotation was possible. There were varying kinds of parody, ranging from playful allusions to the top voice of a song, to the writing of mass sections that were simply contrafacts of the model. Some composers tended to repeat sections or parts of sections literally in the course of the mass, a habit that Obrecht was to take over in several of his works. Some composers used the cantus firmus as a springboard for imitation, or tended to apply imitation on a structural level; others avoided imitation rigorously. Some composers tended to organize or structure their counter-point with repeated motifs or rounded phrases; others pursued melodic irregularity and freedom. To sum up, nearly every composer of the 1470s spoke his own idiom within the broad framework of the contemporary musical language. Because of this, it is not difficult now to distinguish, on stylistic grounds, a mass by Faugues from one by Busnoys, a Martini from a Dufay, a Regis from an Ockeghem—to name but a few of the major composers active in this period. In cases of unknown authorship, it is often possible to pin-point at least the geographical area where a mass must have been composed.

All this is of importance for the question of the origins of Obrecht's mass style. For if the *Missa Petrus apostolus* was written before about 1480, then the compositional choices in that mass should betray Obrecht's own stylistic preferences and backgrounds. That does indeed appear to be

---

[6] For what follows, see R. C. Wegman, 'The Anonymous Mass *D'ung aultre amer*: A Late Fifteenth-Century Experiment', *Musical Quarterly*, 75 (1991), 566–94.

the case. The descriptive analysis of the *Et in terra* has brought to light several features that can have been borrowed from only one man, Antoine Busnoys. The latter's two surviving masses, *O crux lignum triumphale* and *L'homme armé*, both presumably from the years around 1470, display a clearly defined, homogeneous style. It is that style which Obrecht emulated in *Missa Petrus apostolus*.

The first Kyrie of Busnoys's *Missa L'homme armé* serves to illustrate the relationship between the two composers (Ex. 2). The head-motif (bars 1–3) quotes the beginning of the cantus firmus, and effectively relates to the tenor statement as a pre-imitation, as is the case in the Kyrie, Sanctus, and Agnus Dei of *Petrus apostolus*. And just as in the latter mass, the voices are written in a fluent and polished melodic style: they largely avoid leaps larger than a fourth, tend to operate within a restricted range, and are characterized by subtle rhythmic differentiation.

But it is in the combined effect of the voices that the correspondences between the two composers come out most clearly. Most conspicuous, of course, are the frequent cadential progressions, and the unobtrusive way in which they are taken up in the contrapuntal stride. In bars 7–15 we find the two-part cadential formula in the following voice-pairs: C–T, S–C, C–B, C–B, S–T, C–B, S–C, and S–C, respectively. The regular occurrence of 'hidden' cadential progressions is such an essential and distinctive feature of Busnoys's mass style that almost any four-part section from his two cycles could be used to illustrate it. It is found in several of his motets as well (notably *Victimae paschali* and *Anthoni usque limina*). Just as in Obrecht's *Missa Petrus apostolus* the cadential progressions are used, paradoxically, to create a sense of musical continuity. They act as musical catalysts: each time a suspended dissonance is resolved, the next chord is expected as its natural conclusion. But Busnoys takes great care to control their catalytic effect: the cadences can be 'evaded' (bar 15), they may fall during the course of a top-voice line (bars 7, 8, 10, 15), or one of the voices outside the two-part framework may reach its conclusion a minim late (see the bass in bars 8, 12, and 14). Always there is the sense that there is more 'beyond' the cadence—until the very last one is reached.

Whether Obrecht recognized and copied this conspicuous feature consciously is open to question: for him it must have been part and parcel of a style that he sought to emulate as a whole, and apparently knew inside out. If, for instance, bar 18 of his *Et in terra* bears an unmistakable resemblance to bar 12 of Busnoys's Kyrie, this is probably not a conscious quotation, but rather the sort of duplication that is bound to occur in a style so formalized as that of the Burgundian composer. Similar

Ex. 2. Busnoys, *Missa L'homme armé*, Kyrie I (*Van Ockeghem tot Sweelinck*, ed. Smijers, 18)

duplications are found within the latter's own sacred *œuvre*,[7] and indeed within Obrecht's mass. Such resemblances indicate how perfectly the young composer had mastered Busnoys's stylistic idiom.

Busnoys's influence is also conspicuous in the treatment of the cantus firmus. As said earlier, Obrecht repeats the tenor in bars 38–55 of the Et in terra, but in a different mensuration so that its rhythmic shape changes. The inspiration for this procedure, known as mensural transformation, must have come from Busnoys, who applied it systematically in his *Missa O crux lignum triumphale*, and who in turn must have adopted it from Petrus de Domarto's *Missa Spiritus almus* (*c*.1450).[8] The latter two cycles are the only surviving masses before *Petrus apostolus* that mensurally transform a fixed rhythmization of a chant melody.[9] Obrecht's adoption of the very same procedure in what is probably his earliest extant mass confirms that he was influenced by Busnoys more than by any other composer.

One interesting detail of Obrecht's cantus-firmus treatment may shed further light on his compositional backgrounds. In the first Agnus Dei, he transposes the cantus firmus down a fourth, so that it effectively functions as the bass. This recalls similar Agnus Dei 'tricks' in the early *L'homme armé* masses. Ockeghem transposed the *L'homme armé* tune down to the bass range in the Agnus Dei of his cycle, which must pre-date 1467.[10]

---

[7] Compare, for instance, bars 12–13 of *Anthoni usque limina* with the nearly identical bars 12–13 of the Gloria of *Missa O crux lignum triumphale*.

[8] For discussions of mensural transformation in the late 15th-c. mass, see R. C. Wegman, 'Another Mass by Busnoys?', *Music & Letters*, 71 (1990), 5–12, and 'Petrus de Domarto's *Missa Spiritus almus* and the Early History of the Four-Voice Mass in the Fifteenth Century', *Early Music History*, 10 (1990), 244–52 and 258–72.

[9] Edgar Sparks already drew attention to the rarity of the procedure before Obrecht: 'The repetition of a single ornamental version of the c.f. is not at all the practice of Obrecht's predecessors, who, on the whole, prefer to provide a new ornamentation with each new statement' (*Cantus Firmus*, 271). Sparks does not discuss Domarto's *Missa Spiritus almus*, but he stresses the relationship between Obrecht and Busnoys in his discussion of the latter's *Missa O crux lignum triumphale*: 'instead of continuing to ornament the tenor anew each time it appears, the customary way with c.f. elaborations, [Busnoys] chooses to go no further in the direction of ornamentation. He takes the first statement as a model and quotes it exactly from then on . . . Obrecht also prefers to curb the never-ending elaborations; in his Masses on [liturgical] c.f. he often takes one ornamented version of the Gregorian melody as the basis for several movements, achieving variety in the presentation by schematic means just as Busnois had done' (ibid. 172). For an analysis of the cantus-firmus treatment in Busnoys's *Missa O crux lignum triumphale*, see Wegman, 'Another Mass by Busnoys?', 5–6.

[10] Ockeghem's mass was copied in Bruges in 1467/8 (Strohm, *Music in Late Medieval Bruges*, 30). I suggest a date for Busnoys's *Missa L'homme armé* around 1470, since its style is virtually identical with that of the same composer's *Missa O crux lignum*, which is datable to 1467–73 on external grounds (Wegman, 'Domarto's *Missa Spiritus almus*', 262–4). Richard Taruskin's much earlier dating, to 1460 at the latest, is not so much based on internal or external evidence as presupposed by his hypothesis that Busnoys's mass started the *L'homme armé* tradition, and should therefore pre-date Regis's mass, which existed by 1462 (see 'Busnoys and the *L'Homme armé* Tradition', 257–65). This hypothesis has not found wide acceptance, and is contradicted by Taruskin's further

Busnoys seems to have responded by presenting it in inversion (in the same movement of his *L'homme armé* cycle), so that here, too, the cantus firmus functions as the bass. Dufay, in the third Agnus Dei of his mass of the same title, had it sung in retrograde. Obrecht seems to have been aware of these 'tricks'. The third Agnus Dei of his *Missa Petrus apostolus* presents the cantus firmus in retrograde inversion in the bass, a possible combined allusion to Busnoys and Dufay. More importantly, this gives him the opportunity to make a further, and more obvious, allusion to Ockeghem. The first bars of the third Agnus Dei unmistakably hint at the opening of the same section in Ockeghem's *Missa L'homme armé*—one of the most stunning passages in the fifteenth-century mass repertory (Ex. 3). Again Obrecht shows us how much he was an exponent of the Ockeghem–Busnoys generation when he composed the *Missa Petrus apostolus*.

The historic circumstances under which Jacob Obrecht might have become influenced by Busnoys have been outlined in Chapter 2: his father's long-standing association with the court of Charles of Burgundy may well have given him several opportunities to meet Busnoys in the years 1467–70. Significantly, these are precisely the years in which the older composer seems to have developed the peculiar idiom that Jacob sought to emulate. The style is to some extent there in Busnoys's motet *In hydraulis* of 1466–7, but appears fully matured only in the *Missa O crux lignum triumphale* (which I have elsewhere dated 1467–74),[11] the motets *Gaude celestis domina* (which pre-dates 1472–3) and *Anthoni usque limina*, and the *Missa L'homme armé*. If Jacob Obrecht met Busnoys during these crucial years, as seems likely, it is not surprising that the creative developments from that period should have influenced him. Consequently, his *Missa Petrus apostolus* should post-date the early 1470s, just as it is likely to pre-date 1481, the year when his more forward-looking mass *Beata viscera* may have been in existence.

The actual date of *Petrus apostolus* probably lies closer to 1480 than to 1470, for there are a number of features in the mass that hint very tentatively at later developments. One such feature can be observed in bars 38–47 of Ex. 1: it is Obrecht's tendency to structure a contrapuntal line (usually the bass) by means of repeated motifs or phrases. This procedure returns in several of Obrecht's later masses, where it is often handled with great skill, sometimes on a structural level (for instance, *Missa Pfauen-*

hypothesis that Busnoys's mass was composed for Charles the Bold, a patron with whom the composer was not associated until late 1466.

[11] Wegman, 'Domarto's *Missa Spiritus almus*', 263–4.

Ex. 3. (*a*) Obrecht, Agnus Dei III of *Missa Petrus apostolus*, bars 1–5;
(*b*) Ockeghem, Agnus Dei III of *Missa L'homme armé*, bars 1–5 (*Collected Works*,
i. 114-15)

schwanz; see Ch. 8). It is not found in either of Busnoys's surviving
masses. Similarly, we find some brief sequential patterns involving all four
voices, for instance, in the Sanctus, bars 25–8, and Agnus Dei, bars 87–8.
In the context of the mass as a whole these are just passing moments that
do not break the stylistic homogeneity of the cycle (as they would in
Obrecht's later masses). But again the feature is absent in Busnoys's
sacred music, and this may suggest a later date. Finally, there are some
brief homorhythmic passages, at the beginning of the Qui tollis and
Et iterum, and also in bars 196–9 and 210–17 of the latter section. Nothing
of the kind occurs in Busnoys's masses.

One section in the *Missa Petrus apostolus* abandons Busnoys's style
altogether: this is the second Kyrie (whose music is repeated in the
Et exspecto). Obrecht presents here the cantus firmus in imitation between the tenor and bass, in such a way that one voice sounds while the
other rests. We find this same practice in many other Obrecht masses
based on chant cantus firmi (for instance, *Beata viscera*). Basically, the
second Kyrie of *Petrus apostolus* consists of antiphonally responding duos,
each voice-pair stating self-contained musical units rounded off by firm
cadences. This section is thus the most lightly scored of the entire mass
(not counting the tenorless duos and trios). In that respect it directly
anticipates the style of the *Missa O lumen ecclesie*, which will be discussed
later in this chapter.

These forward-looking features, although modest compared to what
happens in *Beata viscera*, *O lumen ecclesie*, and *Sicut spina rosam*, suggest
that the *Missa Petrus apostolus* may have been written in the late rather
than early 1470s. Obrecht tentatively asserts his independence in some
respects, but on the whole he operates within the framework of Busnoys's

style. He handles that style with remarkable confidence and skill. Although early, *Petrus apostolus* is a fine and competent work by a talented young composer who had fully mastered the art of composition, and was ready to transform it.

Missa Beata viscera

The *Missa Beata viscera* already seems to be a transitional work, despite the early *terminus ante quem* of 1481 indicated by the apparent copying date of SienBC K.1.2.[12] Like *Petrus apostolus*, this mass takes the style of Busnoys as its point of departure.[13] But new elements creep into that style that seem to disturb its delicate, almost 'classical' balance: rapid passage-work, leaps, quick traversals through the voice ranges, sequences that are carried on for just about too long, extended homorhythmic passages, and so on. Busnoys's mass style had reached its perfection in the early 1470s: after that it could only be imitated and copied (as in *Petrus apostolus*), not refined any further. In *Beata viscera* we see the first signs that the style is breaking down. Seen from the past, that development can only be described in negative terms. But from the perspective of Obrecht's later masses, we can recognize several new features in the budding stage. The -

---

[12] For this mass, which is based on the Communion at Mass for the Blessed Virgin Mary (*NOE* 2, p. xii), see Meier, *Studien zur Meßkomposition*, 18; Kyriazis, *Die Cantus firmus-Technik*, 59; Salop, 'The Masses of Jacob Obrecht', 27–8 and 140–1; and Sparks, *Cantus Firmus*, 272–4. Although *Beata viscera* is undoubtedly an early mass, I would express some doubts about the copying date for SienBC K.1.2 proposed by Frank D'Accone ('A Late 15th-Century Sienese Sacred Repertory'). The paper of SienBC K.1.2 bears a type of watermark that is not documented anywhere in Europe before 1491; in Siena, where the choirbook must have been compiled, paper of this type has been found only in the period 1495–1524 (C.-M. Briquet, *Les Filigranes: Dictionnaire historique des marques du papier* (Geneva, 1907), nos. 5920 and 5922–4). D'Accone's dating, based on a tentative identification of SienBC K.1.2 with two 'books of figural music' described in a payment of 1481, seems problematic in that it precedes the earliest documented use of this paper-type by ten years, and at Siena in particular by fourteen years. Besides, as Jeffrey Dean has pointed out to me, the script and spelling variations of the main scribe appear to be typically Italian, whereas Matheus Gay, who copied the two choirbooks in 1481, is consistently described in the documents as a Frenchman. *Beata viscera* is otherwise transmitted in MunBS 3154, where it was copied on paper dated 1491–3 (see T. Noblitt, 'Die Datierung der Handschrift Mus. ms. 3154 der Staatsbibliothek München', *Musikforschung*, 27 (1974), 36–56).

[13] A curious notational detail in this mass, which is also found in many later cycles by Obrecht, confirms the composer's debt to Busnoys: this is the pleonastic habit of indicating 'minor color' by coloration as well as a figure '3' underneath the relevant notes (*NOE* 2, p. xvii). This is an exceedingly rare practice, but it was typical of Busnoys: Tinctoris described it in his *Proportionale musices* of 1472–3, stating that it occurs only in Busnoys's works (*Opera theoretica*, iia. 52). It is found in his *Missa L'homme armé*, *Gaude celestis domina*, *Victimae paschali*, *Regina celi* I, and *Magnificat Octavi toni* (Wegman, 'Another Mass by Busnoys?', 4–5 n. 15). Obrecht masses featuring this device include: *Sicut spina rosam* (*NOE* 11, p. xliv), *De Sancto Martino* (*NOE* 3, p. xxxv), *Salve diva parens* (*NOE* 11, p. xxxii), *Ave regina celorum* (*NOE* 1, p. xxxii), *Caput* (*NOE* 2, p. xxiv), *Rose playsante* (*NOE* 9, p. xxxii), and *Sub tuum presidium* (*NOE* 12, pp. liii–liv).

Missa Beata viscera is a pivotal and seminal work; it merits careful consideration.

Ex. 4, the first Agnus Dei, shows how closely the mass is still linked to *Petrus apostolus*.[14] The rhythmization of the chant melody in the tenor is identical to the one used in the Kyrie (the 'primary' version); in all other movements the rhythmizations are free. The primary version also appears in the head-motif of every movement (bars 1–5). This links *Beata viscera* with *Petrus apostolus* and *O lumen ecclesie*. An additional correspondence is the quasi-imitative relationship between the motto and tenor. In the *Missa O lumen ecclesie*, and later in the masses *Sicut spina rosam* and *Ave regina celorum*, Jacob Obrecht was to transform that relationship, a process of which the first signs can be observed in *Beata viscera* (see below).

The style of the first Agnus Dei still breathes the spirit of Busnoys. The tenor is again embedded in a stream of four-part counterpoint. Although cadential progressions occur with lesser frequency than in *Petrus apostolus*, they are handled in very much the same way: the basic two-voice framework is stated by a different voice-pair each time, the remaining voices soften their cadential effect (compare the bass, bars 15–17, with bars 6–8 of the bass in Ex. 2), and the sense of continuity prevails. But on the whole the contrapuntal writing appears to be bolder and more energetic. This can already be seen in the head-motif, whose top voice rapidly descends a seventh, leaps up an octave, and then gradually focuses on the final note, G, which is reached in bar 5. The next top-voice line, in bars 5–9, follows more or less the same pattern. The tendency towards more energetic writing can also be observed in bars 13–17, where the extended line in the top voice starts with off-beat rhythms, presents two scalar passages in quick succession, and finally reverts to the more polished writing of *Petrus apostolus*.

All these forward-looking elements pale in comparison with what happens in some of the other movements, however. Ex. 5 shows bars 12–35 of the Patrem. The introductory duo has been left out of the example, since it follows the same pattern as the Et in terra of *Petrus apostolus*: the head-motif (bars 1–5) is followed by free, imitative extensions, until the cadence in bar 15 triggers off the four-part counterpoint. The tenor enters here with a free rhythmization of the *Beata viscera* melody. The surrounding voices are at first slow to gather speed. Just as in *Petrus apostolus* (see

---

[14] An additional feature that links the two cycles is statement of the cantus firmus in equal semibreve notes: compare the Et unam sanctam of *Beata viscera* with the Qui tollis, Et iterum, Sanctus, Osanna, and Agnus Dei III of *Petrus apostolus* (see also pp. xxix–xxxi of *NOE* 8). With the possible exception of the *Missa De Sancto Martino* (which presents several of its cantus firmi in equal breves), no other Obrecht mass exhibits this particular type of treatment.

Ex. 4. Obrecht, *Missa Beata viscera*, Agnus Dei I

Ex. 5. Obrecht, *Missa Beata viscera*, Patrem, bars 12–35

(Ex. 5, *cont.*)

Ex. 1, bars 13–14), Obrecht seems concerned to let the four-part sonority 'sound out' before stepping up the pace. (We find the same practice in the Et in terra of *Beata viscera* and the Patrem of *Petrus apostolus*.)

Full rhythmic activity is reached only in bar 17, and again the contrapuntal writing is noticeably more dynamic and less restrained than in *Petrus apostolus*. The scalar passages, leaps, and quick melodic ascents and descents (often in parallel motion with the bass) inject a new sense of energy into Obrecht's musical idiom. That idiom is still recognizably early, however, at least up to bar 29: the busy contrapuntal texture flows steadily, without any marked change or interruption, and does not appear to aim for any particular harmonic or melodic goal. It is the *quality* of flowing that Obrecht is still most concerned about, a quality he achieves by pursuing (as in *Petrus apostolus*) rhythmic differentiation and contrapuntal independence.

But the counterpoint has lost its 'cadential' quality. It is as though there is no place for subtle suspended dissonances in Obrecht's new writing. Ironically, the composer's concern for greater dynamism and energy will later lead him to discover the powerful effect of cadences if they are stripped of all contrapuntal subtleties and stated bluntly in long note-values (see Ch. 8). This is just one example of his tendency to redefine the function of individual musical ingredients, and to put them to new effect. This process, which we shall trace several times in the course of the present study, usually follows the same pattern. The ingredients are isolated from the stylistic idiom of Obrecht's early masses, where they are still integrated, then reduced to their most elementary level, and placed in a chain of musical events in such a way that their effect is fully exploited.[15] It is in this sense that the 'Busnoys style' begins to break down in *Beata viscera*.

A further example of that development can be found in bars 29–33: it is the use of an extended four-voice sequential passage. What is significant here is not the fact of the sequence itself, but the way it is handled. In *Petrus apostolus* the few four-voice sequences were still brief and inconspicuous moments within the broader contrapuntal flow. Here, the homorhythmic writing, the energetic rhythmic patterns, and (particularly) the number of repeats, set the passage apart from the music that precedes it.[16] In every sense the sequence is a transgression of the rules of balance, proportion, and restraint that Obrecht had adopted in the *Missa Petrus apostolus*. But what is a transgression from one perspective can be an innovation from another. It was only by isolating and cultivating the device that Obrecht could discover (and eventually exploit) its inherent powers.

Once this general trend is recognized, it is possible to find more examples. Certainly the last part of the Et resurrexit merits discussion (Ex. 6). Up to bar 191, this section has followed the traditional textural layout that

---

[15] This tendency was observed by Otto Gombosi as early as 1925: 'Obrechts Musik sieht die Wege der Entwicklung und zeichnet sie bedeutend intensiver vor als alle seine Zeitgenossen. Er geht bis zu den Wurzeln der Formbildung, schafft Normen, die zwar keine direkte Weiterbildung erfuhren, aber eine Vorausahnung des erst später Werdenden sind'; *Jacob Obrecht: Eine stilkritische Studie* (Leipzig, 1925), 131.

[16] Similar extended four-voice sequences are found in the Qui sedes, bars 115–25, and Et resurrexit, bars 177–82.

Ex. 6. Obrecht, *Missa Beata viscera*, Et resurrexit, bars 191–228

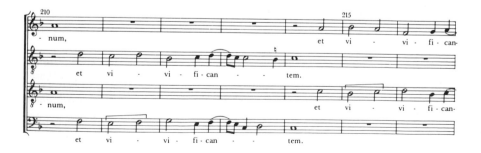

we have observed in the previous examples: imitative duos and trios provide relief against the full passages. But then Obrecht breaks away from this division. The extended three-voice passage involving the tenor (bars 192–202) would be unusual in any mass written before about 1480. But at least in the first few bars the voices behave as though the bass had only temporarily dropped out—something that is seen several times in the course of this mass (see also Ex. 1, bars 40–1). It is in bar 195—when Obrecht shifts over to a quasi-fauxbourdon style and carries on writing in that style for six bars—that something truly new is happening. Again a device is isolated and extended in such a way that it can only appear to be an extraneous element within the total stylistic context. And again we are dealing with a musical ingredient that Obrecht would later put to great effect.

The remainder of the section is structured in a way that resembles that of the second Kyrie of *Petrus apostolus* (see above). The tenor and bass state the cantus firmus in non-overlapping imitation. The contratenor is linked to the bass, and the top voice to the tenor, so that we have in effect a series of alternating duos. The passage contrasts sharply with the sorts

of sections we have seen in Exx. 1–5. It is structured in relatively brief
units, each of which is rounded off with a clear cadence. Consequently, the
cantus firmus has to be divided into several short phrases, each of which
is rhythmized in such a way that it can be easily imitated by the bass. The
duos respond to each other as equal partners. The contrapuntal role of
the tenor thus appears to be transformed: the voice no longer dictates the
structure, but is adapted to a preconceived textural layout; it is no longer
the centre of gravity, but is reduced to a role equivalent to that of the bass.
That Obrecht was particularly fond of this procedure is shown by the
opening of the Qui sedes (bars 88–100), which is also structured quasi-
antiphonally. The contratenor and top voice first state a brief, ornamented
cantus-firmus phrase in imitation. As soon as they have finished, the bass
and tenor repeat this imitation literally. The entry of the cantus firmus
(traditionally the central musical event in mass sections) is thus played
down and reduced to a mere link in a preconceived musical chain.

Before summing up our findings, it is necessary to point out another
significant feature of the *Missa Beata viscera*. The Sanctus employs
a procedure that recurs in several other chant-based masses from the
1480s: the writing of canon (or quasi-canon) based upon cantus-firmus
material.[17] In the first section of the movement, the bass imitates the tenor
strictly, although the time-intervals are varied through the insertion of
irregular numbers of rests. Most of the time the voices overlap, so that
four-voice counterpoint is maintained more or less throughout the section.
The first Osanna is based on a strict canon at the fifth between the top
voice and tenor; quite possibly Obrecht originally wrote out only the
top voice and supplied it with a verbal canon. The second Osanna employs
the same type of quasi-canon as the Sanctus; unlike that section, however,
the canon is between the top voice and tenor. Again the voices overlap for
most of the time, so that full scoring prevails.

To conclude, the *Missa Beata viscera* shows a mixture of conservative
and progressive traits. Obrecht's point of departure is still the stylistic
idiom of the 1470s, and several sections, particularly the first Kyrie and
Agnus Dei, maintain that idiom fairly faithfully. But the concern for more
energetic and dynamic writing leads him to dissolve the style in other

---

[17] Quasi-canon, at shifting time intervals (through the insertion of irregular numbers of rests) is
found in *Petrus apostolus*, Kyrie II (= Et exspecto); *O lumen ecclesie*, Benedictus; *Ave regina celorum*,
Et in terra (bars 26–41), Qui tollis (up to bar 223), Sanctus, Osanna, and Agnus Dei II; *Sicut spina
rosam*, Patrem (bars 44–78); *Libenter gloriabor*, first Kyrie. Strict cantus-firmus-based canon is found
in *De Sancto Martino*, Et in Spiritum (interval: four breves); *Sicut spina rosam*, Et resurrexit
(interval: four breves); *Libenter gloriabor*, Crucifixus (interval: four breves). *Beata viscera* seems to be
the earliest mass to contain both types of canon.

sections and to present its constituent elements in isolation. In doing so he 'discovers' the inherent potential of such devices as sequence, quasi-fauxbourdon writing, chordal declamation, and chain-like structuring— devices that he will put to great effect in his later masses, and that will become an essential part of his mature style. Meanwhile the overall stylistic picture of the *Missa Beata viscera* remains uneven. Some of the finest sections, such as the first Agnus Dei, derive their qualities from the very style that Obrecht breaks down elsewhere. It seems as though he is experimentally developing a new musical language, without daring as yet to depart from the one he had inherited. It is in this sense that the *Missa Beata viscera* appears to be a transitional work.

Missa O lumen ecclesie

The *Missa O lumen ecclesie* seems to be almost a response to *Beata viscera*.[18] The progressive devices that still appeared as extraneous elements in the latter mass are now applied with greater consistency, and thus provide the stylistic unity and homogeneity that *Beata viscera* appeared to lack. This applies particularly to the type of antiphonal chain structure observed in the second Kyrie of *Petrus apostolus* and in the Et resurrexit and Qui tollis of *Beata viscera*. The *Missa O lumen ecclesie* is a virtual study of this type of structure. The extensive use of the device makes the cycle the most thinly scored mass in Obrecht's *œuvre*: full passages make up

---

[18] For *Missa O lumen ecclesie*, which is also known under the title *O quam suavis*, see Meier, *Studien zur Meßkomposition*, 14–16; Kyriazis, *Die Cantus firmus-Technik*, 14, 41, 45, and 61–4; Salop, 'The Masses of Jacob Obrecht', 11–15; Sparks, *Cantus Firmus*, 272 4. Ludwig Finscher included the mass, along with *Petrus apostolus* and *Beata viscera*, among Obrecht's earliest works (*MGG* 9, col. 1820). Edgar Sparks drew attention to *O lumen ecclesie*'s structural resemblance to *Petrus apostolus* (*Cantus Firmus*, 272). Barton Hudson has pointed to its stylistic similarity to *Missa Sicut spina rosam*; since he dated the latter mass in the 1490s, he proposed a date in that decade for *O lumen ecclesie* as well ('Obrecht's Tribute to Ockeghem', 11 n. 17). The connections between *O lumen ecclesie* and *Sicut spina rosam* do indeed appear to be pronounced, but the peculiar style of these two cycles can be explained more convincingly by assuming that they were written between *Beata viscera* and *De Sancto Martino*, that is, before about 1486.

The identity of the cantus firmus is still uncertain. Two sources, JenaU 22 and LeipU 51 (of which the former was copied in the Netherlands), have the tenor underlaid with the text of *O quam suavis*, an antiphon of Corpus Christi, while the Roman manuscript VatSM 26 identifies the chant as *O lumen ecclesie*, the Magnificat antiphon at second Vespers for the feast of St Dominic in the Dominican rite. Barton Hudson has argued that the latter chant is in closer agreement with Obrecht's tenor than the former, although the two chants are evidently related (*NOE* 8, pp. xii–xvii) and several other chants use the same melody (e.g. the antiphon *O Christi pietas* for St Donatian; Strohm, *Music in Late Medieval Bruges*, 215–19). That Obrecht composed the mass for a Dominican endowment is not impossible: Reinhard Strohm has discovered an endowment with polyphony from 1488 in the archives of the Dominican convent at Bruges (ibid. 63). Barton Hudson has speculated that Obrecht's mass might have been composed in the 1490s for the Dominican cloister at Antwerp (*NOE* 8, p. xvii).

only about a third of its total length. Perhaps partly for this reason, the cycle contains only one tenorless section, the Et incarnatus.[19] The Christe, Pleni, Benedictus, and second Agnus are all written for four voices. Perhaps the lucid scoring of the full sections removed the need for textural relief on the level of sections.

Greater unity is also created by stricter cantus-firmus treatment. While *Beata viscera* was based on eight different elaborations of the original plainchant (one of which was repeated in the course of the mass), *O lumen ecclesie* rhythmizes its tenor only once, and repeats that fixed version literally (or almost literally) in every movement. The technique of mensural transformation, which we already recognized as a Busnoys-inspired feature in *Petrus apostolus*, now returns: with one exception, every part of the tenor is restated at least once under a different mensuration.[20]

Ex. 7 shows the first Kyrie of *O lumen ecclesie*.[21] Much here is familiar from the masses discussed earlier, but there are shifts of emphasis that betray a new concern for short-term organization. The motto (bars 1–9) is again based upon the cantus firmus, but it quotes such an extended part of it that the tenor can do no more, in the remainder of the section, than restate the very same part: the top voice has given everything away. As a consequence, the relationship between motto and cantus-firmus statement can hardly be described any longer as a 'pre-imitation', as was the case in the previous masses. It has assumed *structural* significance: basically the Kyrie is built over two successive and identical statements of the same cantus-firmus phrase. To ensure the balance between these statements, Obrecht deprives the second, 'proper', one of the textural emphasis that it traditionally received. The entry of the cantus firmus does not mark the shift to four-part writing: the tenor is simply part of a duo that counterbalances the head-motif. Thus not only the function of the tenor is transformed, but that of the head-motif as well. The duo is no longer an introduction in the traditional sense, for what it 'introduces' is simply its own repetition. Once again we see how Obrecht isolates and exaggerates one ingredient from the mass style of the 1470s (in this case the motto-tenor imitation) and, by so doing, gives it new meaning and impact.

Obrecht cleverly avoided giving undue weight to the tenor entry by postponing the full four-voice scoring. But this left him with a problem in

[19] This is also a feature of the masses *Sicut spina rosam* and *Caput*. In the latter mass, however, the absence of tenorless sections was determined by the layout of the anonymous English *Caput* mass, which Obrecht took as the basis for his setting.

[20] Compare, for instance, the tenors of Kyrie I/Christe with Sanctus/Pleni/Osanna I, and Kyrie II, bars 117–33, with Osanna II.

[21] For another discussion of this section, see Sparks, *Cantus Firmus*, 272–4 and 298.

Ex. 7. Obrecht, *Missa O lumen ecclesie*, Kyrie I

the second half of the section: how to arrive at four-part writing without disturbing the structural balance that had just been achieved. His answer was to let the remaining voices enter as unobtrusively as possible. Unlike any of the movements we have seen so far, the entry of the full texture is not presented here as a major musical event. The contratenor drops in on the last off-beat of bar 11, on a note that could well have been stated here by the tenor. The entry of the top voice is likewise inconspicuous: it steals in on the brief moment of suspended dissonance that precedes the cadence on C in bar 13. The remaining four bars of busy and highly imitative four-part counterpoint bring the section to a quick conclusion.

The problems of structural and textural balance that Obrecht faced in the tight space of one short section were obviously absent in the larger movements, and it is illuminating to see him at work in a section like the Et in terra (see Ex. 8). Almost predictably, perhaps, the composer now uses the opportunity to do what had been impossible in the first Kyrie. Bars 1–17 consist of two fully identical duos, and are organized in a perfectly symmetrical bisectional layout. The basic idea that underlies the Kyrie has thus been carried through to its logical conclusion. Motto and tenor statement have become equal partners: they relate to one another as counterbalancing subclauses in a sentence. The four-voice texture is postponed until the final chord in bar 17.

Four-part writing immediately follows, but is maintained, significantly, for only just over four bars. In the next twenty bars, Obrecht systematically explores the technique of embedding the tenor in a lucid, chain-like structure—a technique he had applied only tentatively in the masses *Petrus apostolus* (second Kyrie) and *Beata viscera* (Et resurrexit; Qui sedes). Every parameter is now used to articulate that structure. The individual units tend to be two or three bars in length, generally consist of self-contained melodic phrases, are rounded off with clear cadences, and are interconnected by means of imitation.

Particularly noteworthy is the passage in bars 30–6. The brief tenor phrase is presented here as the third in a series of three interconnected units—a procedure somewhat related to that of the beginning of the section, but applied on a much smaller scale. In these modest six bars we see the beginnings of a powerful device that Obrecht was to extend and exploit in later works, particularly in his closely related masses *Fortuna desperata* and *Libenter gloriabor* (both presumably from the early 1490s): it is the chain-like build-up towards the cantus-firmus entry.

The *Missa O lumen ecclesie* is still far removed from these cycles, however. Its chain structure lacks the sense of clear direction and mounting

Ex. 8. Obrecht, *Missa O lumen ecclesie*, Et in terra, bars 1–40

energy that those in the two later works have. Although Obrecht has broken down the continuous writing of *Petrus apostolus* into a sectionalized structure, the sense of quiet continuity prevails. This has partly to do with the fluent and gentle melodic writing. Another factor is the relative brevity of the individual units: in the space of two bars one can hardly build up the melodic tension that is needed for a powerful drive. Finally there is the number of units. Chain structures can quickly generate musical energy (if handled in the right way), but by themselves can hardly sustain that energy beyond the third or fourth unit. To maintain musical interest it is imperative to introduce a new idea or device at just the right time. Obrecht would prove himself an unequalled master in that practice, but in *O lumen ecclesie* he was clearly not concerned to do anything of the kind. The extended chain-like structure in Ex. 8 does not lead to a point beyond itself; it is carried on steadily, until the four-voice texture returns in bar 41. So what sets *O lumen ecclesie* apart from the other two cycles is a difference of degree, not of principle. Again the main line of chronological development appears to be Obrecht's tendency to cultivate and expand individual devices in isolation.[22]

Obrecht also introduces another type of chain structure in *O lumen ecclesie*, one in which the tenor is stated in long note-values while the other voices exchange and imitate brief motifs around it (see the opening of the second Kyrie in Ex. 9). The tenor neither dictates this structure (as in Ex. 7 and Ex. 8, bars 1–17), nor is it split up in brief phrases to allow it to be imitated in successive units (Ex. 8, bars 30–6). The structural voice simply follows its own course, independent of any short-term organization. Again the basic idea is simple, and lends itself to development. Good examples of the effective structural use of the device in later masses are *De Sancto Martino*, second Kyrie, and particularly *Grecorum*, Et in terra, bars 1–57 (see below, Ex. 29).

A few additional features need pointing out. In the Benedictus there is a quasi-canonic relationship between tenor and bass, very similar to the one in the Sanctus of *Beata viscera* (see above). But a significant novelty is that the two voices are *both* underlaid with the chant text. This is consistent with Obrecht's new tendency to treat cantus-firmus statements in the tenor and the other voices as equal partners. If literal imitations of the cantus firmus assume a musical significance equal to that of the tenor (see Exx. 7 and 8), it seems natural to extend that development and 'emancipate' the imitations textually as well.[23] In this respect the Benedictus anticipates the *Missa Sicut spina rosam*, where Obrecht tends to identify *all* cantus-firmus citations outside the tenor with the appropriate chant text—even if there is no direct imitative connection with the structural voice.

Another important feature is in the Patrem, bars 18–71, where the bass is organized by means of repeated motifs. We have already observed a brief instance of this in the Et in terra of *Petrus apostolus* (see Ex. 1, bars 38–47), but in *O lumen ecclesie* the practice is pursued more consistently. Obrecht does not yet aim for full consistency, however: he uses ten different motifs; these are not repeated sequentially; and occasionally he inserts free material (bars 24–5, 67–8, and 70–1). But given his apparent tendency

---

[22] It seems likely that the actual elaboration of the phrase was shaped here by Obrecht's apparent intention to place it in a chain structure: only the last two notes appear to be based on the cantus firmus (*NOE* 8, p. xiii).

[23] See above, n. 4. This procedure is extremely rare, but can be found in a number of sacred works from the 1470s: Busnoys's *Anima mea liquefacta est / Stirps Jesse* (Wegman, 'Domarto's *Missa Spiritus almus*', 241–2), the anonymous *Missa Regina celi letare* (TrentC 91, fos. 32ᵛ–33ʳ), and the anonymous motet *Incomprehensibilia / Preter rerum ordinem* (VerBC 755, fos. 101ᵛ–104ʳ). I have tentatively attributed the latter motet to Busnoys on notational grounds (see 'Another Mass by Busnoys?', 4–5 n. 15).

Ex. 9. Obrecht, *Missa O lumen ecclesie*, Kyrie II, bars 77–87

to isolate and develop individual devices, the logical line of development should be towards one motif, strictly sequential treatment, and complete absence of free material (see particularly *Pfauenschwanz*). Once again *O lumen ecclesie* turns out to be a work that tentatively develops and explores techniques that were to become characteristic features of Obrecht's mature style.

To sum up, *O lumen ecclesie* is a successful attempt to extend and elaborate a musical idea consistently, raise it to a structural level, and thus achieve a high degree of stylistic homogeneity. Obrecht was not to write another mass in quite this style: in many ways *O lumen ecclesie* stands alone in his œuvre. But several devices explored here for the first time would be further developed in later cycles. We can trace the first steps of that development in the *Missa Sicut spina rosam*.

Missa Sicut spina rosam

In the mid-1480s Jacob Obrecht seems to have become increasingly pre-
occupied with the musical style of Johannes Ockeghem. A mass that
attests to this preoccupation is *Sicut spina rosam*, which not only quotes
explicitly from the older master, but is clearly indebted to his stylistic
idiom. The same debt is to be found in the masses *De Sancto Martino* and
De Sancto Donatiano (of 1486 and 1487, respectively), which moreover
contain similar, if less prominent, quotations from Ockeghem's music (see
Ch. 6).

Several features in *Sicut spina rosam* connect the work closely to the
three previous cycles.[24] It is based on seven freely elaborated versions of
the chant cantus firmus (four of which appear in the Credo). This recalls

[24] For this mass, which is based upon the final portion of the Great Responsory *Ad nutum Domini*
for the Blessed Virgin Mary, see Meier, *Studien zur Meßkomposition*, 10–12; Kyriazis, *Die Cantus
firmus-Technik*, 46–8; Salop, 'The Masses of Jacob Obrecht', 28–33; Sparks, *Cantus Firmus*, 274–6;
B. Meier, 'Zyklische Gesamtstruktur und Tonalität in den Messen Jacob Obrechts', *Archiv für
Musikwissenschaft*, 19 (1953), 298. The cantus firmus was identified by Manfred Bukofzer, *Studies in
Medieval and Renaissance Music* (New York, 1954), 309. Important research concerning the back-
ground and possible origins of the version used by Obrecht has been carried out by M. J. Bloxam,
'Plainsong and Polyphony for the Blessed Virgin: Notes on Two Masses by Jacob Obrecht', *Journal
of Musicology*, in press. (I am grateful to Jennifer Bloxam for sending me a copy of this article in
advance of its publication.)
   A particularly perceptive discussion of *Missa Sicut spina rosam* is Hudson, 'Obrecht's Tribute to
Ockeghem'. I would, however, express some reservations concerning its main contention, that
Obrecht composed *Sicut spina rosam* in commemoration of Johannes Ockeghem's death in 1497.
Hudson dates the mass in the 1490s on the basis of three criteria (ibid. 6–8). The first concerns the
writing of canon based upon cantus-firmus material. Hudson argues: 'In what we take to be his
earlier works canon, if it occurs at all, usually appears only in brief segments incidental to the larger
structure and may be treated quite freely. Apparently Obrecht did not achieve mastery over the
device early in life. It does seem, however, that as he grew older, when he employed canon, he used
it with increasing ease and strictness, particularly where the canonic voices paraphrase the cantus
firmus' (p. 6). What would argue against this point, as it stands, is the occurrence of a strict and
quite skilfully written canon based on cantus firmus in one of Obrecht's earliest masses, *Beata viscera*
(Osanna I). Hudson's second criterion concerns the combination of different pre-existent melodies
(p. 7), a procedure that is in fact quite rare in Obrecht's mass *œuvre*. It seems open to question
whether this can be used to arrive at datings of individual works. (To the three examples mentioned
by Hudson could be added the Osanna of the *Missa Grecorum*, which combines the *Grecorum* melody
with the Easter sequence *Victimae paschali*, and the Credo of *Plurimorum carminum I*, which quotes
Credo I besides various song tenors.) The argument that Obrecht achieved greater skill in the device
as he grew older rests mainly on the assumption that the *Missa Fors seulement* (whose Credo
combines different melodies as unambitiously as the Osanna of *Grecorum*) is an early work—an
assumption that I would question on stylistic grounds (see below, Ch. 8). Hudson's third criterion
concerns the use of head-motifs, which he argues became more ingenious in the course of Obrecht's
career (pp. 7–8). While *Sicut spina rosam* certainly shows more variety in this respect than Obrecht's
incontestably early masses (*Petrus apostolus*, *Beata viscera*), I believe that its motto treatment nevertheless points to a date in the 1480s (see below). A broad range of features in *Sicut spina rosam*
suggest that the work is closely contemporary with such masses as *O lumen ecclesie*, *De Sancto
Martino*, and *Ave regina celorum*. The same conclusion was reached by Ludwig Finscher in *MGG*
9, col. 1820.

the *Missa Beata viscera*, which has eight different elaborations. Just as in the latter mass (and *Petrus apostolus* and *O lumen ecclesie*), the version presented in the Kyrie returns later on: it is entirely restated in the Gloria, and its first part appears in the Sanctus. In both the latter movements, the Kyrie version is subjected to mensural transformation, a procedure that recalls the masses *Petrus apostolus* and *O lumen ecclesie*. Yet we can no longer speak of a 'primary' version, since the elaboration does not appear in either of the two head-motifs. That function is now taken over by the first elaboration of the Gloria, which is quoted entirely in the head-motif of that movement as well as that of the Credo. The head-motif used in the Kyrie, Sanctus, and Agnus Dei is borrowed from Ockeghem's *Missa Mi–mi*.

Although recombined to some extent, all these features are familiar from the previous masses: free elaboration of a chant cantus firmus, strict repeats of the Kyrie version, mensural transformation, and a cantus-firmus-based head-motif. These elements were to recur (albeit less and less regularly) in the masses *De Sancto Martino* (1486) and *Ave regina celorum* (later 1480s), and some traces are detectable even in *Libenter gloriabor* (?early 1490s). By the end of the decade, however, Obrecht's ideas about structuring mass cycles had changed fundamentally.

Despite its continuation of existing developments, the *Missa Sicut spina rosam* enters a new path in terms of contrapuntal style. Just as in the *Missa Petrus apostolus*, smoothness once again appears to be the keyword. Compared with the earlier mass, however, this general aim is now pursued within a less formalized textural framework, thanks to the dissolution of Busnoys's idiom in the masses *Beata viscera* and *O lumen ecclesie*. The rigid alternation between full and reduced sections that characterized *Petrus apostolus* had become increasingly loosened in the other two cycles; *Sicut spina rosam* exploits the new opportunities that had thus been created.

Bars 1–44 of the Patrem provide a good starting-point for our discussion (Ex. 10). The passage has a bipartite structure, and is built over two identical statements of the cantus firmus: top voice (bars 1–21) and tenor (bars 21–41).[25] One can still recognize here the outlines of the traditional motto-tenor imitation, but Obrecht has expanded that imitation to unprecedented lengths. In *Petrus apostolus* and *Beata viscera* the head-motifs still functioned as brief reminders of the cantus firmus: each quoted only five bars from the tenor (Exs. 1 and 4). In *O lumen ecclesie* the quotation

[25] The relationship between bars 1–21 and 21–41 is strengthened by several motivic recurrences: (1) bass, bars 21–3 = contratenor 1–3; (2) contratenor, bars 30–1 = same voice, 10–11; (3) bass 32–3 = contratenor 12–13. The unorthodox resolution of a dissonance in bars 17–18 (see also Et in terra, bars 17–18) has its parallel in bar 45.

Ex. 10. Obrecht, *Missa Sicut spina rosam*, Patrem, bars 1–44

was expanded to nine bars, and the motto was made equal—structurally as well as texturally—to the 'proper' tenor statement (Exx. 7 and 8). This process is now brought to its logical conclusion in the Credo of *Sicut spina rosam*, where the head-motif quotes the entire twenty-one-bar cantus firmus. This has obvious consequences for the usefulness of the head-motif in the mass as a whole: its very length now prevents it from being used in the shorter movements. Consequently, the Kyrie, Sanctus, and Agnus Dei have their own motto, and unity is to some degree impaired. It seems ironic that by logically extending a principle in one movement, Obrecht is forced to break away from it in others.

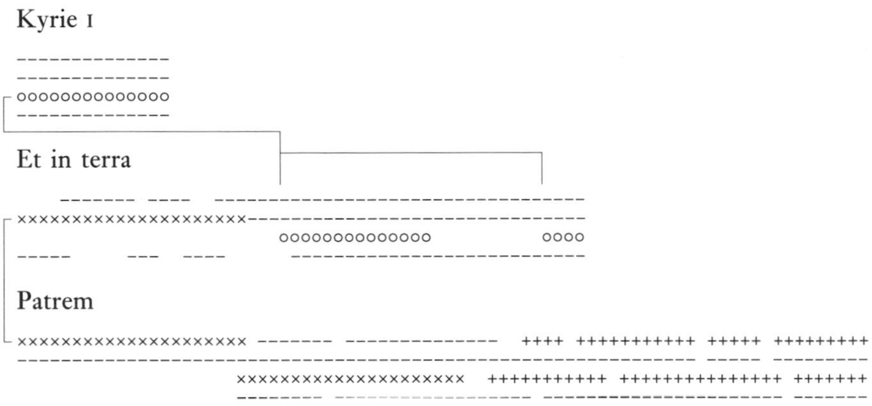

Kyrie I

```
  --------------
  --------------
┌ oooooooooooooo
└ --------------
```

Et in terra

```
                                    ┌──────────────────────────┐
  -------- ----   -----------------------------------  ------
┌ xxxxxxxxxxxxxxxxxxxx----------------------------------  ------
│                      oooooooooooooo                 oooo
│ -----        ---  ----    --------------------------  ------
```

Patrem

```
└ xxxxxxxxxxxxxxxxxxxxxx -------  -------------  ++++ +++++++++++ +++++ +++++++++
  ----------------------------------------------------------  ----- ----------
                       xxxxxxxxxxxxxxxxxxxxx +++++++++++  ++++++++++++++++ +++++++
  --------  -------------------  ------------------------  -------
```

ooooo = first cantus-firmus elaboration (first phrase only)
xxxxx = second elaboration (entire cantus firmus)
+++++ = third elaboration (entire cantus firmus)
----- = free counterpoint

Each symbol is equivalent to one bar in *tempus perfectum*.

Fig. 2. Structural relationships between the Kyrie, Gloria, and Credo of *Missa Sicut spina rosam*

But the extended pre-imitation of the Patrem does 'recur' elsewhere, in the Et in terra, and Obrecht handles it there as a genuine head-motif—not as a structural element equal to the tenor. Fig. 2 illustrates the interrelations between the Et in terra and Patrem. The bipartite structure of the first half of the Patrem, and the subsequent quasi-canonic relationship between the tenor and top voice, can clearly be recognized. The first cantus-firmus statement of the Patrem (marked '×××') is derived from the introduction of the Et in terra. The latter section, however, is not structured in a bipartite layout: its 'proper' tenor statement is simply a twofold repeat (with mensural transformation) of the tenor of Kyrie I. The tenor does not present the entire cantus firmus, but only the first fourteen notes; consequently, it has no direct relationship, either imitative or structural, with the elaboration quoted in the introduction. The absence of such a relationship indicates that the 'introductory' elaboration fulfils here its original function as a head-motif: it is meant to connect the Patrem to the Et in terra, not to structure the section internally.[26] This is

[26] This indicates how little Obrecht's basic approach to structuring a mass had changed since the late 1470s—despite the profound transformation of his style. The Et in terra of *Sicut spina rosam* is a virtual twin of the Sanctus of *Petrus apostolus*: both movements quote one elaboration in the head-motif, and another in the tenor (see Fig. 2).

confirmed by several further correspondences between the introductions of the two sections (bars 1–5, 12–13, and 17–18 of either section). To summarize, the bipartite structure of Patrem bars 1–41 is derived from the motto-tenor imitation of Obrecht's earlier masses. By expanding that imitation to unprecedented dimensions (21 + 21 bars), the composer continues a trend he had started in the *Missa O lumen ecclesie* (9 + 9 bars). Yet he remains aware of the origins of the device: in the Gloria the extended 'pre-imitation' functions as a head-motif in the traditional sense.

Returning to Ex. 10, one of the interesting features of the Credo is its unusual voice-layout. While the other four movements are written in the normal high/two-middle/low scoring, the layout in the Credo is two-high/middle/low. Although the ranges of the top voice and contratenor are virtually identical in this movement (*a–e″* and *g–e″*, respectively), the latter voice generally tends to remain below its companion. This is already a sign that the melodic writing is restrained: leaps and quick runs through the ranges are avoided, and consequently the top two voices rarely get in each other's way. But Obrecht keeps the two parts closely together in the introductory duo: here they are a third or less apart for nearly two-thirds of the time. Since the voices constantly intertwine, and since one of them is cantus-firmus-based, the melodic structure of the duo is shaped by the contours of the chant (see particularly the carefully prepared mid-point climax in bar 10).

The distinctive style of the Patrem comes out most clearly if one compares the section with the Et in terra of *Petrus apostolus* (Ex. 1). The two masses share certain features, particularly the smooth and fluent melodic style, the frequent cadences, and the rhythmic differentiation. But the constant drive and the sense of steady continuity that underlie the writing of *Petrus apostolus* have made way for a more irregular musical flow. This is most clearly seen in the placement of cadences. In the earlier mass, the cadential progressions tended to fall on the first beat of every new *tempus*, and thus they observed and punctuated the underlying rhythmic organization. (This feature is retained in the masses *Beata viscera* and *O lumen ecclesie*.) In *Sicut spina rosam*, however, the cadences are placed irregularly, as the musical flow dictates, in most cases on the second or third beat of the perfection. Consequently, every sense of metric regularity is lost. Moreover, the cadences are not consistently weakened, as in the earlier mass: their cadential effect is regularly enhanced by the leap of a fifth in the bass (bars 26, 35–6, and 38), and some progressions bring the counterpoint to a firm halt (bar 32).

The Phrygian flavour, the smooth melodic writing, delicate use of tone

colour, textural freedom, irregularly placed cadences, and the brief imitative gestures strongly recall the mass style of Johannes Ockeghem. We
find the same features in some of the other movements, notably the Agnus
Dei. This movement is even more closely related to the older composer's
style in that it contains hardly any cadences or imitations (the same is true
of the Kyrie I and the first section of the Sanctus). As is well known, the
Agnus Dei quotes the entire bass line of the Kyrie of Ockeghem's *Missa
Mi–mi*, and combines it with a free elaboration of the *Sicut spina rosam*
melody.[27]

Several other sections, however, bear more clearly the imprint of
Obrecht's methods of short-term organization as we know them from the
three previous masses. Just as the bisectional structure of the Patrem can
be seen as an extension of a principle worked out in the *Missa O lumen
ecclesie*, so other sections in *Sicut spina rosam* seem to develop ideas from
that mass. Once again the keywords in these developments appear to be
isolation, expansion, and structural use.

These principles can to some extent be seen at work in Ex. 11, which
compares the first Osanna of *Missa O lumen ecclesie* with the Qui tollis of
Sicut spina rosam. The structure of the former passage is very similar to
that of Ex. 8, bars 30–6: a brief tenor phrase is presented as the third in
a series of four interlocking units. But whereas the structure in Ex. 8 was
placed in a larger chain of events, the one in Ex. 11*a* opens a section, and
gives the impression of being an introductory point of imitation. This
basic idea is worked out in the Qui tollis of the *Missa Sicut spina rosam*
(Ex. 11*b*), where the cantus-firmus phrase 'genuit' travels from contratenor to top voice, and then from bass to the 'proper' statement in the
tenor.[28] Obrecht goes even further in the Et in Spiritum and Benedictus/
Qui venit of the same mass. In the Et in Spiritum, bars 212–64, the
fourteen-bar phrase 'Iudea' is stated successively in the top voice, tenor,
contratenor, and bass. In the Benedictus/Qui venit, a fourteen-bar rhyth-
micization of the phrase 'sicut spina rosam' is first stated twice in the bass,
and then repeated in the top voice and contratenor, respectively. To sum
up, what had been a mere imitative opening in Ex. 11*a* and *b* has been
developed into a structural scaffold underlying an entire section (Edgar
Sparks called the device 'migrant scaffolding').[29] Obrecht was hardly ever
again to go as far as this (only the *Missa Salve diva parens*, which existed

---

[27] This was discovered by Heinrich Besseler; see 'Musik des Mittelalters in der Hamburger
Musikhalle', *Zeitschrift für Musikwissenschaft*, 7 (1924–5), 44.

[28] Note the curious parallel sevenths in bar 64.

[29] *Cantus Firmus*, 275. Maria Kyriazis labelled the procedure 'ausgedehnte Durchimitation' (*Die
Cantus firmus-Technik*, 36).

Ex. 11 (a). Obrecht, *Missa O lumen ecclesie*, Osanna I, bars 71–8

by 1487–8, contains similarly structured sections), but he clearly remained fascinated with the idea of involving different voices in the presentation of a cantus firmus (*Caput*, Kyrie II of *De Sancto Donatiano*).

Equally interesting is Obrecht's conflation of different devices in the Qui sedes (Ex. 12). This section is based on the cantus-firmus elaboration that had been used previously in the second Kyrie. The tenor entry in bar 122 is preceded by a seventeen-bar, strict pre-imitation in the contratenor, so that there is a dichotomous structure somewhat resembling that of the Patrem. But Obrecht shapes the texture around the contratenor in a way that recalls the second Kyrie of the *Missa O lumen ecclesie* (Ex. 9): the top voice and bass state brief three-bar phrases in alternation, creating the impression of a simple chain structure around a slow-moving tenor. Since there is no audible difference between the contratenor, bars 105–26, and tenor, bars 122–45, the listener is 'tricked' into believing that the tenor has already entered: in this way Obrecht has musically emancipated the pre-imitation in the contratenor. Quite possibly, he intended the imitation to be emancipated textually as well. Although the contratenor of the Qui sedes is underlaid with the appropriate Ordinary text in both sources for the mass, Barton Hudson has convincingly argued that Obrecht's original

Ex. 11 (*b*). Obrecht, *Missa Sicut spina rosam*, Qui tollis, bars 52–68

intention was to have it sung with the cantus-firmus text.[30] In several other sections of the mass, we find that extended imitations of the tenor have been underlaid with the chant text in either or both of the sources (Qui tollis, Et resurrexit, Et in Spiritum, and Qui venit). An early instance of this practice can be found in the Benedictus of the *Missa O lumen ecclesie*.

It is clear from all this that the *Missa Sicut spina rosam* could hardly have been composed without the precedent of *O lumen ecclesie*.[31] The

[30] *NOE* 11, pp. xxxix–xl.
[31] Barton Hudson has already noted their stylistic similarity and apparent contemporaneity,

[*cont. on p. 129*]

Ex. 12. Obrecht, *Missa Sicut spina rosam*, Qui sedes, bars 105–29

Credo in particular abounds with procedures that are found—often in less 'developed' form—in the earlier work.[32] Several examples of cantus-firmus-based canon or quasi-canon (Patrem, bars 44–77, Et resurrexit, Osanna, bars 75–102) recall similar procedures in *O lumen ecclesie* (Benedictus), as well as *Beata viscera* (Sanctus, and the two Osannas). Another significant feature is Obrecht's tendency to organize the bass line by means of repeated motifs. A brief instance of this was found in the *Missa Petrus apostolus* (Ex. 1, bars 38–47). The procedure was expanded in *O lumen ecclesie*, but still not applied systematically (Patrem, bars 22–71). In the Et incarnatus of *Sicut spina rosam*, Obrecht makes a significant step towards the structural use of this device: the bass part repeats the same four-bar motif throughout the section (the only liberty the composer allows himself, a 'free' extension in bars 105–7, is in fact a quotation of a motif handled sequentially in the top voice, bars 83–90).

In several technical respects, then, the *Missa Sicut spina rosam* appears to continue existing lines of development. Given the close links with the other three cycles, it seems significant that the mass moves away from those works in terms of its stylistic idiom. Obrecht clearly abandoned the melodic exuberance and rhythmic energy that had invigorated the Busnoys-inspired idiom of his earlier masses. Instead one finds long and irregularly shaped melodic lines, concern for dark tone-colours, avoidance of leaps or quick runs, and a marked attention to detail. One is tempted to assume that a meeting (or expected meeting) with Ockeghem inspired Obrecht's compositional choices. Since several features of the mass suggest a date in the mid-1480s, it is worth reconsidering the events of August–September 1484 (see Ch. 3). A hypothetical scenario based on those events might be the following.

Jacob Obrecht started work as the new *magister choralium* of Cambrai Cathedral on 6 September 1484. This was two days before the celebration of the Nativity of the Blessed Virgin, the Matins service of which features the responsory *Ad nutum Domini*. Obrecht probably knew in advance that his duties would start around this day (the negotiations were presumably concluded while he was still in Bergen op Zoom), and he may well have agreed to compose a new mass specifically for this major feast. It is unlikely that the composer was aware of the peculiar liturgical practices at Cambrai Cathedral, where *Ad nutum Domini* ended the first Nocturn of

although he tentatively dated the two masses in the 1490s ('Obrecht's Tribute to Ockeghem', 11 n. 17).

[32] For analyses of this movement, see Sparks, *Cantus Firmus*, 275, and Hudson, 'Obrecht's Tribute to Ockeghem', 4.

Matins.[33] In nearby Antwerp, however, this responsory—with its three-fold statement of the phrase 'sicut spina rosam genuit Iudea Mariam'—signalled the culmination of that service. If the same practice existed in Bergen op Zoom, the 'sicut spina rosam' melody would have seemed a highly appropriate cantus firmus for the new mass. While the ideas for the new work were taking shape, Obrecht learned from his 'friend' at St Donatian's that Johannes Ockeghem was to visit that church and meet its singer-clerks. Thereupon he began to explore ways of paying tribute to the older master. In doing so, he discovered that the 'sicut spina rosam' melody could be fitted to the bass of the *Mi–mi* Kyrie. Obrecht finished his mass in time to prepare a copy for the Cambrai *petits vicaires*, who sang the work on 8 September. Its first trial, however, had been at Bruges before Ockeghem, to whom *Sicut spina rosam* pays tribute.

It must be stressed that this scenario is entirely speculative, and will remain so until more evidence is discovered. But it does provide an explanation for the fact that *Sicut spina rosam* refers directly to Ockeghem and at the same time is written for the Nativity of the Blessed Virgin. The scenario is consistent with the early date suggested by several musical features of the mass, and particularly the close links it has with the *Missa O lumen ecclesie*.

Equally close links, but from the other side, exist with the *Missa De Sancto Martino* of 1486. This work shares several features with *Sicut spina rosam* that are already absent in the *Missa De Sancto Donatiano* of the next year, and indeed in nearly all subsequent masses (see Ch. 6). As if to stress the relationship, Obrecht opens his *Missa De Sancto Martino* with the very same motto he had used in the Kyrie, Sanctus, and Agnus Dei of *Sicut spina rosam*. All this may serve as a reminder that the year 1485 does not mark a break in the development of Obrecht's style—as it quite clearly did in his fortunes. With two dismissals, apparent dissatisfaction with his administrative duties, his father's death, and dashed hopes of a position in Italy—against a general background of warfare, economic decline, and famine—the years 1485–91 would be among the most difficult in the composer's life.

---

[33] For this and what follows, see Bloxam, 'Plainsong and Polyphony'.

PART TWO
1485–1491

5 YEARS OF CRISIS

ON 7 February 1485 the chapter of St Donatian's at Bruges discussed the recent resignation of their succentor Aliamus de Groote. Having decided to appoint Johannes Rykelin temporarily in his place, the canons went on to consider the very timely application of *magister* Jacob Obrecht, master of the choirboys at Cambrai Cathedral. He had expressed a strong interest in the position: a friend of his, presumably the singer Jean Cordier (himself a canon at St Donatian's), assured the chapter of Obrecht's ardent wish to become the new succentor. Presumably it was through him that the composer had learnt of the vacancy in the first place. Having taken note of the request, the chapter decided to invite Obrecht to come and discuss the matter in person.[1] So far as we know, he did indeed come over 'two or three times',[2] and an agreement must have been reached fairly quickly, certainly within about four months. By 23 June, Obrecht had promised to take up residence soon—which was all the more welcome as Rykelin had proved inadequate as interim succentor.[3] The chapter of St Donatian's asked Aliamus de Groote to fill in for Obrecht until the latter's arrival, which was now believed to be imminent.[4]

This sequence of events looks normal and unproblematic enough, but puzzlingly, it follows only five months after Obrecht's arrival in Cambrai. The obvious conclusion would seem that his position there had turned out

[1] 'Moreover, the same lords, having heard that *magister* Jacobus Obrechts—up to now master of the choirboys at the church of Cambrai—very much desired to serve this church in the office of succentor, concerning which they were more fully informed through a letter he had written to a certain person, ordered me [the chapter secretary] to write a letter to him, [asking him] to come here soon to discuss this with the chapter, or to write what his intention is, so that the office could be taken by him or by somebody else' (chapter acts, St Donatian's, 7 Feb. 1485; A. C. De Schrevel, *Histoire du Séminaire de Bruges* (Bruges, 1895), i. 159–60).

[2] At Obrecht's installation as succentor on 13 Oct. 1485, the chapter of St Donatian's ordered the payment of 120 Flemish groats 'contra expensas suas bis vel ter eundo et redeundo factas' (ibid. 160). [3] Strohm, *Music in Late Medieval Bruges*, 38.

[4] 'Nevertheless, [de Groote] was told to administer the office of succentor until the imminent arrival of *magister* Jacobus, master of the children of the church of Cambrai, who is awaited to come here to take up residence' (chapter acts, St Donatian's, 23 June 1485; De Schrevel, *Histoire*, i. 159).

to be a disappointment, even though his duties must have been similar to those he had fulfilled for more than four years at Bergen op Zoom. But that is not the whole story. By 23 June Obrecht could have taken up his duties in Bruges at any time he wished, and, given his apparent dissatisfaction with the Cambrai position, one would have expected this to be quite soon. Yet he continued working at the cathedral as though nothing had happened. By 12 September, the chapter of St Donatian's began to wonder what his actual intentions were:[5]

It was ordered to write to *magister* Jacobus Hobrecht, master of the children at Cambrai, to tell him to come, or at least indicate his intention, and, if he knows a tenorist and soprano, to bring them with him to be installed here.

So what were his intentions? If we search for an answer in the documents of Cambrai Cathedral, we find nothing to suggest that the composer had actually decided to leave until he had to resign in late October—a good four months after his promise to leave Cambrai 'soon'. What made him stay at Cambrai? It is unlikely that we shall be able to make much more sense of the composer's moves than the chapters of the two churches. But at least we have both sides of the story, and a tentative answer is suggested if we lay the two parts side by side.

Shortly after the decision of the Bruges canons to invite Obrecht, in early February, we find references to him in the documents of Cambrai Cathedral. These mainly relate to the education of choristers and singers. On 13 March, the composer was paid for having kept 'the little' chorister Martinellus du Caftea from 6 September 1484.[6] On 17 June, two tenorists, Johannes Crassequaule and an unnamed man from Douai, were ordered to visit the composer's house daily for instruction in singing.[7] Eight days later, on 25 June, a singer from Bergen op Zoom was admitted as a *petit vicaire* on the condition that he improve his skills in singing *super librum*; Obrecht was to teach him.[8] By this date St Donatian's was already awaiting the composer's arrival in Bruges.

---

[5] Chapter acts, St Donatian's, 12 Sept. 1485; ibid. 160.

[6] 'Item, to *dominus* Jacobus Obrech, master of the choirboys, for having kept the little Martinelus from 6 September to 13 March . . . £11 12s' (C. Wright, 'Musiciens à la cathédrale de Cambrai', *Revue de musicologie*, 62 (1976), 208).

[7] Doc. 33: '*Dominus* Johannes Crassequaule and another, Longus [or 'tall one'] from Douai, tenorists and *petits vicaires* . . . were told that if they would not visit the house of the master of the choirboys every day, and would not progress further in their lessons than they know at present, they would be sent away, and [the lords] would dismiss both, and take their salaries from them' (chapter acts, 17 June 1485). The two men cannot have made much progress under Obrecht: in Dec. 1485 they were again ordered to improve their singing (A. Pirro, 'Jean Cornuel, vicaire à Cambrai', *Revue de musicologie*, 7 (1926), 194).

[8] Transcription and translation in Wright, 'Musiciens', 207, and the same author's 'Performance Practices at the Cathedral of Cambrai 1475-1550', *Musical Quarterly*, 64 (1978), 313. The singer in

Yet he stayed at Cambrai, carrying out his duties with evident dislike. A month later, on 27 July, scabies had broken out amongst the choir-boys—an event evidently construed as meaning that Obrecht had failed to have their clothes and beddings regularly cleaned. The chapter had no option but to renew the boys' wardrobe, and have the old one destroyed. The composer was berated for not having looked after the children properly (Doc. 34):

[New] linen clothes are to be made for the little children of the choir, and the *magnus minister* is to tell their master that he should look to their government and condition more carefully than he has done so far, for they have contracted scabies, which is not otherwise seen.

Had the chapter decided to dismiss Obrecht at this stage, he could have gone to Bruges immediately, of course. But the matter apparently blew over: more than a month later, on 2 September, the cathedral chapter decided to entrust him with 12 gold crowns to go to the Antwerp fairs and purchase necessities for the choirboys (Doc. 35):

Above his stipends, which the master of the choirboys is to receive from the office of the *petits vicaires*, my lords [of the chapter] have wished 12 gold crowns to be paid so that he can buy necessities at the market of Antwerp, for he will subtract those [crowns] on the next term of payment.

This is a puzzling record. Every fifteenth-century choirmaster had to buy necessities from time to time; such routine expenses must have been calculated in their budgets. Why then did it take a chapter decision to allow Obrecht to buy his 'necessities'? And why was the sum paid from the chapter's own funds, which were not in principle intended for musical expenses? One reason could be that the amount in question was extraordinarily high: around this time, 12 gold crowns equalled roughly 700 Flemish groats, that is, more than the annual income Obrecht had received at Bergen op Zoom in any of the years 1480–4. So we are talking about a sizeable investment here—which must have taken some persuasion to convince the chapter to make. Fortunately, the chapter secretary specified in his minutes what compelled the canons to grant the money: 'for [Obrecht] will subtract those crowns on the next term of payment'. Exactly what this means is unclear, but the most plausible explanation seems that the composer had complained of having to work with inadequate facilities and equipment, demanding the immediate purchase of 'necessities', and threatening to withhold money to that purpose from the

question may have been Quintijne, who had worked under Obrecht at Bergen op Zoom in 1482–4 (Wegman, 'Bergen op Zoom', 222–3 and 241).

allowance of the choirboys. This would obviously be strange behaviour for a man who knew he was leaving anyway—unless, of course, he was looking for an excuse to leave Cambrai. By making excessive demands that the chapter was almost certain to deny, he could blame his departure on the cathedral.[9] If this is indeed the strategy he adopted, Obrecht must have overplayed his hand: the money was granted, and he was left with no reasonable excuse to resign.

We do not know exactly when Obrecht went to Antwerp. The fairs of that year lasted from 28 August to 9 October, so there was plenty of time left after the chapter decision of 2 September.[10] But there was increasing pressure on him to leave Cambrai for a different reason. On 12 September (only ten days after the chapter of Cambrai had ordered the payment of the 12 gold crowns) the canons of St Donatian's sent their letter asking him to come, or explain what his intentions were. A decision on this front was now unavoidable: any further delay could cause Obrecht to lose the position at Bruges. At the same time, this was surely the worst possible moment to submit his resignation at Cambrai Cathedral, having just obtained a generous sum of money to be spent at his discretion. But a way out (at least a temporary one) suggested itself: if Obrecht was to travel away for one or two weeks to Antwerp (which is 140 km. north-east of Cambrai), he could easily make a detour to Bruges, and nobody would be any the wiser. This is of course speculation, but it does fit precisely with the available evidence. The Antwerp fairs ended on 9 October; four days later the chapter acts of St Donatian's tell us that Obrecht had finally arrived:[11]

Before the lords [of the chapter] appeared *magister* Jacobus Obrechts, priest-musician, master of the children of the church of Cambrai, whom my lords had promised by their letter the office of succentor at this church, and who gave his

[9] It is perhaps no coincidence that the chapter decision follows almost exactly one year after Obrecht's appointment in Cambrai. One possible explanation for the curious four-month delay in taking up his position at Bruges is that the composer was under some sort of agreement or promise to stay at the cathedral for at least one year (perhaps even on penalty of a large fine)—something that is often seen in the 15th c. (see Wegman, 'Bergen op Zoom', 243, for a contract from 1497 between the city of Bergen op Zoom and the singer Dominicus Janssoen van Grafft: 'The same Dominicus has tied himself to serve this town and to stay in its service for one year following his arrival, on penalty of [a sum equivalent to 1600 Flemish groats]'). In that case, Obrecht must have approached the chapter of St Donatian's in February simply to secure the position, knowing that he would have to hold out at Cambrai until early September.

[10] There were two annual markets in Antwerp, one starting fifteen days before Whit Sunday, the other on the second Sunday after the Assumption (15 Aug.). Both markets lasted six weeks.

[11] Chapter acts, St Donatian's, 13 Oct. 1485; De Schrevel, *Histoire*, i. 160. The date on which Obrecht was installed happens to be the Eve of St Donatian; it could well be that the canons of St Donatian's had demanded that he arrive before this feast. Similar ultimatums were made to the composer in 1488 (see below).

clerical oath when the choirstall had been conferred on him by the aforesaid presiding [canon], deputizing for the lord dean, and my lords, creating him as a priest, made provision concerning the office of succentor, with its duties, privileges, and incomes, which he accepted; *magister* Johannes Bonivicini installed him on behalf of the lord provost . . . and it was ordered that the receiver of the Equalitas shall pay to the said *magister* Jacobus 120 groats to cover his expenses for travelling back and forth two or three times, and four jugs of wine for him and for [his] companion musicians, who had come with him.

The last-named musicians were in fact the singers whom the chapter had asked Obrecht to bring with him to Bruges (see above). One of these, the soprano Egidius Zelandrinus, lost his voice on arrival.[12]

The chapter of St Donatian's had now been satisfied, but there was more than a little unfinished business in Cambrai to attend to. Obrecht must have asked leave to go back and fetch his belongings there, promising to return within about two weeks. We know that he was in Cambrai again by 21 October, eight days after his installation in Bruges: on this day the chapter acts of the cathedral record his dismissal (Doc. 36):

[It was decided] that the master of the choristers must resign, that [his] accounts should be audited before his resignation, and that he should hand over these accounts to the master of the office of the *[petits]* *vicaires*.

The reason for the dismissal is not specified, but the most likely explanation seems that the canons had been informed of Obrecht's installation at Bruges—in which case they were obviously outraged. Their request to hand over the accounts may have been more than a routine measure. Obrecht had gone to Antwerp with a large sum of the chapter's money, and quite possibly the canons' main concern was to learn how that sum had been spent. In any case, three days later, on 24 October, it turned out that the composer had misappropriated funds from the cathedral (Doc. 37):

[It was decided] that *dominus* Johannes Jorlandi, master of the *petits vicaires*, should speak with the master of the choirboys, come to an agreement with him concerning the songbooks that he is said to have compiled, and will buy those, subtracting the money that he owes the church.

That Obrecht's debt concerned at least part of the 12 crowns seems likely, for it is difficult to see what other debts he could have accumulated without the chapter finding out before 24 October. It was precisely during his travels to Bruges and Antwerp that the composer could most easily have been tempted into making unwarranted expenses. In fact, if we are correct in assuming that he travelled to Bruges while on the journey to

---

[12] Strohm, *Music in Late Medieval Bruges*, 27 and 39.

Antwerp, then this could already have involved making such expenses—
perhaps in the expectation of receiving advance payment from St Donatian's. At any rate, once the misuse of funds was discovered, all Obrecht
could offer as a settlement of his debt were a number of choirbooks he had
copied; these were bought at a price reduced by the amount that he owed
the cathedral.

The assumption that Obrecht had in fact planned to keep the money for
himself may make for a good story, but it is hardly the most obvious
interpretation of the evidence. Quite apart from the question whether he
could seriously have expected to get away with embezzling money from
a cathedral (or indeed whether he would have done it in such a clumsy
way), his financial situation does not suggest that a reasonably normal
lifestyle would ever have presented him with more than short-term li-
quidity problems. Only seventeen months previously, for instance, on
29 March 1484, Obrecht had empowered his father to collect 480 Flemish
groats in revenues from his lands in Hughersluus—more than two-thirds
of the sum given him to spend at Antwerp (Doc. 30). Not that there is any
need to whitewash the composer: his prevarications and neglect of the
choirboys plainly got him in trouble in the summer of 1485. Equally
plainly, however, Obrecht's debt to the cathedral could simply have been
a case of financial miscalculation, and might not even have been noticed
had he not been forced to render account at once. Yet whatever the
composer's motives, all was settled discreetly, and thereafter matters were
rounded off quickly. Two choristers left his house on 28 October. When
the remaining two boys followed, on 1 November, the composer was free
to leave Cambrai, and start work in Bruges.[13]

Bruges and Ferrara, 1485–1488

Obrecht's life in the late 1480s was increasingly overshadowed by a background of war, civic revolt, inflation, soaring food prices, and famine.
These were years of crisis for the Low Countries. Flanders in particular
suffered from the political tensions of the time: it became the principal
scene where the conflicts between France and Maximilian of Habsburg,
Maximilian and the Netherlands towns, and the towns amongst themselves, were fought out. Some of Obrecht's ordeals during these years
have entered the historical record. In the summer of 1488, a particularly
violent year, he feared for his personal safety when he had to travel

[13] Pirro, 'Obrecht à Cambrai', 79.

through Flanders. Around the same time, Maximilian's tactic of breaching the dikes of northern Flemish polders caused extensive flooding: the villages of Steeland and Hughersluus, where Obrecht had inherited several pieces of land, perished for ever. During the Bruges famine of 1490 the composer had to support the choirboys from his own salary. In the words of Reinhard Strohm: 'It must have been difficult for anyone to live a quiet life, dedicated to the arts, in a town lacerated by revolutions and wars, as Bruges was from 1487 to 1491.'[14]

Obrecht's activities in his early Bruges years (1485–7) are not documented beyond a few payment records at St Donatian's (see Pl. 7).[15] But Strohm has convincingly argued that he composed his masses *De Sancto Martino* and *De Sancto Donatiano* in these years, for endowments by the singer Pierre Basin (on 14 March 1486) and the widow of the furrier Donaes de Moor (on 14 March 1487).[16] From the stylistic point of view, Strohm's datings make excellent sense (see Ch. 6); the second of the two cycles, moreover, was copied in Rome in late 1487 or early 1488.[17] Closely related to these works is the mass *Ave regina celorum*, which Strohm has dated 1485–90 since parts from its model appear in three Bruges altarpieces from the 1480s.[18] Another mass likely to date from Obrecht's early Bruges period is *Salve diva parens*, which was copied in a Roman manuscript (now part of VatS 51) presumably in late 1487 or early 1488.[19]

With two masses copied at Rome in 1487, the Italian transmission of Obrecht's works was clearly taking off. This is perhaps not surprising, for Bruges was a centre of international music distribution not equalled by any of the places where the composer had worked thus far. But the quality of his music must have played an ever greater part: in 1487, Duke Ercole I d'Este of Ferrara, a well-known connoisseur, was said to favour 'the musical composition of *magister* Jacob over other compositions'.[20] This is clear evidence that Obrecht's music was increasingly appreciated in Italy. Given the fierce competition between the musical centres there, and given the means they had at their disposal to buy the best musicians of Europe, it was perhaps inevitable that he would soon be invited to come and work in the South.

It was in fact Ercole d'Este who took the initiative. In early September

[14] *Music in Late Medieval Bruges*, 39.   [15] De Schrevel, *Histoire*, i. 160.
[16] *Music in Late Medieval Bruges*, 40–1 and 145–7; see also *NOE* 3, pp. xiii–xv and xxvii–xxviii.
[17] Hudson, 'Obrecht's Tribute to Ockeghem', 11 n. 17.
[18] *Music in Late Medieval Bruges*, 139–40 and 147; see also *NOE* 1, p. xxvi.
[19] See *NOE* 11, p. xix.
[20] 'quod idem dux . . . compositionem musicalem dicti Mg[ri] Jacobi preter ceteras compositiones magnipendat'; chapter acts, St Donatian's, 2 Oct. 1487; De Schrevel, *Histoire*, i. 160.

PL. 7. The church of St Donatian, *c.*1519–20 (British Library, Add. MS 34294, fo. 257ᵛ; used by permission of the British Library)

1487 he sent his singer Cornelio di Lorenzo[21] to Bruges with a letter asking the chapter of St Donatian's to give leave to Obrecht to come to Ferrara. Cornelio travelled through Milan on 5 September,[22] where he was probably joined by the internationally famous tenorist Jean Cordier.[23] Less than a month later, the two singers arrived in Bruges. On 2 October, the chapter of St Donatian's discussed Ercole's request:[24]

A letter from the lord Hercules, Duke of Ferrara etc., was shown by a certain Cornelius of Lilloo, singer of his chapel, in which [the duke] requests the chapter to permit the succentor *magister* Jacobus to come to him and stay there for several months. Having heard the same Cornelius, and also *dominus* Johannes Cordier (who reported that the same duke takes much delight in the art of music, favours the musical composition of the said *magister* Jacob above other compositions, and has long wished to see him), and [considering that] the same *magister* thereupon came before the chapter and consented with the duke's request, [their lordships] permitted him to absent himself for six months after the next feast of St Donatian [14 October], on the condition that he so provided for his office and the choir-boys in the interim period that nothing should be wanting. And since *dominus* Johannes Rykelin was appointed to relieve him from this duty, their lordships were contented, and ordered a favourable letter to be written to the lord duke, and presented the aforesaid Cornelius with two jugs of wine and bread.

Obrecht travelled with Cornelio di Lorenzo through France in the early weeks of November. (On the nineteenth of that month, they were still expected in Milan.[25]) By 1 December they had reached the duke, who at that time was staying in Goito (near Mantua). On that day, Ercole wrote to his wife that 'd. Jacomo Obleth cantore excellente' had come, and that he was expecting to arrive with him at Ferrara on 5 December. The letter throws important light on the esteem in which the composer was held:[26]

. . . it seems to us that Your Ladyship will see to it that the first room, which is

---

[21] Cornelio di Lorenzo was variously described as a native of Antwerp and Lilloo (a village 10 km. north-west of Antwerp); his name in Dutch would have been Cornelis Laurenssone. One of the most famous singers of his time, Cornelio worked at important centres such as Milan, Ferrara, and Florence in the years 1470–1511. It was he who sent the mass by Obrecht to Duke Ercole in 1484. Further biographical details are given in Lockwood, *Ferrara*, 161–5.

[22] Giacomo Trotti, Ferrarese ambassador in Milan, wrote to Ercole on that day, informing him that 'your singer Cornelio was here' (ibid. 163).

[23] Cordier had been given permission to leave Bruges for Milan 'per tres vel quatuor menses continuos' on 10 July 1487, twelve weeks before he was to speak concerning Ercole's request before the chapter of St Donatian's (De Schrevel, *Histoire*, i. 173–4). While in Italy, Cordier undoubtedly did some of the groundwork for Obrecht's later visit to Ferrara. This may well have included bringing some of the works that Duke Ercole was said (by Cordier on 2 Oct.) to favour 'above other compositions'.   [24] Chapter acts, St Donatian's, 2 Oct. 1487; De Schrevel, *Histoire*, i. 160.

[25] Ercole's ambassador at Milan wrote on this day that 'if Cornelio and that other singer, whom he is bringing from France, arrive here, I will send him . . . to Mantua' (where the duke was about to go); Lockwood, *Ferrara*, 163.

[26] The full letter is transcribed and translated in Murray, 'New Light', 505 and 512.

next to the apartment that used to be Paul Antonio's, be put in very good order
for him . . . And see to it that everything is provided for: that a silken drapery
is put on his bed; and let there be in the room a bedstead and bench cover and
any other necessary object. If the window or any other thing is out of order, have
it repaired immediately. And see to it that he is well waited on and welcomed
with much honour, and at our arrival, which will possibly be next Wednesday
[5 December], that everything is in order.

Within days after this letter, Obrecht must have agreed with the duke to
work for him, for the latter immediately deployed his most powerful weapon for recruiting singers: benefices.[27] Already while travelling
through Mantua on his way to Ferrara (between 1 and 5 December)
Ercole had sent a letter to his ambassador at Rome, Buonfrancesco Arlotti,
Bishop of Reggio, instructing him to secure for Obrecht one of two canonries expected to become vacant in the diocese of Tournai. The actual letter
has not survived, but its receipt is acknowledged in a reply from Arlotti,
dated 12 December. This reply makes it clear that the matter was considered to be of the utmost urgency:[28]

. . . one of the three letters you have sent to me from Mantua [is] filled with
affection and an ardent desire that *don* Jacomo receive what he seeks; and well
may it be, so that the most learned of the learned will serve Your Lordship. Since
I understand that this request of yours is one that comes from your strongest
desire, I shall make every effort to persuade the Pope, as I am accustomed to do
in the most important business that you require to be done.

Arlotti happened to be suffering from a severe cold at the time, and his
physicians did not allow him to go out. But by 3 January 1488 he had
recovered, and wrote to the duke that he had finally had his audience with
Pope Innocent VIII, at the Castel Sant'Angelo.[29] We learn from Arlotti's
letter that he raised the matter as earnestly and tactfully as possible:[30]

I tried to make His Holiness understand that nothing at the present time could
please you more than this, and in order that His Holiness might be further
assured of your warmest desire that Don Jacomo be given this benefice, which
would please you more than if a much higher dignity were bestowed upon you or

---

[27] On Ercole d'Este's benefice strategies, see Lockwood, *Ferrara*, 185–95.

[28] Transcription and translation of the full letter in L. Lockwood, 'Music at Ferrara in the Period
of Ercole I d'Este', *Studi musicali*, 1 (1972), 112–13 and 127–8. Lucien van Hoorn, who discovered
the relevant correspondence in 1951–3, pointed to the existence of another letter on Obrecht's
benefices, unfortunately without giving a reference or transcription: 'En effet aux Archives de la
maison d'Este se trouve une lettre de 1487 adressée à la Curie à Rome, signée "Eleonora de Aragona,
Ducissa Ferrariae". Ayant appris que deux bénéfices vacants allaient être conférés à deux prêtres
qu'elle considère comme absolument indignes de cette faveur, la duchesse demande l'un d'eux
pour "don Jacomo nostro capellano", probablement Jacomo Obrecht' (*Jacob Obrecht* (The Hague,
1968), 82).

[29] Full transcription and translation in Murray, 'New Light', 510–13.   [30] Ibid. 512.

your children, I read him your letter from beginning to end, because it seemed most excellently written and in terms suiting this purpose.

Having heard Arlotti's plea, Pope Innocent at first suspected Ercole of trying to steal away a singer intended for the papal chapel. But he had the matter checked, and learned that the name and the diocese did not correspond. Even so, the Pope replied that he was not in a position to promise a benefice to Obrecht in advance. All he could offer at present was his favourable disposition, the advice that Obrecht should raise the matter once either of the canonicates became vacant, and his promise to discuss the matter with the Bishop of Tournai, to whose diocese the benefices belonged.

Ercole was clearly not satisfied with this reply. On 17 January he wrote another letter to Arlotti, pointing out that it was impossible for Obrecht to learn of the vacancy in time to approach the Pope, and urging his ambassador 'to visit His Holiness again and implore him in our behalf that what was his pleasure not to grant for [Obrecht], he may be willing to grant for our particular gratification and satisfaction'.[31] Indeed, every prelate who had any influence on the matter was to be reminded daily of Obrecht 'so that this may never go out of their minds, because we certainly desire above all that this *Messer* Jacomo be favoured'.[32] As regards the Pope's suspicions that the duke was trying to steal his singers, Ercole disavowed having any intention of winning the composer for his own chapel, despite 'the recreation and enjoyment that we constantly receive from him'.

Arlotti followed the duke's instructions to the letter, and replied on 21 February that he had finally made progress: Pope Innocent had given written commission to those in charge that the first of the two benefices to become vacant should be awarded to '*Messer* Jacomo Obreth'.[33] Ercole's agent promised to remain vigilant in the matter, but nevertheless felt that Obrecht would improve his chances if he came to Rome himself:[34]

But *Messer* Jacomo should well understand that nothing any longer is absolutely certain, and that I would advise him to obtain [the benefice] in person; if it is done for him by means of someone else, that other person might be so strongly recommended that our plan might fail; and indeed if he is not in these parts then he should see to it that his friends take care of it for him.

This is the last surviving document on Obrecht's application: when Arlotti and Ercole resume their correspondence on singers' benefices, on

[31] Full transcription and translation ibid., 514–15.　　　　[32] Ibid. 515.
[33] Transcription and translation of the relevant passages in Lockwood, 'Music at Ferrara', 128–9.　　　　[34] Ibid. 129.

12 May, his name is no longer mentioned.[35] We are obviously in the dark as to what happened in the intervening eleven or so weeks. But if the matter was as urgent as the above-quoted letters seem to indicate, there is every reason to assume that Obrecht followed Arlotti's advice and travelled to Rome. His compatriot and fellow composer Johannes Martini —the leading figure of Ercole's chapel and equally favoured by the duke—had done the same almost exactly a year earlier, thereby settling a case that had dragged on for eleven months.[36] The advice of Arlotti was thus well taken. And Martini himself could have pointed out other advantages of travelling to Rome—where at this time two of Obrecht's masses were part of the repertory. First and foremost, of course, was the opportunity to meet fellow composers: Heinrich Isaac at Florence, and at Rome Gaspar van Weerbeke, Marbriano de Orto, and Bertrand Vaqueras (Josquin was absent at the time). But equally tempting perhaps, for a man who would soon have to resume his workload at Bruges,[37] were the sights of Rome. Martini himself had evidently become enchanted by the city during his stay in 1487, for Arlotti then reported to the duke that he was not at all in a hurry to go back to Ferrara: 'These tribes of singers are a terrible thing; they never come to a conclusion. Today he is absent since he has gone on the pilgrimage of the Seven Stations.'[38] If Obrecht spent some time at Rome in order to be in the best position to collect his benefice, this could explain why he arrived in the North almost two months after his leave of absence had expired.[39] It could also shed light on the Roman transmission of some of his masses.[40]

In any case, whether Obrecht waited in Ferrara or Rome, by the middle of May it must have become clear that he was not to receive his benefice. On the twelfth of that month, the first of a new series of exchanges

[35] On 12 May 1488 Arlotti writes to Ercole concerning a benefice at Campiolo for the court singer Mathia of Paris; the correspondence on this matter continues until 7 June (Lockwood, *Ferrara*, 307).

[36] Ibid. 169–71. Martini travelled to Rome again in Oct. 1488, also in connection with a benefice; by doing so, he obtained the latter as well (ibid.).

[37] Since 1480, the succentor's duties at St Donatian's had included the daily *Salve* or *Lof* service (financed by the city), sung after Compline: 'As a consequence, the succentor had to reschedule the 1½ hours' daily teaching of music to the choirboys from the evening to the morning, so that he was now continually busy from matins until lunchtime, besides the actual *Salve* concert in the evening' (Strohm, *Music in Late Medieval Bruges*, 39).

[38] Letter of 15 Feb. 1487; Lockwood, *Ferrara*, 170 and 297.

[39] Obrecht was allowed to be absent until 14 Apr. 1488. Nearly two months later, on 12 June, the chapter of St Donatian's learned that he was at Bergen op Zoom (see below).

[40] If I am correct in assuming that the *Missa O lumen ecclesie* was in existence by this time (see Ch. 4), Obrecht's possible stay at Rome in 1488 could explain why the reading in a manuscript copied at Rome in 1511–20 (VatSM 26) appears to be more closely related to the original version than that of the Netherlands court manuscript JenaU 22 (*NOE* 8, pp. xviii–xx). It should be stressed, however, that Obrecht may have been a singer at the papal chapel in 1503–4 (Wegman, 'Bergen op Zoom', 211 n. 88, acknowledging Richard Sherr, and below, Ch. 11).

between Ercole and Arlotti was written, now concerning a benefice for the singer Mathia of Paris. Obrecht must have left Italy around the same time, for he was in the North exactly a month later—a disappointed man, no doubt.

When Obrecht returned North in early June 1488, the Low Countries were in a politically explosive situation. Maximilian of Austria's attempts to reconquer territories lost to France in the Treaty of Arras (1482) ended in humiliating defeat, and caused increasing resentment in the heavily taxed Flemish towns. Bruges fostered grudges against the rival markets in Brabant, Antwerp and Bergen op Zoom, and accused Maximilian of favouring the latter cities. Ghent—politically the most inflammatory city of Flanders—was still brooding over the loss of its civic privileges in 1485.

In January 1488 Maximilian had convened the Estates of Flanders in Bruges, but he was made prisoner by that town on 2 February. Only on 16 May did he regain his freedom, by swearing an oath that he would defer to a newly forged treaty limiting his powers. Meanwhile the Ghenters had sought the protection of King Charles VIII of France, who not unpredictably confirmed the privileges Maximilian had denied them, and sent a garrison to defend the city. (In the hectic diplomatic activities that evolved in Ghent in the first half of 1488, Obrecht's father Willem—now in the last months of his life—was regularly involved as a letter-bearer and town crier.)

Maximilian's father, the Roman Emperor Frederick III, was outraged over his son's imprisonment, and immediately dispatched an army to the southern Netherlands. The archduke himself joined the forces of revenge immediately after his release, despite the oath he had sworn to Flanders. The main culprits, Ghent and Bruges, could now expect to be punished heavily. But war did not break out. The situation led to a protracted stalemate, in which the two parties kept harassing one another by raids into each other's territories. This situation was not only disastrous for the Flemish economy—as anyone could feel directly in his purse and in his stomach—but made it extremely dangerous for individuals to travel through Flanders, as Obrecht evidently realized. Although two months late, he did not go straight to Bruges but decided instead to travel to Bergen op Zoom (one of Maximilian's most loyal towns), where he waited until the threat of war would have subsided. While Bergen op Zoom was now preparing to assist Maximilian in his war against Flanders, Obrecht received permission from the burgomasters and aldermen to work temporarily as a singer at the Guild of Our Lady. The guild accounts for 1487/8 record the payment to Obrecht of a sum equalling 120 Flemish groats, for forty-eight *loten*.[41] On 12 June 1488 the chapter of St Donatian's finally received news from their succentor:[42]

Having heard the letter of the succentor *magister* Jacobus Hobrecht from the city of Bergen [op Zoom], their lordships instructed me [the chapter secretary] to write to him that notwithstanding the threat of war, he should appear here by the feast of St John [the Baptist, 24 June], that even then he should at least arrange for the choirboys to be housed and taught, since *dominus* Johannes Rykelin asks to be relieved from [his responsibilities for] them. Otherwise it will be necessary for their lordships themselves to provide for another succentor.

The message is clear: the composer should be back within twelve days, wars or no wars. Rykelin had enough of his work as succentor, and urged the chapter to relieve him from his duties as soon as possible. Apparently he kept complaining in the next few days, for the canons—recognizing that the situation was becoming untenable—decided on 18 June to send another letter, demanding Obrecht's immediate return:[43]

Concerning the succentor *magister* Jacobus, recently returned to Bergen [op Zoom] from the duke of Ferrara, whom he had visited with the permission of the chapter, it was again decided to write to him to return here on the forthcoming feast of St John in order to discharge his duties; otherwise it will be necessary for their lordships to make arrangements, particularly since his replacement [Rykelin] absolutely wishes to be relieved.

Only six days were left after this decision. But 24 June passed, and still the succentor had not returned.[44] Another six weeks went by—but the composer remained in Bergen op Zoom. We do not know why he stayed there, whether he wrote to explain his delay, or whether in fact he had any reasonable excuse. But however that may be, he was now clearly being inordinately disobedient. Given the difficulties his absence created for both the chapter and his deputy Rykelin, Obrecht could expect a row of major proportions on his return. The fear of having to face these consequences may well have made him stay away longer: having gone too far anyway, a bit further would make little difference.

[41] 'Item to *meester* Jacop the choirmaster, who had come here, paid [at the command of] the burgomasters and aldermen a certain number of *loten* of 3.75 [Brabant] groats, [together makes] 180 groats' (Wegman, 'Bergen op Zoom', 206).   [42] De Schrevel, *Histoire*, i. 161.   [43] Ibid.

[44] In fact, if Obrecht arrived in Bergen op Zoom on 8 or 9 June (which is three or four days before his first letter arrived in Bruges), it is possible to deduce from the number of *loten* he accumulated at the Guild of Our Lady that he stayed there until at least 17 or 18 July (Wegman, 'Bergen op Zoom', 206). We learn from the chapter acts of St Donatian's that he was still in Bergen op Zoom on 6 Aug. (see below). It is surely no coincidence that 'Cordier den sanghere', undoubtedly Jean Cordier, received 6 *gelten* Rhine wine [*c*.16.5 litres] in Bergen op Zoom around the time Obrecht seems to have arrived there, on 8 June 1488; E. Vander Straeten, *La Musique aux Pays-Bas avant le XIXᵉ siècle* (Brussels, 1867–88), iii (1875), 191.

But the next relevant entry in the Bruges chapter records suggests that he may have been waiting for an important letter from Italy that would get him out of his predicament. In the first days of August the canons of St Donatian's finally received news from Obrecht. He requested to be allowed to return on 15 August, enclosing a letter of thanks from Ercole d'Este that no doubt sang the composer's praises with the same superlatives we find in his correspondence with Arlotti. This evidently appeased the chapter, for on 6 August they decided to grant the composer's request:[45]

Having seen the letter of the lord duke of Ferrara, in which he thanks the chapter for allowing the succentor *magister* Jacobus Hobrecht to travel to him, and having understood the plea of the same *magister* Jacobus, whom, owing to the dangers of the roads between Bergen [op Zoom], where he is now, and Sluis, their lordships granted time to return to his place and office by the feast of the Assumption, just as he had requested.

There can be little doubt that Ercole's intercession was decisive here, for the chapter decision was an extraordinarily generous gesture, given Obrecht's impertinent behaviour. Perhaps the canons were just a little surprised that so powerful a prince as Ercole could be so passionate about this man, who hardly distinguished himself in the performance of his daily duties.[46] It may be no coincidence that the next surviving reference to Obrecht, dated 2 May 1489 (nearly nine months later), is in fact their decision to award him the chaplaincy of St Catherine—which may have soothed somewhat the painful memories of the canonry missed in Ferrara.[47]

Death of a City Trumpeter: Ghent, 1488–1492

1488 was not a happy year for Obrecht. Although it opened with the most promising perspectives, none of these materialized in the end. Within the space of eight months, the wheel of the composer's fortunes had made a cruel downward swing. And there was more to come. About four months after his return to Bruges, Obrecht's father, the trumpeter Willem, 'who was adorned with great probity', died at Ghent.

Willem Obrecht's last years are relatively well documented. Some time

[45] De Schrevel, *Histoire*, i. 161.

[46] Strohm even suggests that 'Obrecht, who hardly possessed the organisational talents of [his predecessor] de Groote, and who had been dismissed from the succentorship in Cambrai for administrative faults, clearly could not cope with the task in Bruges' (*Music in Late Medieval Bruges*, 39).

[47] Strohm, *Music in Late Medieval Bruges*, 39; see also De Schrevel, *Histoire*, i. 161.

in 1484 or early 1485 he moved into the Talboomstraat (today Ursulinen-straat), where he had bought a wooden three-storey house (see Pl. 8).[48] Here Willem and his second wife Beatrijse Jacops lived only 200 metres away from the parish church of St John—where he was a member of the confraternity of Our Lady, regularly gathered with his fellow trumpeters in the chapel of St Andrew and St Lazarus, and might have heard his son's masses and motets being sung by the *cotidiane*. Willem lived only a few houses away from *meester* Arend de Keyser (not to be confused with the city trumpeter), who introduced printing into Ghent and issued an edition of Boethius' *De consolatione philosophiae* in 1485.[49] Yet there were draw-backs to living in the centre of a late-medieval metropolis. In 1486 there were complaints about the prostitutes who had settled in the Talboom-straat and the surrounding streets and alleys—and particularly about the behaviour of their clientele, who accosted married women and maidens with rude remarks (not dissimilar, one supposes, to those set to music in *Meskin es hu cutkin ru*) and caused street fights and unrest during night and day.[50] The city magistrates ordered the prostitutes to exercise their profession 'in the quarter and at such a place as has been appointed by the lords and the by-law in former times'—a remarkably enlightened policy on prostitution.

The first half of 1488 had been a hectic time for Willem Obrecht. Ghent's defiant stand against Maximilian of Habsburg, the preparations for war, the negotiations, the diplomatic initiatives: all this had repeatedly required his (and his fellow trumpeters') activities as a letter-bearer and city crier. On eighteen separate occasions in February to July 1488, Willem had to announce proclamations in the city; nine of these were in June, when the army of the Roman emperor had encamped before the gates of Ghent.[51] As a letter-bearer he had travelled on horse to Dendermonde and Mechlin (27 February–2 March) and to Brussels (13–15 April), and on foot to Nerghem (3 April).[52] Besides all this he kept

---

[48] No contract has as yet been discovered, but Willem Obrecht is mentioned as a neighbour in the Talboomstraat on 8 June 1485 (SAG 301.58, 1485², fo. 13ʳ: 'inde Talboemstrate beneuden Sandt-berghe, Willem Hoebrecht daer neffens ghehuust an den zijde'; see also SAG 301.60, 1489/90, fo. 50ᵛ). Sixteen months previously, on 6 Feb. 1484, the same house had still been owned by Katheline van Calkene (SAG 301.57, 1483/4, fo. 109ʳ; see also SAG 301.55, 1478/9, fo. 140ᵛ; 301.56, 1480/1, fo. 124ʳ; 301.56, 1481/2, fo. 174ᵛ). It is not known where Willem Obrecht lived before 1484–5, but he is listed as having taxable property worth 648 Flemish groats 'beyond the gate of St George' (today Sint-Jorisbrug) in the undated tax register SAG 20.15, fo. 42ʳ (Mattheus Nijs is mentioned on the same folio).

[49] Decavele (ed.), *Gent: Apologie van een rebelse stad*, 344; see also SAG 330.36, 1482/3, rolle fo. 13ʳ.   [50] De Potter, *Gent, van den oudsten tijd*, iii. 385–6.

[51] SAG 400.29 (1487/8), fos. 359ʳ, 361ʳ, 363ʳ–366ʳ, 369ʳ, 410ᵛ, 416ᵛ–423ᵛ, and 428ᵛ. The dates are: 4 Feb.; 28 Mar.; 30 Apr.; 14, 23, and 27 May; 3, 6, 7, 9, 12, 15, 16, 23, and 26 June; and 24, 26, and 30 July.

PL. 8. Willem Obrecht's house in the Talboomstraat, Ghent, on the city map of 1641

carrying out his duties as a city trumpeter. The last known payment to him was made on 30 July 1488.

Willem Obrecht's death was recorded in the city accounts of 1488/9. The entry was made because his estate was assessable for the so-called *exuwe* or *yssue*. This tax was charged on all possessions of non-burgesses that left the town through inheritance, marriage, ordination to the priesthood, or foundations and charitable donations outside Ghent—a measure designed to limit the flow of capital from the city.[53] The *exuwe* receipts were always meticulously recorded in the annual city accounts, and

---

[52] Doc. 38: 'Item Willem Hobrecht, trumpeter, because he went with letters to the court of justice in Dendermonde, and from there to Mechlin; he departed on 27 February and returned on 2 March, total five days on horse, 24 groats per day, 120 groats.' Doc. 39: 'Item Willem Obrecht, trumpeter, because he went with letters to Christoffel Claess in Nerghem [?Meyghem], amounts to one day on foot; done on 3 April 1487 [1488 NS] in Eastertide, 12 groats.' Doc. 40: 'Item Willem Hobrecht, trumpeter, because he went with letters to the court of justice at Brussels; he travelled away on 13 April and returned on the 15th of the same month, amounts to three days on horse, 24 groats per day, 72 groats.'

[53] H. Van Werveke, *De Gentse stadsrekeningen in de middeleeuwen* (Brussels, 1934), 196–7.

Willem Obrecht's case is described in 1488/9 as follows (Doc. 41; see Pl. 9):

Item, concerning the inheritance of Willem Hobrecht, trumpeter: on the entire estate, which was shared by *her* Jacop Hobrecht, priest, was appointed by the magistrates [a tax of] 288 groats, [of which] 18 groats [were] deducted for the announcer, the *exuwe* officials, and the messengers; net residue 270 groats.

It is this document that enabled Berten De Keyzer in 1953 to identify the Ghent city trumpeter Willem Obrecht with certainty as the Guillermus Hobrecht of *Mille quingentis*: both the year of death and the name of the heir match those mentioned in the motet.[54] The city account does not give the exact date of Willem's death, but a *terminus post quem* is provided by the starting date of the financial year, 15 August. This term can be narrowed down by a receipt in connection with Willem Obrecht's death in the accounts for 1488/9 of the Guild of Our Lady in St John's, whose starting-date is 1 October.[55] Various indications in the *exuwe* account moreover suggest that the entry concerning Willem was made in the last weeks of November, thus supporting the date of 22 November mentioned in the motet.[56]

The *exuwe* document casts very little light on the settlement of Willem Obrecht's estate. The tax was almost certainly not charged on his own inheritance (which was exempt),[57] but more probably on an outstanding debt that Jacob claimed in connection with the inheritance of his late mother Lysbette Gheeraerts (which was probably not).[58] As such it could

[54] De Keyzer, 'Jacob Obrecht en zijn vader Willem', 319 (but note that the currencies are incorrectly transcribed there).

[55] Doc. 42: 'Receipts of death fees from the guild brothers and sisters . . . *item* Willem Oobrecht, [handed over to us] by *meester* Jacob vanden Velde, 20 groats.' Death fees were paid to have Requiem services celebrated for deceased members in the chapel of the guild.

[56] Willem Obrecht's case was entered as the 94th of 352 *exuwe* cases in 1488/9. On the face of it, this would seem to indicate that his death was recorded approximately $94 \div 352 \times 365 = 97$–8 days after 15 Aug.; this is 19–20 Nov. 1488, only two or three days before the date mentioned in the motet. For the actual date of death one must obviously deduct the time that was necessary to settle all inheritance matters. Yet there is an important circumstance indicating that the entry was recorded later than 19–20 Nov., thus making up for that delay: this is the Ghent plague epidemic of 1489. That epidemic can clearly be recognized if one counts the numbers of entries in the *exuwe* chapters during the late 1480s: 186 (1485/6), 153 (1486/7), 117 (1487/8), 352 (1488/9), 387 (1489/90), 107 (1490/1). This suggests that mortality in 1488/9 might have been about three times as high as in the previous financial year. This can only mean that the entry was made later than *c.*19–20 Nov., probably a few weeks after the 22nd of that month.

[57] Burgesses like Willem Obrecht were exempt from *exuwe*, and this makes it highly unlikely that the tax of 288 groats was charged on his inheritance. Besides, the sum on which the *exuwe* was charged must have been either 1,920 or 2,400 groats (the rate being 15% for movables and 12% for immovables), and Willem's estate was almost certainly worth a multiple of that sum—given that, for instance, one of his silver trumpets alone yielded 1,464 groats in 1470 (Doc. 25). In fact there are compelling grounds for believing that he left his widow in considerable prosperity (see below).

[58] It so happens that 288 groats is exactly 12% of 10 Flemish pounds (2,400 groats). This in turn

[*cont. on p. 152*]

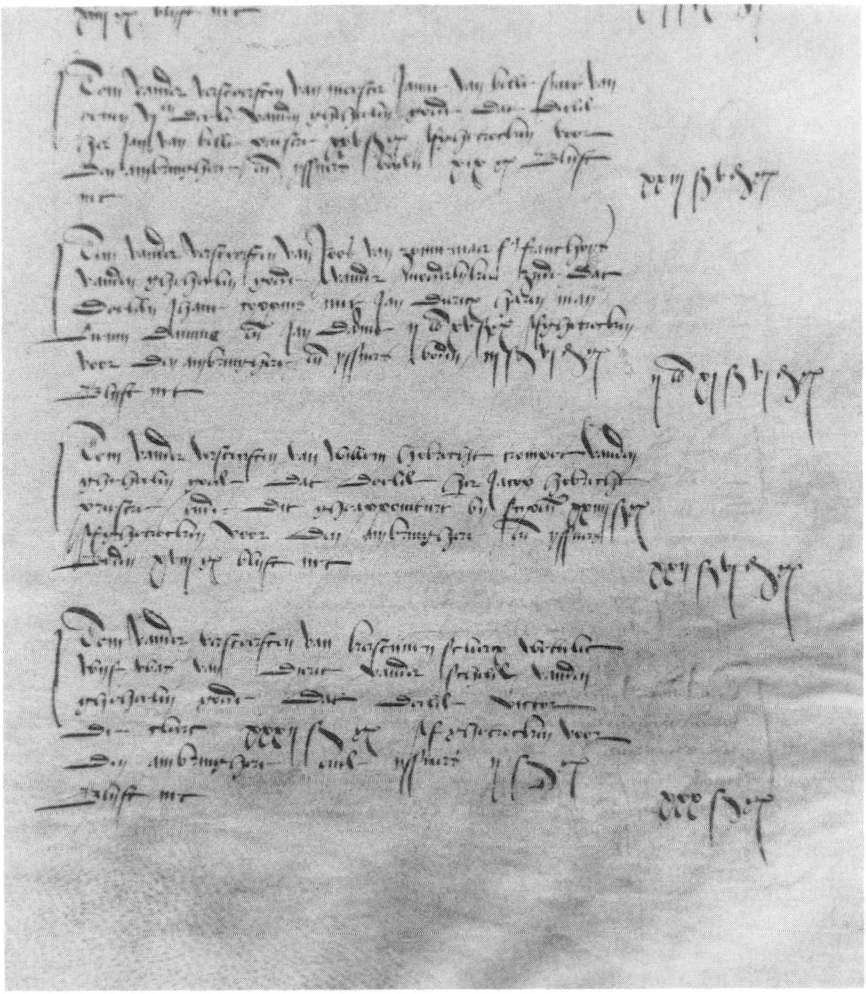

PL. 9. *Exuwe* tax received by the city of Ghent from 'her Jacop Hobrecht priestre', concerning the estate of his deceased father Willem, 1488/9 (Doc. 41)

have been no more than a detail in the division of the entire estate, about which we know next to nothing.

Some general observations nevertheless need to be made, in order to understand better two Obrecht documents written at Ghent in 1492. As the sole heir Jacob would certainly have inherited everything that Willem possessed before marrying Beatrijse Jacops—and this included whatever was outstanding from his mother's estate. Beyond that he was entitled to half the common property acquired by Willem and Beatrijse in marriage (of which portion the widow would nevertheless retain half the usufruct for the rest of her life), and he moreover stood to inherit the remaining half after her death.[59] The common property would normally have been listed and valued, and then either divided (at least on paper) or sold. In this way, for instance, Jacob and his stepmother must have become joint owners of the house in the Talboomstraat, and possibly of any rents or property held in and outside Ghent.

All this means that the financial interests of the composer and his stepmother meshed in a complex settlement that carefully defined the shares, rights, and obligations of both parties. In the long run this settlement might have proved to be restrictive, particularly to Beatrijse Jacops. Despite her age of at least 40,[60] and despite having been married for more than twenty-four years, she could still be an attractive party in the marriage market if Willem had left her a sizeable inheritance. Yet remarriage would inevitably add complications to the settlement with her stepson. For instance, it would have been a matter of some financial concern to Jacob that Beatrijse should marry a man who would prudently manage the property she had acquired with Willem, for Jacob was to inherit it after

happens to be exactly the amount reserved for Lysbette Gheeraerts as a dowry in 1450 (Doc. 2), which Jacob inherited *in toto* after her death in 1460 (Doc. 16), but which his father almost certainly kept until his death in 1488, since a later document refers to 'the sum of money that . . . Willem had in his possession at the time of his death, and that belongs to [Jacob], became his due some time ago, and was left [to him] after the death of Lysbette Gheeraerts, the aforesaid Willem's first wife and [Jacob's] mother' (Doc. 47). The reason why this sum had not been paid during Willem Obrecht's lifetime is provided by Doc. 16: after the death of his first wife Willem had claimed the dowry of 2,400 groats for himself ('an welken x lb. gr. de vornoemde Willem pretendeert recht thebbene'), and even though his claim was probably unjustified, Jacob evidently had never pressed the point. I suggest that Lysbette Gheeraerts, as a native of Hughersluus, did not have citizen's rights, and consequently that Jacob Obrecht could not claim this outstanding part of her inheritance without revealing that the sum was taxable (whereas his father's inheritance could leave the city tax-free). Since the debt had to be paid from Willem's estate, and since this included both movables and immovables (the house in the Talboomstraat), Jacob could choose the more advantageous of the two tax rates, that is, 12% (immovables).

[59] The relevant laws are summarized in Ch. 1, in the paragraph on Lysbette Gheeraerts.

[60] She was married to Willem Obrecht (and consequently had reached the age of consent, 15) by 1464 (Doc. 20); this points to a date of birth of 1449 or earlier.

her death. (Fortune-hunters like Shakespeare's Hortensio were a notorious threat.) And if, despite her age, she were to have any children with a second husband, these would acquire rights of inheritance as well, thus diminishing his. One way or another, Jacob Obrecht would continue to have a firm financial stake in the movements of his stepmother.

These potential complications provide the explanatory background to two documents drawn up by the magistrates of the by-law and inheritance on 13 November 1492, four years after Willem Obrecht's death. They reveal that Beatrijse Jacops had indeed remarried (her new husband was Zegher de Leenheer, a wealthy trader in precious luxury products) and that the newly-wed couple quite understandably sought to come to a final settlement with Jacob Obrecht. This alone confirms that Beatrijse had been a desirable match for financial (if for no other) reasons, and consequently that Willem Obrecht must have left both her and his son a substantial inheritance.[61] The two documents of 1492 are complementary, yet they reveal only the outward legal form of what must have been a much more complex division. Document 46 shows what Jacob Obrecht gained in the agreement. In it, Zegher de Leenheer declares that he has sold Beatrijse's half of the house in the Talboomstraat:

Zegher de Leenhere has come before the magistrates of the by-law in Ghent, [and] stated and declared that he has sold well and fairly to *meester* Jacoppe Hoobrecht *filius* Willems, priest, one-half of a house and stead situated down at the Zandberg in the Talboomstraat, being a *loove* [a house whose long axis runs parallel with the street], Pauwels Blijc living on one side, and all the heirs of Pieter den Buelen on the other . . . This sale was made for the sum of 288 groats, which the vendor declares to have received from the aforenamed *meester* Jacop, his purchaser, and he therefore acquits him of [that sum] . . . Done on 13 November 1492.

The sum of 288 groats was a pittance, of course, given that the house next door had been sold for 6,720 groats in 1485.[62] One reason for this must be that Jacob stood to inherit Beatrijse's half of the house anyway, so that he could not be expected to pay its full value. But a more important reason is that the composer agreed, on the very same day, to surrender all rights to the remainder of Willem Obrecht's estate, thereby freeing his

---

[61] This is one of the reasons for concluding that the *exuwe* in 1488/9 could have been charged only on a small portion of Willem Obrecht's estate, namely that portion which Jacob claimed as his due from his late mother's inheritance (see above, nn. 57 and 58).

[62] SAG 301.58, 1485² , fo. 13ʳ (8 June 1485): sale of a house 'situated in the Talboomstraat down at the Zandberg' to Pauwels de Blijc. Willem Obrecht is mentioned as one of the neighbours, and Pauwels de Blijc, in turn, is mentioned as a neighbour in Doc. 46.

stepmother and her new husband from all future obligations towards him (Doc. 47; see Pl. 10):[63]

Meester Jacop Hobbrecht, priest, living at Antwerp, heir to the estate of Willem Hoobrecht, trumpeter, his late father, has come before the magistrates of inheritance at Ghent, stating and declaring that he, concerning all the effects pertaining to the estate of the aforesaid Willem, nothing excepted or excluded, has fully shared, settled, squared, and agreed with Beatrijse Jacops, former holder, widow of the aforenamed Willem and presently the wife of Zegher den Leenheer, and that he has received his rightful share. And he also declared that the aforenamed Beatrijse and the aforenamed Zegher, her husband, have fully satisfied and contented him concerning the sum of money that she and the aforesaid Willem had in their possession at the time of his death, and that belongs to [Jacob], became his due some time ago, and was left [to him] after the death of Lysbette Gheeraerts, the aforesaid Willem's first wife and [Jacob's] mother. And with this he fully and legally indemnifies the aforesaid Zegher and his wife Beatrijse, now and in eternity, against all that he might or could ever claim from them in connection with the aforesaid bequeathed sum of money or otherwise, generally or specifically, without any more reproach or revocation. Done on 13 November 1492.

Evidently the sum of 288 groats had only notionally been the price of Beatrijse's half of the house in Ghent: effectively it must have been the sum left for Jacob Obrecht to settle after the definitive division of his father's estate, a division by which he acquired a permanent source of revenue in Ghent, and Beatrijse and Zegher capital (and possibly property) that was free from any claims or obligations. The initiative for the final settlement had probably come from the couple. Although it is possible that Jacob Obrecht had insisted on a division (for instance, if he had little trust in Zegher de Leenheer), what brought him to Ghent in November 1492 was more probably his readiness to co-operate, and a desire to consolidate his financial position.

Yet the acquisition of property could have benefits beyond the composer's lifetime. A clear example is provided by the case of Pierre Basin, the well-known singer and canon of St Donatian's, who had worked with Willem Obrecht and Antoine Busnoys at the Burgundian court in 1467, and became Jacob's immediate successor as succentor in Bruges in 1491. Basin, too, held property in Ghent,[64] and it was with such property that he funded the endowments of services for St Martin for which Obrecht composed the *Missa De Sancto Martino* in 1486 (see above). For Obrecht

---

[63] Document kindly brought to my attention by Daniël Lievois.

[64] See, for instance, SAG 301.58, 1484/5, fo. 85ʳ ('her Pieters Basin, presbyter canuenic van Sente Donaes te Brugghe'; 15 Jan. 1485), 301.65, 1498/9, fo. 36ʳ (sold by his brother Adrien Basin, as single heir; 3 Dec. 1498).

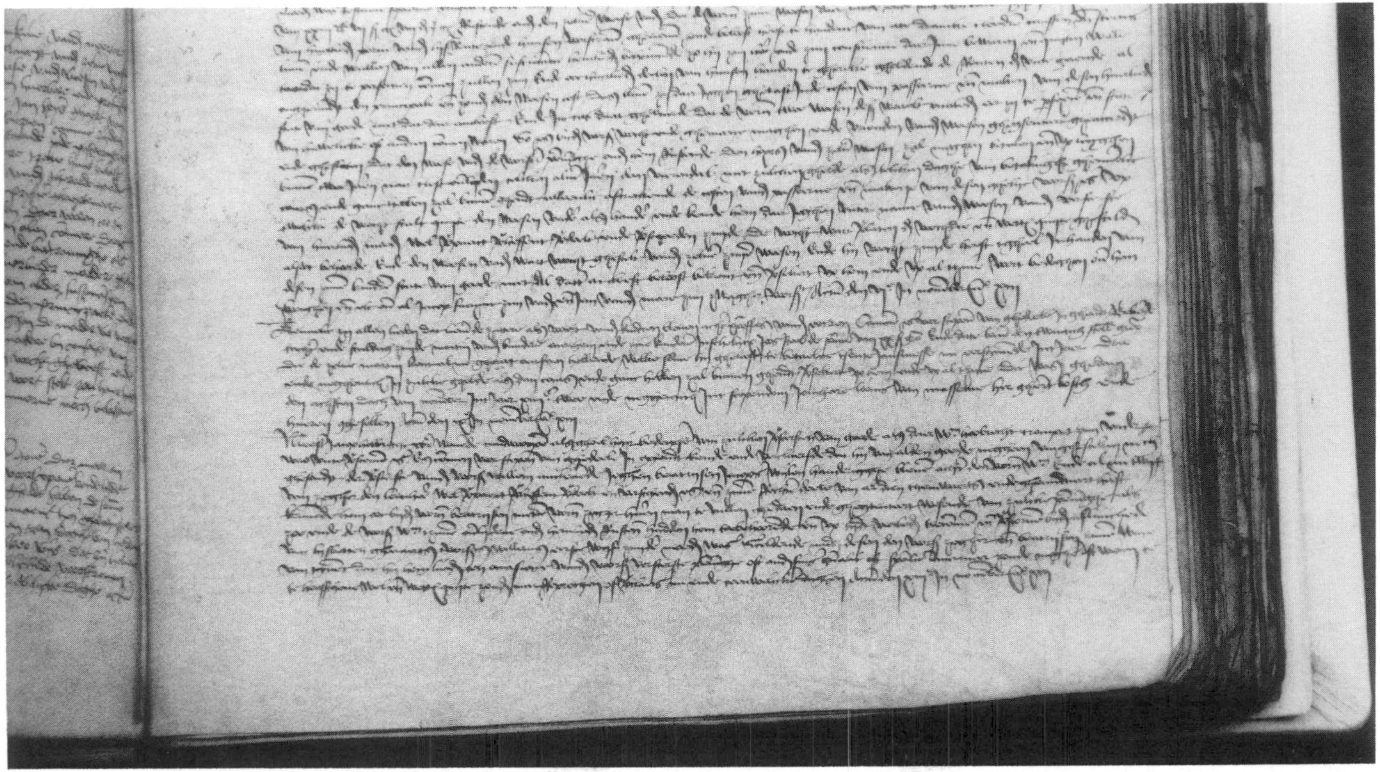

PL. 10. Quitclaim from Jacob Obrecht concerning the settlement of his father's inheritance with Beatrijse Jacops and her new husband Zegher de Leenheer, 1492 (Doc. 47)

himself, too, property could become a means of securing the salvation of his soul (and those of his ancestors) through endowments and foundations of services in perpetuity—and this was no doubt an underlying motive in many of his financial dealings. No direct documentation has as yet come to light, either for the house in Ghent or for the lands in Hughersluus (which became permanently flooded in 1488).[65] Yet the case of *Mille quingentis* suggests that memorial services with polyphony for at least the composer's father were established some time after 1488 (see Ch. 1).

Bruges, 1488–1491

In 1489 and the first months of 1490, none of the events in Obrecht's life was unusual or irregular enough to enter the historical record. But perhaps it was in these years that he composed many of his Middle Dutch songs, possibly as theatrical pieces. As succentor of St Donatian's Obrecht may have been closely involved with the production of Flemish morality plays, a tradition initiated by his predecessor Aliamus de Groote. De Groote wrote his own plays and provided them with music; they proved so popular that he had to be given leave, in 1483, to stage them in the streets, the choirboys acting on a carriage.[66] Although Obrecht left the rehearsing of the moralities to De Groote, it is quite possible that several of his Middle Dutch songs have their origins in this theatrical context— particularly as many of them appear to be based on monophonic popular tunes. Connections with a morality play have been demonstrated for at least one of his songs, *Wat willen wij metten budel spelen, ons ghelt es uut* ('What boots it more with purse to play, our money is all gone'). The

---

[65] Daniël Lievois, an expert on the architectural history of Ghent, has kindly traced all subsequent documentation on Willem Obrecht's house in the Talboomstraat, but was unable to find any reference to rents due in connection with an endowment. His results can be summarized as follows (private communication, 15 Oct. 1992). Document 46 mentions a land tax of 34 groats due to the Table of the Holy Ghost in the church of St John; a 15th-c. register of that institution lists several successive owners, including Katheline van Calkene, but not Willem Obrecht (RAG K1420, fo. 17ʳ). Document 46 also mentions a hereditary rent of 72 groats, payable to the Infirmary of St Elizabeth in Ghent; this rent had been sold on 19 Oct. 1467 by Gillis de Meestere, who had owned the house before Katheline van Calkene (SAG 301.49, 1467/8, fo. 14ʳ). Unfortunately, documents relating to this rent record the ownership of the house only from 1549 (Joosyne Ramont) to 1721 (RAG S489, fo. 109ᵛ, and S309, fo. 140ʳ). It is not known who acquired the house immediately after Jacob Obrecht, and when, but documentation is undoubtedly to be found in the yearbooks of the by-law. Willem Obrecht's house in the Talboomstraat remained structurally intact until after the Second World War; it has since been destroyed, to make way for a hideous police station. The house can be identified as item Q 360 in the land register of 1793 (SAG 153.1, no. 195, fo. 90ʳ), and item 43/3 in the detailed city map of 1811–13, where the façade is described as being 7.5 m. wide (UBG 3066/1, section du centre, deuxième partie, dite section B, îlot 43, rue des Ursulines no. 3).

[66] Vander Straeten, *La Musique aux Pays-Bas*, iii. 15–16; De Schrevel, *Histoire*, i. 158–9; and Strohm, *Music in Late Medieval Bruges*, 34 and 39.

music of this piece appears in a sixteenth-century painting depicting a brothel scene associated with Prodigal Son plays; moreover, there are close parallels with its text in Flemish versions of these plays.[67] Other songs seem to elaborate the same 'faulte d'argent' theme, for instance, *Ic hebbe gheen ghelt in mijn bewelt* ('I have no money in my possession'), or are situated in a brothel, for instance, *Meskin es u cutkin ru* ('Maiden, is your little $%!*&@ rough?'). The latter song incorporates a textual-musical dialogue between a prostitute and a prospective client, as it might have been staged in the streets of Bruges;[68] a similar dialogue song is probably *Waer sij di Han! Wie roupt ons daer?* ('Where are you, John!' 'Who's calling us?'). Obrecht's music in these settings is merry and uncomplicated, playing to an audience that evidently wanted to be entertained as well as spiritually uplifted.[69]

Firm documentation on Obrecht's biography finally resumes on 26 May 1490. On that day, the canons of St Donatian's summarily dismissed their succentor, without explaining their decision:[70]

It was decided that the succentor Jacobus Obrecht was to be dismissed if he would not ask his leave himself . . . And that Father de Hoya should persuade him that, for the sake of his honesty and honour, he had better come to the chapter to ask his leave, rather than being dismissed by their lordships.

The events that led to this decision are unknown, but it is clear that Obrecht must have committed a grave offence to be sentenced so harshly. Chapters were generally quite lenient with musicians: dismissal was the last resort, if only because one might end up with worse musicians. Nevertheless, whatever the composer may have done to incur the indignation of the canons, their decision was not implemented: in the following eight months he kept working as succentor. In fact there is reason to believe that his relations with the chapter soon returned to normal. Only half a year later, when Obrecht complained that the exorbitant wheat prices prevented him from sustaining the choirboys properly (see below), the

[67] H. C. Slim, *The Prodigal Son at the Whores'—Music, Art, and Drama* (Distinguished Faculty Lecture, 1975–6, University of California, Irvine), 16–21. A similar connection, to a French Prodigal Son play, has been proposed for Obrecht's *Tant que notre argent dura* (ibid. 11–12).

[68] See the reconstructed text in B. J. Blackburn, 'Two "Carnival Songs" Unmasked: A Commentary on MS Florence Magl. XIX. 121', *Musica disciplina*, 35 (1981), 141–4. It should be pointed out that the spelling 'Meiskin es *hu*' in some sources points uniquely to Flanders, where there was a tendency to write an 'h' before words starting with a vowel (cf. Obrecht/Hobrecht).

[69] An example of polyphony being sung in a Flemish theatrical context is provided by the late 15th-c. anonymous play *Het Spel van de V vroede ende van de V dwaeze Maegden*, ed. M. Hoebeke (The Hague, 1979), 117–19 (vv. 251–75): the five foolish virgins of Matt. 25: 1–13 sing 'a verse or two' of a *doncker auweet* (night-watch song), even though Hoverdie (Pride) and Zottecollacie (Folly) have protested that they can sing only 'discant' and 'fosset' (falsetto), respectively.

[70] Wegman, 'Bergen op Zoom', 207, acknowledging Reinhard Strohm.

chapter replied 'ex maxima amicitia' that he should try to hold fast—which seems a generous formulation even if one allows for the possibility of overstatement. And when the composer was finally discharged, on 17 January 1491, the chapter's decision was phrased in markedly more cordial terms than it had been eight months earlier (see below). Whatever its causes, the crisis must have been resolved, either through Obrecht's own pleas or apologies, or through the intercession of his friends.[71]

For Bruges, the year 1490 was dominated by the blockade of Count Philip of Cleves at Sluis. In 1488 the count had vouched for Maximilian's oath to Flanders. When the latter broke his oath, Philip felt bound by his honour to lead the subsequent Flemish revolt against the archduke. In 1490 he was forced to withdraw to Sluis, a strategic point from which he posed a continuous threat to Maximilian's income from the Flemish trade, by raiding merchant ships and paralysing the Bruges market. (This played directly into the hands of the city's main rivals in Brabant, Antwerp and Bergen op Zoom, who sided with Maximilian.) Bruges initially supported Philip, but famine soon forced the city to surrender (Peace of Damme, 29 November 1490). These events provide the background for two records involving Jacob Obrecht in 1490.[72] In October of that year, the composer received a letter from Count Philip asking him to come to the castle of Sluis with four fellow singers to provide musical entertainment. Obrecht asked the chapter of St Donatian's on 15 October whether he could go with the singer-clerks Petrus Zouburch and Christianus Baelde (the other two singers who accompanied him are unknown, and presumably came from another church):[73]

The succentor *magister* Jacobus showed a letter of the lord Philippus de Cleves, in which [the latter] commands him to come to Sluis with four singer-clerks to raise morale there; [Obrecht showed the letter] to ask my lords to grant permission to himself together with *domini* Christianus Baelde and Petrus Zuburch. My lords agreed to his request for [a period of] six or eight days, out of regard to the lord Philippus.

[71] It is tempting to assume that it was Jean Cordier who might have persuaded the chapter to repeal its decision. Being a canon of St Donatian's himself, and one of the most celebrated singers of his time, he would have carried special authority. Cordier spoke on Obrecht's behalf in 1487, as we have seen, and would do so again in 1500, when the composer was too ill to appear before the chapter of St Donatian's (see Ch. 9).

[72] A third record survives in the Bruges city accounts of 2 Sept. 1489 to 2 Sept. 1490 (fo. 166ᵛ): 'Paid at the command and with the consent of my lords of the law, the captain, and the deans of this city, to Jacob Obrechts, priest and cantor [*recte*: succentor] of the church of St Donatian in Bruges, and his companions, because they have sung the daily *Lof* and Salve every night in the aforesaid church, to the honour and dignity of the glorious Virgin Mary, together with bell-ringing, organ-playing, and candle-lighting, for one year [which] passed in May [14]90, 4,800 Flemish groats.' The payment is transcribed in Vander Straeten, *La Musique aux Pays-Bas*, iii. 183.

[73] De Schrevel, *Histoire*, i. 51–2.

More than five weeks later, on 22 November, Obrecht approached the chapter with another request. At this time the Bruges famine was at its worst: only a week later the city would surrender. The composer had supported the choirboys from his own income 'for a long time', in loyalty to the church and its rulers. But now he could no longer cope, and asked the chapter to provide relief:[74]

On 22 November 1490 *dominus* Jacobus Hobrecht, succentor of this church, appeared [before the chapter], declaring that [although] corn has been very expensive for a long time, and still is, he has so far quite willingly fed the choristers, on account of the honour of the church and its lords, from whom he has received much income, in which support he has lost much [money]; [but] because corn is valued beyond all reason, and can hardly be found for any money whatsoever, he is not able to support the said choristers properly if their lord-ships do not make provisions from above. My lords, aware of the abundance of money and the scarcity of corn in this city, and [of the fact] that one can hardly buy a *hoet* of wheat [166-72 litres] for 720 groats, nevertheless replied to the succentor in greatest friendship that he should have patience until the day of the chapter-meeting, and meanwhile they would make arrangements.

[note in the margin:] The succentor answered that he could not support the choristers.[75]

The times of severest hardship were soon over, but Obrecht did not stay at Bruges much longer. Two months later, on 17 January 1491, he was discharged by the chapter of St Donatian's (his last recorded activity at the church was on 22 January):[76]

And it was then decided that *dominus* Petrus Basyn should have the government of the choirboys of this church until the church should have provided for a [new] succentor, and I was charged to tell [Obrecht] amicably that my lords had dismissed him because of the better (*propter melius*).

The reason for Obrecht's discharge is specified in only one word, 'melius', which may mean almost anything in this context, including better

[74] Transcription in Vander Straeten, *La Musique aux Pays-Bas*, iii. 184.

[75] It was evidently Obrecht's *non possum* that compelled the chapter, at their meeting two days later, to relent, and to allow the choristers to have their meals in turns at the table of the canons (De Schrevel, *Histoire*, i. 45).

[76] De Schrevel, *Histoire*, i. 164. Obrecht evidently left of his own accord, and apparently without prior notification, for the chapter of St Donatian's had great difficulty in finding a successor. The church recruited an interim succentor, Pierre Basin, from among its own canons. On 14 Mar. 1491 Aliamus de Groote, one of the church's chaplains, came in his place. Two weeks later another chaplain, Johannes Blijman, was elected, but he turned down the offer. Only on 20 Apr. did the chapter finally succeed in attracting a permanent succentor, Hieronymus de Clibano of 's-Hertogen-bosch, but since he did not take up his duties until twenty months later, Pierre Basin was once again asked to fill in. See for this ibid. 164-5, and J. Bouws, 'Jeronimus de Clibano van 's-Hertogenbosch (±1460-1503), zangmeester in Brugge en Antwerpen', *Vlaamsch jaarboek voor muziekgeschiedenis*, 2/3 (1940-1), 77-8.

payment (or a lighter work-load) elsewhere. It is clear in any case that Obrecht and the church of St Donatian parted on friendly terms. Not only was the chapter happy to reappoint the composer eight years later 'in locum suum pristinum',[77] but nothing in the preceding eight-month period suggests that he was out of favour.

The composer's moves in the eight to seventeen months following his final discharge are unknown; he may have found employment elsewhere, but it is also possible that he stayed at Bruges for a while. In any case, he reappears more than a year later, on 24 June 1492, in the annual accounts of the Guild of Our Lady at Antwerp, where he is paid for activity as a choirmaster over an unspecified period (though certainly less than about eight months). Obrecht's move to Antwerp coincides with the rise of that city's economic fortunes, and the return of peace and stability to the southern Netherlands. The next six years of his life would be comparatively uneventful: the years of crisis, so far as we can tell, had ended.

---

[77] This chapter decision, made on 31 Dec. 1498, is transcribed in Vander Straeten, *La Musique aux Pays-Bas*, iii. 183 (a translation is given below, Ch. 9).

6 THE CRITICAL PHASE

As succentor at St Donatian's, Jacob Obrecht faced a demand for new mass music that must have been greater than at any other time in his life.[1] His tasks included the writing of a new mass every year for the Feast of Cripples (celebrated on Thursday in Whit week). The Rogation Days similarly required an annual newly composed mass—and this in competition with his colleagues at St Saviour's and Our Lady's. From 1488 the *beianenfeest* (the feast of the Newcomers to the school; Easter Monday), and from 1489 the Feast of Asses (in the week after Epiphany), required annual polyphonic masses; the responsibility for supplying these fell again to the succentor. For Obrecht this increasing burden meant writing two new masses per year in 1485–7, and four per year after his return from Ferrara in late 1488—a maximum total of thirteen during his period of service in Bruges. And the almost explosive growth of commemorations and other private services raised the demand for new polyphonic cycles even more. It is likely that the composer wrote settings for such occasions as well; in two cases it is virtually certain that he did.[2]

[1] For this and what follows, see Strohm, *Music in Late Medieval Bruges*, 33–59.

[2] It is quite unusual to find 15th-c. musicians being expected to supply polyphony on a regular basis. The only other documented example known to me is that of Durham Cathedral Priory, which from 1487 onwards required its cantor and master of the Lady Chapel choir to compose each year a new mass in four or five parts in honour of God, the Virgin Mary, and St Cuthbert; see F. Ll. Harrison, *Music in Medieval Britain* (London, 1958), 187 and 429–30. Obrecht, however, was not so much contractually obliged as expected to provide polyphony. His predecessors and successors in Bruges (Aliamus de Groote, Pierre Basin, and Hieronymus de Clibano) have left hardly any mass settings at all. (A 'Missa nova domini Aliani [de Groote]' was copied at St Donatian's in 1476–7; see A. Dewitte, 'Boek- en bibliotheekwezen in de Brugse Sint-Donaaskerk XIIIe–XVe eeuw', in *Sint-Donaas en de voormalige Brugse Katedraal* (Bruges, 1978), 93). Possibly their music was not valued highly enough to be transmitted, like Obrecht's, in German and Italian sources. It is equally possible that they did not supply as much polyphony as Obrecht probably did. Relevant here is Roger Bowers's observation: 'As a general rule, it seems that for his employers, any musician's talent for composition was just a windfall—a bonus they were probably glad of when it manifested itself, but one which they had no particular right to expect, and did not normally attempt to demand, of any of their musicians' ('Obligation, Agency, and *Laissez-faire*: The Promotion of Polyphonic Composition for the Church in Fifteenth-Century England', in I. Fenlon (ed.), *Music in Medieval and Early Modern Europe: Patronage, Sources and Texts* (Cambridge, 1981), 11).

So in terms of what his position required, Obrecht should have composed at least fifteen masses during the years 1485–91. How sure can we be that he did? There is no reason to doubt that he was capable of writing new compositions at great speed: his 'quickness of invention and abundance of creativity' were to become legendary.[3] And it so happens that the church fabric accounts of St Donatian's show a sudden increase in the number of copying payments for masses exactly in the period of Obrecht's activity in Bruges (1485/6–1491/2). Eight of the twenty-two masses copied in these years are described specifically as 'new'—an adjective not used since 1476/7 (for a mass by Obrecht's predecessor Aliamus de Groote) and not used again until 1498/9 (when Obrecht was again succentor).[4]

In fact the possibility of a creative outburst in these years is independently suggested by musical evidence. The indications are that within one or two years after his move to Bruges, Obrecht left the compositional paths he had been pursuing until then. While the early 1480s had been a period of gradual stylistic evolution, the second half of that decade witnessed rapid changes in his musical idiom. The exact course and chronology of these developments are hard to establish. The earliest datable work from the Bruges period, the *Missa De Sancto Martino* of 1486, still links up with the stylistic trends of the previous years. The same is true of the more forward-looking *Missa Ave regina celorum*, which was presumably written in the mid- to late 1480s as well. But in other masses from these years it is more difficult to discern clearly any continued trend. The *Missa Salve diva parens*, copied in 1487–8, has some elements in common with earlier cycles, but on the whole it stands alone in Obrecht's mass *œuvre*; several of its features are so uncharacteristic of the composer that one might well be tempted to question his authorship. Closely contemporary with it is the *Missa De Sancto Donatiano* of 1487, likewise a highly atypical work, albeit in an entirely different way. The pronounced stylistic differences between these four masses, written within the space of perhaps

---

[3] Glareanus, *Dodekachordon*, 456: 'ingenii celeritas ac inventionis copia', a quality that Obrecht demonstrated, according to the theorist, by writing a mass in one night. See also 296: 'Iacobus Hobrechth ut qui copia omnes suae aetatis cantores . . . superabat'.

[4] See Dewitte, 'Boek- en bibliotheekwezen', 92–5, for excerpts from the fabric accounts (my italics): 1485/6 ('pro scriptura *nove* misse decantate in festo claudorum'), 1486/7 ('pro notatione unius misse *nove* decantate in Ardenburch in festo claudorum'), 1488/9 ('pro scriptura 4or missarum *novarum*' and 'pro scriptura misse in festa beianorum *confecte*'), 1489/90 ('pro scriptura misse *nove* decantate in festo pape azinorum'), 1491/2 ('pro scriptura unius misse *nove* composite per magistrum Jacobum Hobrecht'; see also Doc. 45), and then not until 1498/9 ('pro scriptura unius misse *nove* edite ter crepelfeeste'). By contrast, the payments for the copying of a set of sixteen masses in 1468/9 and another set of sixteen masses in 1470/1 (ibid. 90–1) do not use the adjective *novus*, and more likely reflect scribal activity after the arrival of substantial mass repertories from elsewhere.

two or three years, suggest that major changes of compositional direction took place around 1486–7.

There are no firmly dated pieces from the next few years, and consequently we lose track of Obrecht's stylistic development. But from slightly later evidence it can be deduced that this period must have been among the most productive, and stylistically most innovative, phases in Obrecht's career. Recent manuscript studies have independently indicated that several of the composer's most advanced masses—including two that were previously thought to date from the last years of his life[5]—existed in fact as early as about 1491–3, that is, more than a decade before his death. The masses in question are *Je ne demande* (paper dating: 1487–91), *Fortuna desperata* (paper dating: 1489–93), *Rose playsante* (paper dating: 1491–3), *Plurimorum carminum I* (copying date: 1487–90), and *Plurimorum carminum II* (paper dating: 1491–3).[6] These dates are unexpectedly early: stylistically the five masses seem much further removed from *De Sancto Martino* than the chronological distance of only five years would suggest. More problematically, perhaps, if an unquestionably 'late' work like *Fortuna desperata* existed by 1493, one wonders how Obrecht's style developed in the remaining twelve years of his life: with the exception of *Maria zart*, no mass moves beyond its style firmly enough for us to say with confidence that it cannot be earlier. But however that may be, the evidence seems to suggest that the rate of stylistic change reached a peak in the years 1485–91, and slowed down thereafter. This in turn supports what was suggested by the documentary evidence: the Bruges period must have been an extraordinarily productive one for Obrecht. The masses he composed there as succentor must cover the entire stylistic range between *De Sancto Martino* and *Fortuna desperata*. This might suggest a total of more than fifteen pieces, and would leave little more than a handful of works for the last decade of the composer's life—chief among them *Maria zart*, *Sub tuum presidium*, and probably *Si dedero* and *Cela sans plus* (see Ch. 10).

Obrecht's career may thus follow a pattern that we find in several other

---

[5] *Je ne demande* and *Fortuna desperata*; see Finscher, *MGG* 9, col. 1820.

[6] For *Missa Fortuna desperata* see M. Just, *Der Mensuralkodex Mus. ms. 40021 der Staatsbibliothek Preußischer Kulturbesitz Berlin: Untersuchungen zum Repertoire einer deutschen Quelle des 15. Jahrhunderts* (Tutzing, 1975), ii. 28. For *Plurimorum carminum I*, see *NOE* 10, p. xii. For the other three masses, see Noblitt, 'Die Datierung', 49. The anonymous *Missa N'aray-je jamais*, which is closely related to *Je ne demande* and *Rose playsante*, and probably by Obrecht as well (see Ch. 8), was copied on paper dating 1492 (Just, *Der Mensuralkodex*, ii. 27). It is true that watermark evidence needs to be handled with a margin of error, even if the identification with dated paper is absolutely certain (in which case the margin can be reduced to about two to four years on either side). In the present case the evidence is, however, highly consistent: several closely related masses survive independently on different types of paper, all of which are documented in the years around 1491–3 (see also Ch. 8, n. 1).

composers' biographies: the rate of production depends not so much on individual creative impulses as on necessity and demand. Most fifteenth-century choirmasters, particularly those working in the North, wrote as much or as little liturgical music as their positions required. There was no financial incentive for them to write polyphony, merely the expectation that they would provide it when necessary, in return for an assured and regular income. If the demand for new polyphony was small, so much the better, for the work-load was heavy to begin with, and it made no difference financially. Even for a man as talented as Obrecht, composition was not a profession in the accepted sense of the word: in terms of income, social position, and everyday activities he was primarily a singer, teacher, and priest.

In the following chapters our goal will be to reconstruct, by interpolation, the stylistic developments between the fixed chronological points of 1486–7 and 1491–3. In doing so it will emerge that Obrecht's idiom became increasingly formalized towards the early 1490s. In contrast to earlier masses, each of which seemed to adopt a different approach to compositional issues, most of the mature ones appear to be realizations of one and the same stylistic concept. This process towards stylistic uniformity may well reflect the increasing speed with which the works were written. Before his mature style emerged, however, Obrecht seems to have gone through a critical phase in the years 1486–8: a brief period during which he was apparently unsure whether to continue the stylistic trends of his earlier works, and experimented with various other styles. Besides the three firmly dated masses *De Sancto Martino*, *De Sancto Donatiano*, and *Salve diva parens*, I would assign to this phase *Adieu mes amours*. The internal chronology of this group is difficult to reconstruct, for each mass is in a number of respects unlike the others, and some are in fact totally unlike anything else Obrecht ever wrote. If any feature holds these masses together, it is probably the new emphasis on freedom and irregularity—in style and structure, as well as in tenor treatment. These are qualities one would not immediately associate with Obrecht; they seem to have been the result, at least initially, of his continued emulation of the style of Johannes Ockeghem.

Missa De Sancto Martino

The *Missa De Sancto Martino* is the most conservative of the masses written around 1486–7.[7] Stylistically it is closely linked to the cycles discussed so far; the main difference is that it is based upon a series of chants rather than on one recurring tenor. The chants, eight antiphons and an invitatory from the Office of St Martin of Tours, are stated successively in the course of the mass. Masses with multiple cantus firmi, dedicated to one feast, seem to have been widespread in the Low Countries. Besides Obrecht's masses for St Martin and St Donatian there are the masses *De Sancto Livino* by Mattheus Pipelare, *De Sancto Job* and *Pascale* by Pierre de La Rue, *Super Maria Magdalena* by Nicholas Champion, and the anonymous mass *De Sancto Johanne Baptista* (see Ch. 7).[8]

Although the masses of this type are very similar structurally, they have little in common stylistically. Each composer used the common layout merely as a framework, filling in the contrapuntal details according his own stylistic habits and preferences. This is certainly true of the *Missa De Sancto Martino*, in which one can recognize several of Obrecht's favourite early devices: free elaboration of a chant melody with mensural transformation, strict repeats of the Kyrie version, and cantus-firmus-based head-motifs. The continued application of these devices is of considerable interest: it is as though Obrecht deliberately conflated two different types of mass layout, in such a way that the nine cantus firmi of *De Sancto Martino* parallel the seven or eight different rhythmizations of *Beata*

---

[7] For this mass, see Meier, *Studien zur Meßkomposition*, 5–7 and 99–100; Salop, 'The Masses of Jacob Obrecht', 80–6; Sparks, *Cantus Firmus*, 278–82. For the historical background, see Strohm, *Music in Late Medieval Bruges*, 40–1, and *NOE* 3, pp. xxvii–xxviii. For the cantus firmi, see M. J. Bloxam, 'A Survey of Late Medieval Service Books from the Low Countries: Implications for Sacred Polyphony, 1460–1520' (Ph.D. diss., Yale University, 1987), 288–98, and ead., 'Sacred Polyphony and Local Traditions of Liturgy and Plainsong: Reflections on Music by Jacob Obrecht', in T. F. Kelly (ed.), *Plainsong in the Age of Polyphony* (Cambridge, 1992), 140–77. Bloxam, while not questioning that *De Sancto Martino* was written for the endowment of 1486, nevertheless believes that Obrecht cannot have written the cycle at Bruges, since two of the antiphons do not occur in a breviary of St Donatian's printed in 1520 ('A Survey', 292–6). Postulating the notion of a unified 'usage of Bruges', represented by this single surviving breviary, she argues that Obrecht wrote the mass at Antwerp after 1491 (one of several places where the antiphons do happen to be documented). This hypothesis seems somewhat implausible, even disregarding the stylistic incongruity with works that have been reliably dated in the early 1490s (see Ch. 8). By 1491 Obrecht was no longer required to provide music for the endowment, and would not have needed to write a mass, since *some* setting by him must have been available since 1486 anyway. Moreover, the 1520 breviary was printed for the main altar of St Donatian's, whereas Obrecht's mass was composed for the side-altar of St Martin; there would almost certainly have been differences in usage, particularly in the liturgy for St Martin, who was the patron saint of the side-chapel.

[8] The cantus firmi of these masses are discussed in Bloxam, 'A Survey of Late Medieval Service Books', and 'Sacred Polyphony and Local Traditions'.

viscera or *Sicut spina rosam*. For instance, the chant presented in the Kyrie (*Martinus adhuc cathecuminus*) is the only one to be used in more than one section: it recurs literally in the Osanna. The Kyrie tenor is presented in three different mensurations; although this does not affect its rhythm (the melody is written entirely in breves), we are reminded of the Kyrie tenors of *Beata viscera* and *Sicut spina rosam*, which are given similar prominence by restatement in different mensurations.

Free elaboration with mensural transformation plays an important role in the mass. To mention one example, the rhythmization of *Dixerunt discipuli* that is stated in the Et in terra recurs under a different mensuration (and consequently in a different rhythmic shape) in the Qui tollis. Likewise, the Patrem is based on a twofold statement (with mensural transformation) of a single notated chant paraphrase of *O virum ineffabilem*. This recalls similar procedures in the Glorias of *Petrus apostolus* and *Sicut spina rosam* (see Ch. 4). The only difference with the latter masses is the presence of a verbal canon instructing the singers to leave out all the rests in the repeat.[9]

Cantus-firmus-based head-motifs are found in the Gloria and Credo.[10] The main difference from earlier masses, of course, is that the head-motifs now vary according to the chants being used, and fulfil no unifying role: they are mere relics of an older practice. Thus the Et in terra opens with a duo that quotes about a third of the tenor melody, *Dixerunt discipuli*. This 'pre-imitation' is not entirely literal (as was the case in all previous masses); only in bars 5–9 does the introduction correspond exactly with the tenor, bars 16–20. In the Patrem the opening duo states the entire

---

[9] 'Dum replicas tantum sine pausis tu tenorisa' (*NOE* 3, p. xxxii). This procedure, which recalls the canon 'Clama ne cesses' in the Agnus Dei III of Josquin's *Missa L'homme armé super voces musicales*, does not affect the rhythm, since the tenor contains breve rests only. Obrecht's verbal canon recalls a similar instruction in the Et in terra of an anonymous *Missa Sine nomine* in SienBC K.1.2, fo. 150ᵛ: 'Dum replicas canta sine pausis tu tenorista'. This interesting work shares a second feature with the *Missa De Sancto Martino*: the top voice of the Et incarnatus quotes the relevant portion of Credo I, in a version identical in every variant to the one used by Obrecht in his Et incarnatus (see below). The mass in the Siena manuscript does not appear to be based on one recurring tenor, but there are several internal repeats of what appear to be cantus firmi. The tenor of the Et incarnatus, for instance, is literally restated in the bass of the Et resurrexit. Since the latter section is a trio, we are reminded here of two three-voice sections in the *Missa De Sancto Martino* that state the cantus firmus in the bass (Domine Fili and Pleni). Moreover, like the cantus firmi of several three-voice sections in Obrecht's mass, the tenor shared by the two sections is rhythmized in equal breves, and is divided into brief phrases by means of breve rests (see below). It is perhaps suggestive that the *Sine nomine* mass immediately precedes Obrecht's *Missa Beata viscera* in the Siena manuscript. The scope of this study does not allow further discussion of the possibility of his authorship.

[10] Although the Sanctus has a long introductory duo (bars 1–13), this opening does not quote the cantus firmus of that section, *Adoremus Christum*. However, the contratenor of the duo appears to quote the first half of *Martinus episcopus* (which itself appears in the Et resurrexit).

cantus firmus of that section (*O virum ineffabilem*) before it appears in the tenor. The only other known mass by Obrecht to present a full statement of the cantus firmus in a head-motif is *Sicut spina rosam* (see Ch. 4). But Obrecht avoids the strictly bipartite motto-tenor structure maintained in that mass, by compressing the 'pre-imitation' rhythmically. As a consequence, the relationship in length between duo and tenor statement (not counting breve rests in the latter) is 13 + 31 bars. The reason for Obrecht's flexibility here is not difficult to imagine: a bipartite structure of 31 + 31 bars would be impractically long.

As regards cantus-firmus treatment, the *Missa De Sancto Martino* looks to the past rather than the future. One of the many features linking it to the four cycles discussed so far is canon or quasi-canon based upon cantus-firmus material (Et in Spiritum). Noteworthy too is the variety of treatment, a feature typical of early masses by Obrecht: in some sections the chant melodies are freely ornamented into graceful melodic lines, while in others the tenors are cast rigidly in equal breves. This recalls the masses *Petrus apostolus* and *Beata viscera*, where free paraphrase is likewise alternated with equal-note treatment (see Ch. 4). But this time Obrecht's motivation in applying the equal-note procedure seems to be different. In the Pleni the chant *Ego signo crucis* is not only stated in equal breves, but each group of notes underlaid with one word is separated from the next such group by a breve rest. Similar 'punctuation' by means of breve rests occurs in the Domine Fili, Et incarnatus, Et resurrexit, and Et in Spiritum. Barton Hudson pertinently notes that this procedure 'calls to mind those chant books from the period in which barlines appear after each word or two of the text, without regard to the phrase design of the melody'.[11] That Obrecht was indeed concerned to retain the *visual* aspect of the original notation is clear from his treatment of the doxology of *Ego signo crucis*: rather than resolving the 'euouae' formula into the full psalm plus doxology, he treats it as a melody in its own right—which obviously makes no sense from the liturgical point of view. It is almost as if the composer wanted his singers to be able to perform the tenor part from a chant book.[12] Obrecht's mentality here may be related to his later

---

[11] *NOE* 3, p. xxvii.

[12] It is possible that Obrecht alluded in these sections to singing *super librum* (improvised counterpoint), which he is known to have taught to a Cambrai singer only a year before *De Sancto Martino* was written (see Ch. 5). The fact that the composer does not resolve the 'euouae' formula confirms that he looks at the original chant notation with mensural eyes only, interpreting square notes as breves and vertical dashes as breve rests. This procedure was described by Johannes Tinctoris in his treatise on counterpoint, bk. 2, ch. 22 (*Opera theoretica*, ii. 119): 'Indeed, a similar counterpoint is made over a plainchant when the notes of that plainchant are measured according to their shapes, which are those of longas, breves, and semibreves, in whatever mensural relationships

tendency to notate mensural mass tenors exactly as he finds them, down to the minutest scribal details.[13] Another feature that is to recur in some later works is quotation from Credo I in the Et incarnatus: this also happens in the mass *Grecorum*, while *Fors seulement* and *Plurimorum carminum I* present the entire melody in the tenor and top voice, respectively, of the Credo. Obrecht uses the same melodic version of the Et incarnatus in all four masses, and interestingly, that version differs considerably from the known versions of Credo I. This may indicate that the four cycles were written in the same place, a possibility that is supported by other evidence (see below, Ch. 8).

The general stylistic impression of *De Sancto Martino* is one of moderation, even of modesty. Unlike many of Obrecht's later cycles, this is not an outgoing, showy piece, nor does it display the variety and wealth of invention of masses like *Sicut spina rosam* or *Salve diva parens*. It is a work of competent craftsmanship, as befits the purpose for which it was written. Devices like imitation and sequential repetition are used with restraint: the only major exception is the second Kyrie, which exhibits a type of chain structure that recalls *O lumen ecclesie*: the tenor is stated in long note-values, while the other voices exchange and imitate two-bar motifs around it. This lends a sense of lucid periodicity to the section uncharacteristic of the mass as a whole. In most sections the polyphony flows forward without marked interruption: cadences or changes of scoring are not dramatized but tend to be played down; the imitations do not generate momentum, but are taken up in the contrapuntal stride; the melodic lines flow gently, and avoid leaps or energetic rhythmic patterns. Taken together, these qualities recall the style of Ockeghem, to whose *Mi–mi* mass Obrecht seems to refer once again, in the very first bars of the mass.[14] *De Sancto Martino* seems closer to Ockeghem than *Sicut spina rosam* in that various procedures common to both works are handled with a greater degree of flexibility and irregularity. As we shall see below, Obrecht was to move even closer to Ockeghem in the *Missa De Sancto Donatiano*.

To sum up, the *Missa De Sancto Martino* is the sort of work one might have expected Obrecht to write for a private liturgical occasion in a side-chapel shortly after his arrival in Bruges. He still relies on stylistic and

[*quantitates*] you like' (my translation; I am indebted to Andrew Kirkman for drawing this passage to my attention).

[13] This is almost certainly a Busnoys-inspired feature. A similar concern with the visual aspect of the original notation of a mass tenor characterizes the anonymous *Missa L'ardant desir* of about 1470, which I have argued elsewhere must be by Busnoys (Wegman, 'Another Mass by Busnoys?', 7–11).

[14] First noted by David Fallows in his review of Strohm's *Music in Late Medieval Bruges*, in *Early Music History*, 6 (1986), 283.

technical devices explored in earlier works, but clearly has no intention of exploring them further. The devices figure as the most progressive elements in a contrapuntal idiom that is otherwise remarkably conservative—and they are handled with little apparent enthusiasm. Given this attitude, it is perhaps no coincidence that one of Obrecht's very next masses would be virtually purged of even those elements: the *Missa De Sancto Donatiano* of 1487 is arguably one of Obrecht's most conservative works, a cycle, indeed, that would not have looked out of place in a choirbook from the early 1470s. But other stylistic directions were also possible, and Obrecht explored these as well: the *Missa Salve diva parens* (copied in the same year that *De Sancto Donatiano* was composed) is an exuberant, virtuoso work that foreshadows if not the style, then certainly the temperament of Obrecht's mature masses.

Missa De Sancto Donatiano

The *Missa De Sancto Donatiano* is a multiple-cantus-firmus mass of the same type as its companion, *De Sancto Martino*.[15] All movements are based on chants taken from the liturgy of St Donatian; two additional cantus firmi that have no relation to the saint appear in the Christe and Et resurrexit. (In the former section, unusually, it is a Dutch devotional song, *Gefft den armen gefangen*.) The two masses are thus related in structure and layout. Yet although they were written within the space of one year, there is one major difference between them: nearly all of Obrecht's favourite early devices, while still present in *De Sancto Martino*, have disappeared in *De Sancto Donatiano*.

For instance, although the antiphon *O beate pater Donatiane* functions as a 'primary' cantus firmus comparable to *Martinus adhuc* (it is stated three times in the Kyrie, and twice each in the Sanctus and Agnus Dei), none of its seven shapes is notationally identical with any of the others. Consequently there is no opportunity for mensural transformation.[16] Given Obrecht's prominent and consistent employment of that technique in all cycles discussed so far, particularly with Kyrie tenors, it is difficult

---

[15] For this mass, see Meier, *Studien zur Meßkomposition*, 7–9; Sparks, *Cantus Firmus*, 472–3; Salop, 'The Masses of Jacob Obrecht', 77–80; A. B. Wathey, 'Isoperiodic Technique in "Cantus Firmus" Organisation, *c.*1400–*c.*1475' (Research Paper, St Edmund Hall, Oxford, 1979), in particular ch. 2, 26–44 ('Obrecht's "Missa Sancti Donatiani" as a Descendant of Ockeghem's "Missa Ecce ancilla Domini"'). I am grateful to Dr Wathey for sharing a copy of his research paper. For the cantus firmi, see Bloxam, 'A Survey of Late Medieval Service Books', 275–88, and *NOE* 3, pp. xi–xiii. For the historical background see Strohm, *Music in Late Medieval Bruges*, 146–7, and *NOE* 3, pp. xiii–xv (Strohm).

[16] A minor exception is the internal repeat in 2 : 1 diminution in the Christe.

not to regard this as a conscious choice. The mass also differs from all previous works in that its six-bar head-motif is not chant-based; consequently there are no bipartite motto-tenor structures in the cycle, not even of the modified type used in *De Sancto Martino*.[17] Cantus-firmus-based canon or quasi-canon is not employed at all, although there are some passing reminiscences of the device in the Gloria (bars 32–41 and 47–50) and Sanctus (bars 14–24). Rigidly maintained chain structures, already rare in *De Sancto Martino* (second Kyrie), are abandoned altogether. Likewise absent is the equal-note-rhythmization of chant cantus firmi that was used so prominently in *De Sancto Martino*: flexibility and freedom of treatment have become the norm.[18]

On all fronts, then, Obrecht breaks with the stylistic traditions he had been pursuing thus far. This is perhaps the clearest sign that the years 1486–7 represent a critical moment in his creative career. At the same time, however, the composer continues a trend that we observed for the first time in *Sicut spina rosam*: emulation of the style of Johannes Ockeghem. It is surely no coincidence that each of the devices omitted from *De Sancto Donatiano* is schematic in nature: Ockeghem himself avoided these same qualities in his mature works. What remains is a mass so uncharacteristic of Obrecht that one would scarcely have suspected his authorship without the manuscript attribution. Most conspicuous by its absence is the composer's typical tendency to extend and develop individual devices with relentless logic. Imitation, sequence, and other motivic devices are used sparingly, and hardly ever is the composer tempted to maintain them for more than a few bars: most of the time he seems content merely to enliven the counterpoint with brief hints of imitation or gentle motivic play. His guiding principles here seem to be restraint and 'good taste'.

The Patrem provides a good illustration of Obrecht's changed attitude (see Ex. 13). For the first time since *Petrus apostolus* all five movements have exactly the same opening: the superius and contratenor present this head-motif in bars 1–6. In any mass from the 1460s or 1470s the cadence

---

[17] The only other mass to use a freely invented head-motif (i.e. without a pre-emptive imitation of the cantus firmus) is *De Sancto Johanne Baptista*. Bipartite motto-tenor openings recur briefly only in two masses, *Salve diva parens* (Credo) and *Ave regina celorum* (Gloria and Credo). None of Obrecht's later masses makes use of head-motif procedures of any kind.

[18] Among the very few features that link *De Sancto Donatiano* to earlier masses is the migration of the melody *Gefft den armen gefangen* in the second Kyrie: bars 61–85 of the contratenor are literally restated (though transposed down a fifth) in bars 87–111 of the bass, while the tenor states the cantus firmus *O beate pater Donatiane*. This somewhat recalls the 'migrant scaffolding' in the Et in Spiritum and Benedictus–Osanna of the *Missa Sicut spina rosam* (see Ch. 4), but closer parallels to that procedure are found in *Salve diva parens* (see below).

concluding the head-motif would function as a signal either for imitative extensions (as in the Gloria of *De Sancto Donatiano*) or for the entry of the tenor in long note-values, as in the Kyrie, Sanctus, and Agnus Dei. In the Credo, however, Obrecht seems intent on deceiving the listener. When the voice labelled 'tenor' joins the top voice–contratenor duo, it does everything this part is traditionally not meant to do: it enters prematurely, before receiving its 'cue' from the cadence, and rather than presenting pre-existent material in long note-values, it drops in on an off-beat, with free material. Bars 6–14 present a freely composed extension of the head-motif, in which the three voices anticipate the entry of the proper cantus firmus. When this passage is concluded with a cadence on A in bar 14, the tenor suddenly starts behaving as though it *were* the cantus firmus: on the down-beat of the cadence, right on cue, it 'enters' with a note on A lasting three bars. Since this drawn-out note is immediately surrounded by two voices moving in parallel tenths (bars 14–16), the listener could be forgiven for thinking that somehow the cantus firmus has finally made its appearance. In fact that is precisely what happened, but one would have to listen very carefully to hear the actual entry, half a beat late, and cleverly placed in the parallel tenths accompanying the tenor: it is the bass that sings the responsory *O sanctissime presul*, in the most subservient contrapuntal role possible.

The subsequent music very much recalls the freely flowing 'Ockeghemian' quality of *Sicut spina rosam* (cf. Ex. 10 in particular): irregular textural changes, almost impressionistic painting with shades of dark and bright tone colour, exchanges of brief motifs (bars 28–30; too short to call them imitations), and irregularly placed cadences (which even led the editor to reinterpret the metre of bars 25–38). The main difference between the two works is the total absence of *any* schematic procedure of internal organization in *De Sancto Donatiano*. After Obrecht's faithful adherence to such procedures in all masses discussed so far, even in *De Sancto Martino*, their absence here can only be interpreted as a deliberate decision.

Quite possibly it was the example of Ockeghem that led him to make that choice: two quotations discovered by Andrew Wathey confirm that Obrecht had Ockeghem in mind while writing the St Donatian mass.[19] First, the first seven notes of the bass in Obrecht's Kyrie I are identical with the corresponding notes in Ockeghem's *Missa Ecce ancilla Domini*. While this could conceivably be coincidence, that objection cannot be raised to the second correspondence discovered by Wathey: the first five bars of four-part writing in Obrecht's Osanna are identical with the

[19] 'Isoperiodic Technique', 31–2.

Ex. 13. Obrecht, *Missa De Sancto Donatiano*, Patrem, bars 1–31

same passage in *Ecce ancilla*. The relationship is unmistakable, and yet, compared with other tributes in Obrecht masses (e.g. *Sicut spina rosam*, *L'homme armé*, and *Caput*), the two allusions strike us as untypically casual and brief: would one not have expected the composer to quote in a more rigidly schematic fashion? The fact that he does not seems significant; it shows, I believe, how consistent and well-thought-out a piece *De Sancto Donatiano* is. For even while alluding to Ockeghem, Obrecht appears to be emulating him, by exercising the very same restraint that characterizes his handling of devices such as imitation and sequence. Whatever his reasons for imitating the older master, Obrecht did it with deliberation and fore-thought. The result is not a slavish copy but an imaginative reflection on Ockeghem's style.[20]

But there is another side to this coin. Although Obrecht shows a vir-tuoso command of a style that was very difficult to emulate, the writing of stylistic replicas, no matter how skilfully, could hardly be his composi-tional destination in the long run. Masses like *O lumen ecclesie, Sicut spina rosam*, and even *De Sancto Martino* reveal a distinctive musical person-ality, yet in *De Sancto Donatiano* that personality is hidden under Ockeghem's shadow. Obrecht's strength, in early as well as late works, lies in the tenacity with which he pursues individual ideas, the directness and force of his expression, the simplicity of his means, the rhythmic energy of his lines, and his peculiar sense of rationality that seems at once rigid and playful. Yet in *De Sancto Donatiano* he goes out of his way to avoid those very qualities. We do not know whether Obrecht wrote the mass as a mere exercise in style (as though to prove a technical point to himself), or whether it may represent something of a creative identity crisis. Either way, it is in the nature of a faithful stylistic imitation that there is little point in writing another. In its outspoken conservatism the *Missa De Sancto Donatiano* occupies an extreme position within Obrecht's *œuvre*, a position that could only be relinquished once it had successfully been reached. But the writing of this mass had not been pointless. By com-pletely abandoning the habits and practices he had cultivated for so long, Obrecht in a sense wiped the slate clean, and created for himself the freedom to move on to new compositional challenges: beyond Ockeghem as well as Busnoys. By some coincidence this crucial development took place just weeks or months before the composer was invited to come to one of the most stimulating musical environments in Europe. On 14 October 1487, the day that the mass for St Donatian would have been first performed, his leave of absence to travel to Ferrara had taken effect.

---

[20] Shortly before this book went to press I had the opportunity to hear a recording of Obrecht's mass by The Orlando Consort, and this provided persuasive confirmation that *De Sancto Donatiano* must be a deliberate exercise in Ockeghem's mass style. Not only is the cycle pervaded with the spirit of Ockeghem in ways that are—like the latter's style itself—almost beyond verbal description (compare, for instance, Kyrie, bars 13–14, with Ockeghem's Gloria, bars 64–5), but there are numerous further resonances with parallel passages in *Ecce ancilla Domini*. To cite some of the more obvious examples: the climactic drive to the final cadence in Gloria, bars 166–70, is based on the same four-note motif as the parallel passage in Ockeghem's Gloria, bars 180–3 (*ut–re–ut–fa, re–mi–re–sol*); the final cadential flourish in the contratenor of Credo, bars 200–1, contains a slightly abridged quotation of the top voice in the parallel passage of Ockeghem's Credo, bars 244–6; the openings of the final Agnus Dei sections are based on similar tenor incipits, and an explicit reminder is given in bars 53–4, which recall bars 63–4 of Ockeghem's final Agnus Dei (all bar numbers of *Ecce ancilla Domini* cited from *Collected Works*, i. 79–98).

Missa Salve diva parens

When Obrecht departed for Italy, his *Missa Salve diva parens* was probably already in existence: it was copied in the Sistine Chapel by the same scribe who copied *De Sancto Donatiano*, presumably in late 1487 or early 1488.[21] *Salve diva parens* is a singular work; without the copying date it would have been difficult to place it anywhere in the composer's stylistic development. The isolated position of the mass suggests that it was written at a time when Obrecht was fundamentally reviewing his stylistic premisses.[22] The *Missa De Sancto Donatiano* confirms that this must have been the case around 1487.

One major difficulty in assessing the style of *Salve diva parens* is the uncertainty whether the mass is based on a pre-existent tune. Although four of the five tenors share the same opening motif of four to six notes, thereafter all obvious similarities disappear.[23] No melody with the incipit 'Salve diva parens' has so far been identified. Puzzlingly, however, there are some indications suggesting that a cantus prius factus may have been used. For instance, Ottaviano Petrucci labelled the mass as '*super* salue diua parens' in his *Misse Obreht* of 1503,[24] a description that clearly implies the use of pre-existent musical material. On the other hand, Petrucci may well have taken the presence of a cantus firmus for granted, even if he could not discover one himself, for the title has a chant-like ring. More persuasive is the fact that two sources for the mass, VienNB Mus. 15495 and LeipU 1494, have various parts of the tenor underlaid

---

[21] For this mass, see Meier, *Studien zur Meßkomposition*, 17–17a; M. Staehelin, 'Obrechtiana', *Tijdschrift van de Vereniging voor Nederlandse Muziekgeschiedenis*, 25/1 (1975), 20–3; Todd, 'Retrograde, Inversion', 62–4; Strohm, *Music in Late Medieval Bruges*, 148; Edgar Sparks, 'Obrecht, Jacob', *The New Grove*, xiii. 482; Hudson, 'On the Texting', 108–15. For the apparent date of the Sistine Chapel copy (VatS 51), see Hudson, 'Obrecht's Tribute to Ockeghem', 11 n. 17, and *NOE* 11, p. xii. The identity of the scribal hand with that of *De Sancto Donatiano* in VatS 35 was first observed by J. Llorens, *Capellae Sixtinae Codices musicis notis instructi sive manu scripti sive praelo expressi* (Studi e testi, 102; Vatican City, 1960), 72, and was confirmed by Jeffrey Dean (personal communication).

[22] Another possibility is that the mass is not by Obrecht at all, particularly since it is ascribed to him in only one of the six complete or substantially complete sources (Petrucci's *Misse Obreht*). Possible doubts about the authorship were dispelled, however, by Barton Hudson in *NOE* 11, p. xvi. From the stylistic point of view *Salve diva parens* is indeed much easier to accept as a work by Obrecht than, for instance, *De Sancto Donatiano* or *Adieu mes amours*: close inspection of the music reveals a number of features that recall the composer's early mass style (see below); such features are absent in the two other masses.

[23] Bernhard Meier reconstructed the first seven notes of a hypothetical cantus firmus and, very tentatively, a continuation of eight more notes, while stressing that *Missa Salve diva parens* may well present a mixture of freely composed and cantus-firmus-based music (*Studien zur Meßkomposition*, 17, and below, Ex. 16*b*).   [24] See *NOE* 11, p. xiii.

Pl. 11. Kyrie of *Missa Salve diva parens* (VienNB Mus. 15495; used by permission of the Österreichische Nationalbibliothek, Vienna)

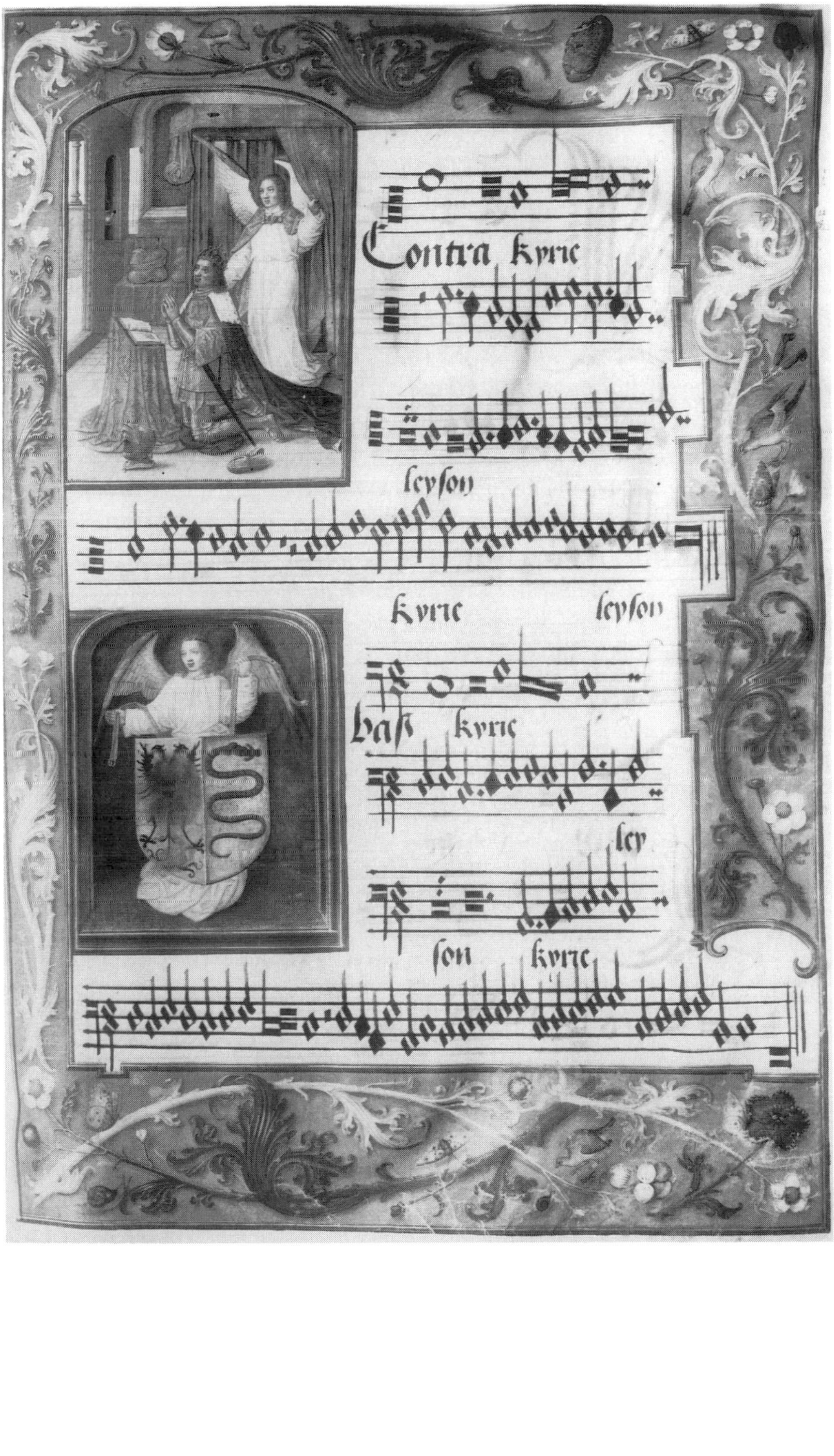
Contra kyrie
leyson
kyrie
leyson
Bass kyrie
ley
son
kyrie

with the same rhymed Latin poem (Pl. 11).[25] The full text as given by these sources runs, in Martin Staehelin's 'classicized' version:[26]

> Salve diva parens prolis amoenae,
> Aeternis meritis virgo sacrata,
> Qua lux vera, deus, fulsit in orbem
> Et carnem subiit rector Olympi.

Tenor underlay of this kind would normally suggest the presence of a pre-existent melody, particularly in a mass by Obrecht: with the exception of *Beata viscera* all cycles discussed so far, and three works to be discussed below (*Ave regina celorum*, *De Sancto Johanne Baptista*, and *Sub tuum presidium*), have the tenors underlaid with the appropriate cantus-firmus text in at least one source. Given this precedent, it would be difficult to explain similar underlay in the tenor if a mass were freely composed. A further important consideration is the fact that the metre of the poem ('sālvē dīvă părēns | prōlĭs ămēnē') is extremely rare but certainly post-classical, as Staehelin pointed out.[27] Reinhard Strohm has discovered a direct context for the poem. The hymn *O quam glorifica luce coruscas*, by the ninth-century Flemish musician Hucbald of Saint-Amand, is in the very same metre as *Salve diva parens*, a coincidence that suggests, as Strohm observes, that the possible cantus firmus is likely to be a hymn stanza.[28]

[25] See also the colour reproduction of VienNB Mus. 15495, fos. 1ʳ–2ʳ, in Heinrich Besseler and Peter Gülke, *Schriftbild der mehrstimmigen Musik* (Musikgeschichte in Bildern, 3/5; Leipzig, 1973), 114–15. Noteworthy is the illuminated initial for the top voice, which depicts a Nativity scene, and thus suggests that the *Missa Salve diva parens* may have some connection with Christmas.

[26] 'Obrechtiana', 21–2. For the manuscript readings, see *NOE* 11, pp. xxxii–xxxiii. Interestingly, LeipU 1494 also gives the incipit 'salve diva parens' at the beginning of the Confiteor: 'Confiteor [cancelled] Salve diva parens' (see *NOE* 11, p. xxxiv). Since the word 'Confiteor' is crossed out, performance of the non-Ordinary text was apparently the preferred option in this manuscript. More importantly, the placement of the incipit 'Salve diva parens' in the course of the Credo suggests that if the mass is based on a cantus firmus, the original tune may well appear more than once in each movement. The tenor of the Confiteor opens with a motif identical with that of the Cum sancto tenor, and with that used in the head-motif of the mass (see Meier, *Studien zur Meßkomposition*, 17).

[27] 'Obrechtiana', 22.

[28] *Music in Late Medieval Bruges*, 148. I am grateful to Leofranc Holford-Strevens, who writes as follows: 'The metre is discussed by two late-imperial grammarians, Terentianus Maurus (3rd c. AD), vv. 1939–56, ed. H. Keil, *Grammatici Latini*, vi (Leipzig, 1873–4), 383–4, and Aelius Festus Apthonius, ibid. 120. 12–121. 2, both probably drawing on Caesius Bassus (1st c. AD). The examples cited are artificial, but Apthonius asserts that it was frequent in the Greek poetess Sappho (early 6th c. BC); a possible example survives among her fragments, and a few in Greek drama. Though not used by classical Latin poets, it is found in Carolingian and later writers; the four-line stanza, though in any case appropriate for a hymn, perpetuates a feature of Horatian lyric even in a non-Horatian metre.'

Strohm notes a similarity between the tenor of *Salve diva parens* and the cantus firmus of Antoine Févin's *Missa O quam glorifica*. Barton Hudson objects that 'the similarity is at best vague and does not provide a basis for the assumption that [Févin's mass] has the same cantus firmus as *Missa Salve*

All this suggests not only the likelihood that pre-existent material was used, but offers concrete clues as to what that material might have looked like: we should be looking for a hymn stanza or hymn-like melody of at least $4 \times 11 = 44$ notes. In spite of this persuasive evidence, however, vertical alignments of the various tenor statements of *Salve diva parens* yield no clear results. Edgar Sparks's verdict thus remains valid: 'if there is [a cantus firmus], it is stated in such a way that it is impossible to be sure what the original notes are'.[29]

Part of the problem may lie in the way we try to solve it. Vertical alignments reveal melodic similarities, if any, between successive tenor statements, but they do not take account of how the tenor interacts with its counterparts, and what this interaction may tell us about its nature and treatment. In *Salve diva parens* the functional relationships between the voices appear to be shifting continuously, so that the presence of a cantus firmus is strongly suggested in some passages, but can be virtually ruled out in others. For that reason alone the tenor will defy vertical alignment if that method is applied indiscriminately to all its music. But even if we do carefully assess the changing role of the tenor, the evidence remains so consistently contradictory that one is tempted to assume that the ambiguity was intentional—in the same way, perhaps, as the deception in the Credo of *De Sancto Donatiano*. That, ultimately, seems the more relevant issue. The question whether *Salve diva parens* is a freely composed or cantus firmus based mass has to do with Obrecht's compositional point of departure. The observation that the end-product persistently appears to be both has to do with his compositional objectives. It is these, surely, that our analysis must aim at ascertaining.

So we must set the question of basic structure aside for the moment, and focus our attention on the finished work as we have it. From that perspective one thing becomes immediately apparent: there is a marked contrast between the ambiguity Obrecht maintains with regard to cantus-firmus usage, and the outspoken rationality with which he handles other devices. Chief among these devices is motivic writing—a feature that is conspicuously absent in his other two masses from 1486–7. The first signs of this are found in the bass of the Christe, which, from bar 60 onwards, states the same six-note motif three times in succession (Ex. 14*a*). The passage is not remarkable by itself—we have observed similar motivic

diva parens' (*NOE* 11, p. xv). It seems worth pointing out, however, that since the similarities between Obrecht's tenor statements themselves are at best vague to begin with, their similarity to the actual cantus firmus (if there was one) cannot by definition be any clearer. But some candidates evidently come closer than others; I would include Févin's cantus firmus among these (see below).

[29] *Cantus Firmus*, 245.

Ex. 14. Obrecht, *Missa Salve diva parens*: (*a*) Christe, bars 60–71 (bass); (*b*) Domine Deus, bars 145–58 (bass); (*c*) Pleni, bars 77–108 (bass); (*d*) Osanna I, bars 120–55 (bass); (*e*) Cum sancto, bars 212–29 (tenor)

repetitions in the Credos of *Missae O lumen ecclesie* and *Sicut spina rosam* (see Ch. 4). Nor are the motivic sequences in the bass parts of Et incarnatus, bars 196–207, Qui cum Patre, bars 262–274, and Sanctus, bars 1–17, particularly innovative. But the Christe motif recurs in the Domine Deus (bars 145–58; Ex. 14*b*), where it is subjected to a new procedure: motivic transformation. At every repetition the motif is expanded by the insertion of a new note; by the last statement it comprises eight notes. Obrecht was evidently fascinated by the idea of transforming a melodic idea in this kind of stepwise process. Another variant of the Christe motif appears in the bass of the Pleni (bars 77–108; Ex. 14*c*), where it undergoes exactly the same kind of expansion as in the Domine Deus, in six successive statements.[30] The most sophisticated treatment is reserved for the next section, the first Osanna (bars 120–55; see Ex. 14*d*). A motif in the bass appears here in three pairs of permutations, the second of every pair being an inversion of the first. The initial motif consists of a longa E and a five-note motif that is moved up a step in each following statement, and consequently down a step in each inversion.[31]

Interestingly, motivic devices of this kind are even applied to the *tenor* of one section, the Cum sancto Spiritu (Ex. 14*e*).[32] In bars 214–26 of the Cum sancto, a phrase consisting of two four-note motifs is stated four times, but on every repetition the second motif is presented a step lower, and a connecting note is inserted to preserve stepwise motion. The resulting process of transformation combines motivic repetition, sequence, and expansion. In the subsequent bars, a scalar motif is stated four times, ascending one note higher each statement, until it spans a sixth. It is significant that Obrecht is prepared to apply these techniques to the tenor, for they seem inherently incompatible with quotation of pre-existent material. Clearly his fascination with motivic devices overrides here whatever allegiance he may have felt towards a cantus firmus. The question whether the composer does in fact use, in some cryptic fashion, a pre-existent tune, is immaterial. He intends to be *seen* not to use one—and that observation is more fundamental to the style of *Missa Salve diva parens*.

Still, it is difficult to explain these devices in terms of Obrecht's stylistic development, for none of the other masses from around 1486–7 provides a context for them. Incidental use of additive techniques is made in the following works, which are likely to post-date *Salve diva parens*:

[30] A very similar 'additive' procedure was noted by Thomas Noblitt in the Gloria of the *Missa Veci la danse Barbari* ('Obrecht's *Missa Sine nomine* and its Recently Discovered Model', *Musical Quarterly*, 68 (1982), 114 and ex. 5).

[31] For another discussion of this passage, see Todd, 'Retrograde, Inversion', 63.

[32] This passage is also discussed ibid., 63–4.

Caput, Qui tollis, bars 114–21
De Sancto Johanne Baptista, Benedictus, bars 140–58
Fortuna desperata, Benedictus, bars 218–32
Je ne demande, Et incarnatus, bars 172–92
N'aray-je jamais, Et resurrexit, bars 162–84
Plurimorum carminum II, Benedictus, bars 197–211
Veci la danse Barbari, Gloria, bars 171–80

In none of these cases, however, are the techniques handled with the persistence and imagination that we find in *Salve diva parens*. Outside Obrecht's *œuvre* motivic devices of this kind are exceedingly rare. Only three works provide clear examples: Busnoys's *Anthoni usque limina* (on 'ut per verbi misterium'), the anonymous *Missa L'ardant desir*, which is almost certainly by Busnoys as well,[33] and the Sanctus *Iste puer magnus*, based on an antiphon for the feast of St John the Baptist.[34] The latter two works must pre-date the mid-1470s, and both are historically significant in that they extend compositional procedures typical of Busnoys beyond the points represented by his known works. The Sanctus is a particularly important work. The composer of this extraordinary setting most probably worked in a southern Netherlands urban centre like Bruges, where private endowments of single mass movements on saints' feast-days were common.[35] I have pointed out elsewhere that the Sanctus is a fore-runner of the type of multiple-cantus-firmus mass cultivated by Obrecht in Bruges.[36] The spontaneous introduction of techniques of motivic trans-

---

[33] In the Pleni of this mass a three-note motif is expanded in the course of seven successive statements; each repetition adds one to four notes to the motif, until it comprises sixteen notes. The *Missa L'ardant desir* survives uniquely in VatS 51, but in an earlier layer than *Salve diva parens* (fos. 90ᵛ–104ʳ, dating from the 1470s). For a discussion of this work, see Wegman, 'Another Mass by Busnoys?' Richard Taruskin has argued that the *Missa L'ardant desir* is musically inferior to the two attributed Busnoys masses, and he therefore questioned Busnoys's authorship; see the relevant exchanges in *Music & Letters*, 71 (1990), 631–5, and 72 (1991), 347–50.

[34] In the first section of the Sanctus, the tenor entry is preceded by a three-voice introduction lasting thirty-four bars. The bass here presents the tenor melody in long note-values (bars 2–15), and then picks up a motif from the top two voices (bars 16–19). This motif is subsequently given five more statements, in each of which it is expanded with one more note (bars 20–33). A similar additive procedure is found in the last twenty-six *tempora* of the Benedictus: the bass starts with a two-note motif G–A, which ascends one more note in each of the seven successive statements, until it spans a ninth. It is worth pointing out that the anonymous composer did not limit his application of such techniques to these passages. Noteworthy are the rigidly sequential organization of the bass in bars 1–14 of the Pleni, the motivic repetitions in the bass and top voices in bars 32–5 of the same section, and the extraordinarily tight motivic integration of the Benedictus (in particular bars 28–38). The concentration of such devices in one movement is highly unusual for the mid-1470s, and suggests a creative mind akin to Busnoys or Obrecht. The Sanctus *Iste puer magnus* survives in MunBS 3154, fos. 137ᵛ–141ʳ. On the basis of watermark evidence, the date of this part of the manuscript has been established as *c.*1476 (Noblitt, 'Die Datierung').

[35] Strohm, *Music in Late Medieval Bruges*, 23 and 29.

[36] R. C. Wegman, 'Another "Imitation" of Busnoys' *Missa L'Homme armé*—And Some Observa-

formation in *Salve diva parens*, and the virtual absence of these techniques outside Busnoys's orbit, may suggest that the cycle was written shortly after Obrecht became acquainted with a composition like the Sanctus—possibly even the setting itself.[37]

Obrecht's concern with schematic melodic organization is also evident in other passages of the tenor. A good example can be found in bars 118–30 of the third Agnus Dei, where the tenor is involved with the other three voices in an extended sequence. In the course of that sequence it states the same five-note motif six times, descending a step on every repetition, and continuing the sequence alone with two further statements of a slightly variant motif. If this passage is cantus-firmus-based at all, the underlying melody is most likely to be a descending octave scale (as in *Missa Ave regina celorum*; Et in terra bars 14–21; see Ex. 20 below). The more plausible assumption, however, is that the passage is freely composed. Elsewhere the tenor is involved in less extensive sequences, for instance the Kyrie, bars 11–13, and the Credo, bars 26–9. Internal repeats of motifs and phrases can be found in the Credo, bars 279–84, and the Sanctus, bars 36–43. These procedures do not always rule out the presence of a pre-existent tune, but obviously they need to be taken into account in vertical tenor alignments.

Moving now to the opposite end of the spectrum, there are several other passages where Obrecht's adherence to established norms of tenor presentation strongly suggests the presence of a cantus firmus. In every movement except the Credo the tenor starts with the same melodic gesture E–C–D–[C–D]–E. Brief and unremarkable though this motif is, Obrecht invariably sets it apart from the surrounding counterpoint by delayed entry and statement in long note-values. He goes furthest in this respect in the Gloria, where the motif is expanded to nine bars, and enters after eleven bars' rest. The tenor is made to stand out so manifestly in this passage that few listeners could have doubted the presence of a pre-existent tune. Just as in the Cum sancto, there can be no doubt here as to what the composer intends to be *seen* to be doing. And even though he

tions on *Imitatio* in Renaissance Music', *Journal of the Royal Musical Association*, 114 (1989), 190–1 n. 8.

37 This is the only explanation I can think of for the prominent use of these techniques in *Salve diva parens*—unless we question Petrucci's attribution or the copying date of the Sistine Chapel manuscript, for which I see no compelling stylistic grounds. It is tempting to suggest that Obrecht became acquainted with the techniques only after he moved to Bruges, but this hypothesis is obviously undermined by the fact that the Sanctus *Iste puer magnus* was available in Austria as early as 1476. Josquin adopted the techniques in his *Missa Gaudeamus*; see H. Osthoff, *Josquin Desprez*, i (Tutzing, 1962), 139.

appears to be doing quite different things in the two sections, that intention could be regarded as one of the mass's binding compositional threads.

Another example is the Genitum non factum, which is constructed with
'migrant scaffolding' technique: a thirteen-bar phrase is stated successively in the top voice, tenor, contratenor, top voice, and tenor. This
structure immediately recalls the Et in Spiritum and Benedictus–Osanna
of the *Missa Sicut spina rosam*, where fourteen-bar phrases (both containing cantus-firmus material) are given identical treatment (see Ex. 11*b*).
The close structural similarity not only confirms the chronological proximity of the two cycles, but suggests that pre-existent material should have
been used, if anywhere, in the thirteen-bar phrase of the Genitum. Unfortunately, the phrase is not very distinctive melodically: two rotations
around B are followed by one on A. The counterpoint of *Salve diva parens*
is virtually saturated with rotations of this kind, and we should therefore
be cautious in trying to identify the Genitum phrase elsewhere in the
mass.[38]

Brief chain structures are regularly found in the mass, and sometimes
these involve the tenor in such a way as to suggest the presence of cantus-
firmus material. Thus the Patrem opens with what appears to be a bisectional motto-tenor imitation of $5 + 5$ bars in the style of *O lumen ecclesie*.
Again, however, this yields only a brief and undistinctive figure rotating
around E. Another technique worth discussing is found in the opening of
the third Agnus Dei (bars 73–101; see Ex. 15). This section starts with
brief imitations between the top two voices, over a long-held note on E in
the bass (the Domine Deus opens in a very similar way). After the tenor
has entered in bar 83, the bass accompanies it with a four-bar phrase that
is subsequently restated in the top voice and contratenor before it finally
appears in the tenor (bars 85–100). To all appearances this is a 'prepared'
tenor statement in the traditional manner (cf. the first Osanna of *O lumen
ecclesie* and the Qui tollis of the *Missa Sicut spina rosam*, Ex. 11; a similar
passage in *Salve diva parens* is Agnus Dei I, bars 22–8). In terms of
a possible cantus firmus, the harvest is richer this time; but the actual
phrase has few obvious parallels elsewhere in the mass. Extended imitation
between tenor and bass often indicates involvement of a pre-existent tune,
as we have seen in *De Sancto Donatiano*. Possible examples in *Salve diva
parens* are Kyrie, bars 33–50, Gloria, bars 88–107, Credo, bars 177–96.

At this point we have gained sufficient insight into Obrecht's treatment

[38] Migrant scaffolding of a somewhat more modest kind can be seen in the Benedictus, bars 183–
210: a six- to eight-bar phrase is stated in the tenor, contratenor, top voice, tenor, and bass. Again
the phrase is too brief and undistinctive to be able to relate it firmly to tenor material elsewhere in
the mass.

of the tenor voice to be able to discuss a possible candidate for the cantus firmus. Reinhard Strohm has pointed out that the tenor melody of Obrecht's mass seems similar to that of Antoine de Févin's *Missa O quam glorifica*.[39] Fortunately, it is not difficult to reconstruct the basic outline of Févin's cantus firmus, as he treats it relatively straightforwardly (Ex. 16a). Comparison with a tentative reconstruction of Obrecht's cantus firmus, made by Bernhard Meier in 1952,[40] does indeed reveal striking similarities (cf. Ex. 16b): against twelve corresponding notes there are only three divergences. The first of these, the absence of the second note on C, is actually shared by the opening of the Credo tenor, the motto of every movement except the Agnus Dei, and the tenor openings of the Confiteor (which is labelled 'salve diva parens' in LeipU 1494) and Cum sancto.

The similarity is encouraging, but it is difficult to prove further correspondences without falling prey to the danger of special pleading. Févin's cantus firmus is divided into four melodic phrases A–D; if the melody is fundamentally identical with Obrecht's tenor, then these phrases must correspond to lines 1 4 of the *Salve diva parens* poem. That assumption can be tested objectively, for two sources for the mass have different parts of the tenor underlaid with that poem. Comparison yields the following results:

1. VienNB Mus. 15495 distributes the four lines of text over the three sections of the Kyrie as follows: [1/2/3, 4]. Phrases A, B, and C can be recognized relatively easily in the relevant places (bars 5–10, 31–57, and 72–8, respectively), but not without presupposing some amount of ornamentation and free writing; the passage underlaid with line 4 (bars 81–92) has no resemblance to phrase D. The layout of the Kyrie thus seems to be [A/B/C*x*].

2. LeipU 1494 provides the text of lines 1 and 2 in the tenor of the Et in terra. Phrase A can be discerned in bars 12–43, but the remainder of the tenor shows no obvious similarity to phrase B. However, the latter phrase can easily be recognized in the next section, the Domine Deus: except for a free interpolation (bars 65–9), it appears there unadorned (bars 63–78). After nine bars' rest, the tenor re-enters (bars 88–122), but phrase C cannot be recognized here (unless we assume that it is buried under the most excessive ornamentation). Curiously enough, though, the next major tenor statement begins with a virtually unadorned version of phrase D (bars 138–51). On musical grounds, then, the first two sections of the Gloria seem to have the layout [A/B*y*D*z*].

Ex. 15. Obrecht, *Missa Salve diva parens*, Agnus Dei III, bars 73–101

Ex. 16. (*a*) Févin, *Missa O quam glorifica*, cantus firmus (reconstructed); (*b*) Obrecht, *Missa Salve diva parens*, cantus firmus (tentative reconstruction by Bernhard Meier)

3. The tenor of the Confiteor is underlaid in LeipU 1494 as follows: 'Confiteor [cancelled] Salve diva parens'. This carries the implication that at least the first phrase of the cantus firmus returns in this section. Discounting the motivic repetition in bars 279–84 on the grounds discussed above, one can clearly recognize phrase A in bars 277–8 + 284–5. The remainder of the section appears to be freely composed.[41]

Admittedly, all these cases presuppose varying degrees of ornamentation. But then it was known beforehand that Obrecht's mass dwells in the border area between heavy embellishment and free composition. If that circumstance is taken into account, Strohm's candidate passes the test with flying colours.

The second objective test is to examine the passages identified above as likely to contain pre-existent material. These do turn out to show similarities to Févin's tenor, although it would only be honest to admit that the relationship is never entirely clear-cut. Thus the opening chain structure

---

[41] The Cum sancto seems to parallel the Confiteor: its tenor opens with the very same two-bar motif (which, incidentally, appears also in the head-motif of every section except the Agnus Dei). The subsequent bars are structured with techniques of motivic transformation (see above, Ex. 14*e*). The starting phrase in the transformation (bars 214–16) is a variant of the opening motif. As it happens, the final transformed version of that phrase (bars 223–6) appears to be a slightly ornamented form of phrase A. The overall layout of the Gloria may thus well be [A/B*y*D*z*/A].

of the Patrem seems to quote the first three notes of phrase A. The structural scaffold in the Genitum non factum closely resembles phrase B. The migrant phrase in the third Agnus Dei can be seen as an elaboration of phrase D. It is possible to detect more resemblances in the course of the mass,[42] but the obvious methodological danger is that one can prove the presence of almost any tune if every degree of elaboration can be postulated. Although it is difficult to imagine a stronger candidate than the one proposed by Strohm, definitive proof can only be established outside Obrecht's mass: this would be the discovery of a tune carrying the *Salve diva parens* melody—most probably in a fifteenth-century Flemish hymnal.

Salve diva parens is as extrovert as its contemporary *De Sancto Donatiano* is introvert. Against the balanced, unassuming style of the latter work we have here a mass bursting with invention, displaying a wide variety of styles, and demanding the utmost from the technical abilities of its performers.[43] No single movement could suffice to illustrate the extraordinary variety and technical mastery displayed in this work: careful scrutiny and attentive listening will reveal new details at every turn. If *De Sancto Donatiano* was written for a private ceremony in a side-chapel, it is tempting to associate *Salve diva parens* with the kinds of public mass competitions in which Obrecht must have regularly engaged as succentor of St Donatian's.[44] The mass is a 'public' composition in the sense that Obrecht seems constantly concerned with what he is *seen* to do on the contrapuntal surface. His work could be regarded as an elaborate exercise in musical deception of the kind we briefly encountered in *De Sancto Donatiano* (and the above discussion illustrates how successful that exercise remains to this day). But Obrecht's attitude in *Salve diva parens* is better described as one of stylistic impressionism. He plays with different textures and techniques in quick succession: motivic devices, imitations of

[42] Phrase A: Credo, bars 20–5, Sanctus, bars 15–31, Agnus, bars 8–16. Phrase B: Credo, bars 112–34, Sanctus, bars 32–6, Agnus, bars 16–23. Phrase C: Sanctus, bars 36–40 and 40–4, Agnus, bars 26–30. Phrase D: Sanctus, bars 120–57.

[43] A particularly complex passage rhythmically is Sanctus bars 36–46, in which dotted rhythms are interlocked in different voices, resulting in a total loss of the perceived semibreve beat. It may be no coincidence that one source for the mass, VienNB Mus. 15495, omits this passage altogether in what appears to have been a systematic attempt to simplify the style of the work (see *NOE* 11, p. xix).

[44] Strohm, *Music in Late Medieval Bruges*, 54: 'On Monday to Wednesday before Ascension, the clergy of the three major churches of Bruges, together with city representatives, participated in three processions to the parish churches of the Holy Cross, St Catherine, and St Mary Magdalene, respectively, all three outside the town walls. The singers of the churches were required to sing in turn one mass in discant at the place of arrival. This amounted to a kind of public musical competition, especially as the succentors of each church (St Donatian's, Our Lady's, St Saviour's) had to compose their respective masses every year. The succentors had the same duty on the occasion of the annual *crepelenfeest* in Aardenburg.'

varying kinds, antiphonal exchanges, chordal styles, sequences, writing in parallel tenths, and so on. The result is a kaleidoscopic series of impressions, none of which reveals, on closer analysis, any deeper compositional design than the impression itself. Obrecht's overriding concern here is the listener's experience as opposed to intellectual construction. Not surprisingly, *Salve diva parens* was among the composer's best-appreciated works: it is one of his three most widely distributed masses, even discounting the independent transmission of the Qui cum patre as a *bicinium*. It is particularly interesting to know that the mass was available in Italy by 1487. It may explain why it was in this particular year that Ercole d'Este invited Obrecht to Ferrara, even though he is known to have appreciated his music several years earlier.[45] The modesty and conservatism of *De Sancto Martino* and *De Sancto Donatiano* would have made this move difficult to understand. But the composer of *Salve diva parens* was plainly worth fetching at once, wherever he lived.

Missa Adieu mes amours

On 17 January 1488, some seven weeks after Obrecht's arrival in Ferrara, Duke Ercole referred in a letter to 'the recreation and enjoyment that we constantly receive from him'. No doubt he was thinking primarily of Obrecht's skills as a singer, but it is very likely that newly written works much contributed to his delight. No fewer than five masses are believed to have been composed in the first Ferrarese period, mainly on the basis of patterns of transmission; the evidence is inconclusive.[46] A possible candidate, now lost (if it ever existed), was mentioned by Glareanus. In his *Dodekachordon* he singled out a *Missa Hercules Dux Ferrarie* as a work in which Obrecht 'seems to have wanted to demonstrate' his productivity.[47] Since the treatise must have been meticulously proof-read, one wonders

---

[45] Lockwood, *Ferrara*, 162–3.

[46] Barton Hudson has made an eloquent case for *Fortuna desperata* and *Malheur me bat*, on the basis of their transmission as well as that of their models. See 'Two Ferrarese Masses by Jacob Obrecht', *Journal of Musicology*, 4 (1985–6), 276–302. Using the same methods, he suggested that the *Missa Cela sans plus* might also have been written in the Ferrarese period (ibid. 299). These cases rest heavily on the assumption that a mass composed at Ferrara could not have been distributed from the North, and consequently that Obrecht did not bring any of the masses composed at Ferrara back with him to Bruges in 1488. Doubts concerning the methods employed by Hudson were expressed by Reinhard Strohm in his review of *NOE* 7 (*Notes*, 47 (1990), 554). Italian origin for the incomplete *Missa Scaramella* has been proposed on the grounds that its model was one of the most famous Italian popular tunes in the later 15th c.; on the basis of its style, Barton Hudson has judged the mass to be from Obrecht's first rather than second stay in Ferrara (*NOE* 11, p. xxxvi; see also 'Two Ferrarese Masses', 299). Martin Staehelin has suggested that the *Missa Plurimorum carminum II* could have been composed during Obrecht's Italian stay, since all but one of its models appear in the Ferrarese chansonnier RomeC 2856 ('Obrechtiana', 27).   [47] *Dodekachordon*, 296.

whether this statement should not be taken at face value rather than rejected as an error; few composers surely had as much reason to pay homage to the duke as Obrecht. If he composed a mass *Hercules Dux Ferrarie*, then his setting may well have been the first in the long tradition of such works, which otherwise includes masses by Josquin des Prez, Jachet of Mantua, Maistre Jan, Lupus, and Cipriano de Rore.

Among the surviving works, the strongest candidate on stylistic grounds seems *Missa Adieu mes amours*.[48] Like the two previous masses discussed in this chapter, this cycle bears hardly any of the hallmarks of Obrecht's style: once again it is the manuscript attributions that compel us to accept it as his. Without those attributions more likely candidates for its authorship would have seemed composers working in Italy such as Gaspar van Weerbecke or Josquin des Prez, for the mass clearly betrays their influence. Among Obrecht's works *Adieu mes amours* makes less apparent sense, unless we assume that it was written at a time of stylistic reorientation, possibly as an exercise in the 'Italian' style.[49]

The events of 1487–8 fit this description extremely well. As observed above, the composer was no longer entrenched in a fixed personal idiom when he departed for Ferrara in October 1487:[50] this cleared the way for him to steep himself in the musical styles prevailing at the north Italian courts, and thus to please the taste of his newly found patron.[51] At the same time, there is evidence pointing to increasing stylistic uniformity after his return, a trend that rapidly culminated in works like *Fortuna desperata*, *Rose playsante*, and *Je ne demande* (all existing by about 1491–3). Moreover, it is difficult to see what could have inspired Obrecht in the

[48] For this mass, see Meier, *Studien zur Meßkomposition*, 72–83; Sparks, *Cantus Firmus*, 255–9.

[49] Cf. Bernhard Meier's concluding remark in his discussion of *Adieu mes amours*: 'Nicht unbedeutsam, vielleicht sogar vor den anderen Messen Obrechts, scheint endlich der Einfluß Italiens' (*Studien zur Meßkomposition*, 83). The possibility that Obrecht might have wanted to emulate Josquin is raised in *NOE* 1, p. xvi.

[50] There are, however, some hints in *Adieu mes amours* that suggest that masses like *De Sancto Martino* and *Salve diva parens* were still fresh in the composer's mind. The openings of the second Kyrie and the Et in terra, for instance, recall these same openings in *De Sancto Martino*, while the opening of the Sanctus recalls bars 13–14 of the latter mass's Patrem. More strikingly, the curious motivic exchanges between bass and contratenor in Gloria, bars 45–8, directly parallel the similar exchanges in Gloria, bars 46–50, of *Salve diva parens*. Quite possibly these passages in the two masses are to be sung to the same words ('Domine Fili unigenite Iesu Christe'). However, it is difficult to be sure whether the resemblance was intentional.

[51] In terms of general stylistic idiom as well as cantus-firmus treatment, one is particularly reminded of Gaspar van Weerbecke's *Missa Princesse d'amourettes*, which circulated in Italy by the late 1480s; see *Gaspar van Weerbeke: Missa Princesse d'amourettes*, ed. W. Elders (Exempla musica neerlandica, 8; Utrecht, 1974). It was copied in VatS 35 by about 1488, along with Obrecht's *Missa De Sancto Donatiano*, and had reached Ferrara by May 1490 (Lockwood, *Ferrara*, 164–5). According to Ercole's singer Cornelio di Lorenzo, it was a mass that would 'please' the Duke's taste. As pointed out in Ch. 5, Obrecht is likely to have visited Rome in 1488, where he would almost certainly have met Gaspar in person.

North to write such a singular piece as *Adieu mes amours*. Although the composer was to be back in Italy by December 1504, the mass must pre-date that second stay: it was copied in SegC s.s. before 1503, together with three masses that date almost certainly from the Bruges years 1485–91.[52] More importantly, *Adieu mes amours* must pre-date a significant change in Obrecht's mensural habits, which presumably took place shortly after 1487–8: while the mensurations O and ₵ are used with equal frequency in his earlier works, in later masses ₵ has become the predominant (and in several cases unique) mensuration. The only exceptions occur when Obrecht borrows a structural plan from an existing mass (*Caput*, *L'homme armé*, *De Sancto Johanne Baptista*), or constructs his setting according to an elaborate numerological plan (*Sub tuum presidium*). *Adieu mes amours*, together with *Ave regina celorum*, must be among the last works pre-dating this significant change.

Few of Obrecht's masses are written in such a relaxed, carefree style as *Adieu mes amours*. There is a new sense of freedom and spontaneity breathing through this work: it is as though Obrecht has deliberately done away with the self-imposed bounds within which he usually likes to operate. Unlike *Sicut spina rosam* or *Salve diva parens*, the mass is not packed full with musical ideas, nor does the composer display his usual fondness for intellectual games and constructive devices. The counterpoint is less dense and involved, the texture more transparent, and there is a general air of speed and fluency about the mass, which makes it an easy work to listen to. If imitative devices assumed structural significance in cycles like *O lumen ecclesie* and *Sicut spina rosam*, here they are brought back to the motivic level. The temporal interval between successive entries is shortened, sometimes to as little as a minim (Gloria, bars 12–13, 133–41; Credo, bars 30–3, 46–7, 56–8; Agnus Dei, bars 10–13). Imitation is not used to structure extended stretches of polyphony, but rather to generate energy, particularly to secure musical continuity after cadences. Consequently, Obrecht does not hesitate to place firm, quasi-final cadences in the course of the sections: all it takes to continue the motion is a new motivic gesture, which may or may not be imitated in the other voices. Sometimes the effect of these cadences is so strong as to suggest a sectional division (Gloria, bars 37, 100, 118; Credo, bars 29, 85, 94; Sanctus, bar 19). This underlines another important quality of *Adieu mes amours*: the music is organized into distinct units, often starting with an imitation and

---

[52] Fos. 25ᵛ–30ʳ; for the earliest copying dates of *Rose playsante* (fos. 30ᵛ–38ʳ) and *Fortuna desperata* (fos. 38ᵛ–45ʳ), see above. *Libenter gloriabor* (fos. 18ᵛ–25ʳ) is a stylistic twin of *Fortuna desperata*, and like that mass it must be from *c*.1491–3 or earlier (see Ch. 8).

ending with a firm cadence. This division is not imposed by the structure of the cantus firmus, but rather by the text, which Obrecht observes and underlays with unusual care.[53] The cantus firmus itself is not a primary focus of compositional attention. It is neither deliberately disguised through excessive ornamentation, as in *Salve diva parens*, nor fixed in one or more mensural shapes, as in most masses discussed so far. Ornamentation or statement in long note-values are applied as the musical flow dictates: with freedom and little apparent calculation.[54] It is therefore difficult to say whether Obrecht based his mass on the tenor of Josquin's *Adieu mes amours* or (like that tenor) on the monophonic tune itself: the cantus firmus resembles both equally well.[55]

Ex. 17 shows the Et in terra, bars 1–40, of *Adieu mes amours*.[56] The section opens with an imitative duo for the top two voices (bars 1–7). Contrary to appearances, this is not the head-motif: there is none in the mass. This underlines a point that could be coincidence but more probably reflects a chronological development. With the exception of *Ave regina celorum* and *De Sancto Johanne Baptista* (to be discussed in the next chapter), none of the masses to be considered in the remainder of this study employs motto procedures of any kind. Together with the change in Obrecht's mensural habits, mentioned earlier, this suggests that the 'critical phase' of 1486–8 inaugurated significant and lasting changes in Obrecht's compositional habits.[57]

Several of the typical stylistic features outlined here are already apparent in the opening bars. The imitations in bars 3–6 follow at a distance of only one semibreve, which heightens the sense of speed. The cadence in

---

[53] Hudson, 'On the Texting', 121.

[54] For a discussion of Obrecht's cantus-firmus treatment in this mass, see Sparks, *Cantus Firmus*, 255–9.

[55] The cantus firmi of Obrecht and Josquin share a melodic variant that seems to be unique to their settings (cf. *NOE* I, p. xii). See for this Sparks, *Cantus Firmus*, 259; and Martin Picker, 'Josquiniana in Some Manuscripts at Piacenza', in *Josquin des Prez: Proceedings*, 253–4 (also includes discussion of another *Adieu mes amours* setting by Josquin that has the same variant). Obrecht does not consistently borrow the most distinctive feature of Josquin's setting, quasi-canonic imitation between tenor and bass, even though this was a favourite technique of his (two minor exceptions are Gloria, bars 151–72, and Credo, bars 137–86). The possibility that Obrecht's mass was based on some other four-voice setting is suggested by some restatements of polyphonic complexes across sections (compare Kyrie, bars 84–5, with Gloria, bars 95–9, and Credo, bars 123–7).

[56] For another discussion of the same section, see Meier, *Studien zur Meßkomposition*, 75–7.

[57] This was already observed by Ludwig Finscher in his *MGG* article on Obrecht: the early masses are distinguished from the late ones by, amongst others, 'Überwiegen des tempus perfectum, [und] identische oder verwandte Satzanfänge' (col. 1820). Barton Hudson has also pointed to Obrecht's changing use of head-motifs, from 'a strict, routine manner' in early masses to 'greater variety' in later ones ('Obrecht's Tribute to Ockeghem', 7–8). Hudson overlooked the variety of motto treatment in masses copied by 1491–3 (*Fortuna desperata, Rose playsante*, and *Je ne demande*), and consequently concluded that the change took place after the mid-1490s.

Ex. 17. Obrecht, *Missa Adieu mes amours*, Et in terra, bars 1–40

(Ex. 17, *cont.*)

bar 7 is followed by another *stretto* imitation, based this time on a mere motivic gesture (evidently inspired by the scansion of the text). Yet another such imitation, at a distance of a minim, is to be found in bars 12–13. All this is quite uncharacteristic of Obrecht's normal working methods: thus far his imitations have tended to be strict, extended, and temporally distant.

It is not until the cantus-firmus entry in bar 15, however, that the Italianate flavour of this mass becomes truly apparent. The slow-moving tenor is immediately placed in a tissue woven out of brief, stereotyped motifs—a procedure more typical of Josquin than of Obrecht. The cantus firmus is not contrapuntally essential to this motivic interplay, as is shown by the tenorless continuation in bars 20–1. This highlights another important quality of *Adieu mes amours*: the contrapuntal voices are uncommonly unresponsive to the tenor. Its presence or absence rarely seems to alter their musical course in any significant way. The concern with speed and continuous motion apparently overrides that of cantus-firmus articulation. This is seen, for instance, in bars 23–30, a passage in which the counterpoint does little more than move from one cadence to the next. The expected place for the cantus firmus to enter would surely be bar 23: its entry here would have coincided with a cadence (the first since bar 15) as well as with a textural expansion, from two to four voices. Moreover, after the two-voice preparation in bars 21–2 it would have been natural for the tenor to supply the missing note in the cadence on G (the contratenor evades it with a leap to *b♭*). Instead, however, the structural voice enters one bar later, when the new passage is already under way, and where, rather than supplying any 'missing' note, it simply doubles the contra-tenor in its cadence on C.[58]

---

[58] Noteworthy is the brief melodic figure in the top voice, bar 23. This is one of several

The attitude underlying this treatment of the tenor is characteristic of
Adieu mes amours as a whole. It seems significant, for instance, that even
though the mass is virtually saturated with imitations, hardly any of these
involve the tenor.[59] A typical example of this can be seen in bars 31–7.
This passage has all the earmarks of a 'prepared' tenor statement such as
we have just encountered in *Salve diva parens* (Ex. 15, bars 85–100):
a clearly outlined two-bar phrase migrates from contratenor to top voice,
in such a way that one would normally expect it to make its final appearance in the tenor, bars 35–7. This expectation seems all the more justified
as we are in the midst of an extended passage bridging two major cantus-
firmus statements (bars 28–54). The tenor is temporarily released here
from its duty to carry pre-existent material, and since it is thus free by
definition, nothing stops it from quoting the two-bar phrase. Moreover,
the cadence in bar 37 is one of those, mentioned above, which, by bringing
the counterpoint to a firm halt, suggest a sectional division: what better
way of preparing such a quasi-final cadence than through an imitative
build-up, in which the tenor has the final say? It thus comes as something
of a surprise to find that the structural voice merely presents contrapuntal
'filling', of the simplest kind (bars 35–7).[60] In terms of Obrecht's usual
procedures, an opportunity has been missed here. But this merely underlines how different his compositional objectives are in *Adieu mes amours*.
The composer clearly is not interested in using imitation to organize
extended stretches of polyphony. Imitation is no longer the structure, but
the very *substance* of the counterpoint.

That this is true is shown by those passages in *Adieu mes amours* where
Obrecht indulges in continuous imitation of a single motif, passages that
are all speed and no development. Good examples are Kyrie, bars 21–9,
and Sanctus, bars 7–8, but the most eloquent instance is Credo, bars 102–
18 (Ex. 18). Here, nine bars of music are produced through the imitation
of one and the same motif. Such procedures recall the mass style of
Weerbecke or Josquin, and in fact this passage has its direct counterpart
in one of the latter composer's works. As it happens, this is the *Missa*

---

stereotyped motifs that Obrecht uses to retain motion after cadences (see also Gloria, bar 54, and
particularly Credo, bar 19). Other motifs with a similar function appear in the bass, bars 10 and 30.

[59] Typically, one of the few exceptions involves a tenor phrase that is embellished beyond
recognition; see Credo, bars 59–63. The other exception is Agnus Dei, bars 10–13.

[60] Edgar Sparks has already drawn attention to the free material in the tenor in this passage: 'The
tenor of the Gloria is uneventful except in one respect. In the interim between the statement of A₁
and A₂ Obrecht does the unpredictable thing and gives the tenor a few notes which apparently are
not from the original voice at all but are added for the sake of sonority, in order to make a full
cadence in four voices in a [passage] which is otherwise all duos and trios (m. 35–37)' (*Cantus
Firmus*, 257).

Ex. 18. Obrecht, *Missa Adieu mes amours*, Et incarnatus, bars 102–18

Hercules Dux Ferrarie, Gloria, bars 16–24, where a nearly identical motif is similarly repeated and imitated.[61] The motif itself is obviously too stereotyped for us to be able to speak of a conscious allusion on the part of either composer. But the point lies precisely in its stereotyped nature. Throughout *Adieu mes amours* Obrecht is sharing in the general motivic vocabulary of composers working in Italy such as Josquin and Weerbecke. He is talking their language. Imitation of the kind shown in Ex. 18 is virtually absent in Obrecht's masses datable before 1487. Yet in his mature mass style (which was to be established by around 1490) it plays a significant role, along with the older, structural type of imitation. Several of Obrecht's mature masses employ both types.[62] The assumption that *Adieu mes amours* was written in 1487–8 as an exercise in the Italian style might explain this expansion of the composer's palette of imitative procedures.

It must be stressed that the proposed date and place of composition remain hypothetical, since *Adieu mes amours* cannot be placed in any continuous stylistic development. Like *De Sancto Donatiano* and *Sicut spina rosam*, it stands alone in the composer's mass œuvre. For that very reason, however, we have suggested that the mass originated in the only known period in Obrecht's life when he was given to far-reaching stylistic experimentation. The lucid counterpoint, the generally thin scoring, the abundance of imitation, the responsiveness to the text, and the absence of strict formal designs—these are all qualities that point to the South. Significantly, the composer is known to have stayed there during this very period, and he was not to make another journey until after the earliest surviving source for the mass was copied. *Adieu mes amours* must have been written before the change to ¢ as the predominant mensuration in Obrecht's masses, a development that is likely to have been imminent on his return to the North in 1488. A date close to that change is suggested by the absence of head-motifs, something this mass shares with all but two of the works to be discussed in the remainder of this study. The two exceptions, *Missae Ave regina celorum* and *De Sancto Johanne Baptista*, will be the subject of the next chapter.

The *Missa De Sancto Martino* was the last in a series of works in which free tenor elaboration alternated with strict, mensurally transformed restatement. The next three masses discussed in this chapter abandoned

---

[61] That this passage had some special meaning for Josquin is suggested by the fact that it reappears literally in his Circumcision motet *Quando natus es* (bars 57–65, on 'descendisti').

[62] Compare, for instance, *Grecorum*, Gloria, bars 1–16, with Credo, bars 8–15 (based on a somewhat simpler form of the motif in Ex. 18) and bars 160–70.

strict cantus-firmus treatment altogether: they show a degree of freedom not found in any of the composer's other settings. Perhaps Obrecht needed to go through a stage like this to rediscover the cantus firmus as the focus of structural and intellectual meaning. It was in the critical phase that the earlier coexistence of the two kinds of approach was abandoned, and freedom and irregularity became the rule. After it, the balance swung to the opposite end. With the exception of *Ave regina celorum*, all Obrecht's later masses show the kind of consistently rigid procedures for which the composer has remained famous to this day. But changes in cantus-firmus treatment rarely stand on their own: they are symptoms of a composer's changing perception of musical style. In the years around 1490 Obrecht fused the different styles and techniques of his earlier works in a new, highly individual idiom. This creation of a new style would become the most significant development in his creative career.

7 TOWARDS A NEW LANGUAGE

OBRECHT'S mature style seems to have emerged quite suddenly in the late 1480s; watermark evidence indicates that it had reached full bloom by 1491–3, with such works as *Fortuna desperata* and *Rose playsante*. The idiom in these and other mature works is so distinct from everything we have seen so far that a break with the past rather than a smooth transition must be suspected. This major turning-point in Obrecht's creative career cannot be dated with accuracy, but several influences and pressures may have co-operated to bring it about: the fundamental reconsideration of his stylistic premisses during the critical phase (1486–8), fresh impulses from the Ferrarese musical environment (1487–8), and the increased demand for new mass settings that he faced on his return to Bruges in 1488 (see Ch. 6).

The mature style may have started as yet another 'experiment' during the critical phase—one that turned out to be so felicitous that it became a virtual recipe for subsequent masses. Around 1488 the time was certainly ripe for Obrecht to develop a successful personal style. One can see this, for instance, in the *Missa Ave regina celorum*. This work adopts several of the favourite structural and formal devices of Obrecht's earlier masses, but these are now rearranged and handled more freely. The mass seems to sum up and reflect upon the composer's past, and does so in a remarkably confident stylistic idiom—itself apparently a reflection on the various styles Obrecht had come to master during the 1480s. *Ave regina celorum* shows a tendency towards integration that sets it apart from the diversifying trends of the critical phase. A similar tendency must have led to the creation of the mature style. I suggest that the mass was written on the eve of that development, some time around 1488.

The *Missa De Sancto Johanne Baptista* must be of approximately the same date. Like its counterparts, the masses for St Martin and St Donatian, it is a work of moderation and restraint, reflecting its probable purpose as a private commemoration mass. There are links with works from the critical phase, *Salve diva parens* in particular, but its structural relationship with Busnoys's *Missa L'homme armé* connects it to one of Obrecht's mature cycles, his own *L'homme armé* mass. A tissue of recurring motifs in these works as well as in *Ave regina celorum* suggests a date around the close of the critical phase.

Independent evidence strengthens the assumption that the two masses were written in Bruges in the late 1480s. The special significance accorded to Frye's *Ave regina celorum*, the model of Obrecht's mass, is well attested in Bruges during these years. The format of *De Sancto Johanne* parallels that of two masses that were almost certainly written in Bruges in 1486–7: *De Sancto Martino* and *Donatiano*. And although Busnoys's *Missa L'homme armé*, on which the St John mass was structured, enjoyed fame throughout continental Europe, its author was a colleague of Obrecht in Bruges in the years before 1492.

Missa Ave regina celorum

Beyond Busnoys, beyond Ockeghem, beyond Weerbecke and Josquin: in the *Missa Ave regina celorum* Jacob Obrecht speaks his own language.[1] A new quality pervades this work that cannot be caught in accounts of cantus-firmus usage, imitative procedures, or motivic treatment alone. It has a richness of sound, a sense of natural poise and momentum—innate to the counterpoint itself—that appears to flow spontaneously from the composer's invention. That 'outward' quality seems as effortless and uncontrived as it is difficult for the scholar to pin down. Yet it conceals an inward structure that is highly schematic, almost arbitrary in its construction: the tenor of an antiphon setting by Walter Frye is presented in various mensural permutations. There is a tension here between rigorous construction and spontaneous invention—a tension that will become increasingly acute in Obrecht's mature masses, where the rationality of the overall planning is consistently stepped up. In modern analysis that schematic component is inevitably overemphasized. Only performance can truly reveal how easily Obrecht's musical imagination transcends the narrow bounds of structure. In actual sound, the sheer directness of the

---

[1] For this mass, see Meier, *Studien zur Meßkomposition*, 23 and 100–1; G. Reese, *Music in the Renaissance* (rev. edn., New York, 1959), 200–1; Salop, 'The Masses of Jacob Obrecht', 21–6, 131–3, and 161–2; Strohm, *Music in Late Medieval Bruges*, 147; Sparks, *Cantus Firmus*, 254–6; *NOE* 1, pp. xxii–xxxv; R. Strohm, 'The Close of the Middle Ages', in J. W. McKinnon (ed.), *Man & Music: Antiquity and the Middle Ages* (Basingstoke and London, 1990), 307–8.

musical event pushes rational considerations to the background: no matter how rigidly laid out we know the tenor to be, in his best works it is always made to appear freshly invented along with the other voices—as though all lines were conceived in a single creative act. *Ave regina celorum* is such a work. The mass must be ranked among Obrecht's finest compositions.

The choice of an English motet as the model for a mass was unusual for composers of Obrecht's generation, but then Walter Frye's *Ave regina celorum, mater regis angelorum* was an unusual work. Short and tuneful, it enjoyed a truly spectacular career in continental Europe, where it survives in no fewer than thirteen manuscripts copied from the mid-1450s onwards. As a choirboy and son of a trumpeter Obrecht must have virtually grown up with this piece, hearing and performing it on many occasions—public, votive, and domestic. Even after English music ceased to be transmitted to the Continent, in the 1470s, *Ave regina celorum* remained a piece of special significance. Two altar-pieces painted in Bruges in the 1480s show the Virgin surrounded by angels glorifying her in song; and the music they sing is Walter Frye's *Ave regina celorum*.[2] These are to be taken as more than playful references to a well-known and much-loved piece of music. What the anonymous painters depicted, with meticulous realism, was an actual reality, constantly present in the minds of the faithful, remembered and reflected in prayer and worship at every moment of the day (Pl. 12). To envisage Frye's setting as part of that heavenly reality is high honour for a human creation indeed. The motet's perceived role as the angelic song in praise of Mary gives it an almost sacred aura, as though it were a liturgical chant.[3] By selecting it as the model for his mass, Obrecht, like the two anonymous painters, was not so much concerned with paying tribute to Walter Frye as to the Virgin, the Queen of Angels.

[2] The painters are known as the Master of the Embroidered Foliage and the Master of the Legend of St Lucy. See R. Hammerstein, *Die Musik der Engel: Untersuchungen zur Musikanschauung des Mittelalters* (Munich, 1962); E. Winternitz, 'On Angel Concerts in the 15th Century: A Critical Approach to Realism and Symbolism in Sacred Painting', *Musical Quarterly*, 49 (1963), 450–63; S. Kenney, 'Four Settings of "Ave Regina Coelorum"', A. Vander Linden (ed.), *Liber amicorum Charles Van den Borren* (Antwerp, 1964), 98–104; P. E. Carapezza, '*Regina angelorum in musica picta*: Walter Frye e il "Maître au Feuillage Brodé"', *Rivista italiana di musicologia*, 10 (1975), 134–54. The musical notation of the motet also appears in the context of angelic praise in the ceiling paintings of the oratory of the castle of Montreuil-Bellay, France, probably dating from about 1485–8. See G. Thibault, 'L'Oratoire du château de Montreuil-Bellay: Ses anges musiciens—son motet polyphonique', in *Memorie e contributi alla musica dal Medioevo all'età moderna offerti a F. Ghisi nel settantesimo compleanno (1901–1971)* (*Quadrivium*, 12; Bologna, 1971), i. 209–23.

[3] Details of Obrecht's text underlay suggest that he did indeed treat Frye's tenor as though it were a liturgical chant: the Netherlands source VatS 160 regularly provides the text of the motet at the relevant places of the cantus firmus (see *NOE* 1, pp. xxxii–xxxiv). This is otherwise known to have been done only in masses based on chant cantus firmi (see Planchart, 'Parts with Words and without Words', and Hudson, 'On the Texting of Obrecht's Masses').

PL. 12. *Mary, Queen of Heaven*, by the Master of the St Lucy Legend (*c*.1485–1500). Samuel H. Kress Collection (© 1993 National Gallery of Art, Washington, DC)

The scene depicted in the two altars had a direct parallel in everyday life. It was mirrored in the daily *Salve* or *Lof* service, in which singers gathered around the image of the Virgin just as the choirs of angels surrounded her in the heavens. The parallelism was probably intentional, and suggests that Frye's *Ave regina celorum* was a favourite piece in this kind of votive context. As choirmaster and succentor at Bergen op Zoom and Bruges, Jacob Obrecht must have directed hundreds of *Lof* services, many of which no doubt featured the motet. This may explain his writing of yet another work based on Frye's tenor: his four-part motet *Ave regina celorum* quotes that tenor literally, albeit transposed down a third (to suit the original antiphon melody that he quotes in the top voice) and re-notated in ₵.[4] Obrecht's setting undoubtedly served in the same kinds of context as its model, and provides additional testimony to its continued use and significance on the Continent.

Several strands of meaning thus came together in the *Missa Ave regina celorum*: Frye's motet had a history, stretching back to the years of Obrecht's youth, and an everyday actuality, linking human and angelic song in synchronous praise. The significance of this can hardly have escaped Obrecht in his mass, for such a link was specifically implored in the Preface before the Sanctus. The analogy may well have inspired two striking moments in the Patrem and Benedictus where the top voice of Frye's motet suddenly appears in the top voice of the mass—moving imperturbably in its own mensuration, as though subject to different laws of time, and yet harmonizing wonderfully with the busy counterpoint beneath it. Ex. 19 shows the effect of this procedure in the Patrem (bars 49–77). The first bar of the example shows the final chord of a cadence on F that marks the end of an extended cantus-firmus statement. The contrapuntal voices immediately deflect this into a cadence on B-flat, and thereafter proceed in duos. In bars 53–8 there is an extended imitation between contratenor and bass, at a temporal interval of only one minim. If this recalls similar 'stretto' imitations in *Missa Adieu mes amours* that may not be coincidental, for when the top voice finally starts quoting Frye's top voice, from bar 58 onwards, another procedure typical of that mass makes

---

[4] This was discovered by Manfred Bukofzer (*Studies in Medieval and Renaissance Music*, 309–10). The tenor was probably renotated by Petrucci's editor, to bring it mensurally into line with the other voices (the motet is uniquely transmitted in 1504³). Obrecht presumably used Frye's original notation in O, employing a C₄ rather than C₂ clef; the mensural layout of his motet would thus have been identical with that of the Et iterum of his *Missa Ave regina celorum*. There exists a musical parallel between Obrecht's two settings: the superius of the motet, bars 11–15, is identical with that of the Christe, bars 15–19 (cf. *NOE* 1, p. xxv). It is, however, difficult to say which work was written first; there is no basis for the assumption that the mass was based on the motet (*NOE* 1, p. xxv). One of Agricola's *Salve reginas* also parallels Obrecht's motet (Strohm, *The Rise*, 613–15).

its appearance: the continuous imitation of the same motif, in a passage that is all motion and no development (cf. Ex. 18). The device may seem simplistic, but it is in fact highly effective here: it generates a sense of pure drive, thus heightening the contrast with the slow-moving cantus firmus. That this contrast was intentional appears from the next few bars, in which Obrecht steps up the rhythmic activity: minim–semiminim movement becomes the norm, and is slowed down only in the approach to cadences (bars 64–5, 67–8, 70–1, 73–5). The texture abounds in imitations of brief motifs, mostly scalar patterns, at short time-intervals. This is Obrecht at his best: he invests the lower voices with so much musical energy that the top voice seems almost other-worldly by comparison.[5] The top part would probably have been performed by boys, who in Bruges were required to have a 'vox angelica'.[6] Together with the more 'earthly' men's voices, this passage would have been a telling representation of the musical conjunction between heaven and earth.[7] Obrecht used this device more often, usually as part of elaborate structural schemes (*Caput, Malheur me bat,* and *Sub tuum presidium*); invariably he put it to great effect.

   Structurally *Ave regina celorum* points to the past; it recalls *O lumen ecclesie* and *Sicut spina rosam* in particular. As in the latter work, the Gloria and Credo are set apart from the other movements by a common head-motif; like that of *O lumen ecclesie* this head-motif presents the beginning of the cantus firmus in alternating voice-pairs structured in bipartite layouts. The remaining movements open directly with four-part writing, a feature that links them to the corresponding movements in *Sicut spina rosam*. The presence of head-motifs, however limited, and the prominent use of *tempus perfectum* would suggest a date of about 1488 or earlier (see Ch. 6). Although Obrecht prefers to quote Frye's tenor in its original notation, he sometimes presents it in free elaborations (Et in terra, Qui tollis, Patrem, Agnus Dei II). The alternation of a main notational version of the cantus firmus with several free paraphrases is yet another feature that links *Ave regina celorum* with earlier works: it recalls similar treatment of the tenor in the masses *Petrus apostolus, Beata viscera,* and *Sicut spina rosam*. Again the link is closest with the latter work, in that the Gloria–Credo

---

[5] The passage recalls Glareanus' well-known comment: 'It also gave [Heinrich Isaac] pleasure to show his versatility especially in tones remaining unchanged in any one voice, but with the other voices running about and clamoring around everywhere, just as waves moved by the wind are accustomed to play about a rock in the sea; it is well known that Obrecht also did this, although in a certain other way' (quoted after *Dodecachordon*, trans. Miller, i. 278).

[6] Strohm, *Music in Late Medieval Bruges,* 49.

[7] This order is reversed in the final Agnus Dei, where, as so often in Obrecht's Agnus Dei settings, the cantus firmus appears in the bass.

Ex. 19. Obrecht, *Missa Ave regina celorum*, Patrem, bars 49–77

head-motif is not based on the Kyrie version but on a later elaboration.
Another feature, which these two works share with *De Sancto Donatiano*,
is mensural transformation of a repeated tenor fragment within a single
section (*Sicut spina rosam*, Sanctus; *De Sancto Donatiano*, Christe; *Ave
regina celorum*, Kyrie; see also *Petrus apostolus*, Et in terra). This technique
was to be applied on a structural level in the masses based on segmented
cantus firmi. Finally, the use of cantus-firmus-based canon or quasi-canon
links *Ave regina celorum* with all early Obrecht masses up to *De Sancto*

Donatiano.[8] A significant forward-looking feature is the freely composed four-part extension at the end of the Gloria (bars 223–31); extensions of this kind are otherwise found only in mature masses (see Ch. 8).

Taken together, these features would seem to confirm Reinhard Strohm's suggestion that *Ave regina celorum* was composed in Obrecht's first Bruges period: there are numerous structural parallels with earlier works.[9] At the same time one has the feeling that the quietly flowing style of *Sicut spina rosam* and *De Sancto Martino* and *Donatiano*, and the direct-ness and force of expression of *Salve diva parens* and *Adieu mes amours*, have merged into a new style. Obrecht's excursions into new stylistic regions during the critical phase seem to have enriched his idiom in *Ave regina celorum*. The voices tend to be more closely co-ordinated rhythmi-cally, while retaining contrapuntal independence. It is as though Obrecht has struck a new balance between contrapuntal and chordal writing—although he does not hesitate to move away from that balance to either extreme when the musical context calls for it. Rhythmic and melodic patterns in one voice are often simultaneously stated in another, some-times in all. As a result, the basic pulse is no longer understated, as in *Sicut spina rosam* or *De Sancto Donatiano*, but receives regular emphasis. Rhythmic co-ordination is often extended to all voices in the approach to cadences, so that these, too, receive stronger emphasis. Since the cadences are often placed in quick succession, they punctuate not only the phrase structure of the music but also its underlying metric order—thus enhan-cing the clarity of diction. Melodic co-ordination is strongest between the top voice and bass, which frequently move in parallel tenths. Melodic interest is concentrated in the top voice: its smooth and graceful lines are chiefly responsible for the sense of spontaneous invention that dominates the counterpoint. The frequent parallel-tenth 'duplication' of these lines in the bass only enhances that quality. Obrecht's style appears on the whole to be simpler but more effective. He subtly controls the musical pace and intensity by shifting the balance between different stylistic ingre-dients. Extremes are avoided: the exuberance and variety of *Salve diva parens*, the contrapuntal rigour of *De Sancto Donatiano*, the imitative writing and speed of *Adieu mes amours*: all these qualities have now merged in a new idiom. Obrecht is moving towards a new language.

The Et in terra may serve to illustrate Obrecht's style in *Ave regina celorum* (see Ex. 20). The bipartite motto-tenor structure in bars 1–9 introduces the cantus firmus in two pairs of imitations; it calls to mind the

[8] Et in terra, bars 26–41, Qui tollis up to bar 223, Sanctus, Osanna, and Agnus Dei III (see also Ch. 4, n. 17).   [9] *Music in Late Medieval Bruges*, 147.

Ex. 20. Obrecht, *Missa Ave regina celorum*, Et in terra

(Ex. 20, *cont.*)

very similar opening of the Et in terra of *Missa O lumen ecclesie* (cf. Ex. 8).
The duo in bars 9–13 seems to initiate a second bipartite structure, and
quite possibly this is what Obrecht originally planned to write: had the
tenor entered in bar 12 with a strict imitation of the preceding duo
(contratenor bars 9–12), it would have made good counterpoint up to the
second minim of bar 13. Its second appearance, moreover, would have
coincided with the first cadence, and with a textural expansion from two
to four parts. But in fact Obrecht did not write a bipartite structure here:
the tenor is 'delayed', and when it finally enters, in bar 14, its rhythmici-
zation differs entirely from the pre-imitation in the contratenor. The
logical continuation that is missing here can be found in the Patrem: there,
the first bipartite structure (bars 1–23) is followed by a complete second
one (bars 23–31), before the full texture is finally established.

By failing to bring one procedure to its logical conclusion Obrecht
could initiate another that he did carry through: a sequence running down
through an entire octave (bars 14–21). This striking passage has often been
singled out as an example of Obrecht's alleged facile contrapuntal writing,[10] but in fact it is quite unusual even by his standards. What makes it
unusual is not only the length of the sequence but particularly its context.
This is clear from a comparison with the only precedent for this passage.
As observed in Ch. 6, a similarly extended though less rigidly maintained
four-voice sequence appears in *Salve diva parens* (Agnus Dei III, bars
118–130). There, however, its treatment was conventional: the sequence

---

[10] 'Of all the musicians of this generation, [Obrecht] is the one in whom many have claimed to
see the greatest resemblance to Josquin; but actually his music, though always pleasant, tends to
sound facile . . . He often extends his ideas by interminable sequences, instead of seeking more
skilful solutions; witness the *Gloria* of his Mass "Ave regina caelorum"'; N. Bridgman, 'The Age of
Ockeghem and Josquin', in *New Oxford History of Music*, iii (Oxford, 1960), 273. See also Sparks,
Cantus Firmus, 255–6.

appeared in the course of a longer passage, in which context it was an accepted ingredient of the contemporary stylistic idiom. Few listeners, however, would have expected the device to occur at such an important and carefully prepared moment as a cantus-firmus entry. After the build-up of fourteen bars it could only have the effect of a witticism. On paper that witticism may seem rather poor, since the entire sequence can be seen there at one glance. Evolving in time, however, there is an obvious element of suspense involved. That, indeed, seems to be the point of the passage. The first link is a perfectly normal opening for a four-voice passage; the second a reasonably normal continuation—assuming that free writing will soon follow. By the third link, however, the opening as a whole begins to appear somewhat unorthodox; by the fourth, Obrecht seems to reach the bounds of stylistic decorum. Had he stopped the sequence at this point, it would have seemed a feeble attempt to remain within those bounds. By firmly transgressing them he makes the 'joke' obvious: not five, not six, but seven successive links. By the time the full octave is traversed (bar 21) the joke is over, and Obrecht quickly rounds it off with a major cadence on F (bar 23). The passage is of course striking and unprecedented, but nevertheless incidental, typical not so much of the composer's perceived contrapuntal laxity as of his musical sense of humour. Similar playful deceptions of the listener's expectations can be found in several other masses from the Bruges period (see Ch. 6).

After a brief imitative duo, proper four-part writing follows in bars 26–43. Although less striking, the latter passage is more typical of Obrecht's writing in *Ave regina celorum*. The tenor and bass are continuously in imitation. Extended imitative pairs involving the tenor can also be found in several other sections (Qui tollis; Sanctus; Osanna; Agnus Dei II). They recall similar canonic or quasi-canonic treatment of the tenor in early masses such as *Petrus apostolus*, *Beata viscera*, *O lumen ecclesie*, *Sicut spina rosam*, and *De Sancto Martino*—another reason for suggesting that *Ave regina celorum* was written early in the Bruges period. Above the freely imitative tenor-bass duo the top voice proceeds in smooth, graceful lines, sometimes picking up brief motifs from the lower voices (bars 35–6, 37–8, and 39–40). But the music is neither generated nor constructed by means of imitation: the individual motifs are submerged in the rich flow of counterpoint. Only when the tenor is silent do the contrapuntal voices engage in highly imitative relationships of the kind we encountered in *Adieu mes amours* (bars 23–5).

The style of *Ave regina celorum* is close to that of Obrecht's impressive five-part motet *Salve crux*—another work that the composer is likely to have written for Bruges.[11] Melodic turns in the mass frequently remind one of the motet; in some places the resemblances are so close as to seem almost explicit.[12] It could be objected that the similarity in style is attributable to the identity of mode (both works are in F Lydian), just as the two Phrygian works *Mille quingentis* and *Missa De Sancto Johanne Baptista*, for instance, seem related in their idiom. But this does not explain everything: other Obrecht masses in F Lydian (*O lumen ecclesie*, *Libenter gloriabor*, *Fortuna desperata*, *Rose playsante*, *Je ne demande*) are quite unlike either *Salve crux* or *Missa Ave regina celorum*. In this context the stylistic relationship between the motet and the mass seems significant. Both works seem to bear witness to Obrecht's increased confidence and greater creative ease in the late 1480s.

Missa De Sancto Johanne Baptista

The *Missa De Sancto Johanne* lacks an attribution in its unique source, VatS 160, but there can be little doubt that Obrecht was the composer.[13] The anonymous cycle has close links with several of his masses. It is a multiple-cantus-firmus setting of the same type as *De Sancto Donatiano* and *De Sancto Martino*. Like *L'homme armé*, it is modelled on the *L'homme armé* mass by Antoine Busnoys, albeit in a less obvious way: not the melody of Busnoys's cantus firmus has been taken over, but only its rhythmic layout, which serves as a kind of notational mould for the plainchant melodies of the St John mass. Another work by Obrecht to be modelled on a pre-existing mass is *Caput*. With the exception of Johannes Ockeghem, no other fifteenth-century composer is known to have modelled mass settings on pre-existing cycles. An intriguing link, moreover, exists with *Ave regina celorum* and *L'homme armé*: each of the three masses has a section opening with the same two-voice imitation of a four-bar

[11] Strohm, *Music in Late Medieval Bruges*, 145, and Bloxam, 'A Survey of Late Medieval Service Books', 335–44. *Salve crux* is edited in Jacob Obrecht, *Opera omnia editio altera*, ed. A. Smijers, ii/1 (Amsterdam, 1956), 17–35. It is probable that Johannes Herbenus was referring to *Salve crux* when he mentioned a setting 'salutiferae crucis' by 'Jacobus Hoberti' in 1496. See J. Smits van Waesberghe, *Herbeni Traiectensis De natura cantus ac miraculis vocis* (Beiträge zur rheinischen Musikgeschichte, 22; Cologne, 1957), 58.

[12] Compare Patrem, bars 47–8, and Sanctus, bars 169–70, with *Salve crux*, bars 71–2, and Agnus Dei III, bars 119–20, with *Salve crux*, bars 45–6.

[13] Edited by N. S. Josephson in *Early Sixteenth-Century Sacred Music from the Papal Chapel* (CMM, 95/1; Neuhausen-Stuttgart, 1982), 1–39. The mass and its cantus firmi have been extensively discussed elsewhere, so I confine myself here to its style. See S. E. Hains, 'Missa De Sancto Johanne Baptista' (MA thesis, Smith College, 1974); Bloxam, 'A Survey of Late Medieval Service Books', 438–51; Wegman, 'Another "Imitation"'; N. S. Josephson, 'Formal Symmetry in the High Renaissance', *Tijdschrift van de Vereniging voor Nederlandse Muziekgeschiedenis*, 41 (1991), 105–33.

motif (see Ex. 21*a*–*c*). This motif seems to have had a special significance for Obrecht. In the Christe of *Ave regina celorum* it reappears in the opening of the bass (Ex. 21*d*); a variant happens to occur at the very same place in *Adieu mes amours* (Ex. 21*e*). Moreover, the final Agnus Dei of *L'homme armé* also opens with the motif, stated this time in parallel tenths by the top voice and bass (Ex. 21*f*). No other mass by Obrecht has sections opening with this distinctive motif—let alone in imitation between the top two voices. To these melodic correspondences can be added others. The Benedictus, for instance, opens almost exactly like the Domine Deus of *Salve diva parens* (a similar opening is in the Qui tollis of *De Sancto Johanne*). Further on in the Benedictus there is another correspondence with that mass: a motivic repetition with stepwise expansion (bass; bars 141–50). While this in itself proves little, the motif in question happens to be almost identical with the ones treated in the same way in *Salve diva parens* (cf. Ex. 14*a*–*c* in particular). The Sanctus and Agnus Dei open with tenorless passages structured by means of three-bar phrases repeated within a single voice; this same technique is found in the Sanctus of *Salve diva parens*.

The *Missa De Sancto Johanne Baptista* thus appears to be linked to several masses Obrecht is known or presumed to have written in the years 1486–8. Within the context of his *œuvre* this approximate date is confirmed by the use of a head-motif. The head-motif of the mass is freely conceived, never quoting any of the cantus firmi. Only one Obrecht mass uses a similar type of motto, *De Sancto Donatiano* of 1487. By comparison, Obrecht's *Missa L'homme armé*, also modelled on Busnoys's *L'homme armé* mass, has no motto at all—nor indeed does any other mass datable after about 1488 or 1489.

The style of *De Sancto Johanne Baptista* is entirely consistent with that of Obrecht, although the mass lacks the dynamism and energy so typical of his mature works. Like *De Sancto Martino* and *De Sancto Donatiano*, the setting is kept comparatively low-key. Imitative devices are mostly reserved for tenorless passages and sections, and seem to be used not so much for generating musical energy as for maintaining the even, flowing pace of the full sections. The melodic style is fluent: energetic rhythmic patterns are avoided, and the writing is markedly less vigorous and agitated than in other Obrecht masses. The use of the Phrygian mode adds to this quality. Cadences are mostly on E and A, and are usually of the VII$_6$–I type (rare in Obrecht), quietly rounding off preceding stretches of polyphony rather than serving as their climactic conclusions. Most of the eight selected antiphons have A or E as their final; the two that do not

Ex. 21. Related openings of sections in masses by Obrecht: (*a*) *Missa Ave regina celorum*, Domine Fili, bars 44–9; (*b*) *Missa De Sancto Johanne Baptista*, Christe, bars 20–5; (*c*) *Missa L'homme armé*, Qui tollis, bars 53–8; (*d*) *Missa Ave regina celorum*, Christe, bars 24–7; (*e*) *Missa Adieu mes amours*, Christe, bars 32–5; (*f*) *Missa L'homme armé*, Agnus Dei III, bars 65–8

(*Johannes vocabitur* and *Apertum est os*) have been transposed, a device also employed to maintain modal unity in *De Sancto Donatiano* and *Martino*. As in the latter two masses, the emphasis on restraint and placidity is probably related to function: all three settings must have been written for private services endowed for the salvation of their donors' souls.

This stylistic picture is brought more sharply into focus by comparison with another companion to *De Sancto Johanne*, Obrecht's *Missa L'homme armé*. In general temperament this work differs markedly from the St John mass, emphasizing speed and climactic effect rather than a smoothly flowing, restrained style. The melodic lines are more athletic, rhythmic co-ordination is closer, four-part sequences are used more emphatically, imitative motifs tend to have a sharper melodic profile, and the whole work breathes a sense of energy that is typical of Obrecht's mature style. Again these qualities are at least partly explicable in terms of function. The use of the *L'homme armé* tune brings this work into the competitive atmosphere of the *L'homme armé* tradition: around 1490, to write a mass on this tune was to invite comparison with a string of other such works by Ockeghem, Busnoys, Regis, Caron, Faugues, Basiron, Tinctoris, Dufay, and possibly Josquin, De Orto, and Pipelare. In the St John mass such comparisons would be inappropriate, for the setting alludes not to the binding thread of the tradition (the *L'homme armé* tune), but to one particular work in that tradition. By removing the actual melody on which that work is based, Obrecht indicates what is his main concern: Busnoys's *Missa L'homme armé* has a significance independent of the *L'homme armé* tradition, and this significance must in some way bear upon the person commemorated in the St John mass.

Unfortunately, the identity of the donor remains obscure. No endowments of polyphonic music in connection with St John the Baptist are known in Bruges documents before 1500.[14] Jennifer Bloxam has put forward Antwerp as a possibility, but virtually nothing is known about endowments made in that city in the 1480s or 1490s.[15] One possible clue is the marked emphasis on the *name* of St John in the selection of antiphons. The antiphon *Johannes vocabitur nomen eius* appears as cantus firmus at the opening (Kyrie I), middle (Et incarnatus), and conclusion (Agnus Dei III) of the mass; this may be significant, as the chant had to be transposed up a fifth to suit the Phrygian mode of the setting.[16] The Confiteor ends with the words 'Johannes est nomen eius', and although these are part of the

---

[14] Personal communication from Reinhard Strohm.

[15] 'A Survey of Late Medieval Service Books', 444–51.

[16] The role of this antiphon thus parallels that of the chants *Martinus adhuc cathecuminus* and *O beate pater Donatiane*, which receive similar prominence in the St Martin and St Donatian masses.

cantus firmus *Innuebant patri*, the same words appear at the end of the Agnus Dei I where this is *not* the case: they substitute for the original words 'benedictus Deus Israel' of the cantus firmus *Apertum est os*.[17] In a commemorative context, such repeated references to the name John could possibly suggest that this was the name of the donor.

Other clues also need to be taken into account. Most intriguing of all, of course, is the relationship with Busnoys's *Missa L'homme armé*. Why would it have been appropriate in a privately endowed mass to fit eight cantus firmi into a pre-existing mass layout? Whatever the reason, one thing seems clear: it must have been Obrecht's personal decision to do so, for neither his position nor the actual endowment could have demanded that he pose himself such a difficulty. If so, it is hard to suppose that he would have considered this an appropriate choice had he not known the donor personally: Busnoys's *Missa L'homme armé* must have had a special significance for the donor, and Obrecht was aware of this. This in turn suggests that the writing of the mass, with the added difficulty of modelling it upon a pre-existent setting, may have been a personal gesture, not part of the composer's normal duties as succentor at St Donatian's. This would place the donor in Obrecht's circle, though not necessarily in Bruges. Bearing in mind the apparent emphasis on the name John, it might have been his friend and fellow musician Jean Cordier, or perhaps his erstwhile guardian, the prominent Ghent citizen Jan Obrecht. Another possibility is that it was his father Willem, who had travelled and worked with Busnoys in the late 1460s, and had probably introduced his son to the composer. Willem was rich enough to endow a mass in polyphony when he died around December 1488 (see Ch. 5). Such a service might have taken place in one of the side-chapels of the church of St John the Baptist at Ghent; it was here that he and his fellow trumpeters founded a chapel for St Andrew in 1459 (see Ch. 2). The Nativity of St John, for which Obrecht's mass was written, was one of the six feasts on which visitors to the chapel would receive periods of remission. It is not impossible that Willem Obrecht might have wished to punctuate this major feast in the chapel with an annual mass for the repose of his soul. Documentary evidence for this speculation is lacking, but a date around 1489 would be consistent with Obrecht's stylistic development, and, as indicated above, is independently suggested by close links with several masses dating from that time or earlier.

*　　*　　*

[17] Noted by Bloxam, 'A Survey of Late Medieval Service Books', 440.

Up to the present point in this study each of Obrecht's masses had to some degree a distinct stylistic profile. It seems as though in his earlier years the composer was concerned to write something new and original each time, while broadly remaining within the same formal–technical framework: free elaboration of a chant melody with mensural transformation, strict repeats of the Kyrie version, cantus-firmus-based head-motifs, bipartite motto-tenor structures, and so on. That framework and its development could be traced in masses as diverse as *Petrus apostolus*, *Sicut spina rosam*, and *De Sancto Martino*, while we witnessed its dissolution in the critical phase. Traces of it were still visible in *Ave regina celorum* and *De Sancto Johanne Baptista*, but with these works we have now reached a major turning-point in Obrecht's creative career.

At this point, it seems, everything changes. Not only do we see the establishment of a new formal–technical framework, but there is a tendency towards much greater stylistic uniformity. Individual works now seem to be realizations of one and the same stylistic concept, rather than stages in an ongoing creative development. For that reason it is difficult to propose a relative chronology of Obrecht's mature *œuvre*. Both the new framework and the new style hold that *œuvre* together, and set it off from the preceding period. Indeed, there appears to be virtually no overlap between the works from before and after this central turning-point. While *Ave regina celorum* and *De Sancto Johanne Baptista* could still be regarded as late examples of an ongoing development, stretching back to the 1470s, little connects these to the works that follow. Obrecht's style will now develop within a changed set of stylistic parameters. To chart and describe these parameters will be the goal of the next chapter.

8 THE MATURE STYLE

SOMEWHERE in the four years between 1487 and 1491 Obrecht hit upon a creative formula that unlocked his full artistic potential. This discovery was the central turning-point in his career. The few securely dated works on either side of the four-year period leave no doubt that he virtually underwent a creative rebirth. On the one side are the masses of 1486–7, in which Obrecht is still a searching, exploring composer. He wrestles with the received idiom and consciously absorbs others, in an attempt to create new forms, new modes of expression. On the other side are the 1491–3 masses, which include such masterpieces as *Rose playsante* and *Fortuna desperata*. Here, Obrecht seems almost overconfident as an artist. He controls his material with consummate ease, voluntarily stepping up the technical difficulties in the assurance that nothing can stem the flow of his invention. To compose, now, is to channel that flow, to discipline the wealth of his ideas. The tension between spontaneous invention and rigorous construction that we observed earlier in *Ave regina celorum* is raised to an extreme point: the new masses are brimming with musical energy, yet this quality is held in check by an almost conspicuous rationality of organization. Obrecht is at the height of his creative powers.

What had happened in those four years? How could the composer have resolved his earlier creative problems so quickly and successfully? How in fact did he resolve them? What was the answer that had eluded him in previous years? These questions are not easily answered, but one thing seems certain. The stylistic gap between the masses of 1486–7 and those of 1491–3 cannot be explained by assuming a continuous line of evolutionary development: the creation of the new style must have been a fresh start. There is a context for such a radical change of tack, of course, in the various 'false starts' of the critical phase. Yet while these never led to more than isolated experiments, the final change evidently released the potential for further development—which potential had been realized by 1491–3.

Taking the 1491–3 masses as our starting-point, we may attempt to sketch the stylistic developments that preceded them. Unfortunately, there are very few datable works to go by: only *Je ne demande* and *Plurimorum carminum I* are likely to pre-date *Fortuna desperata* and *Rose playsante*, since they were copied in about 1487–91. Yet these works do provide, as might have been expected, a picture of a style in development: not quite as magisterial as *Fortuna desperata* or *Rose playsante*, yet clearly breathing the same spirit, and demonstrably sharing the same compositional outlook. A large group of undated masses paint exactly that picture. In the final section of this chapter it will be suggested that these works may predate the 1491–3 masses as well. If so, the late 1480s must have been the most productive and innovative years in the composer's career. With the creation of the new, mature style, Obrecht became the composer as he was to be remembered by posterity: proficient, prolific, exuberant, playful, and, above all, highly individualistic.

The '1491–3' Masses

Before departing into considered hypothesis, however, we must proceed, for the time being, on firm ground. And so the 'new' masses copied by 1491–3, which provide us with a solid chronological anchor-point, must be our point of departure. The most advanced of the new masses is certainly *Missa Fortuna desperata*.[1] It is breathtaking in its boldness, in

---

[1] For this mass, see Gombosi, *Jacob Obrecht*, 112–16; Reese, *Music in the Renaissance*, 201; M. Antonowytsch, 'Renaissance-Tendenzen in den Fortuna-desperata-Messen von Josquin und Obrecht', *Musikforschung*, 9 (1956), 1–26; Osthoff, *Josquin Desprez*, i. 147–8; Sparks, *Cantus Firmus*, 248–9; Todd, 'Retrograde, Inversion', 61–2; Hudson, 'Two Ferrarese Masses'; Strohm, *The Rise*, 620–33. For the copying date, see Just, *Der Mensuralkodex*, ii. 28. Just's dating of gathering 14 of BerlS 40021, which contains Obrecht's mass, is supported by the fact that gatherings 5–15 comprise ten different paper-types (often intermingled within gatherings), all of which are documented within the period 1488–96. It is an established principle of paper research that the date of an individual type of paper is more secure if that type is found intermingled with different paper-types documented in the same years. The paper on which Obrecht's mass was copied (watermark: Bischofshut 19) is dated 1489–93, and found intermingled with another paper-type, dated 1491–4, in gathering 11 (Krone 1). The latter in turn is found intermingled with two other paper-types, both dated 1492–5, in gatherings 2 and 9 (Ochsenkopf 7 and 8). Of these, Ochsenkopf 7 is found intermingled with two more paper-types, dated 1492–6 and 1488–92, in gatherings 8 and 13 (Ochsenkopf 11 and 5). (See Just, *Der Mensuralkodex* ii. 196–200 for reproductions.) Given the overwhelming consistency of these datings (1488–92, 1489–93, 1491–4, 1492–5, 1492–6), any argument that Obrecht's mass might have been entered in BerlS 40021 later than, say, 1492 or 1493 would have to be based on more compelling grounds than a vague uneasiness about watermark evidence in general. (I accept Noblitt's similarly consistent datings of MunBS 3154 for the same reason.) Gombosi pointed out that the first seven bars of Obrecht's Osanna correspond almost exactly to the same bars of the Agnus Dei II of Josquin's *Missa Fortuna desperata* (*Jacob Obrecht*, 115–16; see Osthoff, *Josquin Desprez*, i. 148, for a musical example). The question who quotes whom is difficult to answer as long as we do not have a clear picture of Josquin's musical development. *Prima facie*, however, it seems likely that Obrecht's mass was composed first, since Josquin, so far as we can tell, had scarcely made a name for himself as a mass composer by the early 1490s.

its conception totally different from anything seen in previous chapters. Despite its early date, *Fortuna desperata* already seems to be the culminating achievement of the mature period. It sums up, in concentrated form, much of what is typical of these years, and adds to this the touch of genius. Not surprisingly, scholars have included the mass among the composer's latest surviving works. The present study would certainly have concurred —were it not for the recently discovered (and surprisingly early) copying date of 1489–93. The new dating evidence necessitates a fundamental reassessment of Obrecht's creative development, the focus of this chapter.

The new conception is already evident in the first Kyrie, a section built with an almost classical sense of symmetry and periodicity (Ex. 22). The basic structure of the opening is simple. In bars 1–5 the contratenor and bass present a brief two-voice unit cadencing on F, which is immediately repeated in the top voice and contratenor (bars 5–9). The two melodic phrases of the unit are then separated, and distributed over the next two periods: the bottom phrase in bars 9–13 (top voice), and the top phrase in bars 13–17 (tenor). Only at the latter point does it emerge that the top phrase is in fact the cantus-firmus incipit, and the preceding units therefore pre-emptive statements reminiscent of the old motto-tenor structures.

Yet such words are no longer helpful in this context. It is immediately clear that this 'terraced' opening is far removed from genuine motto-tenor structures (despite their late appearance in such works as *Salve diva parens* and *Ave regina celorum*). Although there is a superficial resemblance, the underlying *conception* has changed: the tenor entry is not the focal point of the 'introduction', but merely one of several steps in a continuous musical development. Purely in terms of structure there is of course no development: each unit presents the same material, and there is a cadence on F after every four bars. Yet the repetitiveness on this level merely helps to bring out the extraordinary sense of development on others. The bottom phrase of bars 1–5 moves up an octave in bars 5–9, and yet another octave in bars 9–13. In the third unit it not only dominates the texture, but is given extra emphasis through parallel-tenth duplication in the bass. Other parameters reinforce this development. The third unit combines the two-part scorings of the previous ones in a three-part texture, thus providing a sense of textural accumulation. The disappearance of the slow-moving top phrase, moreover, enables Obrecht to step up the rhythmic drive. All this culminates in the fourth unit, which sees the final expansion to four-part texture, and concludes the sixteen-bar development with a cadence on F (bar 17).

Ex. 22. Obrecht, *Missa Fortuna desperata*, Kyrie I

Periodicity and continuity are held in a new balance. For instance, Obrecht's previous tendency to understate or evade cadences so as not to interrupt the contrapuntal flow (cf. Ex. 20, bars 27–30) has disappeared. Indeed his means of achieving continuity are now so powerful that even emphatic cadences figure as mere punctuation marks. For a cadence now to be truly 'final', it needs to be given extra emphasis. Obrecht does this by lengthening and drastically simplifying the chord progression. Thus, while a cadence like that in bar 13 would have been firmly 'final' by the standards of five years ago (cf. Ex. 20, bar 43), it now needs to be outdone by an almost exaggeratedly blunt progression (bars 15–17). Here we touch on an essential feature of *Fortuna desperata*. Obrecht is able to generate such an extraordinary sense of motion that he needs extra-strong means of articulation to control it. And since it is mainly by *lengthening* progressions that he acquires those means, his sense of musical proportion and symmetry is profoundly influenced as a result. That sense is not so much rational as intuitive, and often a combination or compromise between the two.

An example of such a compromise can be found further on in Ex. 22. After the cadence in bar 17 Obrecht retains rhythmic energy by immediately introducing an imitation based on the top phrase of the previous bars. The phrase is quoted strictly in the contratenor (bars 18–22), and bridges a brief tenorless period. In these bars the music is in full motion, and thus it comes as no surprise that it ends with a cadence designed to outdo even the previous one (bars 29–31). Once again Obrecht lengthens the basic progression, and for this he is now even prepared to depart temporarily from strict cantus-firmus quotation. If he had remained faithful to the original tune, bar 30 should have immediately followed bar 28—quite possibly this is what he originally wrote. The 'insertion' of bar 29 is structurally unwarranted, yet one can easily understand why it was put here: it adds force to the cadence, and thus helps to control the sheer drive of the music. This is a typical example of how Obrecht's concern with controlling motion influences his intuitive sense of proportion, and occasionally even overrides the rationality that has so often been seen as more typical of his music. Of course, the composer usually manages to create the same effect *within* the constraints of the cantus firmus. Yet there are more 'random' licences in his later masses than one might think, and these show that he was and remained musician first, architect second. Although the licences obviously diminish the rational elegance of his ground-plans, their musical effect is invariably powerful.

The remainder of the first Kyrie shows this even more clearly. Bars 31–49 are an extension in which the tenor states free material in place of the cantus firmus. Structurally this passage is an afterthought, and perhaps it was so in terms of the compositional process as well. There is no obvious reason why the Christe could not have followed directly after a final cadence in bar 31—except perhaps that the first Kyrie might then seem too short in relation to the musical energy it had generated. It is exactly this problem that the extension appears to remedy. In structure as well as length it balances the chain structure in bars 1–17, yet there is one fundamental difference: it winds down where the opening section built up. The melodic line in the bass, bars 1–5, not only ascended by an octave, but was itself transposed up an octave on each repeat. By contrast, the top-voice phrase in bars 31–6 *descends* by an octave, and is, moreover, transposed down an octave in its second statement (bass, bars 34–40). By the time the cadence in bar 40 is reached, Obrecht has released enough steam to allow himself a textural expansion—or rather thickening, for bars 40–6 give the impression of spinning-out rather than building up. Only in the approach to the final cadence, in bars 46–9, is there a real expansion of the combined texture, yet this is merely to create a fitting conclusion to a section that has now truly come to rest.

As a structural licence the freely composed coda in bars 31–49 is obviously more extended than the 'insertion' of bar 29, yet the difference is one of degree, not of principle. Both cases can be seen as modifications of a rigidly predetermined form, motivated by the desire to control musical momentum. There is a sense here that a musical process, once set in motion, dictates exactly the amount of time needed for it to wind down— no more, no less. If the cantus firmus cannot accommodate, it will have to be adjusted, or supplemented with free material. The Kyrie of *Fortuna desperata* shows that Obrecht had no hesitation to do this even in his most advanced works.

It hardly needs pointing out that there is no context for any of the new features in earlier masses. Despite the short temporal distance from the critical phase, we seem to be talking about a different composer altogether. It is not just that musical parameters are handled differently. That is merely the effect of an underlying cause: a totally new *interaction* between parameters. The parameters have changed because they are fine-tuned to each other in a new complex of functional relationships. The sound to which they add up is not floating, as in *De Sancto Donatiano* or *Ave regina celorum*, but seems firmly rooted in the earth.

This is already evident on the most basic level, that of rhythmic structure. Although there are plenty of dotted rhythms and syncopations, these are contained in stereotyped rhythmic patterns that, when strung together, constantly reaffirm the beat. The horizontal interplay of these patterns gives the sound a strongly pulsating quality. The rhythmic patterns are articulated by the melodic motion, which is predominantly triadic in outline, and held together by tight phrase structures. The melodic phrases, in turn, are articulated by heavily emphasized cadences, and held together by the clear sense of harmonic direction and coherence that these provide. Cadences are central to the style of *Fortuna desperata*, not merely as the two-part frameworks described in contemporary theory, but as full chord progressions. They are Obrecht's punctuation marks, and as such they tend to be firm, frequent, and overwhelmingly on the final. At every turn the listener is encouraged to expect an imminent cadence on F, particularly when the music is structured, as in Ex. 22, in short periods. Indeed, often such periods themselves seem little more than elaborated cadential progressions (see, for instance, Ex. 22, bars 13–17, or Ex. 23 below, bars 135–9 and 214–18). Everything here, from the minute detail to the broader structure, co-operates, interlocks, dovetails: no ingredient can be isolated from this complex, and considered separately. The Kyrie of *Fortuna desperata* is the work of a composer who knows exactly what he wants, and who takes the most efficient and direct way to achieve it.

We see many of the same principles in the Qui tollis, though applied with much greater freedom (Ex. 23). The section is based on the full cantus firmus (here the second voice from the top), whose treatment is identical with that of the preceding Et in terra: the first half is stated in retrograde (bar 163 back to 110), the second *ut iacet* (bars 164–218). On paper the rationality of layout is conspicuous, yet in sound this rational element is firmly pushed backstage by the sheer wealth of Obrecht's invention.

Much of the writing seems familiar. At the very beginning there are two six-bar units (bars 110–15 and 116–21), both internally organized by motivic repetitions in the bass, and both cadencing on F. There is no attempt to build up musical energy (the parallel passage in the Et in terra starts with a point of imitation), for the section continues where the Et in terra had left off. We see, rather, the reverse: rhythmic energy is maintained so as to set off the entry of the cantus firmus (bar 122), which is emphasized with solemn semibreve chords.

At this point Obrecht shifts from F to C as a secondary centre of tonal gravity, cadencing on that degree in bars 125, 128, and 129. (By 'secondary' centre of tonal gravity, or tonal plane, I understand a degree that is temporarily given a measure of self-sufficiency, usually through repeated cadences; this is a stylistic feature, and does not affect the modal unity.)

Ex. 23. Obrecht, *Missa Fortuna desperata*, Qui tollis

(Ex. 23, *cont.*)

(Ex. 23, *cont.*)

To some extent he is forced to do so by the cantus firmus, although it would have been possible to remain in the F sonority (a cadence on F is possible in bar 126, as is shown by the parallel passage in Et in terra, bar 17). In any case, in a mass so persistently and firmly centred on the final, any departure is bound to seem a dramatic musical event. Obrecht increases that sense by prolonging the departure, thereby stepping up the tension that the eventual return to the final releases. Once again a comparison with a mass written a few years earlier is helpful. *Missa De Sancto Donatiano* of 1487 cultivates, as we have seen, an Ockeghem-like 'floating' sound: cadences tend to be understated, irregularly placed, and fairly random as to the tonal degree. In Ex. 13, for instance, fifteen cadential progressions can be identified, only four of which are on the final.[2] The floating quality here is tonal as well as contrapuntal: there is no persistently emphasized centre of gravity, as in *Fortuna desperata*. A departure as in bars 122–9 of Ex. 23 would have meant little in *De Sancto Donatiano*. In *Fortuna desperata* it can only appear to be a decisive musical shift.

There are more such departures in the example, all prolonged: one to B flat in bars 141–52, and one to A Phrygian in bars 176–88 (suggested by the cantus firmus), which is immediately followed by one on D in bars 189–94. In between there are brief passages that bring back the final F in as powerful a way they can. After the first departure to C, Obrecht returns to F with the cadence in bar 135; the unit that follows in bars 135–9 is basically a prolonged and virtually unadorned cadence, confirming the final in exceedingly simple yet powerful fashion.

The same is true of bars 152–77, in which each of four successive cadences rams the final home with stronger emphasis. Again this is a matter of increasing retardation: the first cadence comes after two bars,

---

[2] Bars 6, 9, 11, 18, and 25–6; the other cadential progressions are in bars 5, 7, 8, 10, 14, 17, 20, 22, 25, 28, and 30 (four on A, three on C, and four on D).

and has the dissonance on the minim (bars 153–4). The second comes after four bars and has the dissonance on the semibreve (bars 157–8). The third cadence concludes a period of six bars, and, in bars 161–4, repeats the strikingly prolonged cadence we have seen at the end of Ex. 22. In the following passage of twelve bars—surely one of the most unusual in all fifteenth-century music—this progression is slightly altered so as to remove its cadential effect, and stated six times in an impressive build-up towards the fourth cadence (bars 175–6), which crowns the entire twenty-five bar 'F period'. Given the length of that period, it seems hardly surprising that the third and longest tonal departure (to A and D, bars 176–95) should be followed by a longer 'F period' than the remaining nine bars of cantus firmus allow (bars 196–204; see above). The 'final' cadence in bar 204 would have been conclusive enough by the standards of five years ago, yet here it can only appear premature. The thirteen-bar extension is necessary to establish a balance with the central 'F period' in bars 152–76: it consists of three four-bar periods, each cadencing on F, of which the third is simplest and most powerful.[3]

Obrecht's music, some scholars have argued, represents an early stage in the development of harmonic tonality.[4] If that term is perhaps anachronistic (as indeed the very act of describing this music), the phenomenon it describes is genuine. *Fortuna desperata* shows a drastically simplified harmonic language, a tendency to think in distinct tonal 'planes', and a consequent sense of formal symmetry and balance. One could scarcely describe the creative process in this mass as a matter of merely adding voices to a pre-existing tune. The ultimate challenge for Obrecht was to create coherent, long-term developments in which the tenor—even though predetermined—is so naturally involved that it seems spontaneously invented along with the other parts. The Qui tollis is a virtuoso demonstration of his ability to do so. One can describe the section entirely in terms of musical developments, as has been done here, only to realize afterwards that Obrecht created those developments under severe structural limitations. For instance, the thirteen-bar extension in bars 206–18 seems natural and indeed necessary after what preceded it: one feels there has got to be an extension, that the music would be less effective without it. Yet if one looks at the tenor notation,[5] it comes almost

---

[3] Other examples in this mass are: Et in terra, bars 96–109; Patrem, bars 99–109; and Et incarnatus, bars 208–18.

[4] See in particular A. Salop, 'Jacob Obrecht and the Early Development of Harmonic Polyphony', *Journal of the American Musicological Society*, 17 (1964), 288–309, and R. D. Ross, 'Toward a Theory of Tonal Coherence: The Motets of Jacob Obrecht', *Musical Quarterly*, 69 (1981), 143–64.

[5] See the reconstruction, printed in *NOE* 4, p. xxxiii.

as a surprise that the extension would have had to be there anyway, whether motivated musically or not: the placement of the rests is symmetrical, so that those at the end mirror those at the beginning. This is Obrecht at his best: even the most arbitrary features of the rigid tenor are somehow made to seem musically essential.

Before moving on to our next mass, *Rose playsante*, it is worth pointing briefly to close parallels in *Libenter gloriabor*, a mass whose stylistic idiom is so similar to that of *Fortuna desperata* that it must be of approximately the same date.[6] The Qui tollis of *Libenter gloriabor* in particular shows how closely the masses are related: the first twelve bars of the tenor are introduced in two preceding units that are identical in everything except scoring. The Patrem shows the application of the same principles, though in an entirely different situation. The actual tenor is transformed,[7] yet the opening bars of the section seem to prepare the way for an untransformed version: quasi pre-emptive statements are given in three successive seven-bar units, moving up an octave each time (bars 1–8, 8–15, and 15–22). At the expected entry-point there is an evaded cadence (bar 22). After yet another statement (bars 23–30), a new succession of four-bar units leads directly into the actual entry-point (bars 30–4, 34–8, and 38–42). The balance between continuity and periodicity in these and other terraced openings of *Libenter gloriabor* is exactly the same as in *Fortuna desperata*:

---

[6] For previous discussions, see Meier, *Studien zur Meßkomposition*, 87–92; Sparks, *Cantus Firmus*, 276–8 and 471–2; T. Noblitt, 'Chromatic Cross-Relations and Editorial *Musica ficta* in Masses of Obrecht', *Tijdschrift van de Vereniging voor Nederlandse Muziekgeschiedenis*, 32 (1982), 30–44. Much of the discussion on this mass has centred on the use of sequence, and its implications for *musica ficta*; see M. van Crevel, 'Verwante sequensmodulaties bij Obrecht, Josquin en Coclico', *Tijdschrift der Vereeniging voor Nederlandsche Muziekgeschiedenis*, 16 (1946), 119–21; E. E. Lowinsky, 'Secret Chromatic Art *Re-examined*', in B. S. Brook, E. O. D. Downes, and S. van Solkema (eds.), *Perspectives in Musicology* (New York, 1972), 91–135; M. Bent, 'Diatonic *ficta*', *Early Music History*, 4 (1984), 34–40. Bent has argued that the correct application of rules of solmization in the sequence ending the Kyrie II/Osanna/Agnus Dei III inevitably turns this into a passage running down the circle of fifths, so that the final F *ut* sounds as our pitch F♭. Although this view has recently been challenged (Berger, *Musica Ficta*, 43–8), and has not been adopted in *NOE* 6, it has the merit of being consistent with 15th-c. theory. The notion of pitch stability, on the other hand, which has been advanced by Bent's opponents, is by definition anachronistic, since it cannot be defined in terms of medieval theory. If applied to the sequence in question, it would involve a violation of contemporary rules of solmization. This is a much more serious problem than the proliferation of editorial flats in a modern transcription of the passage (see the musical example in Bent, 'Diatonic *ficta*', 37–9). The latter 'problem' simply reflects the fact that modern notation lacks the efficiency and elegance of mensural notation, which Obrecht's music here presupposes.

[7] The voice survives in what must be a resolution. The basic principle of the canon was discovered by Sparks, *Cantus Firmus*, 471–2, but he was unable to explain it entirely. The original notation was almost certainly in equal longas, with various longa rests functioning as incises between words (except after 'libenter'), in the same way as in *De Sancto Martino*. These longa rests are included in the canon; each is equal to one note. Sparks counted two successive longa rests also as equal to one note, however, so that the order of selection seemed to reverse at some points. (More on the cantus-firmus treatment in *Libenter gloriabor* below, n. 25.)

individual units are delineated by tight phrase structures and emphatic use of cadences, yet there is a clear sense of development, achieved through changes of scoring and a vigorous upward melodic drive.

Libenter gloriabor also closely parallels *Fortuna desperata* with respect to its harmonic language. Cadences are mostly on the final F, and they serve as articulation-points in a lucid contrapuntal structure, in much the same way as in *Fortuna desperata*. Departures to other tonal planes are few, and always followed by repeated reconfirmations of the final. Freely composed extensions after the final note of the tenor can be found in various sections. For instance, in the Qui tollis the last cantus firmus note comes in bar 192, yet this cadence is followed by a twenty-one-bar coda in which the tenor itself is involved with free material (bars 192–213). A similar extension involving free tenor material comes at the end of the Credo (bars 199–211).[8] Yet it is in the melodic content and the overall idiom that the close relationship between the two masses is clearest: at every turn they sound strikingly similar. If *Fortuna desperata*, compared with settings from the critical phase, seems the work of an altogether different, reborn composer, then the author of *Libenter gloriabor* was clearly the same man. Laying the two masses side by side, there can be little doubt that they are closely contemporary: if *Fortuna desperata* existed by 1491–3, then so, in all probability, did *Libenter gloriabor*.

We turn now to the next mass copied by 1491–3, *Rose playsante*.[9] This is one of Obrecht's so-called segmentation masses.[10] In works of this type, the pre-existent melody is not given a full statement in every section or movement, but split up into a number of segments. Each of these segments is allotted to one mass section, and repeated there in several proportions or mensurations before the next one is taken up in the following section. The Agnus Dei invariably presents the entire tune in full. Segmentation would appear to be the *ne plus ultra* in rigid construction, yet in fact it allows much greater flexibility than other types of rational treatment. The composer is free to determine the length of each segment, the number of statements, and their successive proportions. By balancing these choices judiciously, any section can be covered with segments of any length. For instance, a relatively short segment may suffice for a short

---

[8] The well-known sequence at the end of the Kyrie II/Osanna/Agnus Dei III is at least partly a freely composed extension (from bar 88 onwards in the Kyrie).

[9] For discussions of this mass, see Meier, *Studien zur Meßkomposition*, 83–7; Reese, *Music in the Renaissance*, 202–3; Sparks, *Cantus Firmus*, 266–8. For the date, see Noblitt, 'Die Datierung', 49.

[10] Obrecht's technique of segmentation has been discussed extensively in the literature; see Kyriazis, *Die Cantus firmus-Technik*, 14–19; Salop, 'The Masses of Jacob Obrecht', ch. 3 ('The Segmented *Cantus Firmus*'), 66–75; Sparks, *Cantus Firmus*, 259–68; Just, *Der Mensuralkodex*, i. 298–309.

mass section, but it can also be used in a more extended movement by repeating it more often (up to six times), or expanding it to larger proportions (up to 9 : 1). To some extent an element of artistic control is thus brought back: the division-points, repeats, and proportions can be endlessly adjusted to suit the composer's design.

No doubt this concern for flexibility was a major impulse behind the invention of structural segmentation. More important, however, was the composer's fondness for the 'layered' sound, in which the tenor and the contrapuntal voices seem to be moving in different time-dimensions (as in *Ave regina celorum*; Ex. 19). Segmentation offered the opportunity to cultivate such a sound on a scale not available in conventional works. It allowed Obrecht to state a tenor in up to ninefold augmentation, but at carefully selected and controlled points—usually the first statement in a section of the Gloria or Credo. By reducing the proportion in successive statements he could make sure to use the device with discretion, and to alternate the layered sound with more integrated textures. The technique of segmentation is therefore not the invention of a man who delighted in rational construction *per se*. For Obrecht it was a flexible method of creating specific textural effects wherever he wanted them. Rather than subjecting him to the cantus firmus, the technique limited its constraints.[11]

This is borne out by the *Missa Rose playsante*. In its Gloria and Credo sections, the first entry of the segment is usually preceded by series of brief units that exchange one or more self-contained phrases; each of these units ends with a cadence on the final. The cantus-firmus segment is invariably in its most expanded form in the first presentation. Obrecht either underscores this with chordal writing in the other voices, or puts it into relief by writing busy, frequently imitative or sequential counterpoint around the tenor. Departures to other tonal regions are mostly found in these passages; if there is no return before the end of the segment, the subsequent tenorless passages will bring back the final and confirm it one or more times before the tenor re-enters. As the segment is successively reduced in the next presentations, the texture becomes more integrated, the structure more clearly articulated, and the harmonic language more firmly centred on the final.

[11] For this reason I doubt that the cycle of six *L'homme armé* masses in NapBN 40, dating from the 1460s or early 1470s, can be regarded as a direct historical precedent for Obrecht's segmentation technique. The anonymous composer of the cycle divided the *L'homme armé* tune into five segments, each of which was used as the basis for one mass; the sixth mass is based on the full melody. See J. Cohen, *The Six Anonymous L'homme armé Masses in Naples, Biblioteca Nazionale, MS vi E 40* (Musicological Studies and Documents, 21; American Institute of Musicology, 1968). Although there are obvious similarities, Obrecht's handling of the technique appears to be motivated by different artistic concerns.

This broad contrapuntal layout is carefully planned. If the tenors of segmentation masses can be endlessly manipulated in order to produce just the right formal design, then obviously there is much less structural 'coincidence' in these works than in masses like *Fortuna desperata*, where strict quotation or transformation of the cantus firmus is the ideal. Yet in a sense it makes little difference whether formal layouts have to be recognized in a rigidly fixed tenor, created by departing from rigid quotation, or deliberately engineered, as in the segmentation masses. The crucial point lies in the sense of long-term coherence that Obrecht seeks to create. Composing is now less than ever a matter of writing one bar after the other, introducing cadences, imitations, or other devices as the opportunity arises. Distant passages have to be functionally related: they must be written with awareness of one another, so that a compositional choice at one point is bound to have ramifications at another—in the same way that a sonata theme presupposes its elaboration and return at various key points in a movement.

The Et in terra of *Rose playsante* illustrates Obrecht's skill in long-term planning (bars 1–54 are shown in Ex. 24). Much here is familiar. The extended passage preceding the tenor entry in bar 28 is organized entirely in self-contained units. All cadences are on F, and material is shared between units. A sense of drive and development is created by the rhythmic intensification in bar 13, the dynamic upward motion of the phrases exchanged between units, and the tendency to state these phrases an octave higher on repeat. Yet the actual tenor entry is not the culmination-point: the cadence in bars 27–8 has not enough weight to give a sense of arrival, and the three contrapuntal voices do little to suggest that anything momentous has happened. Harmonic motion remains quick, but the unchanging cantus firmus in bars 28–36 limits the available triads to A, C, and F, of which Obrecht uses only the latter two. Whatever sense of development there is comes from the top voice, which is involved in a stepwise upward sequence (F to G to A). When the cantus firmus moves to *d'*, the top voice does not continue its sequence, but it does continue the stepwise upward motion (*bb'*). Harmonic and rhythmic motion are now slowed down, finally lending weight and momentum to the four-part polyphony. The bass starts a sequence in bar 39, moving upward quickly to the real culmination-point, bars 43–4, where the top voice reaches the highest note heard so far (*c''*), and all other voices are in the top ends of their ranges. This is rounded off quickly with a cadence on F, albeit evaded (bar 47), which is immediately followed by yet another, this time truly conclusive (bar 53). When the latter cadence is reached, one has the

Ex. 24. Obrecht, *Missa Rose playsante*, Et in terra, bars 1–54

(Ex. 24, *cont.*)

clear sense that a major internal part of the section has been concluded, even though the first segment has yet to be finished.

The means by which Obrecht achieves this culmination-point are simple: basically the top voice moves up a fifth, and takes sixteen bars to do so. Yet once this development is set in motion, and is underscored by developments in the other voices, it acquires a compelling logic, and lends purpose and coherence to a passage that might otherwise have consisted of purely perfunctory counterpoint (particularly since the cantus firmus seems distinctly unpromising to begin with). Simplicity of means—bringing back parameters to their bare essentials so as to increase their effectiveness—is the keyword in Obrecht's new style.

There are plenty of parallels in other segmentation masses. Perhaps one of the most striking is the Crucifixus of *Malheur me bat*, a cycle that has the cantus firmus in the top voice (Ex. 25).[12] The overall pattern is familiar: the first segment enters after twenty-four bars' rest (bar 142), and is presented in sixfold augmentation (with mensural transformation). The period that precedes it is not structured in distinct units, but Obrecht does make sure to hit the final A in a series of cadences (bars 126 and 130–3), and he returns to the A sonority after a brief excursion to E (bars 134–6).[13] The cantus-firmus entry marks a sudden and decisive shift to another tonal plane. The long-held G in bars 142–7 limits the available triads to C,

[12] Earliest copying date: 1497 (Just, *Der Mensuralkodex*, ii. 31). Discussions in Gombosi, *Jacob Obrecht*, 91–3; Reese, *Music in the Renaissance*, 199–200; H. C. Wolff, *Die Musik der alten Niederländer (15. und 16. Jahrhundert)* (Leipzig, 1956), 44–7; Osthoff, *Josquin Desprez*, i. 148–51; Sparks, *Cantus Firmus*, 260–6; Hudson, 'Two Ferrarese Masses'.

[13] Although the model for *Missa Malheur me bat* is in E Phrygian (see the transcription in *NOE* 7, pp. xiv–xv), Obrecht consistently reinterprets it in A Aeolian: each movement ends with a cadence on A, and although several internal sections end on E, these cadences on the dominant are invariably weak and evidently intended to raise the tonal tension (similar procedures can be found in several other masses by Obrecht).

Ex. 25. Obrecht, *Missa Malheur me bat*, Crucifixus, bars 118–74

(Ex. 25, *cont.*)

E, and G, of which Obrecht clearly prefers the dominant E.[14] Although it would have been possible to return to A in bars 148–9, he makes no attempt to do so: just as in *Fortuna desperata* Obrecht prolongs the departure, postponing the expected return to a carefully prepared point. Indeed, he makes it quite clear that with the cantus-firmus entry the music has moved into a different situation: in bars 142–5 harmonic motion has come to a complete standstill, leaving the inner voices to maintain rhythmic impetus with 'filler' material. These bars, more than anything seen before, show Obrecht's skill in writing music that is all speed and no development. When the harmonic stillness is finally lifted, cadences are mainly on C (bars 148, 151, 153). Only in bars 158–61 does Obrecht prepare the final return to A, in a cadence so elementary that it lacks nothing in weight. Rhythmic motion is slowed down in all voices, and the penultimate chord of the cadence lasts a full two bars (160–1), increasing the tonal suspense before its final release in bar 162. At this point the contratenor is triggered into rapid passage-work, reaching its top note (c'', the highest heard so far in this section) immediately after the cadence (bars 162–5). Hereafter the music quickly winds down, reconfirming the final A in a series of cadences before the segment makes its second appearance.

Once again the means by which Obrecht achieves this culmination-point are simple: basically he shifts to another tonal plane, stays in it for twenty bars, gives massive weight to the return, and makes sure to reach

[14] This striking shift must have been deliberately planned: all Obrecht would have needed to do to avoid the move to the dominant was to omit the first note of the segment (since it had already been stated in the previous segment anyway), and to start with the second note (on E), which might have allowed a chord on the final. The seemingly arbitrary decision where to make the cut clearly had far-reaching implications for the tonal layout of the Crucifixus. This confirms the element of artistic control inherent in the technique of segmentation (see above).

a melodic peak at that point. Although the means are different from those applied in the Et in terra of *Rose playsante*, and yet again from those applied in the Kyrie of *Fortuna desperata*, the underlying aesthetic is the same: Obrecht thinks in terms of long-term goals. Once he has set himself such a goal, all that comes before and after it is turned in its service, and contributes to making it stand out as a high point.[15]

From the small-scale elements in the Kyrie of *Fortuna desperata* we have moved to the large-scale design in the Crucifixus of *Malheur me bat*. Yet there is no sharp dividing-line between the two extremes: every aspect of style is governed by a single aesthetic vision. Fundamentally, Obrecht's concern seems to be to dramatize musical events that by themselves seem undramatic: a cadence, a melodic peak, a rhythmic change, a textural expansion, a shift in sonority. To dramatize is to simplify the event, but more than that. For each event, to be truly dramatic, presupposes an appropriate preparation and conclusion. In that recognition lies the key to the magnificent sense of long-term formal proportion that underlies the four masses. Yet from that recognition one can also go back again to the details, and appreciate them in a new light.

Returning to Ex. 25, for instance, the climactic cadence in bar 162 obviously presupposes the shift to the dominant in bar 142. That shift itself is dramatized in turn, and thus presupposes the low-key introduction on the final that precedes it. Beyond this broad outline, however, it is exceedingly difficult to disentangle the complex web of interacting parameters, and particularly to establish musical cause and effect. Let us take a simple example. The cadence in bar 162 is dramatized partly by the rhythmic deceleration in the preceding bars. For that development to be particularly effective, these bars will have to present the slowest rhythmic motion heard so far (which they do), and particularly there will have to be a point of extreme motion earlier on *from which* they decelerate. That point can easily be recognized: in bars 142–6 Obrecht abandons the careful

[15] The relationship between *Rose playsante* and *Malheur me bat* is especially close in the final Agnus Dei. In both masses, this section recapitulates the full cantus firmus after its segmented presentation in the preceding movements, and also has an ostinato-like bass part consisting entirely of a single, repeated pattern: in *Rose playsante* a circulation around the dominant (C), in *Malheur me bat* an oscillation between the final A and the dominant E. The harmonic language is thus restricted, yet the music is far from monotonous. In both cases it is the dominant that receives constant, repeated emphasis: the cadence on the final is postponed until the very end. This is the same principle as the one applied in the Crucifixus of *Malheur me bat*, but now extended to an entire section. The final Agnus Dei is kept in a permanent tonal suspense, which is released only when the cantus firmus reaches its final note. (Other significant examples in *Malheur me bat* are Gloria, bars 67–73, and Sanctus, bars 65–85.) Professor Chris Maas drew my attention to the string of parallel six-four chords in the final Agnus Dei of *Malheur me bat*, bars 188–91. This is extremely unusual in the 15th c.; the only other instance known to me is in the final Agnus Dei of the anonymous *Missa De septem doloribus dulcissime Marie virginis* in BrusBR 215–16 (*tempora* 21–3 and 25–7).

melodic phrasing and 'cadential' writing of the previous introduction, and writes 'filler' material in the inner voices so as to create pure rhythmic drive. The sense of drive is particularly pronounced here because every other parameter is kept stationary, in particular the harmony: the passage is literally all speed and no development. That is all Obrecht needs to create the necessary relief to the later reduction of speed, and thus to dramatize the cadence following that reduction in bar 162.

Yet this is only one way of looking at the passage. It is true that the harmonic standstill in bars 142–5 helps to give relief to the rhythmic motion in the inner voices. Yet it also has a purpose in itself: after the relatively lively harmonic rhythm of the introduction, the standstill can only serve to dramatize the shift to the dominant, and thus to emphasize that the music has moved into a new situation. Why does this need emphasizing? Of course: because the cadence in bar 162 will end that very situation—and the more firmly we seem locked into it, the more effective the release will be. This is a different way of looking at the same music. Yet from both points of view, the passage in bars 142–6 took exactly the shape that it had to.

What role does the cantus firmus play in all this? Without the knowledge that it was predetermined, it might have seemed just another voice, which enters at exactly the right time, and then does exactly the right thing. The textural expansion created by its entry in bar 142 underscores the shift to the dominant, and its static nature in the next five bars helps to emphasize the harmonic standstill and to give further relief to the active inner voices. This is yet another way of looking at the passage. From this point of view, Obrecht could have written no better music for the top voice than he in fact had to. The viewpoint is a factually incorrect one, of course: the cantus firmus *was* predetermined. Yet even if we know that the cantus firmus was the cause and everything else the effect, Obrecht has tightened the web of functional relations to such an extent that every element here seems both the cause and the effect of every other element. The web cannot be disentangled. Take it apart, and the very genius that made it the way it is evaporates.

Earlier Mature Masses

The 1491–3 masses *Fortuna desperata* and *Rose playsante*, and their associates *Libenter gloriabor* and *Malheur me bat*, are among the best Obrecht ever wrote. They lift him from the level of accomplished mastery to that of artistic brilliance, and place him firmly in the ranks of the greatest composers of the Renaissance. Had Obrecht died around 1488, the eight or nine masses written by that date would have earned him a position equal to that of a Barbireau or Pipelare—composers who produced masses of superb quality, yet whose outlook remained essentially conventional and conservative. It is Obrecht's central achievement that he went beyond this outlook and created a radically new and thoroughly personal sound world, governed by its own aesthetic laws: a world of balance and proportion, of skilfully controlled and directed motion, of economy and cohesion, in which the ingredients of fifteenth-century style, although entirely re-shuffled, interacted in purposeful and effective ways.

Two other masses belong to the same world, yet they are different, and we know from their copying dates that they must be earlier: *Je ne demande* (paper dating 1487–91) and *Plurimorum carminum I* (copied 1487–90). Both settings merit close attention, for they seem representative of a larger group of mostly undated masses, and may help us to place these in the chronology of Obrecht's style. In what ways are the two settings, and the group they seem to represent, different from the four cycles discussed so far? That question can best be answered in terms of the narrative structure of the previous paragraph. There, we have described the new style starting with the smaller elements, and gradually moving up to ever higher levels of musical design. If we were to do the same for *Je ne demande*, *Plurimorum carminum I*, and their associates, we would find that the comparison always ended at some point beneath the highest level. In some masses all one can recognize is the new contrapuntal idiom: the typical rhythmic patterns, the pulsating rhythms, the triadic outlines, the ceaseless melodic drive. While this is enough to make them look strikingly different from the works discussed in previous chapters, these works are still some way off from the greatest achievements in the new style. What they lack is regular phrase structure, clarity of articulation, harmonic planning and, ultimately, the large-scale design of the highest levels. Other masses introduce these latter elements piecemeal, and yet others do so more and more frequently and with increasing confidence.

Plurimorum carminum I shows all the 'low-level' signs of a mature work. It was copied in 1487–90; the absence of head-motifs and the virtual disappearance of perfect *tempus* would suggest a date not before about 1488. *Plurimorum carminum I* is based on a series of cantus firmi borrowed from contemporary songs, and thus resembles somewhat the pot-pourri; it was given its title by the editors of the *New Obrecht Edition*.[16] Other

---

[16] See A. Smijers, 'De Missa Carminum van Jacob Hobrecht', *Tijdschrift voor Muziekwetenschap*,

settings of a similar type include a second mass of the same title (see below), and settings by Isaac and Pipelare. Obrecht invariably quotes the borrowed melodies in their original form, and does not manipulate them in any way. Their lively character is thus maintained, and this is matched by equal liveliness in the other voices. In the words of Edgar Sparks: 'All [Obrecht] does is write new counterpoints to the melodies . . . The Mass consists essentially of a series of new settings of the chanson melodies, and because different ones are quoted one after another the work can hardly be considered as a unified Mass cycle.'[17]

It is difficult to describe the style of *Plurimorum carminum I*, for there is very little in the music to hold on to. Imitations, motivic devices, sequences, antiphonal exchanges, and changes of scoring are used in moderation, so that one is basically left with a dense and involved contrapuntal tissue, in which few musical events really stand out. Indeed, the very lines of the counterpoint are undistinctive: one scarcely encounters a phrase that is given the time and space to unfold freely, and to attract attention for its melodic qualities. All lines are moving forward relentlessly, breathlessly, constantly infusing the dense texture with rhythmic and melodic energy: Obrecht often spins them out indefinitely, from a limited vocabulary of typical patterns and turns. The dotted and off-beat rhythms, the syncopations, leaps, and scalar patterns have been heard many times in different contexts, yet they recur again and again in endlessly varied permutations. In this basic vocabulary lies the key to the new style; fundamentally it is the same vocabulary as in *Fortuna desperata* or *Rose playsante*. At its root lies a perception of contrapuntal lines as carriers, not so much of melodic content, as of sheer motion. The main difference with later masses, of course, is the virtual absence of attempts to control and steer that motion. It is as though Obrecht has struck a new well of invention but is not as yet concerned with managing it: ideas gush out in rough and inarticulate form, lacking in focus and direction. Disciplining the flow of his invention would require Obrecht to redefine every other element in the musical language: motifs, phrases, cadences, textures, and so on. The final stage of that development has been described in the previous paragraph. In *Plurimorum carminum I* and similar works lies its beginning.

Given that the mass is unlikely to post-date the critical phase by more

17 (1951), 192–4; Reese, *Music in the Renaissance*, 195–6; Meier, *Studien zur Meßkomposition*, 27–8; Salop, 'The Masses of Jacob Obrecht', ch. 4 ('The Quodlibet Masses'), 76–89; Sparks, *Cantus Firmus*, 247 and 467; Staehelin, 'Obrechtiana', 25–7. For the date, see *NOE* 10, p. xii.

[17] Sparks, *Cantus Firmus*, 247.

than one or two years, it seems striking that in so many respects it is the opposite of the works from that period. *Plurimorum carminum I* is not a work of contemplation or reflection; it aims to solve no creative problems, does not experiment, and is not at all self-conscious about style. On paper its ambitions would indeed seem quite modest: basically, as Sparks observed, the setting consists of a series of new song arrangements, ordered and adapted to the mass format, and written in a style that pleases and entertains rather than displays erudition and learning. The mass breathes a sense of carefree spontaneity, as though the act of writing it was a diversion rather than a major creative effort. There is a notable tendency, for instance, to simplify the contrapuntal framework: the top voice and bass keep relapsing into parallel-tenth relationships—the simplest possible around a pre-existent tune. Obrecht neither seeks nor avoids those relationships: they seem to be the unwitting consequence of a fairly spontaneous creative process. In this spontaneity also lies the main redeeming feature of the mass. For although the writing never moves between extreme highs and lows, as in later works, the straight line of the musical discourse is propelled by unprecedented rhythmic and melodic vigour. One can easily believe that this is where the new style began: sheer, unrelenting motion. This is the most basic level, the lowest common denominator, of the mature idiom.

It will not be necessary to illustrate the style of *Plurimorum carminum I* here with a musical example, for all it would reveal is the absence of distinctive features, and the pervasive presence of a basic idiom that can be seen in all other examples in this chapter. Rather, it will be helpful to take a brief look at the mass's companion, *Plurimorum carminum II*, a work that shows the same idiom, but with added 'higher-level' elements. Comparison seems particularly appropriate since the two settings belong to the same type of multiple-cantus-firmus mass, and are, moreover, closely contemporary (*Plurimorum carminum II* was copied on paper dated 1491–3).[18]

Where the two masses differ, the second invariably shows that Obrecht is taking control of the musical discourse. This reveals itself first of all in the selection of cantus firmi. While the first mass is based on no fewer than twenty different tunes, and therefore lacks the space to do anything but straightforward three- or four-part arrangement, the second reduces this number to five: one for each movement. This enables Obrecht to

[18] For literature, see Meier, *Studien zur Meßkomposition*, 27–8; Salop, 'The Masses of Jacob Obrecht', 88; W. Elders, *Studien zur Symbolik in der Musik der alten Niederländer* (Utrecht, 1969), 27–8; Staehelin, 'Obrechtiana', 25–7. For the date of the MunBS 3154 copy, see Noblitt, 'Die Datierung'.

introduce twofold augmentation in some sections, so that the original tunes are less restrictive in the new context, and their melodic curves direct larger stretches of polyphony. The second major difference indicates a new concern with control of motion and formal balance: all movements, and most of their internal sections, end with freely composed extensions ranging in length from two to nine bars. All these extensions introduce free material in the tenor-bearing voice, and thus they constitute a notable departure from the otherwise obsessively strict cantus-firmus treatment. There is an obvious link here with the more spectacular codas in masses like *Fortuna desperata* and *Libenter gloriabor*.[19] The final major difference is one that has profoundly affected the musical character of *Plurimorum carminum II*: instead of quoting the tenors of the songs, Obrecht selects their top voices and places these in the bass of his setting. Harmonic motion is thus steered by unusually song-like basses, traversing their ranges with smoothly shaped arches rather than sudden leaps. As a consequence, there are many 'in-built' highs and lows that Obrecht may choose either to exploit or to ignore.

A look through the score of *Plurimorum carminum II* quickly confirms that he did indeed capitalize on such predetermined opportunities. Although the basic contrapuntal idiom is identical with that in the previous mass, there is now a tendency to single out key events, mainly through stylistic differentiation. This can be seen, for instance, in the second Kyrie (Ex. 26). The cantus firmus, Barbireau's *Scoen lief* ('Fair beloved'), is quoted in twofold augmentation up to bar 91, thereafter *ut iacet*. It is clear in several places that Obrecht aims to capitalize on the most distinctive features of the cantus firmus. Usually he does so simply by writing parallel tenths in the top voice. In this way he highlights, for instance, the melodic rise in bars 80–5, the melodic peak in bars 92–6, and the rapid upward sequence in bars 107–11. The inner voices are written in such a way as to heighten the effect in each case. In the slow-moving bars 80–3, for instance, they state rhythmic 'filler material' very similar to that used in *Malheur me bat* (Ex. 25, bars 142–6). And in the melodic peak in bars 92–6, the contratenor, too, moves to the top end of its range, while the disappearance of the voice labelled 'tenor' helps to keep the texture bright. And in bars 107–11, both the inner voices fully co-operate in the sequence, generating rhythmic and melodic energy before the freely composed extension in bars 114–17 brings the final cadence. This latter exten-

[19] But it should be pointed out that a very similar extension is found in *Ave regina celorum* (Qui tollis, bars 223–31); this is puzzling, for that mass otherwise seems typically early in formal respects (see Ch. 7).

sion itself is an example not only of Obrecht's developing sense of formal balance, but also of his increasing awareness that cadences, to be powerful, need to be slowed down.[20]

The stylistic differentiation in *Plurimorum carminum II*—the very quality that was lacking in its companion—is conspicuous even at first glance. Yet it was not an aesthetic goal in itself. It seems rather that Obrecht was simply concerned to play his best card in each predetermined situation, to capitalize on every opportunity for musical effect. As a result, *Plurimorum carminum II* contains a wealth of stylistic felicities and truly inspired moments. The other side of the coin, however, as Ex. 26 shows, is that the moments are little more than just that: moments. There is no long-term strategy that might have turned their succession into a musically motivated discourse. In the 1491–3 masses, for instance, one would have expected the gradual rhythmic intensification in bars 75–90 to culminate in bar 93, so that it would have coincided with the central melodic peak of the section: two effects reinforcing each other. Instead, however, there is a complete standstill separating the two effects (bars 91–2), a contrapuntal hiatus that seems unmotivated musically. It must be immediately added that this, of course, is to judge *Plurimorum carminum II* by standards of which it is as yet innocent (however much it contributes to their development). Obrecht's style is in transition: he is handling the new idiom with increasing confidence, broadening its scope, developing its grammar, yet never losing that sense of spontaneity and energy that invigorated the writing of *Plurimorum carminum I*.

A picture thus begins to emerge of the early development of Obrecht's mature style. The next mass, *Je ne demande*, copied on paper dated 1487–91, reinforces and extends that picture.[21] Its model is the tenor of Busnoys's four-part song *Je ne demande*, segmented and distributed over the various mass sections in the same manner as in *Rose playsante* and *Malheur me bat*. The mass is deliberately designed on a large scale. Even by the standards of the segmentation masses it is an expansive work: not only does the number of segments, eleven, exceed those in the other segmentation masses, but Obrecht presents more, and generally larger, segments in five- and sixfold augmentation.

[20] Several of the free extensions in this mass, particularly the ones in the Sanctus (bars 39–43) and Agnus Dei III (bars 173–7), linger deliberately on the dominant, a procedure evidently motivated by the same aesthetic as the 'insertion' of the extra bar in the central cadence of *Fortuna desperata*'s Kyrie I (see above).

[21] For discussions, see Gombosi, *Jacob Obrecht*, 96–9; Reese, *Music in the Renaissance*, 203–4; Salop, 'The Masses of Jacob Obrecht', 67–72; Sparks, *Cantus Firmus*, 469–70; Elders, *Studien zur Symbolik*, 28; T. Noblitt, 'Problems of Transmission in Obrecht's *Missa Je ne demande*', *Musical Quarterly*, 63 (1977), 211–33. For the copying date, see Noblitt, 'Die Datierung', 49.

Ex. 26. Obrecht, *Missa Plurimorum carminum II*, Kyrie II

If *Je ne demande* is large in comparison with its structural counterparts, compared with *Plurimorum carminum I* and *II* its scope is absolutely vast. A single segment, stated in five- or sixfold augmentation, gives Obrecht almost as much ground to cover as an entire song tenor stated *ut iacet*. And an expansive framework requires expansive treatment. Although Obrecht is free to deal with each drawn-out tenor note as a separate contrapuntal situation, the absence of restrictive detail in the cantus firmus should obviously encourage him to look ahead and plan musical events in advance. To capitalize on features of the tenor is now inevitably to develop long-term musical strategies.

Does this mean that we are entering a higher level of musical design? Yes and no. There are certainly elements of long-term design in *Je ne demande*; examples will be discussed shortly. On the other hand, Obrecht's vision rarely reaches as far as it does in later works. A telling sign of this is his often unquestioning acceptance of tenor entries and exits as formal division-points, particularly in first statements. One consequence of this is that the long tenorless introductions have to stand as self-contained sections, and do not introduce developments that might continue beyond the tenor entry. In later works the introductions were usually either written in such a way as to create maximum contrast with the four-part writing that followed, thus dramatizing the cantus-firmus entry (Exx. 23 and 25), or designed to generate musical momentum, so that the entry was merely one of several steps in a cumulative development (Exx. 22 and 24). In *Je ne demande*, by contrast, Obrecht often seems indifferent as to the structure of his introductions. In quite a few cases he simply reverts to the 'song arrangement' procedures of *Plurimorum carminum I*: voices from the model are quoted *ut iacet*, so that the problem is reduced to that of responding to predetermined situations with *ad hoc* counter-point.[22]

This can be illustrated, for instance, in the Patrem (bars 1–62 are shown in Ex. 27). The tenorless introduction is based almost entirely on the contratenor *primus* of the song, the first twenty-three bars of which are quoted literally in the contratenor of the mass (bars 1–23, but with octave transposition from bar 7). Other voices from the model are quoted as well: the opening of the tenor appears in bars 1–11, and bars 7–11 of the second contratenor are used to bridge a silent passage in the contratenor (bars 11–15).[23] This falls, strictly speaking, under the heading of parody, but one may well ask whether that term is appropriate here. It fails to cover close parallels in *Plurimorum carminum I*: in the Patrem and Sanctus of this mass

---

[22] Extended quotations from the song contratenor also feature in Kyrie I, bars 1–5, Et in terra, bars 1–8, Et incarnatus, bars 113–19. Material taken from the top voice is found in Kyrie I, bars 4–8 and 26–37, Patrem, bars 100–12, Sanctus, bars 1–18, 105–16, and 119–30, Agnus Dei, bars 14–27 and 177–86 (brief references to the top voice of the song are abundant in this mass). Material from the second contratenor also appears in Et in terra, bars 7–29. There are also quotations of entire parts of the model in the Pleni and Benedictus, discussed below.

[23] Similar extended quotations from the model can be found in other tenorless introductions, for instance in the Et in terra (bars 1–29 of the second contratenor quoted in top voice, bars 1–29) and Agnus Dei I (bars 1–10 of first contratenor quoted in top voice, bars 6–15, and linked with a quotation from top voice, bars 17–31 which appear in bars 14–27). Random quotations can be found throughout the mass, particularly towards the endings of sections (e.g., Et in terra, bars 67–75, Patrem, bars 100–11); see also Gombosi's detailed analysis of the Kyrie, *Jacob Obrecht*, 96–7.

Ex. 27. Obrecht, *Missa Je ne demande*, Patrem, bars 1–62

(Ex. 27, *cont.*)

(and possibly the Et in terra), the tenorless introductions are similarly structured on extended, literal quotations from songs. These quotations happen not to meet our definition of parody (since they never cite more than one voice), yet they do provide a direct context to the procedures in Ex. 27. The point in this example is surely that Obrecht decided to be 'guided' through the introduction by pre-existent material, and consequently that the amount of new music he had to write is very small (just over one-third, to be exact).

Given the severe restrictions, it is surprising that the introduction is actually quite well written. The outline is simple: the first major cadence, in bar 11, concludes the opening duo; the second, in bar 19, brings a shift to the dominant, while the third, in bar 25, returns to the final. Although contrapuntal options are limited, Obrecht succeeds in articulating this basic outline effectively. It is clear, for instance, that he carefully prepared the move to the dominant in bar 19—through textural expansion, a general melodic rise in all voices, and increased rhythmic impetus—and dramatized the event itself, through a harmonic standstill and a radical simplification of the contrapuntal tissue. Tonal tension is raised here not just because there is a cadence on C (there is a minor one in bar 13 as well), but because Obrecht wants that cadence to be a central musical event, and because he is careful to sustain the tension in the next few bars—saving it up for the final release in bar 25. In this period of sustained tonal tension (bars 19–25) all melodic interest is concentrated in the top voice, yet its extended flourish can scarcely conceal that the passage is in fact a simple cadence, stretched out over seven bars.

These procedures are familiar from works like *Fortuna desperata* or *Malheur me bat*, yet they are applied here on a lower level of musical design. Contrary to what happens in the two later works, the introduction remains a self-contained section, so that it would be impossible to predict from anything *before* the tenor entry what will happen *after* it. Yet the advance over *Plurimorum carminum II* should be evident: even in its first twenty-five bars the Patrem of *Je ne demande* has greater cohesion than the Kyrie based on *Scoen lief.*

It will be useful to compare the tenor segment, stated for the first time in bars 25–54, with that of the Et in terra of *Rose playsante* (Ex. 24). While the latter is almost devoid of melodic interest, the one in *Je ne demande* is a beautifully shaped arch—gently rising up an octave (bars 25–39), reaching a peak exactly in the middle (39–41), and slowly descending again to the lower octave (41–54). There are tantalizing opportunities here—at least in terms of the fully developed mature aesthetic. Bars 36–42, for instance, provide an ideal framework for a slowed-down cadence on the dominant, which might be all the more effective if not just the tenor but all voices reached the upper ends of their ranges. Having established this as the moment of supreme tension (by analogy, perhaps, to bar 19 in the introduction), one might write the preceding bars in such a way as to maximize the effect, fine-tuning the parameters in the same way as in the Crucifixus of *Malheur me bat*. Certainly the return to F should be powerful; a period of sustained tonal tension on its dominant C is possible in bars 47–54.

It is clear from Ex. 27 that Obrecht did not think along these lines when he wrote the Patrem. That is not to imply criticism of the piece: all it probably means is that the terms on which *Je ne demande* can be criticized are different from those of *Rose playsante* or *Malheur me bat*. And this in turn might be seen as consistent with the somewhat earlier copying date. The sound that Obrecht aspired to in this particular passage was one of Ockeghem-like solemnity and gravity. It is significant, for instance, that when the tenor reaches its peak, in bars 35–45, all other voices go down under it, so that the overall tone colour does not change significantly. What does change radically, however, is the rhythmic and harmonic motion. In bars 28–35 the texture had become more and more involved rhythmically—semiminim patterns being introduced in the bass, and then gradually infusing the other contrapuntal voices; but the emergence of the tenor as the leading voice has put all activity to a stop. What follows is a moment of musical suspense, a stillness sustained for so long that the context seems to disappear—an effect usually reserved for texts proclaiming the mysteries of the faith. Obrecht is not known for his sensitivity to the Credo text, and one suspects that the intended effect here was musical rather than rhetorical. As such it is powerful, and cleverly contrasted with the rhythmic activity in the preceding passage. Once again it is increased coherence that distinguishes *Je ne demande* from *Plurimorum carminum II*: the new grammar is taking shape.

Signs that *Je ne demande* aspires to even higher levels of the mature style can be found occasionally, for instance at the opening of the Qui tollis. Here, too, the tenor segment (stated in fivefold augmentation) is suggestive of musical development: it rises up a fourth from *g* to *c'*, and then down a fifth to *f* (bar 123), on which note it gradually zooms in in a 'circulating' approach. Obrecht cleverly emphasizes this implied development. In the bars preceding the tenor entry he has the bass move up a fifth in the same rhythm as the tenor, so that the first four notes of the tenor segment complete a melodic sequence comprising a full octave: the introduction and tenor entry are joined together almost seamlessly. The stepwise octave rise is underlined by the use of sequence, so that the passage has a simple yet inescapable logic: the high point is reached after eighteen bars (bars 99–100). In later mature masses this climactic development would have been rounded off with a cadence on the final, particularly since the high point represents a moment of heightened tonal tension (a single triad on the dominant, held for nearly three bars) and a firm cadence on F would be possible at any point in next few bars (101–3). Given this, the actual music here seems disappointingly inconclusive. The tension built up in the first twenty bars is not released in a single, forceful cadence, but simply evaporates: the contratenor drops out, and the outer voices state a phrase of little melodic interest in parallel tenths. Only eight bars later is a firm cadence on F finally reached (bar 111), yet it comes too late to be really effective.

Once again we should be careful not to imply criticism. The point surely is that *Je ne demande* introduces new trends, not that it is less perfect than works that build on its achievements. If the mass compares unfavourably with those later works, then all this shows is what we knew already from the copying date: that it is *not* a later work. As a work of art *Je ne demande* creates its own aesthetic frame of reference. Within that frame one might not even have expected the Qui tollis to proceed as it might have done in *Fortuna desperata* or *Rose playsante*. It is true that Obrecht raises tonal tension with great effect in several places (e.g. Ex. 27, bars 19–24), and we have given special attention to this practice because of the importance it was to have to the full-blown mature style. Yet in the context of the mass itself it is one of several possible effects—hit upon when the context allows it, but not pursued systematically. Obrecht's prime concern in *Je ne demande* still seems to be to generate and sustain motion, not to control and target it: cadences, for instance, tend to be weakened rather than dramatized. And so, to return to the Qui tollis, it may have been this aesthetic that dictated that the tonal tension in bars 98–100 be discharged measuredly rather than in a single cadence. That, too, is a form of control.

With the discussion of *Missa Je ne demande*, we have now gone as far as the available dating evidence will allow us to go. Yet the picture that emerges from the seven masses discussed so far is a consistent one, and may be plausibly extrapolated to include other, undated works. Before doing so, however, it will be necessary to pause awhile, and to consider the new picture in the broader context of Obrecht's stylistic development.

A few elements stand out immediately. Contrary to the critical phase, the mature period is not one in which Obrecht aimed to realize all his ambitions at once in a single work. In this respect the earliest datable mass in the new style, *Plurimorum carminum I*, is the very opposite of the self-conscious and deeply considered works of the critical phase—with which it must be closely contemporary. The impression one gets is that Obrecht lowered his artistic ambitions and gave himself over to unpremeditated creative impulse, barely giving conscious thought to what he had written. Perhaps it was sheer time pressure that forced him to do so; in Chapter 6 we have pointed to the increased demand for new mass settings that Obrecht faced from 1488 onwards. If a short-term need for polyphony forced Obrecht to resort to basic craftsmanship, and to leave more ambitious projects until later, he must have found that the exercise brought unexpected gains. Freed from the burden of writing in artful and erudite fashion—which had weighed heavily upon him in the critical phase—he discovered new resources of creative energy. His idiom acquired a fresh sense of vitality and vigour that, although lacking as yet in focus, was worth cultivating in the long run. This is the lowest common denominator of the new style, and its most directly audible 'Obrechtian' quality.

It is true that the new style eventually became more ambitious, but it never lost its initial sense of vitality and vigour. Indeed, there is every reason to believe that an element of spontaneity remained inherent in the creative process. Free to write as his invention led him, Obrecht played with the musical material, discovering new effects almost accidentally. (Playfulness and sheer creative pleasure are qualities that very much typify the mature style.) In *Plurimorum carminum II* the succession of musical effects seems impressionistic and unpredictable: its writing shows a lack of deliberation and planning that seems compatible with spontaneous composition. Yet, as *Je ne demande* shows, the consistent pursuit of certain effects over others caused Obrecht's idiom to be transformed under his very hands. Again, he did not try to realize all ambitions at once: the 'high-level' syntax was not invented overnight, but must have evolved in a series of masses written in quick succession.

Three other features have not thus far been emphasized because they are not intrinsic to contrapuntal style, yet they unify the seven masses as a group, and set them apart from earlier works. The first of these features is the virtual disappearance of O, and the almost exclusive use of ₵. Of the masses discussed so far, four employ ₵ as the unique mensuration; the three others employ O never in more than one, brief section.[24] In the present context this important change in mensural habits (which was universal in continental Europe around 1490–1500) is of interest only as a criterion for dating. The wider issues, mainly relating to the history of notation, cannot be discussed here; they are explored in Appendix II.

The second feature is the conspicuous rationality for which Obrecht has become renowned: schematic treatment of cantus firmi, and rigid mass construction according to overarching rational plans. Although elements of strict tenor treatment (mainly mensural transformation) featured in all masses pre-dating the mid-1480s, free elaboration remained at least equally prominent in these works, and in fact began to dominate in the critical phase. This trend was reversed in the mature period. In all masses discussed so far except *Libenter gloriabor*,[25] strict quotation and schematic manipulation are the norm—albeit one from which musically motivated departures remain possible. The importance of the rational procedures has

---

[24] Of the *Plurimorum carminum* masses the first uses O only in one section (Kyrie I), as does *Malheur me bat*, and the second only in a nine-bar passage (opening of Et in terra).

[25] *Libenter gloriabor* is a somewhat curious exception since Obrecht seems to revert briefly to older procedures: the Kyrie version is restated in the Sanctus (but with the rests differing in length), the Qui tollis and Crucifixus present ornamented forms of the tenor, canons or quasi-canons involving the cantus firmus are employed in the Kyrie I and Crucifixus, and the brief tenor-based opening of the Kyrie is restated at the beginning of the Sanctus. The devices could scarcely be described as more than isolated relics of past procedures: only the knowledge of precedents makes them worth singling out from their neighbours. For detailed analyses, see Meier, *Studien zur Meßkomposition*, 87–92; Sparks, *Cantus Firmus*, 276–8 and 471–2. The treatment of psalm tone 8, in the bass of the Christe, recalls *De Sancto Martino*: the melody is stated in breves, with breve rests after various groups of notes (see Ch. 6). Since neither the number of repeated recitation notes nor the placement of the rests can go back to chant notation, one might speculate that Obrecht originally supplied the text of a verse here, it being replaced later by Mass Ordinary text. In that case the verse may have consisted of 3 + 5 words or 7 + 8 syllables, the arrangement of syllables being: 2 2 3 / 1 3 1 1 2. The second quotation of the psalm tone (Gloria, bars 168–75) likewise incorporates 15 or 7 + 8 notes. The third (Pleni, bars 101–8), however, has 14 or 7 + 7 notes (at least according to BerlPS 40634; *NOE* 6, p. xxvii). The antiphon *Libenter gloriabor* was sometimes sung with the verse 'quando autem infirmor, tunc fortior sum et potens', which fits Obrecht's notes exactly. See W. H. Frere, *Antiphonale Sarisburiense* (repr., Farnborough, 1966), 453. Like the text of the antiphon itself, this is a paraphrase of St Paul's words in 2 Cor. 12: 9–10: 'libenter igitur gloriabor in infirmitatibus meis ut inhabitet in me virtus Christi . . . cum enim infirmor tunc potens sum.'

been overemphasized, however. As we have aimed to demonstrate in this and the previous paragraph, one can evaluate Obrecht's music perfectly well without needing even to be aware of this fundamentally schematic aspect. Because of this, and since Obrecht's cantus-firmus usage has been dealt with extensively in the literature,[26] we shall confine ourselves to dealing with it as one of a broad range of features that changed as he entered the mature period.

Connected with Obrecht's changing cantus-firmus usage is a new habit of quoting the cantus firmus in sections in reduced scoring; the only precedents to this practice can be found in *Ave regina celorum* (Et resurrexit) and *Adieu mes amours* (Agnus Dei II). In *Je ne demande*, the Pleni is structured on the top voice of the model (quoted in the top voice), and the Benedictus on the bass (quoted in the bass). *Rose playsante* goes a step further, and structures three sections on the three parts of its model: the Pleni on the top voice, the Benedictus on the tenor, and the Agnus Dei II on the bass. The Benedictus and Agnus Dei II of *Malheur me bat* are based on the tenor of the song, quoted in the tenor and bass, respectively. And finally, the Pleni of *Libenter gloriabor* quotes the cantus firmus (verse plus antiphon). Since sections with reduced scoring in Obrecht's masses tend to be self-contained in nature, contemporaries frequently isolated and transmitted them as independent textless settings, sometimes with the designation 'Obrecht in Missa'.[27] For this reason it has been suggested that several of Obrecht's surviving textless pieces may have been part of masses now lost.[28]

The third feature is perhaps the most interesting, because it touches on issues of contrapuntal style and design: the disappearance of head-motifs. The significance of this change can be appreciated only in the light of developments stretching back perhaps as much as ten years. Obrecht had wrestled with head-motifs throughout the 1480s, and although he arrived at quite different solutions in different works, a brief review will show that his underlying artistic concerns never changed—not even after head-motifs had disappeared altogether.

---

[26] For general discussions, see Gombosi, *Jacob Obrecht*; Kyriazis, *Die Cantus firmus-Technik*; Meier, *Studien zur Meßkomposition*, 3–28; Salop, 'The Masses of Jacob Obrecht', 1–96; Sparks, *Cantus Firmus*, ch. 9 ('The Masses and Motets of Jacob Obrecht'), 245–311; Todd, 'Retrograde, Inversion'. A study of Obrecht's cantus-firmus usage in motets is M. E. Nagle, 'The Structural Role of the Cantus Firmus in the Motets of Jacob Obrecht' (Ph.D. diss., University of Michigan, 1972).

[27] J. Zanger, *Practicae musicae praecepta* (Leipzig, 1554), fo. L^v–Liii^r: 'Obrechtus in Missa' (Osanna of *Ave regina celorum*), and Petrucci, *Canti B*: 'Obrecht in Missa' (Osanna I of *Cela sans plus*). See *NOE* 1, p. xxii, and Staehelin, 'Obrechtiana', 7–8.

[28] Cf. Staehelin, 'Obrechtiana', 9–10, and Fallows, review of Picker, *Johannes Ockeghem and Jacob Obrecht*, 249.

Obrecht adopted head-motifs, introductory duos, and texturally emphasized tenor entries as mere conventions in his early masses *Petrus apostolus* and *Beata viscera* (Exx. 1 and 4). In *O lumen ecclesie* and *Sicut spina rosam* he tried to motivate his use of those conventions by redefining head-motifs as structural elements equivalent to the tenor. This balance could be achieved in two ways: by expanding the head-motif, or by withholding textural emphasis on the tenor entry. Obrecht did both in *O lumen ecclesie* (Exx. 7 and 8), but thereafter seems to have continued on the first path, that of expanding the head-motif. In the Patrem of *Sicut spina rosam* the head-motif quotes the entire cantus firmus in an extended pre-imitation (Ex. 10). This extreme point was maintained only in the Credo of *De Sancto Martino*, yet here Obrecht was already forced to compromise on the strictness of the imitation. After this retreat he seems to have proceeded instead on the second path, that of understating the tenor entry. In this respect only one mass, *Ave regina celorum*, directly copies the example of *O lumen ecclesie*: both settings have movements in which the actual tenor entry is made part of antiphonal introductory duos, textural emphasis being reserved for a later part of the cantus firmus (compare Exx. 8 and 20). A very similar procedure is found in the Agnus Dei of *Adieu mes amours*: its tenor is first made part of a typically imitative introduction in reduced scoring, and assumes its proper, tenor-like appearance only after the cadence in bar 14. The tenor entry was understated in a more subtle way in the Credo of *De Sancto Donatiano* (Ex. 13), but the basic principle remained the same. In all cases the cantus firmus temporarily assumed the *appearance* of a freely composed voice—whether as a quasi-preparatory statement in a duo or trio (*Ave regina celorum, Adieu mes amours*), or as a quasi-contrapuntal part against a 'tenor-like' contratenor (*De Sancto Donatiano*). This fascination with the appearance and identity of the tenor was of course typical of the critical phase. *Salve diva parens* was in this respect the most far-reaching exercise: the main reason why this is such an inscrutable work is that the tenor continually changes its appearance.

All these experiments show the same concern to integrate the tenor into a continuous musical discourse—either by upgrading what precedes it, or by downgrading its own entry. Against this background it seems hardly surprising that Obrecht finally abandoned the conventions with which he had wrestled for so long. The initial reaction seems to have been one of indifference. In both *Plurimorum carminum I* and *Je ne demande* introductory passages tend to be straightforward arrangements of pre-existent material, with little opportunity to establish a musical continuity in which the tenor might be incorporated. That concern, it seems, was abandoned along with the head-motifs. But it returned in later masses, and we have seen examples in *Fortuna desperata* and *Rose playsante*. In the Kyrie I of the former, for instance, it is impossible to say whether the tenor entry is downgraded or the 'introduction' upgraded. There simply is perfect continuity, such as Obrecht had never established before the mature period— just as, paradoxically, there is perfect periodicity. The sense of 'arrival' that traditionally accompanied the tenor entry is now postponed to the end of the tenor statement (bars 29–31). The Kyrie does not stand alone in this respect. It is almost the rule in the most mature masses that movements open with either imitations or repetitions of texturally varied units. These devices seem to have been used primarily to generate musical momentum; the tenor entry does not usually come as the culmination-point, but often functions as one of several cumulative steps towards that point, just as in the *Fortuna desperata* Kyrie. It is apparent from this that despite the radical break that marked the beginning of the mature style, there are elements of continuity in Obrecht's *œuvre*. In some ways the creation of the new style was a fresh start, but in others it enabled the composer fully to realize artistic concerns that had occupied him throughout the 1480s.

The Mature *Œuvre*

In this final paragraph the mature style will be explored once again from the basic contrapuntal idiom up to higher levels of musical design. The only difference this time is that the nine masses discussed below cannot be shown, on external evidence, to pre-date 1491–3. Yet they are all to varying degrees part of the same picture as the seven masses discussed above, and for that reason alone they should properly be discussed here. Whether all nine masses actually date from the years around 1490 is another question. The picture that emerges from the dated and undated masses together shows such considerable homogeneity that it seems difficult not to regard that as at least highly suggestive (if circumstantial) evidence. Moreover, the possibility of a creative outburst in the later Bruges years seems to be supported by documentary evidence (see Ch. 6). This possibility could be problematic, however, in that one would necessarily have to assume a sharp decline in productivity after the early 1490s. That problem could be remedied either by assuming that *Fortuna desperata* and *Rose playsante* do not provide a *terminus ante quem* for less advanced mature works, or by questioning their copying dates. Neither alternative is favoured in this study, but in a sense the issue of time-scale is immaterial. What is crucial is that the mature *œuvre* is a distinct and unified corpus, which must have originated after about 1487–8, and which can be understood and appreciated, if necessary, without an absolute temporal dimension.

Before starting our final journey up the levels, it may be useful to devote a few words to the anonymous *Gracioulx et biaulx*. This mass, based on a song by Barbireau, is something of a puzzle. It survives uniquely in the Ferrarese choirbook ModE M.1.2, where it is preceded by three and followed by two securely ascribed Obrecht masses. Although the work lacks an attribution (due to the loss of its first page), Martin Staehelin has persuasively argued that the systematic arrangement of the choirbook strongly suggests Obrecht's authorship.[29] On first examination of the score the composer's fingerprints do indeed appear to be abundantly present: motivic repetitions, extensive use of sequence, ostinati, or quasi-ostinati in the bass, and typically Obrechtian witticisms (such as the persistent C–D oscillation in the top voice of the Qui tollis, bars 81–115). Four other features suggest a kinship with the mature masses: there are no head-motifs, $\mathvarnothing$ is the predominant mensuration, the cantus firmus is quoted and treated in rigid and schematic fashion, and one section in reduced scoring, the Et incarnatus, is based on a literal statement of the song tenor (in the contratenor). One feature of the cantus-firmus treatment may even indicate proximity to the segmentation masses: while five sections of the mass are based on full statements of Barbireau's tenor, five others isolate its first sixteen notes and present this 'segment' in various proportions and mensurations—the very technique we have seen above in *Je ne demande*, *Rose playsante*, and *Malheur me bat*.[30] In view of all this, the attribution of *Gracioulx et biaulx* to Obrecht would seem plausible on both internal and external grounds.

Yet although the mass fits neatly into the mature picture on these grounds, other features place it firmly outside that picture. The contrapuntal idiom of *Gracioulx et biaulx* is not mature, even on the most basic level. The style seems strangely archaic, recalling in places even the late masses of Dufay. Melodic lines are gently curved, stepwise motion prevails, and the composer rarely seems concerned with generating rhythmic drive (exceptions are usually found in tenorless passages or in places

[29] M. Staehelin, 'Möglichkeiten und praktische Anwendung der Verfasserbestimmung an anonymen Kompositionen der Josquin-Zeit', *Tijdschrift van de Vereniging voor Nederlandse Muziekgeschiedenis*, 23 (1973), 85–6; id., 'Obrechtiana', 5–7.

[30] The alternation between the two types of treatment is conveniently shown in Staehelin's schematic representation, 'Obrechtiana', 6.

where the tenor itself speeds up). This may be partly attributable to the model, whose stamp the mass bears to a greater extent than is usual in Obrecht. For instance, the three-bar cadential phrase that is imitated at the beginning of the song permeates the openings of most mass sections as well. It is in these openings, too, that the composer often follows Barbireau's practice of stating a cadence after every three bars. This lends a sense of predictable regularity to these passages that is to some extent maintained throughout the mass. Yet the cadences do not articulate a lucid periodic structure in the way they do, for instance, in *Fortuna desperata*. In contrast to the neatly parcelled units of the latter work, the counterpoint of *Gracioulx et biaulx* is smoothly flowing and continuous. The treatment of texture, similarly, shows little concern with articulating the counterpoint, and is instead rhapsodic and irregular. Imitation is used in moderation, but motivic techniques of various kinds almost saturate the writing (particularly in the bass).

All this would suggest that *Gracioulx et biaulx*, if it is by Obrecht, was most probably written just before the advent of the mature style. The reason why this could not be argued in the previous chapter is simple: one could not have arrived at the same conclusion without knowledge of the mature picture. In several respects *Gracioulx et biaulx* is part of that picture, but in the most important respect, contrapuntal style, it is not. Unlike the masses discussed in Chapter 7, however, none of its features finds a context in earlier works—except in so far as the very absence of context is typical of the critical phase.

With our next masses, *Caput*, *L'homme armé*, *De tous biens playne*, and others, we move into the primary level of the mature style. At this stage, as argued above, Obrecht aims for an even, continuous flow of vivid counterpoint, in which few devices are treated in any conspicuous way. There are still elements that are readily detectable on paper: imitations, motivic devices, sequences, and so on. Yet Obrecht uses these in moderation, and they hardly ever seem motivated in terms of distinct musical goals. They come and go irregularly, not so much creating the musical discourse as grafted on to it, as ornaments, or figures of speech. The problems for the analyst increase correspondingly. When it makes no real difference to a style whether imitations, sequences, or motivic repetitions are used at a particular point or not, spotting such elements becomes pointless enumeration. On the higher levels, of course, it *was* to make a difference: as Obrecht aimed to give coherence and direction to ever longer stretches of polyphony, he became more and more dependent on conventional devices—redefined and transformed—to hold those stretches together. As a consequence, even a single imitation in a mass like *Fortuna desperata* or *Rose playsante* may tell us something important about the higher mature levels. For it has a context from which it cannot be removed: rather than grafted on to the discourse, it *is* the discourse.

As for the primary level, the problem here is not that the style incorporates many elements that do not seem essential to it—for that in itself is already a helpful observation. The essence of the mature style on its primary level is a contrapuntal quality, overwhelmingly present in sound, yet difficult to capture in words. We have attempted to describe that quality in *Fortuna desperata* and *Plurimorum carminum I*, and Bukofzer, as will be seen shortly, brilliantly described it in *Caput*. To prove its presence in other works that are mature only in so far as they have that quality would require us to describe it again for every single piece, an exercise as repetitious as Obrecht's mature *œuvre* is uniform. The point here is that masses operating on the primary level of the mature style do not aspire to musical individuality; they seem to be realizations of a common stylistic concept, as though they were written in quick succession. It would go too far to say that Obrecht was a *Vielschreiber* in these years, yet it has to be admitted that for all his genius, he did write a number of masses that are remarkable not so much as individuals but as a group. Such works, which include *Caput*, *L'homme armé*, and the three-voice masses, neither ought nor need to keep us long; they will be discussed briefly here before moving on to the higher mature levels.

Caput, like *De Sancto Johanne Baptista* and *L'homme armé*, is a 'remake' of an earlier work, the anonymous English *Caput* mass (composed presumably in the 1440s).[31] In this mass Obrecht follows the direct example of Johannes Ockeghem, who similarly modelled a new setting on the anonymous cycle, probably in the 1450s. As part of a trio of *Caput* masses, Obrecht's setting has received much attention, particularly because the elusive cantus firmus has proved so difficult to identify. It was Manfred Bukofzer who finally solved the enigma. His essay 'Caput: A Liturgico-Musical Study' made musicological history not only because of the discovery itself, but also because of the stylistic analyses of the three *Caput*

---

[31] For general discussions of this mass, see Gombosi, *Obrecht*, 82–5; M. Bukofzer, 'Caput: A Liturgico-Musical Study', in *Studies in Medieval and Renaissance Music* (New York, 1950), 217–310; Reese, *Music in the Renaissance*, 196–7; Salop, 'The Masses of Jacob Obrecht', 6–11; R. Nowotny, *Mensur, Cantus Firmus, Satz in den Caput-Messen von Dufay, Ockeghem und Obrecht* (Inaug.-Diss., Munich, 1970); Taruskin, 'Busnoys and the *L'Homme Armé* Tradition', 275. For the cantus firmus and its performance, see A. E. Planchart, 'Fifteenth-Century Masses: Notes on Performance and Chronology', *Studi musicali*, 10 (1981), 3–29, and W. Elders, 'The Performance of Cantus Firmi in Josquin's Masses based on Secular Monophonic Song', *Early Music*, 17 (1989), 330–41.

masses, to which he devoted over one-third of the study. In the decades
since there has been a tendency to extrapolate Bukofzer's perceptive observations to the respective composers' styles in general. This tendency
has been unfortunate in the case of Ockeghem, whose *Caput* mass is in
many ways an atypical work. Obrecht's own setting is a better representative of its composer: nearly all Bukofzer's comments can be taken as
accurate descriptions of the mature style on its most elementary level.
Indeed, he captured this basic style so eloquently that some of the perti-
nent points bear extended quotation, complementing as they do our own
observations in other masses:[32]

Obrecht's lines are robust and earthy, and breathe the same lusty virility which
characterizes the Flemish canvases of the time. Continual high-pitched activity
and ceaseless rhythmic drive pervade his music. The peculiar melodic vitality is
the result of a thoroughly patterned organization relying essentially on melodic
sequence and even direct repeats of identical or slightly varied ideas. Obrecht is
the master of clearly profiled themes, memorable equally for their rhythms and
for their intervals. Spinning round within a frame of a fourth or fifth and filling
it in by conjunct motion, the themes are interminably and continuously expanded
by means of sequences in asymmetrical patterns which are often closely juxta-
posed in imitation.

   The dynamic vigor of the rhythmic drive springs from an incessant pulse of
strong beats and is heightened by the division of the beat into small units. The
steady and sturdy pulse that underlies all of his music enables him to bring to
play, in triple meter, all sophistications of hemiola rhythm and, in duple meter,
the innumerable possibilities of subtle syncopations, durational accents on and off
the beat, and rhythmic patterns that start on the weak beat and gather momentum as they move to the strong beat.

   . . . The flow of the music is consciously articulated by strong harmonic
cadences, and from them the sequentially spun lines received their direction and
force. As the cadence is no longer as strictly localized as it is in [the anonymous
English composer], Obrecht can build more extended phrases, arch them more
widely, and sustain them longer.

   In general it can be stated that Obrecht's music falls into well-defined harmonic periods of varying length but often symmetrical proportions. Linked
together by melodic means and unified furthermore by imitation, they follow
each other in an orderly procession.

Bukofzer obviously drew attention to features that distinguished
Obrecht's setting from the other two *Caput* masses. In the context of the
composer's own *œuvre* other aspects need emphasizing. Some traits recall
Salve diva parens: tenorless introductions are frequently in three-part
texture throughout—this is a feature of *Gracioulx et biaulx* and *L'homme*

---

[32] '*Caput*: A Liturgico-Musical Study', 293–4, 297, and 299.

armé as well—and the rhythmic writing occasionally reaches extreme levels of intricacy; the same is true, once again, of *L'homme armé* and *Gracioulx et biaulx*.[33] What *Caput* shares with the latter mass is the principle of cantus firmus migration. *Gracioulx et biaulx* has the cantus firmus in the tenor during the first four movements, but the melody appears in the top voice of Agnus Dei I, and then in the bass of the final Agnus. This principle is applied systematically in *Caput*, where the cantus firmus appears successively in the tenor (Kyrie), top voice (Gloria), tenor (Credo), contratenor (Sanctus), and bass (Agnus Dei). It may be significant, in this connection, that the endings of the two masses—surely the points most likely to linger in the memory—are virtually identical.

Several of *Caput*'s movements end with spectacularly long flourishes over the tenor's final longa, usually involving motivic sequences in all voices.[34] Obrecht here exploits the fact that final longas are of indefinite duration, and can therefore be sustained for as long as the other voices continue. The same principle is applied in *Je ne demande* (albeit only in internal sections) and *N'aray-je jamais*, but the closest parallels, with respect to scale as well as writing, appear in *L'homme armé* (where the Osanna flourish is even based on the same motif as the Qui tollis of *Caput*).[35] Although the relationship with the extensions in *Fortuna desperata* and *Libenter gloriabor* is evident, there is one important difference. The latter extensions are genuine continuations of the musical discourse, in which the tenor is either silent or freely composed, and are held in a tight formal balance with the actual tenor-based polyphony. The flourishes in *Caput* and *L'homme armé*, on the other hand, never leave any doubt that the end has been reached, and that all there is left for the voices to do is to sound out while the tenor's final longa is sustained. The procedures are similar, but they are carried out on different levels of the mature style: while *Caput* and *L'homme armé* still reflect the conventional approach, *Fortuna desperata* and *Libenter gloriabor* display Obrecht's new conception of musical form.

The stylistic profile of *L'homme armé* is very similar to that of *Caput*.[36]

[33] For rhythmically intricate writing (which also recalls *Salve crux*, bars 6–18), see particularly Gloria, bars 58–89.   [34] See especially Kyrie, bars 91–9, and Gloria, bars 216–27.

[35] Likewise, the motif treated sequentially in the Kyrie II flourish of *Caput* (bars 91–5) reappears and is given similar treatment in the top voice of *L'homme armé*'s final Agnus Dei (bars 68–72).

[36] The relationship with Busnoys's *L'homme armé* mass was discovered by Oliver Strunk in 1937; see 'Origins of the "L'homme armé" Mass', in *Essays on Music in the Western World* (New York, 1974), 68–9. Discussions of Obrecht's setting have appeared in Gombosi, *Jacob Obrecht*, 59–61; Meier, *Studien zur Meßkomposition*, 26–7; Reese, *Music in the Renaissance*, 197–8; Salop, 'The Masses of Jacob Obrecht', 42–4; Sparks, *Cantus Firmus*, 248 and 458; Todd, 'Retrograde, Inversion', 56–8; Taruskin, 'Antoine Busnoys', 274–5.

Once again the melodic lines show the angularity, patterned structures, and rhythmic energy that typifies the mature style on its primary level. The combined texture is infused with dotted, off-beat, and syncopated rhythms; leaps and triadic motifs abound, and the underlying metric structure receives constant emphasis (particularly in duple time). Yet there are also deviations from the familiar pattern. The highly imitative rhythmic filigree in some passages recalls *Caput*, *Gracioulx et biaulx*, and *Salve diva parens*, but is atypical of the mature idiom, which avoids such extreme intricacies.[37] The extended flourishes at final cadences have already been noted; they have their equals only in *Caput*, although modest parallels can be found in *Je ne demande* and *N'aray-je jamais*. Only one feature in *L'homme armé* points to the past: this is Obrecht's habit of stating freely rhythmized versions of the *L'homme armé* tune successively in different voices of the tenorless introductions.[38] These statements are not strictly speaking pre-imitations, but since they are repeated literally within the introductions, they do create bipartite structures reminiscent of such masses as *Salve diva parens* and *Ave regina celorum*.

De tous biens playne is generally assumed to be among Obrecht's earliest masses.[39] The assumption goes back to Otto Gombosi, who tentatively suggested a date in the late 1460s because of the three-part texture, Obrecht's 'total subordination' to the cantus firmus, and the way in which he treated repetitions and sequences.[40] In the light of new biographical evidence, Gombosi's early date obviously cannot be sustained, but even a date in the late 1470s (when Obrecht was about 20) seems problematic. One would expect any mass written by an adolescent composer to be thoroughly conventional, and faithfully copy the style of the leading masters of the day—as is the case, for instance, in *Petrus apostolus* and even *De Sancto Donatiano*. Yet *De tous biens playne* shows no resemblance to either Busnoys's or Ockeghem's works. Indeed, the mass has several features that would have been quite novel in the 1470s, and yet are typical of Obrecht's mass music after about 1488: the use of ¢ throughout, the absence of head-motifs, the persistent tendency to write parallel tenths

[37] Gloria, bars 36–49, Credo, bars 38–40, Sanctus, bars 24–33, and Pleni, *passim*.

[38] Gloria, bars 1–10 (contratenor) + 10–19 (bass); Sanctus, bars 1–7 (contratenor) + 7–13 (bass). For other pre-emptive statements of the *L'homme armé* melody in contrapuntal voices (one of the mass's more conservative features), see Gombosi, *Jacob Obrecht*, 59.

[39] For discussions, see Gombosi, *Jacob Obrecht*, 45–7; Reese, *Music in the Renaissance*, 198–9; Salop, 'The Masses of Jacob Obrecht', 51–8; Meier, *Studien zur Meßkomposition*, 23–5; Sparks, *Cantus Firmus*, 249–54, 288–93, 469, and 474–5; Todd, 'Retrograde, Inversion', 58–61.

[40] *Jacob Obrecht*, 47. Gombosi's date rested on the assumption that Obrecht had been active in Ferrara in 1474, and that this first 'Italienreise' marked a watershed in the composer's creative development, which *De tous biens playne* could only pre-date.

around the cantus firmus, introductory duos and interludes involving 'parody' quotations as in *Je ne demande* and *Plurimorum carminum I*,[41] and the modelling of a two-voice section on the cantus firmus (Agnus Dei II). The three-part 'chanson' texture (with tenor and contratenor in the same range) is of course an archaism. But then it would have been no less so around 1480 than around 1490, for this particular kind of texture had become obsolete already by the mid-1460s. Obrecht's curious decision to employ it cannot be explained away by assuming a date in the late 1470s.

Amongst the mature masses *De tous biens playne* distinguishes itself in only one respect: its complete lack of contrapuntal ambition. Although the cantus firmus is transformed canonically in three sections, and mensurally in one,[42] most sections are simply straightforward rearrangements of the song tenor, very much like what happens in *Plurimorum carminum I*. As in this latter mass, the counterpoint has a lively, improvisatory character, and relies for its musical interest on rhythmic impetus more than anything else (particularly in the Gloria and Credo). Truly inspired moments are absent: the mature idiom is applied routinely, and there is no apparent desire to handle it with great originality. Here and there the mass gives the impression of a rush job; it seems unlikely that it would have taken Obrecht more than a few days to write a modest setting like this.

Fors seulement and *Je ne seray plus vert vestus* are two other run-of-the-mill works that scarcely invite extended comment.[43] *Je ne seray* is in fact anonymous, but it is an identical twin of *Fors seulement*, and has been tentatively attributed to Obrecht on this ground.[44] The above comments on *De tous biens playne* apply to these works as well: a date before the mature period would seem unlikely because of the absence of head-motifs,

[41] Gombosi, *Jacob Obrecht*, 45, and Sparks, *Cantus Firmus*, 251 and 288–90.

[42] The cantus firmus treatment in *De tous biens playne* has received much comment (see the literature cited above), but the application of mensural transformation in the Osanna II appears to have been overlooked (Loyset Compère already realized the tune's potential for mensural transformation in his motet *Omnium bonorum plena*, of c.1470). The sampling procedures in the Patrem and Et incarnatus connect the mass to *Grecorum* (in both sections the tenor notes are to be sung in order according to their value, just as in the Patrem of *Grecorum*). In the Sanctus the tenor is split up into eight segments that are to be sung in the order 1 8 7 6 5 4 3 2 (*NOE* 4, p. xv). This procedure has sometimes been regarded as a forerunner of Obrecht's segmentation technique, but it is difficult to consider it as more than a sophisticated sampling procedure.

[43] On *Fors seulement*, see Gombosi, *Jacob Obrecht*, 32–4; Salop, 'The Masses of Jacob Obrecht', 38–41; Sparks, *Cantus Firmus*, 247–8, 274, and 285–8; Staehelin, 'Obrechtiana', 16–17. For *Je ne seray plus*, see Just, *Der Mensuralkodex*, i. 292–3; T. R. Ward, 'Another Mass by Obrecht?', *Tijdschrift van de Vereniging voor Nederlandse Muziekgeschiedenis*, 27 (1977), 102–8. The earliest surviving copy of *Je ne seray* is in BerlS 40021 (c.1498; see Just, *Der Mensuralkodex*, ii. 33).

[44] Ward, 'Another Mass by Obrecht?'

the exclusive use of ¢, and the complete absence of any device or procedure that is known to have exercised Obrecht before the late 1480s. The various sections are straightforward rearrangements, with the song discantus in the top voice. Although *Fors seulement* in particular shows greater polish than *De tous biens playne*, the idiom in both settings never moves beyond the basic level of the mature style.

The anonymous *Missa N'aray-je jamais* is the only known segmentation mass not attributed to Obrecht; if his authorship is to be accepted, this work falls into the category of the primary-level mature masses.[45] In several respects *N'aray-je jamais* seems more closely related to *Je ne demande* than to any other segmentation mass. Both cycles tend to structure their opening duos and trios over strictly quoted voices from their models,[46] they have the same kinds of flourishes at final cadences, and they both introduce canons in the Qui tollis indicating fivefold augmentation in the first tenor statement. Major differences between the two masses are attributable mainly to the fact that the song *N'aray-je jamais* is about one-third of the length of Busnoys's *Je ne demande*. Not surprisingly, then, the cycle built on the former has only seven segments, while the one based on the latter has eleven. Yet we have already noted that *Je ne demande* was deliberately planned on a large scale: its eleven longer segments are given thirty-eight statements altogether, while the seven shorter ones of *N'aray-je jamais* receive only thirty-two. The latter mass is not only shorter, but the writing is correspondingly more compact and dense.

Comparison quickly reveals that while *Je ne demande* is a rhapsodic work, incorporating several effects that can be associated with higher levels of the mature style, *N'aray-je jamais* shows the unvarying, relentlessly forward-moving counterpoint of the primary level. Irregular changes of texture, which frequently occur in *Je ne demande*, are found hardly at all. Nor does the composer aim to exploit opportunities offered by the tenor, in the way that we have seen in Exx. 26 and 27. Imitations, motivic sequences, and related devices make random appearances, and do not seem to be motivated by any musical goal except the mere enrichment of the counterpoint. All this points to the primary level of the

---

[45] Copying date: *c*.1492 (Just, *Der Mensuralkodex*, ii. 27). For the mass's authorship, see Staehelin, 'Obrechtiana', 3–5; Just, *Der Mensuralkodex*, i. 297–338; Noblitt, 'Problems of Transmission', 223.

[46] For *Je ne demande*, see above. The following quotations appear in *N'aray-je jamais*: Kyrie, bars 12–15 (top voice of song), Et in terra, bars 1–16 (tenor), 16–22 (top voice), Patrem, bars 1–7 (top voice), 7–21 (top voice), Sanctus, bars 1–19 (top voice). As observed earlier, the practice of structuring introductory passages on literal quotations of pre-existent material seems to be typical of early mature masses; see *Plurimorum carminum I* (Patrem, Sanctus, and probably Et in terra), which existed by 1487–90.

mature style, and would seem to support Martin Just's conclusion that
N'aray-je jamais, if is by Obrecht, must have been his earliest segmentation mass.[47]

With our last two masses, *Grecorum*[48] and *Pfauenschwanz*,[49] we move to
a level of the mature style roughly comparable to that of *Plurimorum
carminum II* and *Je ne demande*. Both works use ₵ as the predominant
mensuration, have no head-motifs, are based on strictly quoted and manipulated tenors (deviations in *Pfauenschwanz* will be dealt with below),
and incorporate sections in reduced scoring based on statements of the
cantus firmus.[50] Both, too, introduce a measure of stylistic differentiation
into the mature style, and show a more advanced sense of musical development and long-term proportion. Just as in *Plurimorum carminum II*, the
tell-tale signs of this latter sense are the musically self-contained extensions beyond the final tenor note. The extension at the end of the Gloria
in *Pfauenschwanz* (bars 249–60) involves free writing in the tenor, and
recalls similar extensions in *Plurimorum carminum II* and *Libenter gloriabor*. In general *Pfauenschwanz* is less concerned with rigidity of tenor
treatment than *Grecorum*. The latter mass is absolutely strict in this respect, and so it comes as no surprise that the longest extension here

[47] Just summarizes his 'basic hypothesis' as follows: 'mit der anonym überlieferten *Missa N'aray-
je* habe Obrecht erstmals jene außergewöhnliche Disposition eines Cantus firmus [i.e., segmentation
technique] erprobt und den Weg zu späteren und im einzelnen konsequenteren Meisterwerken wie
Malheur me bat und *Je ne demande* geebnet' (*Der Mensuralkodex*, i. 338). Unprecedented in Obrecht's
mass œuvre (but not actually out of character) are the first seven bars of the Pleni, in which there
is no polyphony but merely exchanges of brief motifs between the three voices (there may be
a context for this curious opening in the Benedictus of Josquin's *Missa Pange lingua*; see Elders,
Studien zur Symbolik, 127–8). Likewise atypical of Obrecht seems the strict canon for three voices
in the Benedictus (this may suggest the influence of Busnoys; see *A que ville est abominable* and the
Benedictus of *Missa L'ardant desir*).

[48] For literature, see Meier, *Studien zur Meßkomposition*, 4–5 and 96–7; Salop, 'The Masses of
Jacob Obrecht', 44–51; Sparks, *Cantus Firmus*, 249–50 and 468; Staehelin, 'Obrechtiana', 23–5;
Todd, 'Retrograde, Inversion', 65–9. For hypotheses as to the nature and possible identity of the
Grecorum melody, see O. Ursprung, 'Alte griechische Einflüsse und neuer gräzistischer Einschlag in
der mittelalterlichen Musik', *Zeitschrift für Musikwissenschaft*, 12 (1929–30), 219; A. Pirro, *Histoire
de la musique de la fin du XIVe siècle à la fin du XVIe* (Paris, 1940), 194; Finscher, 'Obrecht', *MGG*
9, col. 1820; Staehelin, 'Obrechtiana', 23–5; Sparks, *Cantus Firmus*, 468. One possibility is that the
title refers not to the tenor but to the feast for which the mass was written. In the late 1480s Obrecht
had to write annual masses for, amongst others, the *festum asinorum*, *festum claudorum*, and *festum
innocentium* (see Ch. 6). Given the quotation of the Easter sequence *Victimae paschali* in the Osanna,
the feast might have been that of the newcomers to the school (*beianen*, i.e. 'yellow-beaks', nestlings)
which was celebrated annually on Easter Monday (Strohm, *Music in Late Medieval Bruges*, 35). It
is not known, however, whether 'greci' (or any word resembling it) was ever used as a synonym for
'nestlings', or 'the new boys'.

[49] The mass is discussed in: Meier, *Studien zur Meßkomposition*, 25–6; Salop, 'The Masses of
Jacob Obrecht', 37–8; Sparks, *Cantus Firmus*, 294–8 and 469.

[50] In *Grecorum* the top voice of the Agnus Dei II quotes the entire cantus firmus. In *Pfauenschwanz* the tenor of the model appears in the contratenors of the Christe and Pleni, and in the bass
of the Agnus Dei II.

(Credo, bars 196–202) is written over a period of silence in the tenor, exactly as in the Qui tollis of *Fortuna desperata* (Ex. 23).[51]

Pfauenschwanz seems the less advanced of the two. The setting somewhat resembles *Plurimorum carminum II* in that both masses state their cantus firmi in twofold augmentation as well as *ut iacet*, and exploit the opportunities that the former procedure creates. But there is a difference of degree here. In *Pfauenschwanz* one can almost tell from the nature of the contrapuntal voices whether the tenor is augmented or not, for with the exception of the Et resurrexit (bars 172–236) and third Agnus Dei, they persistently follow the rhythmic movement of that voice (shifting over almost immediately when the proportion changes, as in Sanctus, bar 65). This explains the sharp contrast between the basically chordal writing in such sections as Kyrie I, Sanctus (up to bar 65), and Agnus Dei I, and the typical primary-level style of Kyrie II/Osanna, Et resurrexit (after bar 248), and Sanctus (after bar 65). This is a crude distinction compared with the subtle stylistic differentiation in *Plurimorum carminum II* (Ex. 26). There are more signs that *Pfauenschwanz* scarcely moves beyond the primary level of the mature style. One of the mass's most distinctive features is the structural use of sequence and ostinato in the bass.[52] Yet the device is rarely used with distinct musical goals in mind, and often one has the impression that Obrecht is simply trying to find out how long he can persist in repeating a single motif.[53]

Yet there are exceptions, and these are revealed, paradoxically, by Obrecht's treatment of the cantus firmus. Basically, as already said, *Pfauenschwanz* is structured over a series of straightforward tenor statements. Literal quotations are found in all movements except the Et in terra, Qui sedes, and Patrem. Even in the latter sections, however, Obrecht always takes the original tune as his starting-point. Rather than actively reshaping it, he only allows himself temporary departures from the original. Sparks dubbed these departures 'arbitrary and unpredictable',[54] but it is clear from the musical context that most are in fact motivated in terms of the

---

[51] A further parallel with the Qui tollis of *Fortuna desperata* is the symmetry of the tenor layout, so that the rests at the end exactly mirror those at the beginning. In *Fortuna desperata* the first half of the cantus firmus is stated in retrograde (from the middle backwards to the beginning), and the second *ut iacet* from the middle to the end. In *Grecorum* the entire cantus firmus is first stated in retrograde-inversion (middle backwards to beginning), and then forward in inversion (middle to end), following the verbal canon: 'Tu tenor cancriza et per antifrasim canta cum fueris [orig.: fureis] in capite antifrasizando repete' (*NOE* 5, p. xiv).

[52] Cf. Kyrie, bars 108–17, Gloria, bars 39–42, 43–8, 165–84, Credo, bars 16–27, and Kyrie I and Agnus I and III, *passim*. See also Sparks, *Cantus Firmus*, 297–8 (with example on 294–6).

[53] This recalls the Et resurrexit of *Plurimorum carminum I*, whose top-voice line states a single motif twenty-six times. The intended effect here is surely witty rather than musically motivated.

[54] *Cantus Firmus*, 469.

musical discourse. It is in such passages that *Pfauenschwanz* goes beyond the primary level.

A good example is the Qui sedes (Ex. 28). After the tenor has entered (bar 165) it quotes the cantus firmus faithfully up to bar 170; thereafter it is freely rhythmized. The reason for the departure can be found in the contrapuntal context. With the tenor entry the bass has started a motivic sequence, and the tenor, if maintained strictly, would clash with this sequence precisely in bar 170 (*a* against *B♭* in the bass). Two bars later it would produce parallel fifths with the bass, and two bars after that yet another clash (*e* against *f*). Obrecht was thus forced to compromise between two rigid compositional principles; significantly, he made the tenor give in, not the bass.[55] The sequence is allowed to continue freely until bar 185 (ten statements in all). At exactly that point the tenor resumes strict quotation of the cantus firmus. It is clear that we are not dealing with an Obrechtian witticism here, for if he was trying to find out how long the sequence could be continued, this would have been simply cheating. Rather it seems that Obrecht thought of an appropriate musical development before he actually knew whether or not the tenor could accommodate it; when he found out that it could not, the idea must have seemed too attractive to abandon it for the sake of arbitrary rationality. Such thinking can only indicate that we have moved away from the primary level of the mature style. Although the sequence is not particularly forceful compared with what happens in more advanced masses (especially since no other stylistic parameter co-operates in the development, as in the Qui tollis of *Je ne demande*), it is properly concluded with a firm cadence on the final G, giving the passage a measure of coherence and direction (bar 189).

Once this attitude is recognized, the other departures in *Pfauenschwanz* are easily explained. The Patrem, for instance, starts with a strictly quoted cantus-firmus statement (albeit mensurally transformed through presentation in O), but departs from that course in bar 20. Once again this coincides with a motivic sequence in the bass (bars 16–21), which is continued in the top voice and contratenor in the tenorless passage in bars 22–8. Similarly, the four-voice sequence in Et in terra, bars 39–42, and the motivic sequence in the top voice, bars 43–51, may be responsible for the freedom of tenor treatment in bars 36–52 of that movement. Only one 'unmotivated' departure appears in *Pfauenschwanz*: this is the slightly remodelled version of the last part of the tenor in Qui sedes, bars 249–60.[56]

[55] The opposite happens elsewhere in the mass: in the Kyrie I and Agnus Dei I and III the bass ostinato is modified so as to make it fit with the cantus firmus.

[56] 'Unmotivated' remodellings of this type are extremely rare in Obrecht's mature period. They usually occur in passages written in ⸲, where the tenor sometimes joins the other voices in rounding

[*cont. on p. 276*]

Ex. 28. Obrecht, *Missa Pfauenschwanz*, Qui sedes, bars 141–92

(Ex. 28, *cont.*)

Having allowed himself these freedoms, Obrecht firms them up in a manner only he could adopt. The freely rhythmized passage in the Qui sedes is repeated in a second cantus-firmus statement within the same section. The departure in the Et in terra, bars 39–52, is similarly repeated in the Patrem, bars 48–61 (where it coincides again with four-voice sequences, in bars 49–50 and 51–2). And the mensurally transformed version of the Gloria, bars 13–36, is restated in the second half of the Osanna, bars 175–91. After the various compromises Obrecht thus reintroduces an element of strictness in this mass, in keeping with the new 'rationalistic' attitude of the mature period.

Grecorum shows much more developed skills. Although the cantus firmus is treated here with uncompromising strictness, Obrecht's counterpoint is more effective, mainly, one feels, because he understands his language much better. A sequence as in Ex. 28, although motivated musically and firm in purpose, still seems crude in comparison with the effects that can be created by subtly handling and co-ordinating the basic parameters of style. *Grecorum*, by demonstrating the latter point, makes an important step in the direction of *Fortuna desperata*, *Rose playsante*, and their associates.

Ex. 29 shows bars 1–70 of the Et in terra. It is evident already in the opening bars that we are not on the primary level of the mature style— where the musical discourse does not depend, for its contrapuntal quality, on imitations or motivic devices. In bars 1–16, imitation *is* the discourse: take it away and one is left with little more than the bare structural backbone, the *Grecorum* tune in threefold augmentation. The basic melodic unit is first stated in the contratenor (bars 1–6), disappearing under the tenor in bar 4, still 'hidden' in the second statement (bass, bars 6–11),

off a movement in a quick triple rhythm. This is true of the Qui sedes in *Pfauenschwanz*, and also of the Et unam sanctam of *De tous biens playne*.

Ex. 29. Obrecht, *Missa Grecorum*, Et in terra, bars 1–70

(Ex. 29, *cont.*)

but finally re-emerging in the top voice (bars 11–16). There are clear parallels here with the Kyrie I of *Fortuna desperata*. The music moves in clearly demarcated units, each cadencing on the final, and there is a terraced expansion of sonority and texture. The main difference, of course, is that the tenor starts straight away, so that its entry is neither dramatized nor taken up into the musical discourse. That discourse, a development spanning sixteen bars, is rather projected on to the tenor, whose shape is not at all suggestive of musical development.

This much tells us that Obrecht has moved beyond the mere cladding of the cantus firmus in nondescript, *ad hoc* counterpoint. The 'high-level' sense of purpose and direction, and the balance between continuity and periodicity, are firmly there. This is evident, too, from Obrecht's handling of other parameters. In the first sixteen bars, rhythmic energy is concentrated in the imitative phrase: the other voices are generally slow-moving, thus keeping the expanding texture as sonorous as possible. In bar 16 no further development is possible in terms of either the imitation or the texture. From that point onwards, rhythmic energy begins to infuse the other voices, leading to full rhythmic drive in bars 21–4. Even more telling is Obrecht's handling of tonal planes. While bars 1–16 are kept firmly on the final G, in bar 19 the music moves to another tonal plane, on D, which remains in force until the return to the final in bar 34. Thereafter, too, the tonal planes are easily identified: G (bars 34–43), B-flat (bars 43–60), and a final return to G that marks the end of the first major tenor statement (bar 67). The harmonic language, then, is simplified, and clearly more coherent than in either *Plurimorum carminum II* or *Je ne demande*. Yet Obrecht does not make the language speak as eloquently as in *Fortuna desperata* or *Malheur me bat*. Although the writing remains generally periodic, with motifs exchanged between voices and with cadences after every period (bars 25–31, 34–43, 43–57), the cadences do not have the force of either *Fortuna desperata*'s 'articulation marks' or *Malheur me bat*'s powerful tonal hinges. Still, in these sixty-odd bars Obrecht has written music that is consistently full of interest, drive, and direction, and is perfectly lucid and clear in structure. And that is an impression which holds true for the whole of *Grecorum*. It is one of Obrecht's finest settings, and was rightly included by Petrucci in his *Misse Obreht* (the mass's unique source). Looking at a work like this, one can understand that Obrecht would one day be capable of writing masses like *Fortuna desperata* and *Rose playsante*: the ingredients of the full-fledged mature style are firmly in place.[57]

---

[57] It is worth devoting a few words to the fragmentary *Missa Scaramella*, for it may have some connections to both *Pfauenschwanz* and *Grecorum*. Although the tenor part does not survive, it can be reconstructed in those places where its treatment was evidently strict. The original tune (as given in *NOE* 11, pp. xxxv–xxxvi) was transposed up a fourth. Most statements appear to be literal: Kyrie I and II; Et in terra, bar 46, second semibreve, to 54 (2 : 1 diminution); Qui tollis, bars 160–75; Et incarnatus (three times; each phrase preceded by four breves rest); Et unam, bars 250–65; Osanna II and Agnus Dei II (preceded by three semibreves rest; presented twice, second time in 2 : 1 diminution; no final note in Osanna, final maxima in Agnus Dei); Agnus Dei III, bar 105, second minim, to 116, and 128, last minim, to 140 (both in 2 : 1 diminution). Retrograde is employed in the Sanctus (from bar 25, second semibreve, backwards to bar 1), and followed by straightforward statement (bar 30, second semibreve, to 53; cf. the remark 'Canon: Revertere' in the bass at bar 28, *NOE* 11, p. xxxvii). The cantus firmi in the other sections and passages remain to be reconstructed, although, as in *Pfauenschwanz*, they need not all be entirely strict. ₵ is the predominant mensuration, and, to judge from the surviving voices, no head-motifs seem to have been used (although the

Our approach in this chapter has necessarily been circumspect, because the undated mature masses outnumber those for which we have early copying dates. Five masses are known to have existed by 1493 at the latest (six if *N'aray-je jamais* is included), and these alone tell us that the late 1480s must have been years of stylistic upheaval. The primary level of the mature style was established before 1490 (*Plurimorum carminum I*), the segmentation technique was developed by 1491 (*Je ne demande*), at least three masses employing that technique existed by 1493 (the other two being *Rose playsante* and *N'aray-je jamais*), by which time, also, the mature style had reached its perfection (*Fortuna desperata* and probably *Libenter gloriabor*). At least ten undated masses are so closely related to these works that it would have been perfectly reasonable to date them in the same years, were it not that their number seems almost alarmingly large. For this reason it has been necessary not to pre-empt questions of chronology, for instance by discussing dated and undated masses together in a putative chronological order. Yet such questions cannot be avoided altogether, and we must finally address them briefly.

As far as chronology is concerned there are various ways of interpreting the evidence, each of which is based on suppositions that are inherently unprovable. One such supposition has already been mentioned: that works like *Fortuna desperata* and *Rose playsante* provide a *terminus ante quem* for less advanced mature masses. Self-evident though such an assumption might seem in other contexts, here it would inevitably force us to date all masses discussed above (with the possible exceptions of *Libenter gloriabor* and *Malheur me bat*) before 1493.

Paradoxically, this conclusion seems easiest to draw for those undated works that operate *between* the extreme levels of the mature style (*Plurimorum carminum II*, *Pfauenschwanz*, *Grecorum*). This is partly because the artistic perfection of the 1491–3 masses presupposes an evolutionary development in works of this kind, since such perfection is unlikely to have come about overnight. Also, the ways in which Obrecht realizes his ambitions in these works often suggests that he was simply not aware of opportunities for more effective (and often in fact simpler) writing. Works on the primary level, on the other hand, do not seem to have particularly high ambitions in the first place, and it is entirely possible that Obrecht, even in the 1490s, made a distinction between works of basic craftsmanship and works of art (not unlike the *Kenner/Liebhaber* distinction in the

Gloria and Credo open with old-fashioned introductory duos, much like the same movements in *Pfauenschwanz*). The Credo ends with an extension in which the tenor may have been either silent or freely composed (bars 266–74). Agnus Dei II, bars 86–92, looks more like a cadential flourish, since the final tenor note can be sustained during the entire passage (by analogy to bars 70–3).

eighteenth century). These questions cannot be resolved at present, but we can at least aim to identify the various stylistic layers of the mature *œuvre*, awaiting further dating evidence. Table 1 conflates the three groups of masses discussed in this chapter, and presents the mature *œuvre* in order according to the levels of the mature style. This order may be roughly chronological.

Obrecht's achievement in the mature style is considerable. His new sound world is so fundamentally different from that of the recent past that direct comparisons across the divide do little justice to either. Compared with earlier works, the mature masses often seem to transgress the bounds of stylistic decorum, and seem obsessively emphatic in their gestures, in places even simplistic and crude. Conversely, the earlier masses, judged by the aesthetic of the mature period, seem too subdued and inward-looking, revelling in fleeting sounds while avoiding a commitment to clearly defined musical goals. Yet although qualitative comparisons of this kind are inappropriate, it would be unrealistic to claim that they were never made by Obrecht's contemporaries, and that they might not have influenced the early reception of his music.

Obrecht's new style was bound to polarize the musical world of his time. Judging from transmission, the style found quick admirers, particularly in central and eastern Germany, where Obrecht's mature masses were widely copied throughout the first half of the sixteenth century.[58] Yet, significantly, no mass except *Si dedero* was copied or printed in full in any known Italian source after the composer's death. One of the earliest appraisals of his music is found in Paolo Cortese's *De cardinalatu libri tres* (1510), an encyclopaedic treatise on the rules of behaviour befitting a cardinal.[59] Cortese's words are particularly interesting because it is in the nature of his book that he reports fashionable opinion rather than his own, personal judgement. He cites Obrecht as an important composer of motets, but quickly moves on to the composer's general musical style, pointing out its lack of polish:[60]

In this genre Iacobus Obrechius has been considered mighty in varied subtlety, but in the whole style of composition somewhat rough, and indeed one who has sown more of the keenest sweetness in music with skilful harmony, than would

[58] See the important observations on transmission made by Martin Staehelin in 'Obrechtiana', 19–20.

[59] See N. Pirrotta, 'Music and Cultural Tendencies in 15th-Century Italy', *Journal of the American Musicological Society*, 19 (1966), 146–61, esp. 160.

[60] See the facsimile of the passage, ibid. 151: 'quo in genere Iacobus Obrechius habitus est varia subtilitate grandis, sed toto struendi genere horridior, et is a quo plus sit in musicis acerrimae suavitatis artificiosa concinnitate satum, quam esset aurium voluptati satis, ut qui in gustatu ea magis laudare solent quae omphacium quam quae saccarum sapere videantur'.

TABLE 1. *Stylistic layers in the mature mass œuvre of Jacob Obrecht*

layer	mass	dating[a]	level
1	*Caput*	—	transitional
	L'homme armé	—	
2	*Plurimorum carminum I*	1487–90	primary
	De tous biens playne	—	
	Fors seulement	—	
	? Je ne seray	1498	
	? N'aray-je jamais	1492	
3	*Plurimorum carminum II*	1491–3	intermediate
	Grecorum	—	
	Pfauenschwanz	—	
	Je ne demande	1487–91	
4	*Fortuna desperata*	1489–93	highest
	Libenter gloriabor	—	
	Malheur me bat	1497	
	Rose playsante	1491–3	

[a] earliest known copying date or date of paper

have sufficed to please the ear—just as people, when tasting, praise such things that seem to taste of unripe juice more highly than those tasting of sugar.

Such a verdict would have been difficult to understand if Cortese had masses in mind like *Sicut spina rosam*, *De Sancto Donatiano*, or *Ave regina celorum*, which are among Obrecht's smoothest and most polished works. Yet in such a mass as *Fortuna desperata* one can understand his point of view—and Cortese is, after all, writing within years of its publication by Petrucci.

Henricus Glareanus, writing in the south-westernmost corner of Germany, points out that 'there are many compositions of [Obrecht] everywhere', an observation which then probably applies mainly to countries north of the Alps. Glareanus is particularly impressed by the grandeur (*maiestas*) of Obrecht's music, a quality in which the composer is 'second to none' in the opinion of both himself and Erasmus.[61] His brief assessment differs markedly from Cortese's:[62]

[61] See *Dodekachordon*, 256: 'Primum [exemplum] est Iacobi Hobrechti symphonetae, quod ad copiam attinet ac carminis maiestatem D. Erasmi Roterodami, praeceptoris nostri, atque adeo etiam nostri iudicio, nulli secundus.'

[62] Ibid. 456: 'Omnia huius viri monumenta miram quandam habent maiestatem et mediocritatis

All the works this man has left have a certain wondrous grandeur and an intrinsic quality of moderation. Indeed he was not such a lover of the unusual as was Josquin. He was one who displayed his talent, but without pretence, as if he preferred to await the judgement of the listener rather than to preen himself.

Glareanus praises Obrecht for not showing off his skill, for instance with such notational complexities as the theorist condemns four pages later in Isaac. Pretence is foreign to his music. In so far as Obrecht displays his talent, it is directed to the listener—meaning perhaps that any complexity or artifice is motivated in terms of the listener's musical experience. Writing music of direct appeal, the composer achieves 'a certain wondrous grandeur and an intrinsic quality of moderation'. It may not be too far-fetched to suggest that Glareanus is describing here the paradoxical combination of simple means and effective results that characterizes Obrecht's mature style. One suspects that what is 'grand' for Glareanus, was 'rough' for Cortese. If so, both points of view would be understandable.

To this day Obrecht is known primarily as the composer of the mature masses: it is these that ultimately determined his posthumous reputation. Although the composer had absorbed the idioms of Busnoys, Ockeghem, and Weerbecke or Josquin in earlier years, he firmly did away with them later on. The only standards Obrecht set himself in the mature period were his own, and to these he adhered persistently, never again taking account of other composers' styles. That gives him a highly individual profile even today. As a mass composer he was perhaps not the 'genialer Außenseiter' of the Renaissance, as Besseler described him,[63] but certainly the *genialer Einzelgänger*.

---

venam. Ipse hercules non tam amans raritatis atque Iodocus fuit. Ingenii quidem ostentator sed absque fuco, quasi qui auditoris iudicium expectare maluerit quam se ipse efferre.'

[63] H. Besseler, 'Von Dufay bis Josquin, ein Literaturbericht', *Zeitschrift für Musikwissenschaft*, 11 (1928–9), 18.

PART THREE
1491–1505

9 'JUBILATING ALWAYS IN MY SONGS'

On 17 January 1491 the canons of St Donatian's discharged Jacob Obrecht 'because of the better'.[1] No doubt this motivation, however ambiguously worded, reflected the composer's rather than the chapter's point of view. Only he could now expect a change for the better, not the church, which was ill-prepared for his departure, and would have to struggle with interim succentors for nearly two years.[2] Obrecht was now in his early thirties, and had established himself as the leading composer of northern Europe. His masses and motets were finding their way to musical centres hundreds of miles removed from Bruges, spreading his fame to all corners of the Continent. A man of his stature could do better, much better, than remain a succentor at Bruges, a city starved into surrender only two months earlier. Prices had soared, standards of living fallen. Obrecht's salary—never adjusted to inflation or actual costs of living—was barely sufficient to sustain him. Bruges could not offer anything better at this time, nor, it seemed, in the foreseeable future. Obrecht went to find it elsewhere.

Frustratingly, we lose track of the composer at this very point, and consequently we do not know exactly what 'the better' was, or where he found it. But it is not difficult to guess what Obrecht might have aspired to in these years: a leading position at one of the courtly chapels in

[1] The phrase is no more idiomatic in Latin than it is in English: '. . . et michi [the chapter secretary] etiam injunctum ut gratiose dicerem succentori quod domini mei *propter melius* licentiarunt eum' (italics mine; De Schrevel, *Histoire*, i. 164; see also the translation in Ch. 5).

[2] See Ch. 5. In the two years after Obrecht's departure, the church had to recruit various interim succentors from among its own personnel, and was at one point even forced to house some of the choirboys with the canons. Although Hieronymus de Clibano was appointed succentor as early as 20 Apr. 1491, and repeatedly promised to come soon, he managed to postpone his arrival until 1 Dec. 1492. Within seven months De Clibano was found to be neglecting his duties, and on 26 June 1493 the canons of St Donatian's were forced to threaten him with dismissal. They resorted to this measure four years later, on 16 Aug. 1497. See De Schrevel, *Histoire*, i. 165, and Bouws, 'Jeronimus de Clibano', 77–9.

Europe. Had not all the great composers of his time obtained such positions in their early thirties: Dufay in the papal chapel, Binchois and
Busnoys at the Burgundian court, Ockeghem in the French royal chapel?
And had not Johannes Tinctoris, in 1472, directly attributed the flourishing of contemporary music to the patronage of the courts? It was the
Christian princes, he had argued, who by treating their singers with 'honour, glory, and riches' made them 'most fervently inflamed towards the
study of music'.[3] How then would Obrecht, who had already accomplished so much without that support, prosper in such surroundings?

    This is not just speculation. Direct evidence that it was Obrecht's
ambition in these years to move into courtly circles comes from the motet
Inter preclarissimas virtutes, a musical letter of application addressed, significantly, to the patron of a household chapel (Pl. 13).[4] The composition
of this work has usually been placed in the Ferrarese sojourn of 1487–8,
but the chronology of Obrecht's sacred musical style would now suggest
a date of at least a few years later.[5] The text makes it quite clear that
Obrecht is aiming for an appointment (Doc. 44):

Among your excellent virtues and immense gifts of the mind, is godliness—
which according to the Apostle is 'profitable unto all things'—shining forth
greatly. Thus it is that you always show a ready and benevolent disposition to this
end that, [having adorned many services when ⟨you appointed⟩ strangers and

---

[3] Tinctoris, *Proportionale musices*, in *Opera theoretica*, iia. 10. A clear documentary example is in
Strohm, *Music in Late Medieval Bruges* (rev. edn., Oxford, 1990), 258: on 14 Aug. 1482 the Bruges
singer Johannes de Vos requested leave to go to the chapel of the King of Hungary, 'ad hoc per
quendam magnis promissis allectus et spe multi maioris lucri, quod dicit se vix posse vivere ex lucro
huius ecclesie.' (I am grateful to Bonnie Blackburn for pointing out this reference to me.)

[4] Unique source: SegC s.s., fos. 78ᵛ–81ʳ. See Smijers, 'Twee onbekende motetteksten', 130–3;
A. Dunning, *Die Staatsmotette 1480–1555* (Utrecht, 1970), 14–17; Nagle, 'The Structural Role',
152–74; Wegman, 'Bergen op Zoom', 210. The cantus firmus is the antiphon *Estote fortes in bello*
from the Common of Apostles and Evangelists, transposed up a fourth (*Liber Usualis*, 1118). For
attempts to identify the dedicatee, on the assumption that the cantus firmus text might be his
heraldic motto, see Smijers, 'Twee onbekende motetteksten', 131, and B. Murray, 'Jacob Obrecht's
Connection with the Church of Our Lady in Antwerp', *Revue belge de musicologie*, 11 (1957), 129.

[5] Although *Inter preclarissimas virtutes* is copied next to *Mille quingentis* in the unique source,
SegC s.s., it is clearly the later of the two. *Mille quingentis*, written at the close of the critical phase,
still adopts the O–₵ mensural layout typical of Obrecht's earlier works (using ⊊ as the final sign).
Its three sections are structured on three identically notated statements of the full cantus firmus, the
Introit *Requiem aeternam*, which is mensurally transformed in the manner of Busnoys. Isolated
phrases of the cantus firmus are occasionally quoted in the other voices; in one case the text of the
cantus firmus is quoted as well ('et lux perpetua'), recalling identical procedures in the masses
O lumen ecclesie and *Sicut spina rosam* (see Ch. 4). All this is consistent with a date of composition
before the mature period. *Inter preclarissimas virtutes*, by contrast, is written in ₵ throughout, has no
mensural contrasts (apart from a brief *sesquialtera* excursion in the *secunda pars*), and is based on
a chant fragment that is notated and treated exactly as in a segmentation mass: five successive
statements in each of the first two sections, sixfold augmentation in the first statements, with
successive reduction, until the notes have the same durations as in the other voices. These features
would seem to preclude a date of composition before the mature period, making it likely that the
motet was written around the time of Obrecht's departure from Bruges or later.

poor people],[6] music may be supported through your effort. For the generosity of the clergy gives you praise, for your outstanding magnanimity stands out even more in that it promotes those who deserve it. Glorious is your state before God. You nourish the poor, enrich the virtuous, build the Church, raise the humble—from all which things you are commended as the good savour. 'Be ye strong in war.'

Well then, because of your such considerable fatherliness, I sound forth, jubilating always in my songs, not the praises that I owe but such as I am capable of, and I humbly offer [them], being present through this page which is put together in a crude style of harmony, for the praise of God and your comfort. For what else I can do in service for you now, I do not know. You do not want for money, you are rich in understanding and wisdom, are encouraged by prosperity and joy, rejoice in tranquillity and peace, and are praised among those who look up to men of rank. 'Be ye strong in war.'

Therefore accept this present musical song and me, Jacobus Hobrecht, the humblest of your servants, benevolently and as you please. Command and rule happily and long.

Since the unnamed dedicatee is credited with such qualities as 'the generosity of the clergy' and 'fatherliness', one may suspect that he was a prelate, quite possibly even the Holy Father himself. The latter possibility seems all the more likely as Obrecht seems to allude to the pope's apostolic dignity. He mentions 'the Apostle' explicitly in the first sentence, quoting from the first Epistle to Timothy, and further on alludes to the second Epistle to the Corinthians.[7] In both cases St Paul the Apostle describes qualities that Obrecht sees as characteristic of the dedicatee: godliness, which is 'profitable unto all things', and the 'good savour of Christ'. To underline these references, the cantus firmus, *Estote fortes in bello*, is taken from the Common of Apostles and Evangelists.

The dedicatee is known for his 'ready and benevolent disposition' towards the cultivation of sacred polyphony, in which cause he promotes 'those who deserve it', including strangers and poor people. Obrecht is cleverly praising here the very disposition that might compel the dedicatee to appoint him. He is a stranger, that is, probably, a Northerner: for this reason he has had to send his motet by letter ('this page'). Surely it is for this reason, too, that Obrecht reserves the longest-held chords—in a piece that is generally homophonic and declamatory—for his own surname (two longas, of which the second has a fermata). Apparently he is not expecting the dedicatee to know him. This, and the final valediction 'command and

---

[6] The passage in square brackets is corrupt, and the translation is conjectural (see the commentary in App. I, Doc. 44).

[7] See the commentary in App. I, Doc. 44. Significantly, the passage in the epistle to Timothy follows shortly on a section describing the qualities and behaviour proper to bishops and deacons.

PL. 13. Third opening of Jacob Obrecht's *Inter preclarissimas virtutes*, in the unique source, SegC s.s.

rule happily and long', may indicate that the person in question had taken office not too long before.

Several possible occasions for this work could be suggested,[8] but crucial here is Obrecht's evident ambition to obtain a position in a court chapel. If he realized that ambition in January 1491, it was not to be for long. A year and a half after his departure he is found working as a choirmaster in Antwerp, a position very similar to the one he had left in Bruges. In fact 'the better' was to elude Obrecht throughout the 1490s. His movements in these years—none of which brought any significant improvement—give the impression of a restless, circular quest: from Antwerp back to Bergen op Zoom, from Bergen op Zoom back again to Bruges, from Bruges back yet again to Antwerp. This is the bitter irony of Obrecht's later years: his career stagnated at the very point when it should have brought lasting success. The reason behind that stagnation may well lie in events that evolved in the obscure months after January 1491, and no doubt documentation on this crucial period will one day emerge. But at present we are forced to skip these months, and must resume our account when archival references to Obrecht resurface.

Antwerp and Bergen op Zoom, 1491/2–1498

On 7 August 1491 Jacob Barbireau, choirmaster of the church of Our Lady at Antwerp, died at the age of 36.[9] His death was premature, but it did not come unexpectedly, and it may in fact have followed after weeks of illness during which the chapter, hoping for a recovery, appointed a fellow singer in his place.[10] Now, however, the chapter had to secure

---

[8] Since the motet was sent by letter it could in principle have been written at any time, but some occasions seem more probable than others (see below). It is unlikely that the motet helped secure the position that Obrecht may have held in the chapel of Pope Julius II some time after Nov. 1503 (see Ch. 11), since it survives in the Segovia choirbook, which existed by 1503.

[9] On Barbireau, see most recently J. Van den Nieuwenhuizen, 'De koralen, de zangers en de zangmeesters van de Antwerpse O.-L.-Vrouwekerk tijdens de 15e eeuw', in *Gouden jubileum gedenkboek van de viering van 50 jaar heropgericht knapenkoor van de Onze-Lieve-Vrouwekatedraal te Antwerpen* (Antwerp, 1978), 47–8, and E. Kooiman, 'The Biography of Jacob Barbireau (1455–1491) Reviewed', *Tijdschrift van de Vereniging voor Nederlandse Muziekgeschiedenis*, 38 (1988), 36–58.

[10] Death did not come so suddenly as to prevent Barbireau from writing his will, which provided for annual commemorations on the day of his decease, 7 Aug. (Kooiman, 'Jacob Barbireau', 52). He was apparently still in good health forty-four days before his death, on 24 June 1491, when the payment of his full annual salary for the preceding year was recorded in the accounts of the Guild of Our Lady (ibid. 49). For a hitherto unnoticed document concerning the execution of Barbireau's testament (by Ghijsbrecht vanden Houte *alias* Peterssone, *heer* Janne Roelants, and *heer* Willeme Pouret, priests and chaplains of Our Lady's), see Antwerp, Stadsarchief, Schepenregisters SR 109 (1496), fo. 75ᵛ: on 28 Aug. 1496 the executors bought a hereditary rent worth 320 Flemish groats on two adjacent houses in the Predicheerenstrate. A matching document from the cathedral archive,

a permanent choirmaster. The canons succeeded in this aim much more quickly than did their colleagues in Bruges: within ten months of Barbireau's death they had appointed a man who was to be their choirmaster for more than five years. Named initially 'mester Jacop de sanghmester' in the documents, it is clear by 1494 that he is in fact Jacob Obrecht—who once again has a full-time job looking after choirboys and singing Matins, Masses, Lesser Hours, and Salves every day of the year.[11]

Obrecht must have been quite a catch for the Antwerp church—possibly it is for this reason that the annual salary for one of his duties, the daily singing of the Salve in the chapel of the Guild of Our Lady, was immediately increased by half (in the Flemish equivalent from 480 to 720 Flemish groats). As choirmaster of the church proper he was also responsible for housing, sustaining, and teaching the eight choristers, for which he received at least three times as much in salary, plus expenses, as well as nine loaves every day.[12] Moreover, he was expected to attend Matins, Mass, and Lesser Hours daily in the nave, for which he would receive a *loot* after each service.[13] With this the list of his tasks was not exhausted, for in 1494 he received the chaplaincy of St Judocus, so that he was now also required to say Mass at the altar of that saint every day.[14]

Antwerp offered the political stability and economic wealth that Bruges had so patently lacked in the previous few years. Maximilian of Habsburg generously rewarded the city for remaining loyal to him during the crisis of 1488; thanks to his privileges, Antwerp effectively became the great port of northern Europe, the most affluent city in the Low Countries. Yet Obrecht's appointment at the church of Our Lady was hardly a promotion

dated 13 Nov. 1496, reveals that the hereditary rent was purchased for Barbireau's daughter Jacoba (Van den Nieuwenhuizen, 'De koralen', 48 and 59 n. 197).

[11] Firm proof that Obrecht lived in Antwerp by Nov. 1492 at the latest is now provided by Doc. 47 (see Ch. 5). The account of his activities in Murray, 'Jacob Obrecht's Connection', 127–9, is superseded; see Van den Nieuwenhuizen, 'De koralen', 48, and K. K. Forney, 'Music, Ritual and Patronage at the Church of Our Lady, Antwerp', *Early Music History*, 7 (1987), 43. Important Antwerp documents are transcribed (albeit incompletely) in A. Piscaer, 'Jacob Obrecht', *Sinte Geertruydsbronne: Driemaandelijks tijdschrift gewijd aan de geschiedenis en volkskunde van West-Brabant en omgeving*, 15 (1938), 11–13, and Murray, 'Jacob Obrecht's Connection', 130–3; see also Forney, 'Music, Ritual and Patronage', 42–4.

[12] The choirmaster's duties and payment had been laid down by the chapter in an ordinance of around 1460. In this ordinance the actual amounts, expressed in their Flemish equivalents, are 576 groats 'pro expensis cuiuslibet choralis', and 1,920 groats 'pro laboribus suis' (see the transcription in Van den Nieuwenhuizen, 'De koralen', 63). Quite possibly Obrecht had negotiated higher payment for these duties as well, but no documentation on this survives.

[13] The system is explained in some detail in Van den Nieuwenhuizen, 'De koralen', 34–41.

[14] See the transcription of the relevant document in Piscaer, 'Jacob Obrecht', 12, a payment for the reception of the chaplaincy, as a contribution to the daily distributions of loaves. Like any other newly appointed chaplain, Obrecht received no income from the chaplaincy until two years after it had become vacant (Van den Nieuwenhuizen, 'De koralen', 41).

for a musician of his stature. His work-load had anything but diminished, and for this he still received a fraction of the salary he could have earned in northern Italy. There, good singers were playing off musical centres against one another, bargaining for better pay, allowances, benefices, and favourable working conditions. The Italian rulers cared passionately about music, if only as a status symbol, and were prepared to exert all their political influence to advance singers in the hierarchy of the church—as Obrecht himself had experienced in 1487–8. Singers in the Vatican were even better placed for a successful ecclesiastical career, but even the Burgundian or French courts would have seemed more rewarding and lucrative environments than the church of Antwerp. Yet here he was, sharing the privacy of his house with eight boys, walking them to and from the church several times a day, teaching them 'in moribus, cantu et ceremoniis ecclesie',[15] directing his eleven fellow singers in the nave, and four of them in the Chapel of Our Lady,[16] day in, day out. No doubt life was better than it had been in Bruges, but this was hardly 'the better', by any reckoning.

Biographical information for these years derives mainly from the annual accounts of the Guild of Our Lady.[17] In the financial year that ended on 24 June 1492, Obrecht is mentioned as the third of three choirmasters who served in that year, the first being Barbireau, the second an unknown interim choirmaster.[18] He is immediately paid for a damask tabard, a payment that is repeated, 'after old custom', in each of the following years except the next.[19] More interesting than this are the payments that

[15] Van den Nieuwenhuizen, 'De koralen', 63.

[16] By the 1490s the church and the Guild of Our Lady employed twelve adult singers and eight choirboys on a permanent basis. The twelve adult positions were fixed; they had been created by converting twelve chaplaincies, founded in the 13th and 14th cc., into purely musical positions (a procedure known as incorporation). See Van den Nieuwenhuizen, 'De koralen', 31–46. The Guild of Our Lady employed only four adults selected from this group of twelve permanent singers, plus the choristers and the choirmaster (ibid. 64).

[17] The church proper recorded only Obrecht's presence in services held in the nave, often not even under his own name. The half-yearly accounts of the *loten* distributed after Matins, Mass, and Lesser Hours often mention singers under the name of the last holder of the chaplaincy whose income they receive. This explains why Obrecht's name does not appear in these accounts until about three years after his appointment, in the account written on 24 Dec. 1494. In earlier accounts his payments must be hidden under the name of one of twelve deceased chaplains (Van den Nieuwenhuizen, 'De koralen', 48). The assumption that Obrecht was frequently ill during these years is unfounded (Piscaer, 'Jacob Obrecht', 11–12). His apparent poor attendance of the nave services may have had other causes, and the church could at any rate not compel its singers to come every day—except by not paying them for the services they did not attend.

[18] See the transcription and translation in Kooiman, 'Jacob Barbireau', 41; but note the comment in Wegman, 'Bergen op Zoom', 207.

[19] Since the tabard received by 24 June 1492 did not need to be replaced until more than a year later (see the payment in 1493/4; Piscaer, 'Jacob Obrecht', 12), it may be concluded that it was still quite new by that date, and consequently that Obrecht had only recently been appointed. In his

indicate professional contacts.[20] On 26 February 1493 the Guild of Our Lady paid Obrecht for inviting 'the singers of 's-Hertogenbosch'—no doubt his colleagues from the Confraternity of Our Lady in that city. In 1493/4 he similarly received money to entertain 'singers from elsewhere' and, later on, 'singers from Bruges'.[21]

These were no doubt cheerful occasions, of singing and dining, but in 1494/5 Obrecht received a rather more influential guest: the master of the papal chapel, at this time Bartholomaeus Martini, bishop of Segorbe in Spain.[22] The nature and circumstances of this visit are unknown: the accounts of the Guild of Our Lady merely mention a payment 'to master Jacop the choirmaster, for entertaining the master of the chapel of the pope'.[23] Yet this is surely the most likely moment for the composer to have written his motet *Inter preclarissimas virtutes*. Alexander VI had been pope for about two years, and thus it would have been fitting for Obrecht to wish him many more: 'command and rule happily and long'. Moreover, there would have been a recent precedent for such a gesture—one which the master of the papal chapel would certainly have pointed out. On 9 December 1492, during the celebration of Mass in the Sistine Chapel, the singers of the papal choir had wished to perform a motet in praise of Alexander VI, written by Johannes Tinctoris; the pope, however, had preferred to hear the work some other day in his private chambers.[24] For Obrecht this story would have been most encouraging: if Pope Alexander had wanted to listen to Tinctoris' motet in the privacy of his chambers, then surely a work like *Inter preclarissimas virtutes* would receive a warm reception. Sending his motet through the master of the papal chapel, moreover, would be the surest way of guaranteeing its performance before the pope.

capacity as choirmaster of the church proper, the composer also received on 1 Nov. each year a tabard of eight ells 'from the cloth from which the choirboys are to be dressed' (Van den Nieuwenhuizen, 'De koralen', 63).

[20] For what follows, see Piscaer, 'Jacob Obrecht', 11–12.

[21] Léon de Burbure's claim that the singers came to thank him for a mass he had sent to St Donatian's in 1491 should be treated with extreme caution, since no documentation has ever been cited (it was first published by François-Joseph Fétis, on the basis of private communications from De Burbure, in *Biographie universelle des musiciens*, vi (Paris, 1864), 344). It is true, however, that a newly composed mass by Obrecht was copied in St Donatian's in 1491/2 (Doc. 45). Although the copying payment gives no exact date, it comes between two others dated 10 Mar. and 9 June 1492, respectively, that is, between fourteen and seventeen months after his resignation.

[22] For Martini, see Haberl, 'Die römische "schola cantorum"', 246, who incorrectly states that he was bishop of Segovia. Fétis (*Biographie*, vi. 344) and several authors after him have assumed that Obrecht's guest was Christofano Bordini, Bishop of Cortona, but he had in fact ceased to be *magister capellae* in Oct. 1492; Martini had been appointed master of the papal chapel in Jan. 1494 (Haberl, ibid.).   [23] Piscaer, 'Jacob Obrecht', 12.

[24] The story is recounted by Pope Alexander's master of ceremonies Johann Burchard, who gives the full text of the motet; see *Johannis Burchardi Liber Notarum*, ed. E. Celani, i (Rerum italicarum scriptores 32/1, Città di Castello, 1906), 376.

There is of course no evidence to confirm this scenario. All we know for certain is that the motet—whenever it was written—failed to bring Obrecht what he desired. If it was performed before the pope at all, it may well have failed to strike the right chord. For although the text starts out by praising the dedicatee in the most glowing terms, the actual subject eventually turns out to be Obrecht himself. And although he styles himself 'the humblest of your servants', he does not hesitate to single out his *own* name for solemn recitation—not (as would have been usual) the dedicatee's, which is not even mentioned. This, and the piece's very directness ('for what else I can do in service for you now, I do not know'), could easily have been perceived as immodesty, even insolence. Just as in *Mille quingentis*, Obrecht adopts a musical form with strong public and political overtones, the secular tenor motet, but uses it for purely personal purposes, putting himself, as it were, on a stage reserved for more powerful men than he. Is this *naïveté*, or such professional self-esteem as the composer had grown up with in Ghent?

A sense of self-esteem does in any case emerge from his decision, in the early 1490s, to have his portrait painted, possibly as part of an altarpiece.[25] Although dated 1496, the painting itself may largely have been finished two years earlier. Technical and stylistic features, as well as the sheer quality of the work, have been thought to suggest the hand of Hans Memling, who died at Bruges in 1494. Parts of the portrait, however, in particular the hands, are painted in a cruder style, and several technical details here suggest the work of a different, less accomplished master.[26] This has led the Belgian art historian Dirk De Vos to assume that Memling's death in 1494 left the portrait, and possibly the altar-piece to which it may have belonged, unfinished, these being completed in the next two years by one of his apprentices.

The portrait is of breathtaking quality, striking in its directness, meticulous in its realism.[27] Obrecht is depicted as a healthy, well-nourished, robust man. He is shown in his clerical dress, as he would have worn it during the daily services in the nave of the Antwerp church. Over his bluish-black gown (he received black velvet gowns from the Guild of Our Lady in 1493/4 and 1494/5)[28] he wears a transparent batiste surplice,

[25] Frontispiece; see De Vos, 'Een belangrijk portret', and Wegman, 'Het "Jacob Hobrecht" portret'. The portrait survives with its original frame; possible traces of two hinges, which might have connected the painting to a companion piece of the same size, are visible on the right-hand side (in the joint between the two vertical strips of wood).

[26] In particular the heavy use of white lead (as revealed by X-ray photography), which is known to be untypical of Memling (De Vos, 'Een belangrijk portret', 202–3 and 205).

[27] I am most indebted to Hugh Brigstocke (Sotheby's, London) for allowing me to inspect the painting prior to its being offered for auction.   [28] Piscaer, 'Jacob Obrecht', 12.

which partly covers the lapel. Underneath is a black doublet (only the laced collar is visible), and beneath that a white linen shirt—these are the clothes that he would have worn in everyday life.[29] Obrecht wears an *aumusse* or *almutium* of grey fur over his left arm, indicating that as a chaplain (since 1494) he is entitled to a place in the upper choir-stalls.[30] His shaggily cut, brownish-black hair creeps over his forehead and over his ears. He has thin eyebrows and lashes, and close inspection of the painting reveals light stubble on his upper lip and chin (not on his cheeks). Obrecht's greyish-blue eyes have an expression of calm assurance. Their openness contrasts markedly with the reserved, almost hostile look in Memling's well-known portrait of the Bruges composer Gilles Joye.[31] Joye's lips, too, seem tight and grim where Obrecht's, despite the downward corners, are relaxed.

The shoulders are comparatively narrow, but there is nevertheless a sense of bust-like breadth, since the left arm is resting upon an elbow rest or similar object. This, however, causes the hands to come together in an unusual angle: the second painter was evidently not used to this, for he depicted the hands as though both arms were close to the chest.[32] Compared with the meticulous detail in Obrecht's face, the hands are notably lacking in finish. Shadings are made simply with thin dashes over a basically monochrome undercoat. Notable, too, are the sketchy finger-nails, and the poor anatomy of the third finger and particularly of the left hand.

The light source shines down on Obrecht from a lateral rather than frontal angle, causing the left side of his face to remain virtually in the shadow. Yet this contributes to the almost sculptural quality of the painting, its marked sense of depth and space. Whereas Joye seems narrowly enclosed on all sides by the frame, surface, and background of his portrait, there is plenty of room in Obrecht's, allowing him to stand back at ease, his hands almost projecting into our space. His name—exceptionally for

---

[29] M. Scott, *The History of Dress Series: Late Gothic Europe, 1400–1500* (London, 1980), 80.

[30] Obrecht had been entitled to a lower choir-stall before 1494, but not in an official capacity as chaplain, but merely as the holder of an incorporated chaplaincy—a purely musical position that did not necessarily require clerical status. After receiving the chaplaincy of St Judocus, Obrecht was entitled to a place in the upper stalls of the choir, and was in principle released from the duty of singing polyphony. In 1486, however, Pope Innocent VIII had permitted clerical singers in the Antwerp church to combine their musical positions with chaplaincies (Van den Nieuwenhuizen, 'De koralen', 41–3 and 65–6). The *aumusse* does not necessarily indicate the status of canon, as De Vos states ('Een belangrijk portret', 194–5); see De Schrevel, *Histoire*, i. 158: the chaplain Aliamus de Groote received a 'nigrum almutium' on his installation as succentor of St Donatian's, 5 July 1475.

[31] Painted in 1472; for reproductions, see e.g. Pirrotta, 'Music and Cultural Tendencies', 130 (full portrait), and De Vos, 'Een belangrijk portret', 208 (detail, showing head only).

[32] Note the awkward angle in the left wrist; the right wrist, by comparison, is straight. As a consequence, the hands are not pointing straight forward, as was probably the original painter's design, but are turned slightly to Obrecht's left.

portraits of this type but no doubt following the composer's wishes—is written in ornate Gothic letters of gold leaf, in the style of the well-known escutcheons of the knights of the Golden Fleece. This, then, is Jacob Obrecht in the mid-1490s, as observed by one of the most accomplished portraitists of his time: poised and dignified, at ease in the space surrounding him, concentrated but not tense, unassuming in his self-esteem. The painting offers more than a mere physical likeness: it has individuality and character, allowing a direct visual encounter with the man Obrecht, across the space of five centuries.

Having thus peered, as through a window, into Obrecht's time and space, one inevitably experiences a sense of disenchantment on returning to the documents, and the faint glimpses of his life they reveal. Yet documents, of course, are not all we have. It is Obrecht's music that not only allows us to peer into his world, but actively reaches out to ours— filling the very air around us with sounds as crisp and fresh as were those that have for ever died out. Transmitting those sounds in writing was one of Obrecht's activities at the very time the portrait was finished. The account of the Guild of Our Lady for the year 1495/6 records the usual payments of his annual salary plus bonnet and tabard, but also one 'for copying many motets'—confirming that he continued to copy and distribute his work and that of others in these years.[33]

No doubt it was partly because of these activities that the shock-waves of Obrecht's creative outburst were now being registered throughout Europe. Not only were his masterpieces *Rose playsante*, *Fortuna desperata*, and *Malheur me bat* being copied in Tyrol and Saxony, but there is evidence testifying to the continued reception of his music in Italy. In December 1494 the Venetian trumpeter Giovanni Alvise reported to Francesco Gonzaga in Mantua that he and his fellow musicians were playing an unnamed Obrecht motet in a new arrangement:[34]

In these past few days we have arranged certain motets for instrumental performance, of which I am sending two to Your Excellency. And one of these is a work by Hobert, that is, the one in four voices: two sopranos, a tenor, and a high contratenor. And because there are six of us, I have added two low voices to be played with trombones, so that the motet is now in six parts, and makes a good sound. And for whomever wishes to perform it also in five parts, I have also made another low contratenor . . .

Ercole d'Este of Ferrara, meanwhile, continued to have his agents chase after masses by Obrecht. The following letter, written by Antonio di

---

[33] Piscaer, 'Jacob Obrecht', 12; see also Forney, 'Music, Ritual and Patronage', 38.
[34] The letter is transcribed in Vander Straeten, *La Musique aux Pays-Bas*, viii. 537.

Costabelli from Milan on 14 December 1496, shows that Obrecht's latest music was brought to Italy by singers from the circle of his friend Jean Cordier:[35]

... I have spoken to all these singers in order to obtain the Mass of Hobreth that Your Excellency wrote to me about. But up to now I have not been able to be certain of getting it because they excuse themselves saying that the Mass was in the hands of two singers who have left with Cordiere, who has gone home, although they have the intention of seeing if it will not be possible to find some copies of it, and if they find them they will be pleased to let me have them, in order to be agreeable to Your Excellency.

There is a further intriguing letter to Ercole, written at Antwerp on 27 June 1498, in which his agents Gian Guascon and Girolamo da Sestola promise to return with a bundle of 'about twenty' masses.[36] Obrecht had left the city for Bergen op Zoom one year earlier, but we may assume that his settings dominated the bundle. Perhaps these settings included the seven mature masses that were copied in the Ferrarese court manuscript ModE M.1.2—an anthology not just of Obrecht's music in general, but of his most recent work in the mid-1490s. In 1498, too, the 's-Hertogenbosch Confraternity of Our Lady paid a messenger for fetching a mass in polyphony from Bergen op Zoom—once again probably a work by Obrecht, since he was at that time the only known composer active in that city.[37]

The last Antwerp document from the 1490s to mention Obrecht by name ('meester Jacop de sangmeester') is the account of the Guild of Our Lady of 1495/6. Yet the composer certainly stayed at the church of Our Lady for at least another year.[38] The unnamed 'sangmeester' whose full annual salary was recorded in the next year, 1496/7, had visited Bergen op Zoom two months before that account was written, on 23 April 1497. Documents from that city helpfully confirm that he was still the same man: 'meester Jacobe den sangmeester van Antwerpen'.[39] Yet 'the choirmaster of Antwerp' Obrecht was not to stay for much longer. In Bergen op Zoom musical conditions had dramatically improved since his last activities there, nine years earlier, making it now one of the richest centres in the region. In the summer of 1497, Obrecht's quest for the better led him to move back to that city.

Bergen op Zoom was a changed place when Obrecht returned there in

[35] Transcription and translation in Murray, 'New Light', 515–16.

[36] Lockwood, *Ferrara*, 201.   [37] Wegman, 'Bergen op Zoom', 196.

[38] For this and what follows, see Wegman, 'Bergen op Zoom', 192.

[39] Ibid.; Forney ('Music, Ritual and Patronage', 43) is therefore incorrect in concluding that Obrecht did not stay at Antwerp after 1496.

1497 (Pls. 14 and 15).[40] Like Antwerp the town had done well economically by staying loyal to Maximilian of Habsburg during the troubled late 1480s. Politically, too, it had strengthened, particularly since John III of Glymes had become the new lord, in 1494. John III was a much more internationally oriented, cosmopolitan figure than his father John II had been. He had been made a knight of the Order of the Golden Fleece in 1481, was appointed first chamberlain of the prince-regent Maximilian in 1485, and later became ambassador to Emperor Charles V. Thanks to his political and diplomatic skills, he developed into one of the most powerful and influential noblemen of the Burgundian Netherlands.

Although much smaller than Bruges or Antwerp, Bergen op Zoom was now taking a prominent place on the international political stage. For the reception of important visitors, such as Duke Philip the Fair (1497), Emperor Maximilian I (1508), and the knights of the Order of the Golden Fleece (1496), as well as various ambassadors, officials, princes, and noblemen, it needed a representative musical establishment equal in quality to the finest chapels of northern Europe. Thanks to a decision made by the lord and city in 1474, Bergen op Zoom's market revenues flowed directly into its main musical establishment, the Guild of Our Lady. With these revenues rising steadily, the budget for polyphony was already much larger than in the sister institutions in Antwerp and 's-Hertogenbosch. Moreover, a new recruitment policy, initiated probably by John III, enabled the guild to lure away the best singers from other centres: by reducing the number of singers, it was able to afford more expensive ones, thus outbidding its competitors on the labour market.

Obrecht was attracted to Bergen op Zoom as a result of this new policy; the conditions on which he was hired were considerably more favourable than those in Antwerp or Bruges. To begin with, this was the first time in his documented career that he would not have to look after choirboys: Obrecht was appointed singer, not choirmaster. Yet for his services to the guild he now received twice as much as when he had been its choirmaster, more than thirteen years earlier: the equivalent of 4 rather than 2 Flemish groats per *loot*. Indeed, in the year of his return Obrecht was the guild's best-paid singer. On his arrival, some time between 24 June and 3 July 1497, he was also given a bonus equalling 50 Flemish groats, at the personal command of Lord John. In a musical centre that was now more and more beginning to resemble a court chapel in terms of budget and patronage, Obrecht finally received a measure of recognition.

Since the welcoming bonus had been paid at the lord's command, we

[40] For what follows, see Wegman, 'Bergen op Zoom'.

PL. 14. Bergen op Zoom around 1500 (drawing by Albrecht Dürer; used by permission of the Musée Condé, Chantilly)

PL. 15 The central market square in Bergen op Zoom, dominated by the church of St Gertrude (gouache by Hans Bol, 1587; used by permission of the Gemeentelijke Archiefdienst, Bergen op Zoom)

may assume that he had taken the initiative in appointing Obrecht. No doubt John III considered the famous composer a major adornment to 'his' guild chapel. Obrecht, in return, worked very hard indeed. Although one of the guild's annual accounts for this period is lost, it is clear from the others (1496/7 and 1498/9), that he attended nearly all the daily Salves and weekly Masses. Biographical details are of course not to be expected in these purely administrative documents. Yet it is worth pointing out that one month after Obrecht's arrival in Bergen op Zoom, in late July 1497, Philip the Fair visited the city with his full household.[41] The singers of the archduke, including Pierre de La Rue, joined in singing the Salves in the chapel of Our Lady—yet another occasion for Obrecht to meet and work briefly with colleagues from other institutions. The remainder of his eighteen months in Bergen op Zoom are virtually obscure, and so we lack an explanation why he moved to another city yet again in late 1498. Of all known centres that Obrecht worked for in the 1490s, Bergen op Zoom probably came closest to 'the better'. Yet in December 1498 he returned to the city that he had left 'because of the better' in the first place, and was reappointed succentor at the Bruges church of St Donatian.

Bruges and Antwerp, 1498–1503

If the return to Bruges seemed like defeat for Obrecht, the canons of St Donatian's were glad to welcome him back. In his second Bruges stay, the chapter minutes speak of Obrecht with a genuine sense of benevolence and respect, particularly after the illness that befell him in September 1500. But then St Donatian's had struggled, too, those last few years.[42] Hieronymus de Clibano, who took over the succentorship after much difficulty in December 1492, had been dismissed more than a year previously, in August 1497, after grossly neglecting the choirboys. Jean Cordier came in his place, but left the post in the autumn of 1498. Six weeks before Obrecht's arrival, Johannes Clerici of Saint-Omer had been appointed, but submitted his resignation immediately, after the chapter denied his request for higher reimbursement of expenses. On 23 December 1498, the old and dependable Aliamus de Groote was once again asked 'ut chorales per modum provisionis regeret usque ad tempus'. The succentorship, neglected by De Clibano, turned down by Clerici, taken up

---

[41] Wegman, 'Bergen op Zoom', 208.
[42] For what follows, see De Schrevel, *Histoire*, i. 164–78; Bouws, 'Jeronimus de Clibano', 77–9.

temporarily by Cordier and De Groote, changed hands more often than would have been good for any choral establishment. The church desperately needed a permanent, reliable choirmaster. Obrecht's return must have been a godsend.

Quite possibly St Donatian's had approached the composer with a desperate plea to come back, even though the church could offer little in the way of payment—except possibly the promise to grant him benefices as soon as any became vacant. One of the canons, Obrecht's friend Jean Cordier, must have been in regular contact with him throughout the 1490s, and possibly it was he who won him over. For the 40-year-old Obrecht himself it was perhaps the memory of his productive and hopeful late twenties, spent in a musically thriving if economically declining Bruges, that persuaded him to return. If he now desired to settle for a more stable life, then a city and a church sympathetic to him might offer the best long-term prospects. In any case, on 31 December 1498 he appeared before the chapter, taking his oath to serve the church as succentor:[43]

On the last day of December 1498, according to French reckoning the day of St Silvester, the chapter being assembled in the vestry and the lord Dean presiding, *magister* Jacobus Obrecht was received into the succentorship of this church and in his former place [in the choir-stalls], who by his oath, taken once, promised lawfully to pay obedience, reverence, and honour to the lords Dean and chapter, and also the church, and to instruct and teach the boys in singing and the customs of the church.

Obrecht was back in his old place, carrying out his former duties, and everything seems to have gone well. The next twenty months are a period of documentary silence, interrupted only by the standard annual payment for the daily Salves in St Donatian's, surviving in the city accounts of 1498/9 (Doc. 48), and an isolated payment in the church fabric accounts of 1499/1500, for supplying six quires of paper for a new choirbook 'missarum de *Salve sancta parens* et aliis', and drawing staves in the remainder of the choirbook.[44] It is only when things went wrong

---

[43] Transcriptions in Vander Straeten, *La Musique aux Pays-Bas*, iii. 185, and De Schrevel, *Histoire*, i. 179. The wording 'more gallicano' is puzzling, for St Donatian's celebrated the feast of St Silvester on 31 Dec. at least by the early 16th c. Bruges was, moreover, within the French kingdom.

[44] Dewitte, 'Boek- en bibliotheekwezen', 95. I am indebted to Bonnie Blackburn for pointing out to me that Dewitte published only part of the payment. Her full transcription is as follows: 'Item solutum Anthonio vander Gavere pro ligatura unius libri discantus missarum de *Salve sancta parens* et aliis "metten beslach" in simul, xlviij s. [par.] Item magistro Jacobo Hobrecht pro vi manibus papiri ligatis in dicto libro, l s. [par.] Item eidem magistro Jacobo pro lineacione ad scribendum notulas in dicto libro, l s. [par.]' (Bruges, Bisdom, Kerkfabriek Sint-Donaas, 1499/1500, fo. 37ᵛ.) It

again, in September 1500, that the documents start supplying more information.

The first sign that something was amiss is found in the city account of 1499/1500. Again there is the standard payment to Obrecht and his fellow musicians for singing the daily Salve, copied verbatim, as usual, from previous accounts (Doc. 49):[45]

Heer Jacop Obrecht, priest and cantor of the church of St Donatian in Bruges, for him and his companions the sum of 4,800 groats, because they have sung the Lof and Salve every night in honour of the glorious Virgin Mary in the aforesaid church, including bell-ringing, organ and candle-lighting, and this for a whole year, 4,800 groats.

This time, however, a lengthy comment was added in the margin, explaining that the organization of the Salve—for which Obrecht was responsible—had deteriorated to an unacceptable level, bringing shame to the city and the church. Of the four adult singers whom the succentor was obliged to bring to the services, only two or three usually showed up. According to the account, this frequently caused 'great confusion', meaning presumably that scheduled pieces were not performed, or not performed in full. Since the city nevertheless paid the full sum for the Salves, it was felt that measures should be taken to ensure regular attendance by all four singers. The measure recommended in the account was to introduce *loten* distribution, as used at this time in Antwerp, Bergen op Zoom, and other places:

Nevertheless, one should speak concerning this Salve with my lords of St Donatian, or with the aforesaid choirmaster, to find ways of ensuring that the singers who have to come to this same Salve will attend it better than they have done so far. For it is understood that the same choirmaster is obliged to bring with him, in every Salve, in addition to the children, four of the best companion singers of the church, to whom he has to give one groat each, every time. But now most of the time there are rarely more than two or three singers, which frequently causes great confusion, so that it would be better—for the honour of the church and of the city (since this Salve is commonly attended by all noblemen and foreigners who are staying in this city)—not to sing the Salve rather than to sing it. The commissioners consider, as their advice on this matter, that it would be recommendable, given that each singer has to receive one groat and the choirmaster with the children a double groat, that a respectable person should be appointed

would appear from this that Obrecht supplied six quires of paper in which he had copied masses 'de *Salve sancta parens* et aliis', and drew staves in an unspecified number of blank pages, all of which was bound together by Anthonius vander Gavere.

[45] Compare this with Doc. 48, and with the payment translated in Ch. 5, n. 72. I am grateful to Keith Polk for drawing my attention to this document.

on account of the city, at a salary of 120 groats per year, who handed to each singer who arrived at the same Salve before the singing of the hymn or sequence, and to no other, upon his oath, a token worth one groat, which they could bring to the treasurer every month, who would buy and pay for these in cash. This should nevertheless be left to the discretion of my aforesaid lords of the church and of the law, so that they might find better ways and expedients, if it were possible.

Since the city account covered the financial year ending on 2 September, it must have been around that time that the abuses became a matter of grave concern. This being so, it is not difficult to see a connection between this document and a chapter decision made at St Donatian's on the very next day. On 3 September 1500 Obrecht's friend Jean Cordier appeared before the chapter, explaining that the composer was gravely ill—so ill, in fact, that he dared not hope for a speedy recovery, if indeed he would live at all. There can be little doubt that the disorder in the Salves was the result of Obrecht's inability to exercise any control as choirmaster. He had left the services and their administration to his fellow singers, who evidently decided not to be over-zealous in carrying out their duties (for which they continued to receive payment). The composer being bed-ridden at home, musical standards in the church were declining rapidly.

That his colleagues were letting him down was perhaps the least of Obrecht's worries. We do not know the nature of his illness, but since the disorder in the Salves had been going on for some time ('now most of the time', according to the city accounts), it was probably a disease that had developed slowly, in the course of weeks or perhaps months. During that period Obrecht was able to carry out fewer and fewer duties, yet he must have hoped for a recovery all the time, for he apparently kept silent about his illness. Only when he had lost hope altogether did the composer finally send word to the chapter. By then things were already so bad that Obrecht asked for the choirboys to be removed from his house instantly: he could not cope for even one more day. The canons nevertheless asked Obrecht if he could possibly keep the choirboys in his house for the next four days, so that a solution could be found:[46]

On Thursday 3 September, my lords being assembled in the vestry, *dominus* and *magister* Johannes Cordier explained—being requested (as he said) and urgently entreated by *magister* Jacobus Hobrecht, succentor of this church, at present suffering from grave illness—how the said *magister* Jacobus thanked my lords for all the honours granted to him. And since he suffers at present from grave

---

[46] Transcriptions in Vander Straeten, *La Musique aux Pays-Bas*, iii. 185–6, and De Schrevel, *Histoire*, i. 179–80.

illness—which he fears not to be curable by light or easy means—and therefore lacks the strength to his office of succentorship, he asked my lords to be willing and prepared to absolve him from such office (from which at that time he already absolved himself as much as he could), and to place the choirboys with some honourable person, whom my lords should appoint for this purpose. My lords, grieving over the illness of this *magister* Jacobus Hobrecht, accepted the absolution of this *magister* Jacobus, and absolved him from the said succentorship. But since they could not arrange in the matter concerning the choirboys and their placement, they deputized me, Johannes Dionisii, their secretary, to approach the said *magister* Jacobus and ask him on behalf of my lords whether he would be willing to keep the choirboys in his home and at his expense until the next Monday, which *magister* Jacobus, after I had explained this to him on behalf of my lords, generously undertook to do, offering himself in the service of my lords for so long as he would live.

The next Monday, a solution had indeed been found: the church once again turned to Aliamus de Groote, now in the last year of his life, who immediately accepted the succentorship.[47] Obrecht had struggled for weeks or months in the hope of holding on to his position, but finally lost it altogether. He was now ill, and fearing for his life. Poverty threatened: apart from two chaplaincies in Bruges and Antwerp, and various rents from the inheritance of Lysbette Gheeraerts and Willem Obrecht, he had no regular sources of income. Yet the canons of St Donatian's did not forget him. In late October 1500, nearly two months after the illness had first been reported, they decided to award Obrecht the chaplaincy of the Holy Cross, which had recently become vacant:[48]

On the same day [26 October 1500], my lords, on the nomination of *dominus* Victor Brunync, awarded the chaplaincy of the Holy Cross in this church, being one from outside the choir, lately fallen vacant by the death of *dominus* Jacobus Peckele, who possessed it, to the honourable *magister* Jacobus Hobrecht, submitting to this same *magister* Jacobus a letter in form, saving the rights [of other potential incumbents].

Clearly it was felt that Obrecht should not simply be allowed to go. Even if he had served only as a succentor, and the church no longer had any

[47] 7 Sept. 1500: 'Moreover, on the nomination and recommendation of the reverend *dominus* and *magister* Richardus de Capella, cantor of this church, my lords provided for the succentorship, vacant because of the absolution of *dominus* and *magister* Jacobus Hobrecht, [to be given] to the honourable *dominus* Aillermus de Groote, chaplain from within the choir in this church, who had held this office in former times, charging him to instruct the choirboys diligently in singing and in morals, and to do all things that concern and pertain to the said office, otherwise they would deprive him of the said office. Wherefore he thanked their lordships for the honour bestowed on him, and, accepting this office, promised to see to it diligently, to the best of his ability' (Vander Straeten, *La Musique aux Pays-Bas*, iii. 186, and De Schrevel, *Histoire*, i. 180–1).
[48] Vander Straeten, *La Musique aux Pays-Bas*, iii. 186, and De Schrevel, *Histoire*, i. 180.

formal obligations to him, ties could not just be severed so abruptly. And so more honours were bestowed on the composer three days later, on 29 October 1500. This time the chapter acts say explicitly that the benefices were granted in recognition of his international fame, and in appreciation of his diligent teaching of the choirboys and 'many other agreeable services'. Obrecht's illness and consequent hardship may have added urgency to this—something that may well have been pressed upon the chapter by one of the canons, Jean Cordier, who knew the composer well enough to report on his worsening circumstances. And there is indeed a sense of urgency about the chapter's decisions. Obrecht had not received a single benefice in the preceding twenty-two months, yet now he suddenly received three honours in four days. Beside the chaplaincy of the Holy Cross, he was granted the income from a choir-stall. And since the composer was about to become provost of the church of St Peter in Torhout, the canons felt that he should also be entitled to a place in the upper stalls:[49]

Moreover, since *dominus* and *magister* Jacobus Hobrecht, who is known to be a very famous musician, has contributed to this church in the instruction of the choirboys and with many other agreeable services, my lords granted him the income from one stall in this church, with the usual honours and obligations. And since this same *magister* Jacobus, who possesses the provostship of the church of St Peter in Torhout, and for this reason is in a position of dignity, so that it would be improper for him to remain with the clerks in the low stalls, my lords have consented that the same *magister* Jacobus may wear the dress of chaplain and be seated higher up with the chaplains, and that in processions he shall have the same place as the other chaplains from outside the choir, notwithstanding anything to the contrary.

Were these decisions inspired by reasons of charity, or were they designed to keep Obrecht in Bruges? If the latter, they were evidently not sufficient. Despite his offer to serve the chapter 'for so long as he would live', Obrecht stayed for less than eight months to enjoy the new honours, and to recover from his illness. By 24 June 1501 he had moved once again to another centre: from that date until at least 24 June 1503, 'Obrecht' (or sometimes 'Hobrecht') is listed as a vicar-singer in the church of Antwerp.[50] In this very period, from 1 July 1501 until after 24 June 1503, a 'meester Jacop de sangmeester' returns in the accounts of the Antwerp Guild of Our Lady.[51]

[49] Vander Straeten, *La Musique aux Pays-Bas*, iii. 186, and De Schrevel, *Histoire*, i. 180.
[50] Murray, 'Jacob Obrecht's Connection', 132–3, and Van den Nieuwenhuizen, 'De koralen', 48.
[51] See the transcriptions of payments in Piscaer, 'Jacob Obrecht', 13, and Forney, 'Music, Ritual and Patronage', 38–9 and 42–4. The 'meester Jacob' in the account of 1500/1, who received payment

The two years in Antwerp would be Obrecht's last in the North. Documentation is extremely sparse, and mostly limited to the usual payments of his salary and tabard, by the Guild of Our Lady. The only details beyond these standard items are found in the church fabric accounts. These reveal intense scribal activity on the part of the composer. In 1501/2 he received four quires of double paper, worth 24 Flemish groats, 'for writing masses in', as well as a sum equalling 960 Flemish groats 'for a songbook in polyphony to sing from in the choir on high feast-days'.[52] No doubt this was a lavish parchment codex, equal in quality and value to the best Alamire manuscripts.[53] Had it survived, if only fragmentarily, its value today would have been inestimable. Meanwhile, the international distribution of Obrecht's music continued unabated. A major impulse for the dissemination of his masses came in late March 1503, when Ottaviano Petrucci issued his *Misse Obreht*, a set of four partbooks containing the masses *Je ne demande*, *Grecorum*, *Fortuna desperata*, *Malheur me bat*, and *Salve diva parens*. The publication was quickly circulating in northern Italy and elsewhere; even today six copies survive, in Italy, Germany, Austria, and Belgium. It is possible, given Antwerp's international importance in the book trade, that copies were quick to reach Obrecht as well. If so, it is tempting to think that after all the difficulties of the previous years, this convinced him, in the summer of 1503, that 'the better' might not elude him forever.

Obrecht was now at a crossroads. His quest for the better had turned out to be a tale of three cities: Antwerp, Bergen op Zoom, and Bruges. Geographically these cities comprise a triangle whose perimeter he had travelled twice in the course of twenty-three years, ending up little better than he had started. No doubt his movements in these years had been determined by *ad hoc* opportunities, but looking back in 1503, there must have seemed an uncanny, self-repeating pattern to his unsettled

'for having served until Candlemas', that is, until 2 Feb. 1501, cannot be Obrecht, having been active in Antwerp before the latter became ill in Bruges. This is clear from the amount he received. The annual salary of the choirmaster was 1,080 Brabant groats, which equals twelve monthly payments of 90 Brabant groats. After 'meester Jacop' stopped working, on 2 Feb. 1500, his successor Michiel Berruyer was paid 'for having served from the first day of February to the last day of June'. For these five months he received a salary of 450 Brabant groats, which is indeed five times 90. It follows that 'meester Jacop', who earned 630 Brabant groats, or seven times 90, had been working for seven months. His period of service must therefore stretch back to the beginning of July 1500. This is two months before Obrecht's illness became so severe that he had to stop working in Bruges. The most likely scenario, therefore, seems that an unknown 'meester Jacop' was replaced by Berruyer on 1 Feb. 1501, who in turn was replaced by Obrecht on 1 July of the same year.

[52] Forney, 'Music, Ritual and Patronage', 39.

[53] Alamire had received the equivalent of 480 Flemish groats for a songbook containing motets and Magnificats in 1498/9 (Forney, 'Music, Ritual and Patronage', 37).

career. Obrecht was now 45: breaking away from the pattern could only become more difficult as he grew older. If he was to move abroad and find 'the better', now, if ever, was the time to do it. His compositions had prepared the way for him throughout Europe. In the summer of 1503, Obrecht decided to follow them, in what was to become his last journey.[54]

[54] After this book had gone to the press, Eugeen Schreurs kindly informed me that he had discovered a new Obrecht document in the cathedral archive at Antwerp; I am most grateful to Dr Schreurs for allowing me to discuss his discovery, which he will discuss at greater length in a forthcoming publication. The accounts of the *intrantiae* for 24 June 1492 to 24 June 1493 contain two entries concerning a payment ordered by the chapter to Willem Luydinck, receiver of the vicars and choristers, 'ad dandum Binsois cantori, misso in Franciam, pro magistro Jacobo magistro choralium'. This means that Jacob Obrecht was in France at some point in 1492/3, and that the chapter of Our Lady's decided to send him a sum of money, which should be brought to him by the singer Johannes Binchois. The amount in question was substantial: the equivalent of 468 Flemish groats. The newly discovered payment may shed light on Obrecht's motet *Quis numerare queat*, whose text was also set to music by the French court composer Loyset Compère (see Ch. 10). If the settings by Obrecht and Compère were written after the withdrawal of an invader (see below, pp. 317–18), the occasion might have been the peace of Étaples (3 Nov. 1492) which ended a short-lived invasion into France by Henry VII of England. As it happens, this peace was concluded only ten days before Obrecht happened to be in Ghent, so that there is the possibility that he was then on his way back from France to Antwerp (see above, pp. 153–4).

10 BEYOND FORTUNA

꧁ᘏᘏᘏᘏᘏᘏᘏᘏᘏᘏᘏᘏᘏᘏᘏ꧂

THE news of Antoine Busnoys's death, in November 1492, could hardly have left Obrecht untouched. It closed a major chapter in his life, from possible early encounters in the late 1460s to the six years in which both men worked at Bruges, 1485–91. More importantly, it came at a particularly sensitive time in his own musical career. Busnoys was relatively young when he died, probably under 55, and about fifteen years older than Obrecht himself. Yet this in a sense underlined what Obrecht's recent successes had made so easy to forget: how quickly Busnoys had become a figure of the past. True, he was still a famous man. But his fame rested on works written more than twenty years earlier. The zenith of his international success had been reached by about 1470, when he was in his early thirties, had created his own individual mass style, and brought it to perfection in *L'homme armé* (see Ch. 4). Now, in 1492, Obrecht had achieved exactly this. Like Busnoys two decades earlier, he had become one of the leading mass composers of Europe. He, too, was now in his thirties, had created his own style, and had brought it to perfection—in a work based, ironically, on a song attributed to Busnoys, *Fortuna desperata*.

One cannot improve on perfection; one can only aim for it elsewhere. Busnoys had somehow failed to extend his extraordinary early successes in mass composition. So far as we know, he never went beyond *L'homme armé* and *O crux lignum*: it was Obrecht who went beyond Busnoys. But could he himself now move beyond *Fortuna desperata*, beyond *Rose playsante*, *Libenter gloriabor*, and *Malheur me bat*? Would he, as Tinctoris had said of the *moderni* in 1472–3, continue to write 'new music each day in the newest fashion'? Or would he, like the English, 'always use one and the same manner of composing, which is a sign of the poorest invention'?[1]

---

[1] Tinctoris, *Proportionale musices*, in *Opera theoretica*, iia. 10. Thinking in terms of 'the moderns' was not restricted to Tinctoris. See, for an earlier example, the Cambrai copying payment for four 'books of music of the moderns' in 1449–50 ('libros cantus modernorum'; A. E. Planchart,

Or like Busnoys, once the prototypical *modernus*, would others move beyond him?

The issues of Obrecht's historical position and of his mass chronology become inseparable here. For that position must depend, ultimately, on what happened after *Fortuna desperata*. And any stylistic chronology, conversely, depends to some extent on what kind of composer we think Obrecht was. The present study exemplifies this interdependence. In previous chapters I have suggested dates before 1491–3 for some fifteen undated masses ranging from *Petrus apostolus* to *Grecorum*. Apart from the grounds given *in loco*, there is a fundamental ground that could not be stated until the present point.

It is that Obrecht made pioneering contributions to the mass style in the early 1490s, and that it seems problematic to assume that he would have discarded those achievements thereafter. Had he written such works as *O lumen ecclesie*, *Sicut spina rosam*, *De Sancto Martino*, or *Ave regina celorum* in the 1490s, these masses would have seemed strangely devoid of the truly modern features that showed the composer at his best, and curiously exercised about issues he had already transcended in the mature style. It would mean that Obrecht was a *genuine* conservative, a reactionary even—in the sense that he voluntarily and consciously chose to return to the styles and sounds of an earlier generation, in the face of his international success as a *modernus*.

Yet although this assumption may be problematic, it is not impossible. Even if the opposite assumption, that Obrecht kept moving with the times, seems prima facie more plausible, we still need hard evidence to support it. And hard evidence there is, but it does not come from the masses. It is Obrecht's motets that most clearly show the new directions—and herein lies the final, unexpected twist in our tale. Yes: Obrecht moved beyond, far beyond, *Fortuna desperata*; he remained in the front ranks of the 'Josquin generation' to the end of his life. But so far as we can judge from the surviving works, his masses did not fully partake in these developments, and the central question of this chapter must be why this was so. Why does none of his masses move decisively beyond the mature style, when several motets leave that style far behind? Why did the two genres grow apart?

'Guillaume Du Fay's Benefices and his Relationship to the Court of Burgundy', *Early Music History*, 8 (1988), 142.

Obrecht the Progressive: Late Motets

Although a full assessment of Obrecht's motet *œuvre* would be beyond the scope of this study, it is necessary to look at both sides of the problem. For it is not enough simply to observe that the masses, after the early 1490s, failed to keep abreast of the newest stylistic trends: we have to know what those trends were, and how Obrecht might have applied them in the mass, had he wanted to. The following excursion is necessarily sketchy, but it may serve to outline the most salient developments.

Laudes Christo redemptori, printed by Petrucci in 1505, is a motet that defies all the textbook descriptions of Obrecht's style (that is, usually, his mature style; see Ex. 30).[2] Like Josquin's late works, it aspires to norms of modal propriety that were to be codified only in the course of the sixteenth century. *Laudes Christo* is Obrecht's only sacred work in so-called *a voce piena* texture, in which each of the voices occupies a distinct modal range.[3] This is evident from the clef disposition alone: C_1 C_2 C_4 F_4. Most important here is the distance of a fifth between the altus and tenor clefs,[4] for in virtually all four-part music since the 1440s (Obrecht's included) these two voices had operated in basically the same range. In *Laudes Christo* the composer not only divorces the two parts in terms of mode (the tenor is plagal while the altus is authentic), but he generally keeps them neatly apart in his writing, rigorously avoiding crossings. The distance between top voice and bass has also increased, since each is still a fourth or fifth removed from either of the two middle voices. The combined texture, then, is wide, lucid, and spacious. It is the standard texture of the sixteenth century.

This much tells us that the motet must be late. But there is more, for the new texture cannot be considered separately from the compositional technique with which it was intimately related: pervasive imitation. *Laudes Christo* employs this technique systematically. It has no cantus firmus, and is structured almost entirely in points of imitation. Obrecht handles the imitations in truly modern fashion, that is, by articulating musical periods that, in turn, articulate the syntactic units of the text. This is

---

[2] All bar numbers refer to the edition by Johannes Wolf, *Werken van Jacob Obrecht*, vi (repr. Farnborough, 1968), 75–84. Strikingly, this beautiful setting has not been discussed in the literature since its first publication, some eighty years ago.

[3] See Meier, *Die Tonarten*, 36–74. Obrecht's four-part *Salve regina* in SegC s.s., fos. 71ᵛ–73ʳ, seems to come close to this texture (clef disposition G_2 C_2 C_4 F_3/C_4), yet it is clear from the ranges that no modal differentiation was intended: the bottom voice comprises the entire range of the C_4 part, while the upper voice comprises all but one note of the range of the C_2 part.

[4] Note that Wolf changed the altus clef in his edition, from C_2 to C_3.

Ex. 30. Obrecht, *Laudes Christo redemptori, prima pars*, bars 1–37

clearest in the *prima pars*. It consists of five periods, all except the third and fifth starting with successive imitative entries from the top voice down to the bass,[5] and each ending with a full-textured cadence on the final A (in bars 11, 29, 37, 44, and 64, respectively; the first three periods are shown in Ex. 30).

The contrapuntal style, too, seems to have moved into the new age. The patterned structures of the mature style, its rhythmic drive and emphatic sweeps and gestures, have disappeared. Instead, Obrecht aims for extreme melodic polish, and for a 'classical' balance between stylistic parameters. Melodic motion is generally stepwise and smooth, and the handling of rhythm is so liberal that the *tempus* units between voices gradually shift apart, and irregular 'bars' are presupposed (this is clear from the arrangements of breve and semibreve rests in the source). *Laudes Christo* is not about speed, not about pent-up musical energy and its release, and it needs no tight units or emphatic cadences to contain what it does not aim to generate. Above all, the setting breathes that sense of serenity and balance, even detachment, that the sixteenth century was to relish in its masses and motets.

The few Obrechtian devices that can still be recognized are subordinated to this aesthetic. The motivic repetitions in bars 25–37 of the bass, for instance, serve to guide the polyphony through stable tonal planes, prolonging the dominant E (bars 25–9, followed by a major cadence on A), reaffirming the final (bars 30–4), and yet again prolonging the dominant for another major cadence on A (bars 34–7). Yet this basic harmonic outline is not articulated and reinforced by other parameters, as in *Malheur me bat* (Ex. 25), but virtually camouflaged in the rich contrapuntal texture. An even clearer example of prolonged tonal tension is in bars 63–7 of the second section, again before a major cadence on A. This passage is particularly interesting because it closely resembles one of the freely composed 'extensions' of *Plurimorum carminum II* (Agnus Dei III, bars 173–7; see Ch. 8), confirming that Obrecht had not lost his feel for effective tonal writing.

Despite such passing reminiscences, *Laudes Christo* represents the opposite of what is usually regarded as the typical Obrecht style. Yet it does not come as a total surprise that the composer would be capable of writing works like this at a later stage in his career. Throughout his life Obrecht demonstrated his understanding of contemporary styles in 'un-Obrechtian' works (*Petrus apostolus*, *Sicut spina rosam*, *De Sancto Dona-*

---

[5] Unorthodox, by later 16th-c. standards, is the fact that the entry-points are a fifth apart, so that they do not outline the octave and fifth species of the mode.

tiano, Adieu mes amours). Such works, no less than the 'Obrechtian' ones, show his concern to write 'new music each day in the newest fashion'— whether that fashion had been initiated by himself or by others.[6] *Laudes Christo* shows that Obrecht remained in close touch with contemporary stylistic trends, and ended up writing pieces that come close to the late works of Josquin. The motet undoubtedly dates from the last years of his life, and may well be his latest surviving composition.

Increased sensitivity to the metric and grammatical structure of the text is another feature that marks out several Obrecht motets as progressive. Declamatory passages are compatible with the mature style only as isolated effects, since the most distinctive quality of that style is the rhythmic differentiation of the primary level. So it is not surprising to see that declamatory and mature styles are kept neatly apart in *Inter preclarissimas* (structurally the counterpart of a segmentation mass); the same distinction is maintained in *Laudemus nunc Dominum*. Both motets probably date from the 1490s. *Laudemus nunc* seems the more advanced of the two; it may have been singled out for its prominent declamatory writing by Johannes Herbenus in 1496.[7]

In *Quis numerare queat* Obrecht shows sensitivity not only to grammatical structure, but also, to some extent, to textual content.[8] The poem, which was also set to music by Loyset Compère, has been thought to celebrate a peace treaty, but this seems unlikely. Rather, it expresses gratitude for the *cessation* of war (possibly the withdrawal of an invader or the ending of a civil war), and does so exclusively from the people's point of view. War is seen in terms of the innumerable sufferings and losses inflicted on the people. The poet interprets this as God's wrath at their sins, condemns aggressors in general, and regards peace as God-given rather than man-made. Such thoughts would hardly seem appropriate at the signing of a peace treaty. On such an occasion the absence of any praise for the supreme wisdom of the reconciled rulers—indeed, the explicit denial that man is capable of establishing peace on his own—could only have been regarded as deliberately provocative. The fact that the anonymous author identifies with the people ('nostris peccatis'), and directly addresses the nations of the earth ('queque es in terris natio, funde

[6] In composers like Josquin, whose styles are less easily subjected to generalization than Obrecht's, one would of course take such versatility for granted.

[7] Herbenus mentions a motet 'in honorem consecrationis templi' by 'Jacobus Hoberti' as an example of effective musical declamation; cf. Smits van Waesberghe, *Herbeni Traiectensis De natura cantus*, 58. The other motet 'salutiferae crucis', cited in the same passage, may have been *Salve crux*, although declamatory writing is less prominent in this work.

[8] In *Werken van Jacob Obrecht*, ed. Wolf, vi. 120–30. Discussed in Dunning, *Staatsmotette*, 9–14.

preces'), would seem to point instead to a civic context, possibly a public service of thanksgiving.[9] In purpose the text most resembles a sermon: it draws moral lessons from war and its horrors, emphasizes God's forgiveness in restoring peace, and exhorts the people to be thankful and to pray that the 'given' (rather than concluded) peace may be lasting.

The absence of a cantus firmus in Obrecht's setting likewise suggests that *Quis numerare queat* is not a state motet in the traditional sense. (Compère, by contrast, employed a canonically treated cantus firmus.) Obrecht's writing is best described as rhetorical. Units of the text (which is written in elegiac couplets) are demarcated by clear cadences or half-cadences, simultaneous rests, or changes of musical procedure. Key phrases are underlined by homophonic, declamatory writing, or by special musical effects. In the first section, for instance, each of the three couplets ends with a major cadence on the final G (bars 30, 61, 81; the only such cadence that does not mark the ending of a couplet is in bar 75). Since the divisions between groups of feet likewise coincide with breve chords or full silences (bars 6, 24–5, 46, 58, 70–1, 78), the music acquires the 'stop and go' quality typical of declamatory writing (as in *Inter preclarissimas virtutes* or Josquin's *Tu solus qui facis mirabilia*). Yet Obrecht reserves the chordal, declamatory style for key words and phrases only, and heightens their effect by stepping up the overall stylistic variety.

A telling example of this is in bars 45–61 (see Ex. 31). In the preceding bars Obrecht has set the words 'let the good man count [the losses of the wars], having endured such things', and the text now continues 'but let the bad man who has brought them upon him [?himself], count them'. The first part of this phrase is underlined by a melodic rise in all voices, spanning nine bars, which culminates in bar 56 on 'intulerit', and is then rounded off with a half-cadence on D. In sharp contrast with this is the quick declamatory conclusion in triple rhythm, cadencing on G (bars 59–61), which underlines the desire for justice: let the aggressor be made to count the innumerable sufferings he has caused to himself and others. It is perhaps no coincidence that there is a musical link between this ending

---

[9] Despite the phrase 'fundant preces itali' in the unique source, Petrucci's *Motetti libro quarto*, I am not sure that Obrecht's setting originated in Italy (cf. Dunning, *Die Staatsmotette*, 9–14). Compère's motet on the same text survives in two sources: Petrucci (*Motetti A*) once again gives 'itali', while VatS 15 reads 'galle'. That 'galle' would have been changed into 'itali' in two commercial prints intended for the Italian market is easy to assume; that the reverse might have happened in a papal motet anthology is far from obvious. Compère worked in France from at least 1486 until his death in 1518. His career brought him closest to Obrecht in 1498–1500, when documents record his association with churches in Cambrai (1498–1500) and Douai (1500). Obrecht, in these years, worked at Bruges, part of the same (French) county as Douai, that is, Flanders. But see above, p. 310, n. 54.

of the second couplet and that of the third (bars 79–81), which speaks of the 'deserved rewards' for mankind's sins: the aggressor will be subject to divine justice just as much as everyone else.

In the second part of the motet Obrecht makes no musical division between the first two couplets, probably because they form one sentence. In a series of alternating duos, the text describes how God, having heard the wailing of the people (various melodic flourishes emphasize their grief), took pity and gave them that peace which—and now Obrecht shifts over to full texture—no mortal is able to give. The first major cadence on G concludes the two couplets (bars 48–9). The third and final couplet of the second part, which exhorts the people to express their gratitude, is written in 'stop and go' declamatory style until the final word, 'referat', which receives a point of imitation (bars 50–73).

From the sufferings and their cause (first part) the text has moved to God's forgiveness in restoring peace and the gratitude due to him (second part). Finally it turns to the future: let all men pray that the peace may be lasting (third part). Here the musical writing loses its rhetorical quality, and is instead free in design. Yet Obrecht evidently wished to end his setting on a jubilant and confident note: witness the increased rhythmic drive and imitative density in bars 75–90, and finally the powerful cadential progression in bars 91–6.

Quis numerare queat shows that Obrecht, despite the rigorously abstract thinking in his mature masses, was capable of handling music as a medium to clarify the structure and content of the text. He clearly understood the poem, understood what it meant to those it was addressed to, and this understanding expressed itself in a considered alternation of styles and procedures. In the mature masses Obrecht would have aimed to give such alternation musical purpose and coherence; here that sense is rhetorical rather than musical.

The progressive motets are small in number, yet they obviously could not have been written if Obrecht had remained innocent of the newest stylistic trends, or was a declared and inveterate reactionary. That conclusion is helpful, for although it does not resolve the central question of this chapter, it does rule out possible assumptions on the composer's general frame of mind. Furthermore, we have now some idea of the sorts of trends that exercised Obrecht in the later stages of his career, and this allows us to rephrase the central question: why are these particular trends not discernible in later masses? It is now time to look at the other side of the problem.

Ex. 31. Obrecht, *Quis numerare queat, prima pars*, bars 45–81

Missa Maria zart

Of all Obrecht's masses, *Maria zart* moves furthest beyond *Fortuna despe-rata*, and yet it still shows a strong debt to the mature style.[10] *Maria zart* moves beyond that style in that it modifies its primary level. The higher levels are beyond its aesthetic outlook altogether: there is no apparent interest in dramatizing and planning musical events, and the stylistic differentiation that is the precondition for such writing has disappeared. In this sense Obrecht goes back to where he came from: the primary level. Here, the debt he owes to the mature style is visible mostly in the rhyth-mic and melodic clichés, the motivic fingerprints. Yet these elements no longer make up the very substance of his writing. They are used less often, and this is one of the reasons why the counterpoint generally seems less energetic. The other reason is that Obrecht has relinquished two con-spicuous qualities of the mature style: the rhythmic differentiation (note in particular the lesser frequency of dotted patterns) and the basically triadic conception of the melodic lines. On the whole *Maria zart* seems smoother, more polished in its counterpoint. Yet there is enough vigour of the mature Obrecht left to be able to distinguish the mass easily from truly polished works such as *Petrus apostolus*, *Sicut spina rosam*, or *De Sancto Donatiano*, which have been dated here in the 1480s.

Maria zart is the sphinx among Obrecht's masses. It is vast: close to one hour, in fact. And this is not just a reflection of the cantus-firmus treat-ment (which is a rather intricate variant of the segmentation type). Even the sections in reduced scoring, which generally are also penetrated with the tenor melody, are unusually extended. Two successive duos in the Gloria comprise over 100 bars, two successive trios in the Credo close to 120; the Benedictus alone stretches over more than 100 bars. This already raises questions. Can one envisage an occasion in which the polyphony alone took up one hour? Can one think of a context in which two- or three-part writing could go on for minutes and minutes on end? These questions reflect what is perhaps the most conspicuous difference from *Fortuna desperata*. The latter mass is direct and outspoken, it comes to the point, and makes it abundantly clear at every turn what the point is. *Maria zart*, by contrast, never appears to make a specific point at all. Despite its length, and despite its debt to the mature syntax, the mass persistently

[10] For literature on *Maria zart*, see Meier, *Studien zur Meßkomposition*, 19–22; Reese, *Music in the Renaissance*, 193–5; Wolff, *Die Musik der alten Niederländer*, 47–9; Sparks, *Cantus Firmus*, 262 and 470; Salop, 'The Masses of Jacob Obrecht', 73–4; Obrecht, *Opera omnia editio altera, Missae*, vii, ed. M. van Crevel (Amsterdam, 1964), pp. vii–clxiv.

manages to avoid the suggestion that one should be attentive to anything in particular. The music just goes on, it seems. And by writing in this way Obrecht creates an altogether different sense of time from *Fortuna desperata*. There is no neatly organized agenda packed full with plans and designs. There is just a vast expanse of time, traversed rather than articulated by the music.

Looking through the score, one can see that there are things going on all the time. The analyst can identify those things, and give them names: imitations, sequences, scales, cadences, motifs. Yet there is an air of randomness about these devices that ultimately leaves the impression that such names mean or explain little. To put it differently, if you ask rational questions, *Maria zart* will give rational answers. Yet any attempt to inquire beyond those answers reveals apparent randomness, lack of purpose and design, as though we have expected the mass to be something it is not. One can see this, for instance, in the duos of the Gloria: the Domine Deus and Qui tollis. Reading through these sections, it is difficult to avoid the impression that they just go 'on and on'; no amount of device-spotting can take that impression away. For their length seems somehow disproportionate to their content: can two-part writing sustain interest for such a length of time, can any composer afford to do without textural variety for so long? The catch here, of course, is in the words 'content' and 'interest', for these reflect our own expectations. Listen to this music for a full hour: our expectations may not have been fulfilled, but the mass does create a special experience, an experience that somehow transforms our perception of musical time. That is what the score seems to tell us: be still and listen, ask no questions, expect no answers. Listen.

Is that an excuse for giving up writing about this mass altogether? No: it just means that the more we write about *Maria zart*, the more we end up feeling that this is what the score seems to tell us. Consider the opening of the Et in terra (Ex. 32). On one level one can observe that there is a point of imitation in the first eleven bars, based on the first phrase of the *Maria zart* melody, and that the contratenor (here the third voice from the top) quotes the second phrase in bars 14–20. Yet the imitation does not articulate the musical discourse as a whole (as in Ex. 29, bars 1–16), nor does the musical discourse articulate the imitation. For one thing, the contratenor starts with free material, thus concealing the first statement (bass, bars 1–4), and as soon as it takes its own turn (bars 7–11) it is itself concealed beneath the top voice. An imitation there may be, but the audible *structure* of this passage is hardly imitative, and the writing itself does not depend on the device at all. It is not just that imitation is not the

Ex. 32. Obrecht, *Missa Mariâ zart*, Et in terra, bars 1–54

(Ex. 32, *cont.*)

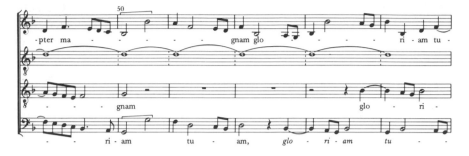

discourse, as was the case, for instance, in Exx. 22 or 29 (take the imitation
away, and one is still left with a reasonably self-sufficient musical discourse). To get a sense of what the quality of the writing is like, one needs
to take only the top voice alone (or either of the other voices, for that
matter), and read it in search of a focal musical point or a firm musical
caesura. The first impression that should occur is that Obrecht persistently avoids either; the second that it matters little to the writing that the
first four bars happen to be cited in the other parts as well. For the quality
is the same as that of the two-part sections in the Gloria. The voice goes
'on and on', it spins out indefinitely. There is no sense of development, no
musical process: the spinning-out *is* the process. Forget the imitation, it
seems to tell us, be still, and listen.

And thus we need not be surprised that when the cantus firmus enters,
in bar 22, the contrapuntal voices take virtually no notice of the event. We
have not been led to expect an entry at this point: for all we know the
spinning-out might have continued. We are not reminded that there is an
entry: the spinning-out does in fact continue. For the spinning-out *is* the
discourse. And if it tells us anything, it must be this. Forget the cantus-
firmus entry; the entry is not the point: listen, and you will hear the point.

From bar 26 onwards the writing becomes motivic, so much so, in fact,
that one might justly say that motivic usage, in the next thirty bars, *is* the
discourse: take the motifs away and one is left with virtually no discourse
at all. To this extent the word 'motivic' is informative; it tells us something about the passage. Yet Obrecht used motivic techniques throughout
his life, and one of the basic tenets of this study is that we should never
stop with the mere observation that devices are being used. Our interest
is in the *ways* in which they are applied, since these, rather than the
devices themselves, tell us something about the composer's aesthetic out-

look. This is not to say that the word 'motivic' does not tell us anything at all: of course it does. But it does not tell us what we would most like to know: what the device expresses.

The most noteworthy aspect of the passage is in fact its lack of rigidity. Only the top voice is strictly sequential for six bars (26–31). Everywhere else Obrecht seems to place his motifs freely, wherever they fit or suit him, and he changes over to a different motif four times (bars 39, 41, 44, and 51). This makes it unlikely that he was attempting to demonstrate his contrapuntal skill. Had this been the point, he would have had to accept such technical constraints as only skill can overcome (for instance, one motif plus strict repetition or sequence). Nor is it easy to think of an Obrechtian witticism. Had that been the point, he would have had to carry on a procedure (be it a repetition or a sequence) to such lengths that there was a clear transgression of the rules of aesthetic decorum: only that would make the witticism truly apparent (as in Ex. 20; see Ch. 7). This, of course, is not the case. For although the motivic writing in *Maria zart* is indeed carried on for nearly thirty bars, its very lack of rigidity prevents the listener from thinking that Obrecht is making a special point.

Yet the motivic passage does seem too long to be able to say that it is perfectly normal and unexceptionable. Can motivic writing sustain interest for such a length of time? Is a thirty-bar passage based on only four motifs (two of which are in fact nearly identical) not dangerously thin in musical content? If the writing does not display musical humour or uncommon skill, what does it display? Facility? That, of course, has too often been the easy way out with Obrecht. The notorious sequence in *Ave regina celorum* in particular has been cited as an example of the composer extending 'his ideas by interminable sequences, instead of seeking more skilful solutions'.[11] Yet do we really believe that Obrecht, in masses as rich as this, was desperately at a loss how to fill seven bars with polyphony? (Note that this is in fact the only sequence in the whole of that mass.) In *Maria zart*, too, such a notion can only seem superficial within the rich context of the work as a whole.

Given the very length and irregularity of the passage, and given that it does not appear to make a specific musical point, the discourse is best described as spinning-out. For that is what happens: the motivic writing goes 'on and on', and avoids, if anything, the suggestion that the music has to lead anywhere in particular. In the opening of the Et in terra we have considered the top voice alone and followed it in search of a focal musical

[11] Ex. 20 in Ch. 7; see Bridgman, 'The Age of Ockeghem and Josquin', 273.

point or clear caesura, so as to gain an impression of the linear writing. In the same way we might now take the musical discourse as a whole and, starting from the (interrupted) cadence in bar 22, read it in search of anything that implies a sense of arrival. There is no such point, of course, not even beyond the example (the section ends with a half-cadence). But some sense of what this mass is about does seem to come through. Compare the music with the neatly measured units and the perfect sense of timing of *Fortuna desperata*. *Maria zart*, although clearly indebted to the mature idiom, creates a different musical experience altogether, because it creates a different perception of musical time. The keyword is experience. That is what the score seems to tell us all the time. Ask no questions. Expect no answers. Listen.

If spinning-out is the discourse of *Maria zart*, what, exactly, is being spun out? The answer can be found on virtually every page of the score: the counterpoint is saturated with allusions to the *Maria zart* melody. Material from the tune is quoted and treated in every conceivable degree of ornamentation, so that the line between citation and spinning-out is in fact very hard to draw. Yet the melody penetrates the writing to such an extent that the aural impression is one of all-pervasiveness: to listen to this mass is to develop a sensivity even to melodic turns that barely seem conscious allusions at all. The peculiar nature of *Missa Maria zart* in this regard becomes apparent if we compare the setting with *Sicut spina rosam*. In the latter work the monophonic melody also appears in the contrapuntal voices, but *always* in direct (and usually strict) imitation of the tenor. In *Maria zart* the tenor and its surrounding voices do not communicate in this sense: they represent two quite distinct layers of cantus-firmus presentation. In this respect the mass closely resembles *Si dedero*, where parody citations infuse the contrapuntal tissue to such an extent that the aural impression similarly is one of all-pervasiveness (see below).

Maria zart has to be experienced as the whole, one-hour-long sound event that it is, and it will no doubt evoke different responses in each listener. Yet there is more to the mass than meets even the ear. It is perhaps not surprising that one reputable Dutch scholar, Marcus van Crevel, lost himself in far-reaching speculations as to a 'secret structure'.[12]

---

[12] Obrecht, *Opera omnia, Missae*, vii, pp. lv–cxlvi. Detailed evaluation of Van Crevel's extensive numerological analysis is beyond the scope of this study. As a general point, however, it must be said that its most serious flaws seem to be methodological. Van Crevel introduced too many auxiliary hypotheses (mainly concerning Obrecht's intellectual leanings) to explain the significance of individual numbers. The combined effect of these hypotheses was not only to increase the length of his commentary (and consequently to diminish the elegance of the alleged secret structure) but, more importantly, to lower the threshold above which numbers appear to be significant. The familiar objection to numerology, namely that one can discover significant numbers anywhere if one adjusts

For there are indeed intimations, suggestions of secrecy and learning, about this elusive and mysterious work. One example is the three-voice Et incarnatus: Gustave Reese discovered that if one removes all note-values other than the semibreve from the bass, one ends up with the first half of the *Maria zart* melody.[13] Why would Obrecht have spent the time and the effort to quote the tune in such a way that no one would ever be able to recognize it again? The question is all the more puzzling as the composer could hardly have expected a longer life-span for his music than two or three decades. Since he gives no verbal commentary of any kind, the Et incarnatus does in this sense indeed contain a musical 'secret'. This is confusing, for if that secret has any message, it is surely this: do ask questions, do expect answers, for you will find answers. (The truth of this is borne out by a subsequent discovery of Chris Maas: the top voice of the same section contains, in the same way as the bass, the second half of the *Maria zart* melody.[14]) And anyone must surely wonder at the complexity of the tenor segmentation, and the dazzling array of mensuration signs (fourteen, all told), which, if anything, must be suggestive of a special ambition.[15] Is there an agenda, a program, to this work after all?

Unfortunately, these tantalizing questions are beyond the scope of this study, for our main interest is in the conservative–progressive issue. Compared with the progressive motets, *Maria zart* is obviously conservative in its idiom, and many contemporaries may indeed have perceived it as a conservative work. At the same time it is clear that Obrecht wanted to do something special in this mass, something for which neither the high-level mature style nor the styles of the progressive motets were suited. One might say that the composer retreated in a sound world all his own, in which the conservative–progressive issue could only appear to be of limited relevance. In this respect *Maria zart* is perhaps the only mass that truly conforms to Besseler's description of Obrecht as the outsider genius of the Josquin period. If Obrecht was an outsider, it is not so much because he was out of touch with new trends (the progressive motets show

one's methods to the desired results, comes down to the same point. For to lower the threshold by means of auxiliary hypotheses is effectively to make it more difficult to find non-significant numbers (whether in the work in question or in others). It is for this reason that the results of numerological analyses often leave readers indifferent. The problem here is the absence of a coherent theory that differentiates clearly between 'meaningful' and 'random' numbers in 15th-c. music. This underlines that the goal of numerological research should not be to find more instances of number symbolism, but to work towards a generally accepted theory and method of numerology.

[13] Reese, *Music in the Renaissance*, 195.

[14] I am indebted to Professor Maas for pointing this out to me.

[15] O, Φ, O2, ☉, ϕ, C, ₵, C2, C3, ₵3, ₵2, ℭ, ₵, Ↄ (see *NOE* 7, pp. xxxvi–xxxvii). For the cantus-firmus treatment, see ibid., pp. xxxii–xxxv, and the analysis in Reese, *Music in the Renaissance*, 193–5 (supplementary comments in Sparks, *Cantus Firmus*, 262 and 470).

that this was not the case), but because in this particular work he chose to be an outsider.

To date *Maria zart* within one or two years on stylistic grounds would be sheer guesswork. Several features suggest a date not before about 1487–8: there are no head-motifs, ₵ is the predominant mensuration, the cantus firmus is segmented, and it appears in various tenorless sections. Although *Maria zart* takes the primary level of the mature style as its point of departure, it is difficult to see this work in close chronological juxtaposition with such early mature segmentation masses as *Je ne demande* or (if it is Obrecht's) *N'aray-je jamais*. On the whole, any date between about 1491–3 and 1505 would seem equally possible from the stylistic point of view. On biographical grounds, however, 1503, or possibly 1504, is by far the most plausible date. In that year Obrecht was active in the very region where the devotional song *Maria zart* originated, and where several other settings of the melody, including a three-voice mass, turn up in the 1500s (see Ch. 11). This would place *Maria zart* very late in the composer's career, and consequently either after or very shortly before he wrote the progressive motets *Laudes Christo redemptori* and *Quis numerare queat*. Is it possible to accept such a sharp stylistic juxtaposition if we earlier rejected one that seems much less sharp? This, of course, is merely to rephrase our central question: why is it that Obrecht did such different things in masses and motets, possibly even in close chronological juxtaposition? To accept 1503–4 as the date for *Maria zart* is implicitly to answer that question, for then we can reach only one conclusion: that Obrecht perceived mass and motet as genres that required quite different approaches. Yet it would obviously be dangerous to base such a far-reaching conclusion on only one mass, particularly when we are dealing with such a singular and inscrutable work as *Maria zart*. What do the other late masses tell us?

Missa Si dedero

The segmentation mass *Si dedero* is written in the mature style, yet it falls outside the picture sketched in Chapter 8.[16] Like *Maria zart* it operates exclusively on the primary level: there is virtually no stylistic differentiation, and consequently no 'dramatic' writing. Yet instead of turning down the most distinctive qualities of that level, as in *Maria zart*, Obrecht steps them up. The constant rhythmic activity in *Si dedero* has a quality of nervous agitation, even mannerism, about it, and contrasts with the

---

[16] The mass is briefly discussed in Sparks, *Cantus Firmus*, 262–3, 299–300, and 475.

sense of relaxed spontaneity and elementary force of the works discussed in Chapter 8. Indeed, there is no mistaking this mass for a genuine primary-level mature work, for it shows an awareness of procedures used (albeit to different effect) on the highest levels. The most significant of these are the points of imitation at the openings of movements and sections, which are not employed in any of the primary-level works. *Si dedero* employs such imitations more often even than *Fortuna desperata*, *Rose playsante*, or *Libenter gloriabor*—at the expense of 'terraced' openings (as in Exx. 22 and 24). Yet, and here lies the crucial difference, the momentum thus generated is not heightened subsequently by means of other procedures, let alone focused on a climactic point. Instead Obrecht seems to employ the imitations merely to get going, contrapuntally speaking, to move into a stable gear for the rest of the section.

Another feature also suggests awareness of the high-level mature works. All three of the mass's tenorless sections are based on voices from the model, the motet *Si dedero* by Alexander Agricola. The tenor of that setting appears in the Pleni (quoted in the contratenor), the top voice in the Benedictus (top voice), and the bass in the Agnus Dei II (bass). The only other mass to treat the three voices of its model in exactly this way is *Rose playsante*.[17] Two of the extended quotations in *Si dedero*, those in the Benedictus and Agnus Dei II, are, strictly speaking, examples of parody. But that term seems unhelpful, since it creates an arbitrary distinction with the third quotation, in the Pleni, which happens to be from the song tenor. It seems better to speak of secondary cantus firmi, since this describes the nature of the quotation (i.e. that it does not appear in the cantus-firmus-bearing voice, which is silent), its contrapuntal treatment, and the relationship with similar quotations in tenorless openings and interludes (as in *Je ne demande*, *N'aray-je jamais*, and *Plurimorum carminum I*; see Ch. 8). *Si dedero* uses the three voices from its model as secondary cantus firmi not only in the three-voice sections but also in such openings and interludes (see particularly the nearly strict quotation of the entire top voice in Et resurrexit, bars 119–72 and 188–203). Yet there are many more citations, and these are often so brief, and their appearance so irregular and unpredictable, that it is fair to say that the mass does contain elements of parody—in the sense that material from the song is reworked and reordered imaginatively in the new context, and that its most salient melodic features penetrate the 'free' writing. The Kyrie I may well have the greatest density of such citations: hardly a bar goes by without an

---

[17] This was noted already by Sparks, *Cantus Firmus*, 263.

explicit reminder of the model. Table 2 illustrates the extent to which Obrecht had finally embraced the concept of parody.[18]

Surveys of this kind, of course, cannot convey the aural impression of all-pervasiveness that such allusive writing creates. Indeed, they may easily create the opposite impression, that Obrecht wrote a mere patchwork of citations. Such an impression would be misguided. For it is evident from the score itself that *Missa Si dedero* is in fact an imaginative attempt to *recreate* the sound world of its model. Obrecht's writing is so homogeneous, and the quotations come and go so unobtrusively, that quotation-spotting is not only a time-consuming exercise but ultimately an arbitrary one. As Edgar Sparks put it: 'even where there is no direct quotation, the voices are conducted so much in the manner of Agricola's motet that they seem to have grown out of it'.[19] This explains the quality of nervous agitation that typifies Obrecht's counterpoint in *Si dedero*: it is a quality he perceived in the model and that he chose to emulate in his own writing— whether with direct quotations or with a more generally allusive style. *Cela sans plus*, as will be seen shortly, relates to its model in the very same way: in so far as its sound world is 'un-Obrechtian' it breathes the atmosphere of the original song.

The novelty of this approach, at least within the context of Obrecht's mass *œuvre*, can best be appreciated if we return briefly to the works discussed in Chapter 8. These masses generally give the impression that they inhabit a uniform, preconceived sound world, in which cantus firmi feature merely as construction material, as compositional pretexts. Only this can explain why settings such as *Fortuna desperata* and *Libenter gloriabor* are so similar in style and sound, even though their tenors could hardly be more different. In later years, as we have seen here, Obrecht seems to have developed a different attitude to his models. The notion of a 'constructive' cantus firmus still remained prominent, but superimposed on it now was a contrapuntal layer replete with allusions to the model. By writing two distinct layers of cantus-firmus presentation Obrecht came close to genuine parody in *Si dedero*, and created a highly individual sound world in *Maria zart*.

The first signs of Obrecht's new attitude can be found in *Malheur me bat*, which we have classed here as a high-level mature mass (and which in any case pre-dates 1497). Otto Gombosi listed a great many quotations from the original song, and went on to conclude:[20]

Bei so großer Inanspruchnahme der . . . Melodien [of the song] ist es nicht

---

[18] See also Sparks, *Cantus Firmus*, 299–300.   [19] Ibid. 475.   [20] *Jacob Obrecht*, 92–3.

TABLE 2. *Quotations from the model in the Kyrie I of Jacob Obrecht's* Missa Si dedero

Kyrie I	voice	model	voice
1–5	S C B	6–11	T
8–15	C	7–15	T
15–19	B	16–20	B
17–23	S	18–24	S
26–31	S	27–32	S
31–4	B	37–41	B
36–9	S	32–6	S
41–54	S	40–53	S
41–5	C	40–5	T
52–4	C	51–3	T
56–8	B	53–5	B
62–7	B	66–71	B
67–9	B	74–5	B

verwunderlich, daß der schon an sich feste, markante, liedmäßige Charakter dieser auch die Stimmen der Messe beherrscht. Diese treten aber viel entschlossener zu Akkordmassen zusammen, die besonders klare Harmonieführung ist die stärkste Seite der Messe.

In the last sentence Gombosi summarizes why *Malheur me bat* is still a high-level mature mass: effective chordal writing and clarity of harmonic organization are the very features to which we have drawn attention in Ex. 25. And it is in exactly this respect that *Si dedero* and *Maria zart* make the crucial step away from the mature sound world. Both masses abandon the stylistic differentiation and the 'dramatic' writing that would inevitably have restricted the possibility of entering imaginatively into the sound world of the model, and of recreating it in an allusive contrapuntal tissue.

In so far as chronology is concerned, *Missa Si dedero* most probably dates from the roughly ten years between about 1491–3 and 1502, the date for the paper on which the mass was copied in MunBS 3154.[21] Any attempt to be more precise must be speculative, since there are virtually no clues to the chronology of Obrecht's mass style in the 1490s and early 1500s. The fact that *Si dedero* seems much closer to the mature style than *Maria zart* is of little help, not only because this may be a reflection of the nature of its model, but also because *Maria zart* was in any case probably

[21] Noblitt, 'Die Datierung', 49. *Si dedero* is likely to post-date 1487–8 for the same reasons as for *Maria zart*: there are no head-motifs, ₵ is the predominant mensuration, the cantus firmus is segmented, and it appears in various tenorless sections.

composed after 1502. As in the case of the next mass, *Cela sans plus*, we can only conclude that the work is 'post-mature', not because it has a recognizably late style, but because its style is a considered reflection on that of its model.

Missa Cela sans plus

The Osanna I of the anonymous *Missa Cela sans plus* was printed by Petrucci in 1502, with what amounts to a clear attribution: 'Obrecht in Missa'.[22] There are no obstacles to accepting his authorship, which was first proposed by Martin Staehelin in 1975. On the contrary: *Cela sans plus* is not only worthy of the composer but, if included in his canon, must count as one of his loveliest masses.[23]

Otto Gombosi, who knew only the Osanna I, held that Obrecht's counterpoint redeemed the shortcomings of the model (a song by Colinet de Lannoy), which he judged 'eine ärmliche, blutarme Komposition von minimaler Erfindung' on account of its thin texture and motivic economy.[24] Now that it is possible to see the Osanna in the context of the mass, and the mass in the context of Obrecht's whole *œuvre*, the relationship between model and mass appears to be different. For it would be incorrect to say that the song merely supplied the construction material, the compositional 'pretext', for a work otherwise thoroughly Obrechtian. Just as the tenor and top voice were augmented to structural scaffolds, so the intimate microcosm of the song was expanded to the stylistic macrocosm of the mass. This is true not only of melodic content, although all the imitations of the model are indeed recombined and expanded many times in the new context. The most distinctive feature of the mass, however, is its relatively high scoring (G_2 C_3 C_3 F_3), a feature evidently inspired by the model (G_2 C_3 C_3). Obrecht capitalized on this by writing counterpoint of extreme lucidity and sonority. Voices are frequently brought close together to form triads or first-inversion chords (usually above middle C), and these sonorities are sustained with only minor

---

[22] The Osanna of Obrecht's *Ave regina celorum* was also transmitted independently under this designation (see Ch. 8, n. 27). For *Missa Cela sans plus*, see Staehelin, 'Obrechtiana', 7–8, and C. Broekhuijsen, 'Obrecht in Missa?' (MA thesis, University of Amsterdam, 1983). Gombosi (*Jacob Obrecht*, 78–9) discusses the Osanna I as the self-contained song arrangement it was thought to be prior to Staehelin's discovery of the mass.

[23] Several features in *Cela sans plus* support the possibility of Obrecht's authorship and suggest that the mass is late. Cantus-firmus treatment is strict, in typically mature or post-mature fashion (see the survey in Staehelin, 'Obrechtiana', 8), the chanson tenor is used as a supplementary cantus firmus in the Pleni and Agnus Dei II, ¢ is the predominant mensuration, and there are no head-motifs.   [24] *Jacob Obrecht*, 76–7.

contrapuntal modifications. As a result, *Cela sans plus* is one of Obrecht's most euphonious masses—the very opposite, in fact, of the rigorously and nervously linear *Si dedero*. Imitations and motivic repetitions are mostly based on motifs from Lannoy's song, whose elegant melodic shapes have inspired Obrecht's part-writing in general.[25] The overriding impression, consequently, is one of contrapuntal luxuriance: the well-shaped melodic lines constantly submerge into and resurface from the mellow sonorities they help to generate. No antithesis is perceived between contrapuntal and chordal thinking: the balance that Obrecht had earlier achieved in *Ave regina celorum*, and that the stylistic differentiation of the mature style had undone, has somehow been re-established.

Obrecht could hardly have perceived Lannoy's song as poor or anaemic. His very decision to recreate its intimate sound world in a large-scale composition can only indicate that he saw a great deal of potential in the piece. By realizing that potential in *Missa Cela sans plus* he created a work that in contrapuntal style is the opposite of *Si dedero*. Yet the stylistic contrast between these two settings is a reflection of the extent to which Obrecht allowed his models to inspire his writing, and to which he modified the mature idiom accordingly.

Beyond *Fortuna desperata*, then, lay greater sensitivity to models and, one assumes, greater care in selecting them. The notion of a constructive cantus firmus continued to be prominent, yet one wonders whether this would have remained the case had Obrecht lived two or three decades longer. Even the song *Cela sans plus*, for all its brevity and modesty, relies so heavily on imitation and motivic writing that it seems somehow inappropriate to dissolve one voice from the texture and turn it into a scaffold. And the long-term trend, in motets as well as in songs, was only towards *more* imitative writing, to a musical conception in which imitation, and imitation alone, was the musical discourse. Obrecht himself contributed to that trend in his *Laudes Christo redemptori*. And so the inevitable question is this: had he been confronted with a model as thoroughly imitative as this motet, would he still have lifted the voice labeled 'tenor' from the ensemble and turned it into a scaffold cantus firmus? Or would he perhaps not have chosen such a model precisely because cantus-firmus quotation would have betrayed lack of musical sensitivity?

All this is a different way of saying that the two distinct layers of cantus-firmus presentation, as we have seen them in *Maria zart*, *Si dedero*, and

---

[25] See also Staehelin's comment: 'Besonders ausgeprägt erscheint . . . das Spiel mit der Imitation, die in grössern Elementen und in kleinen, zuweilen fast krausen Schnörkelfloskeln durch die Stimmen geht oder, auf den Einzelpart beschränkt, ostinat behandelt wird' ('Obrechtiana', 8).

Cela sans plus, were not destined to remain in each other's company for long. The scaffold tenor was on the way out. As potential mass models changed rapidly in style, as pervasive imitation became the stylistic norm, the future inevitably lay in the other layer: the imitative and allusive contrapuntal tissue that had come to surround the tenor. To write a mass consisting entirely of such a tissue was the step Obrecht never took—and that, ultimately, has made him the conservative of our history books. *Cela sans plus* shows how close he came to making that step. For despite the presence of a strictly quoted tenor, Obrecht showed his musical respect for Lannoy's song throughout the mass, by taking over, rearranging, and expanding its imitations—because these imitations were *intrinsic* to the sound world he sought to recreate.

From this perspective the conservative–progressive issue may seem to disintegrate: if 'conservative' is merely a synonym for 'using a scaffold tenor', what does it mean to attach such a label to a composer? Yet the fact remains that Obrecht wrote no masses remotely like *Laudes Christo redemptori* or *Quis numerare queat*. The question as to why he failed to do so is now easily answered: because he chose no models in the styles of either motet, and consequently did not have to 'recreate' such styles in his masses. But this may be putting the cart before the horse. After all, it may well have been a fundamentally conservative conception of the mass that guided his selection of models.

Yet we have also given an implicit answer that seems more important. It is that the song and the motet, around the turn of the century, had become the primary vehicles for stylistic innovation, and that the mass was 'progressive' only in so far as it was based on progressive songs or motets, and took account of their novel features. In this sense Obrecht's late masses are stylistically as conservative or progressive as their models. That they all carry the 'conservative' legacy of the cantus firmus may mean no more than that the critical point—beyond which using a scaffold tenor would have meant being insensitive to the sound world of the model—had not yet been reached, either because Obrecht was not yet ready to go beyond it (and hence chose no models which might have forced him to do so), or because no one was at the time of his death.

In this sense the story of Obrecht's masses ends in mid-air. The composer died at an age, 47, when men like Dufay or Ockeghem were yet to make their most significant contributions, and a composer like Busnoys apparently had little or nothing left to contribute. He died at a time, 1505, when a radical transformation of the mass was imminent, if not already taking place. The clearest sign of that transformation would eventually be the disappearance of the scaffold tenor. Yet this was only the last step in a much longer development, whose inception we have witnessed in Obrecht's late masses. Death cut off that development in so far as he was concerned, and that is why any account of his stylistic development in the mass can only have an open ending. Obrecht's mass *œuvre* was left unfinished. The prospects and promises in his late masses were never fulfilled. There is no swan-song, no musical testament. The rest, literally, was silence.

Postscript: *Missa Sub tuum presidium*

Only one mass remains to be accounted for: *Sub tuum presidium*.[26] We have left this work to the last because it is governed by a rational design that presented such a heavy compositional burden that its stylistic profile is of necessity low. Technical difficulties have moved to the foreground; contrapuntal style is reduced to the mere accompaniment of those difficulties. *Sub tuum presidium*, consequently, is Obrecht's only mass in which it is virtually impossible to move beyond the 'mere' analysis of rational elements. And this is so because it was virtually impossible for Obrecht's own style to move beyond those elements. For the rational design was not shaped with specifically musical concerns in mind. On the contrary, Obrecht found his contrapuntal way around it with the greatest difficulty. This can only mean that his priorities in this mass were different from those in other works: *Sub tuum presidium* has a rational message that is stated through music, but not translated into it.

The chief cantus firmus of the mass, the Marian antiphon *Sub tuum presidium confugimus*, appears in the same shape in every section (quoted in the top voice). This rigid cantus-firmus layout is modified only twice in the course of the work, and these minor modifications, as Marcus van Crevel discovered, have tremendous significance for the structure of the setting. For it is only by virtue of these modifications that the mass comprises a total duration of exactly 888 semibreves, a number that divides up into 333 (Kyrie and Gloria) plus 555 (Credo, Sanctus, and Agnus Dei).[27]

Of course such a layout could still have left Obrecht with all the freedom he needed to write the mass as he liked. Yet he made a second *a priori*

---

[26] For this mass, see Reese, *Music in the Renaissance*, 195; Wolff, *Die Musik der alten Niederländer*, 52–4; Salop, 'The Masses of Jacob Obrecht', 3–6; Obrecht, *Opera omnia editio altera, Missae*, vi, ed. M. van Crevel (Amsterdam, 1959), pp. xvii–li; L. Lockwood, 'A Note on Obrecht's Mass "Sub tuum presidium"', *Revue belge de musicologie*, 14 (1960), 30–9; Sparks, *Cantus Firmus*, 282–5; Elders, *Studien zur Symbolik*, 122 and 135–6; Bloxam, 'A Survey of Late Medieval Service Books', 297–310.

[27] Obrecht, *Opera omnia, Missae*, vi, pp. xvii–xxv.

decision that did bind his hands. From the Credo onwards other Marian chants are quoted alongside the central cantus firmus, and the number of these additional cantus firmi increases by one in every subsequent movement. The Agnus Dei presents the culmination of this development: it incorporates a layer of four pre-existent melodies, one being predetermined in shape (*Sub tuum presidium*), the others freely rhythmized. The technical difficulties in this scheme are considerable, and Obrecht obviously could not have overcome them without extensive rhythmic and melodic manœuvring, not only with the cantus firmi, but also with the freely composed parts.

This process of successive cantus-firmus accumulation was placed in a broader textural development. The Kyrie and Gloria are in three- and four-part texture respectively (the chief cantus firmus plus two or three counterpoints), and with the additional cantus firmi in the next movements this increases to five-, six-, and seven-part texture (see Table 3).

It is clear from Table 3 that direct parallels in Obrecht's mass *œuvre* can be found only for the Kyrie and Gloria. *Fors seulement* and *Je ne seray* parallel the Kyrie in that they employ a similar type of three-part texture and likewise place the predetermined cantus firmus in the discantus. And there are several masses and mass movements that, like the Gloria, are in four-part texture with a cantus firmus in the top voice: the Benedictus of *Ave regina celorum*, the Gloria of *Caput*, *Malheur me bat*, the Credo of *Cela sans plus*, and the Agnus Dei I of *Gracioulx et biaulx*. Comparison with these works quickly reveals that the contrapuntal voices in the Kyrie and Gloria are written in the primary-level style at its most vigorous but also at its least distinctive, and that Obrecht somehow manages to maintain its vigour in the rest of the mass. In a way this is not surprising, for the primary-level style was better suited to overcoming extreme technical difficulties than any of the other idioms Obrecht developed or emulated in his career. And possibly its spontaneity and vigour was the very quality he needed to bring life into the thickening tapestry of cantus firmi. That there was less and less room to handle the style comfortably as the mass approached its 888th semibreve was probably the least of his worries. For the most conspicuous musical quality of the work, its increasing textural richness, was in-built in the design, and would come over whether the counterpoint was particularly imaginative or not. In *Sub tuum presidium*, for once, Obrecht was architect (and speculative mind) first, musician second.

Not surprisingly, then, it is extremely difficult to date the mass on stylistic grounds. A date in the mature period or after is suggested by the

TABLE 3. *Cantus-firmus layout and textural structure (reconstruction) of Jacob Obrecht's* Missa Sub tuum presidium

Voice	clef	Kyrie	Gloria	Credo	Sanctus	Agnus I/II	Agnus III
Discantus 1	C_1	A	A	A	A	A	A
Discantus 2	C_1	—	—	B	C	D	F
Altus 1	C_2	—	—	—	—	E	G
Altus (2)	C_{2-3}	■	■	■	■	■	■
Vagans	C_{3-4}	—	—	—	C	D	F
Tenor	C_{3-4}	■	■	■	■	■	■
Bassus	F_{3-4}	—	■	■	■	■	■

■ = free counterpoint; *A* = *Sub tuum presidium*; *B* = *Audi nos* (from *Ave preclara maris stella*); *C* = *Mediatrix nostra* (from *Aurea virga prime matris Eve*); *D* = *Celsus nuntiat Gabriel* (likewise from *Aurea virga*); *E* = *Supplicamus nos emenda* (from *Verbum bonum et suave*); *F* = *Regina celi*; *G* = *O clemens O pia* (from *Salve regina*).

primary-level style and the absence of head-motifs.[28] Most of the other musical features are determined by the rational design, which by definition stands outside the composer's stylistic development: the design is 'timeless' in the sense that Obrecht could have conceived it at any point in his career. The strictness of cantus-firmus treatment, for instance, would normally point to the mature period or after, yet in the present case it can be explained equally well as a by-product of Obrecht's arithmetic. The prominent use of *tempus perfectum*, conversely, would suggest a date before the mature period, yet the choice of mensuration, too, was obviously part of the grand numerological design. The clefs of the two middle parts in the Gloria are a fifth apart (C_2–C_4), so that the texture here resembles *a voce piena*. Yet it would be hazardous to conclude from this that *Sub tuum presidium* must date from Obrecht's last years, if only because the composer faced considerable textural problems in this work, and may well have found it difficult to maintain the standard textures of his day.

These seemingly conflicting clues highlight a question that has not so far been raised explicitly here: Why do we actually wish to date fifteenth-

[28] Lockwood suggested that the mass might have been composed for the church of Our Lady at Antwerp, that is, in either 1491–7 or 1501–3 ('A Note', 39). Bloxam has cautiously endorsed this suggestion ('A Survey of Late Medieval Service Books', 310). Since the liturgically most specific cantus firmi (*B*, *C*, *D*, and *E* in Table 3) were frequently associated with the Assumption or with Assumptiontide (ibid. 300 and 308), it is tempting to suggest that Obrecht might have provided his setting for the 'missa celebrata in octava assumptionis, cum organis et discantu', which had been sung annually in the nave of Our Lady's since 1490 (Antwerp, Cathedral Archive, Register D, fos. 203ᵛ (1490/1) and 221ᵛ (1491/2); payments of 36 and 42 Brabant groats, respectively). Another possible candidate for this celebration is Barbireau's five-part *Missa Virgo parens Christi*.

century compositions? What is the point of a chronology? The answer that
has been presupposed throughout this study is that we wish to understand
music in its historical dimension. From the viewpoint of method a chronology is no more than a conceptual tool, a mode of thinking that helps us
to arrive at a particular kind of musical understanding, and in which we
try to express that understanding. Thus chronology has been chosen as
the framework for this study, not because dating is an end in itself, but
because this format seemed best suited for a renewed attempt to evaluate
Obrecht's mass *œuvre*. From another point of view, a chronology should
obviously have a claim to historical truth, and should be rejected or
modified if it fails the test of external evidence. In so far as we are trying
to arrive at a *historical* understanding of Obrecht's music, this of course
amounts to the same thing. Yet a case like *Sub tuum presidium* shows that
historical truth and musical understanding can be quite different concerns. Most of this mass's musical features are dictated by a rational
design whose creation was clearly a singular historic event—an event that
intruded into Obrecht's creative development rather than grew out of it.
Such an intrusion could have occurred at any time in his life, whenever
there happened to be an external occasion for writing a deeply symbolic
work. If we knew that occasion, it would mainly be of biographical or
historical interest. For it is in the nature of a once-only intrusion that it
sheds little light on the historical development of a composer's style.

It is perhaps just as well that this last musical chapter should end on
such a note. We have tried to arrive at a historical understanding of
Obrecht's mass *œuvre*, yet from this perspective our understanding of *Sub
tuum presidium* can only be that its distinctive musical profile is 'unhistorical'. That one of Obrecht's best-known and most appreciated masses
should thus end up in a postscript, merely because it fails to answer the
particular question that concerned us, underlines the limitations of that
question. For our understanding can only be incomplete if it cannot
account for the peculiar nature of this mass—except as an intrusion. What
we have obtained is only a slice of the world of Obrecht's music. The
worlds that are outside the picture sketched here, the worlds of chant
and liturgy, of mathematics and numerology, of piety and devotion, of
politics and society, are not just responsible for 'intrusions' into an otherwise neatly sealed-off musical territory. Every Obrecht mass—not just
Sub tuum presidium—inhabits these and many other worlds of fifteenth-
century thought and living. Fuller understanding of his music can be
achieved only if we probe more deeply into those worlds and, ultimately,
can come to perceive their essential unity.

11 THE LAST JOURNEY

IN the summer of 1503 Obrecht disappears from our view. For at least fourteen months after his departure from Antwerp we have only threads of biographical evidence, which cannot be woven into a seamless historical narrative. There are hints that the composer was active at the court of Emperor Maximilian I, and perhaps the chapel of Pope Julius II—but all we know for certain is that he was appointed in Ferrara in September 1504, and died there within eleven months.

Documents are sparse and often difficult to interpret, but it seems significant that all of them now come from courtly circles outside the Netherlands. And so it would appear that Obrecht's career finally did take a turn for 'the better', a turn leading ultimately to his appointment as *maestro di capella* at Ferrara. This should have been the beginning of a new series of chapters, describing ten or twenty more years of activity in the dominant musical centres of Europe, rounded off with retirement in the country of his birth. Yet death, of course, intervened: having finally tasted the fruits of success, and the prospects of a glorious career, all it took was a simple infection of the plague, in July 1505, and his life was over within days. This, then, must be the final chapter: Obrecht's journey in 1503 was his last.

Innsbruck and ?Rome, 1503–1504

The date of Obrecht's departure from Antwerp is unknown. The account of the Guild of Our Lady for 1503/4, which covers the year starting on 24 June 1503, mentions three choirmasters, the first of whom is 'meyster Jacob'.[1] It is clear from this that Obrecht continued working at Antwerp

---

[1] Forney, 'Music, Ritual and Patronage', 44: 'Item, paid to the choirmasters, namely *meyster* Jacob [Obrecht], and Jaspar and *meyster* Jan [Raes], for their salary, [but] since they have not served equally, we have contented them with 1,428 Brabant groats.' The payment requires some explanation. The three choirmasters together received 132 Brabant groats less than the standard annual

for some time after June 1503, although we do not know for how long.[2] The next item of information was recorded more than three months later in Innsbruck. On 6 October 1503, the accounts of the imperial court in that city mention the following payment:[3]

Master Martin [Trumer, tailor], give Jacoben Opprecht fourteen ells of good damask, which we grant him because of a *Missa Regina celi* that he has made for us.

The record seems to come out of nowhere: it is an isolated flicker of light, preceded by three and followed by eleven months of darkness. Yet to have even this much is invaluable, for there is a highly suggestive context to the record: it so happens that on the day before the payment was ordered, Archduke Philip the Fair had left Innsbruck with his full court entourage, having been fêted in the city for more than three weeks by his father, Emperor Maximilian. This encounter had been one of the most splendid events in Innsbruck's history. It included several occasions on which the chapels of the two monarchs, including La Rue and possibly Isaac, joined in singing polyphonic masses in the churches of Innsbruck and Hall. The Burgundian court chronicler Antoine de Lalaing mentions these occasions, and occasionally refers to music:[4]

[17 September] . . . the king [of the Romans] and Monseigneur [the duke], their coats of arms before them, heard Mass in the great church of Innsbruck . . . The singers of the king and of Monseigneur sang the Mass, and played the organ full of all instruments, mentioned above.[5] It is the most melodious thing one could hear.

salary at this time, 1,560 Brabant groats. Since Obrecht had earned this salary in the preceding year, and Raes would continue to receive it in the following years, it was evidently the interim choirmaster Jasper (who did not have a master's degree) whose salary had been cut. Since the standard monthly salary was at this time $1,560 \div 12 = 130$ Brabant groats, it is clear that the reduction of 132 Brabant groats must have been divided over a number of months. The total reduction divides only by 2, 3, 4, and 6: consequently, depending on how drastically his salary was cut, Jaspar worked between two and six months. The latter seems the most likely possibility, for a monthly reduction of $132 \div 6 = 22$ Brabant groats would have left a monthly salary of exactly 9 Brabant shillings (108 groats).

[2] One of the singers of Duke Ercole d'Este, Bartolomeo de Fiandra, visited the church of Our Lady at Antwerp between mid-June and Oct. 1503, and drafted a brief report on six singers there who might be suitable for the Ferrarese chapel (note that this is *half* the number of singers employed at that church). Interestingly, Obrecht is not mentioned in the report, which may suggest that Bartolomeo visited Antwerp after the latter's departure. See for this L. Lockwood, '"Messer Gossino" and Josquin des Prez', in R. L. Marshall (ed.), *Studies in Renaissance and Baroque Music in Honor of Arthur Mendel* (Kassel, 1974), 15–24.

[3] Transcribed in H. Schweiger, 'Archivalische Notizen zur Hofkantorei Maximilians I.', *Zeitschrift für Musikwissenschaft*, 14 (1932), 373: 'Ynnsprug, 6. X. [1503]: Maister Martin, gib Jacoben Opprecht 14 ellen gueten Tamaschk, so wir ime schenckhen von wegen aines Ambts *Regina celi* so er vnns gemacht hat.'

[4] See the edition in *Collection des voyages des souverains des Pays-Bas*, ed. M. Gachard, i (Brussels, 1876), 313 and 316.

[5] Ibid. 310: 'The parish church of Innsbruck has the most beautiful and exquisite organ I have

[26 September] . . . and there [in the church of Innsbruck] were solemnly sung two Masses. The first, a Requiem Mass, was sung by the bishop and the singers of Monseigneur. The second Mass was of the Assumption of Our Lady, sung by the singers of the king . . . And the sackbuts of the king started the Gradual and the *Deo gratias* and *Ite missa est*, and the singers of the king sang the Offertory.

Given this public display of musical splendour, it could hardly be coincidence that one of Europe's most famous composers was in the city at this very time. Although Obrecht was paid only on the day after the meeting had finished, this was for a composition he had already made 'for us', suggesting activity in imperial circles in the preceding weeks. Also there can be little doubt that the actual piece, a *Missa Regina celi* (which does not appear to have survived), resulted from a commission, and was therefore probably written for the occasion. An element of musical competition between the Burgundian and Habsburg chapels is suggested by Lalaing in his description of the service on 26 September: Philip the Fair's musicians sang a Requiem Mass, either the one by Pierre de La Rue or the lost setting by Dufay, while Maximilian's performed a Mass for the Assumption of Our Lady, quite possibly a setting by the imperial court composer Heinrich Isaac.[6] The earlier service of 17 September may well have been a similar occasion. Other Masses were sung by Maximilian's chapel alone on 1 and 2 October,[7] just days before Obrecht was paid for his setting.

Was the composer brought over specially with a view to this occasion? The evidence would certainly seem to suggest so. It would have taken Obrecht at least three weeks to travel to Innsbruck, and so to arrive there in time for the September festivities he should have left the Netherlands by mid-August at the latest. His period of activity in Antwerp after 24 June 1503 is thus unlikely to have been longer than about seven weeks, suggesting that he left straight for the Tyrol. Moreover, even if no documentation survives, we may safely take it that there had been written contact between Obrecht and the imperial court, perhaps even an invitation: the composer would certainly not have abandoned his position and travelled such a distance without any prospect of financial security.

ever seen. There is no instrument in the world that does not sound in that organ, for all [instruments] are contained inside it; it cost more than ten thousand francs to make.'

[6] Martin Staehelin has argued that the setting might have been Isaac's *Missa Virgo prudentissima*; see Isaac, *Messen*, ed. M. Staehelin (Musikalische Denkmäler, 8; Mainz, 1973), ii. 162. Obrecht's *Missa Sub tuum presidium* also seems to be associated with the Assumption of Our Lady (see Ch. 10, n. 28). This is the only known Obrecht mass to incorporate the chant *Regina celi* (in the final Agnus Dei; see Ch. 10, Table 3). For documentary evidence that Dufay's (lost) Requiem mass had been performed by the singers of Philip the Fair two years earlier, in 1501, see W. F. Prizer, 'Music and Ceremonial in the Low Countries: Philip the Fair and the Order of the Golden Fleece', *Early Music History*, 5 (1985), 133–5, 142, and 150.   [7] Gachard, *Collection des voyages*, i. 319–20.

At the same time it is clear that Obrecht was not appointed as a singer: none of the lists of musicians in Maximilian's chapel ever mentions him. Yet we cannot rule out that he served the emperor in a different capacity, perhaps one, like Isaac's, that did not require him to be resident permanently; surely some offer of paid work must have persuaded him to travel to Innsbruck. In this connection it is worth mentioning a tantalizing though unfortunately unsubstantiated claim made by Hugo Leichtentritt over fifty years ago:[8]

While at Florence Heinrich Isaak met his countryman, Jacob Obrecht, also one of the greatest of Dutch musicians. Obrecht had been sent by Emperor Maximilian as diplomatic agent to Florence, with a special mission to Lorenzo. Nowadays one can hardly imagine a musician as ambassador on important political missions. Yet the age of the Renaissance shows us quite a number of great musicians, painters, and architects as ambassadors of kings, popes, princes, who in turn displayed the wide range of cultural interests that is characteristic of the Renaissance mind. Obrecht spent his last years at Maximilian's court at the head of the imperial chapel, where the great Josquin de Près [sic] was his colleague, and Heinrich Isaak and Ludwig Senfl his successors. Obrecht died in 1505 in Ferrara, a victim of the great plague that devastated Italy at that time.

No documentary confirmation for any of the claims concerning Obrecht and Josquin has been found, but perhaps we should not too quickly dismiss them all as fantasy. At least in the case of the alleged mission to Florence there is the possibility that Leichtentritt (or a historian with whom he was in contact) had seen documents not normally explored by musicologists, since they would have mentioned the composer as a diplomatic agent rather than a musician. That Obrecht may have been in Florence at some point after 1500 is independently suggested by Pietro Aaron in his *De institutione harmonica*, when he mentions 'the most outstanding men in this art, especially Josquin, Obrecht, Isaac, and Agricola, with whom I had the greatest friendship and familiarity in Florence'.[9] Since Aaron was born around 1480, any amicable relationship with Obrecht is unlikely to have developed before the early 1500s, when the young Italian was making a modest name for himself as a composer (a frottola of his was printed by Petrucci in 1505).

There is independent musical evidence to suggest continued activity in the Innsbruck region. Obrecht's *Missa Maria zart*, generally accepted to be his latest surviving mass, is based on a devotional monophonic song

[8] H. Leichtentritt, *Music, History, and Ideas* (Cambridge, Mass., 1938), 78–9.

[9] Bk. iii, ch. 10; translation by Bonnie Blackburn, who discusses the passage extensively in 'On Compositional Process in the Fifteenth Century', *Journal of the American Musicological Society*, 40 (1987), 213.

written probably in the Tyrol in the late fifteenth century. The tune became popular as a cantus firmus in the years around 1500, particularly in Innsbruck and the surrounding area. Among settings that provide a context for Obrecht's mass are the Tenorlied by 'quidam dictus Pfabinschwanz' of Augsburg,[10] composed in 1500, two similar settings by Ludwig Senfl, who had close connections with the Innsbruck court, and an anonymous three-voice mass copied in the Innsbruck manuscript MunBS 3154 on paper dated 1504–6.[11] The only known settings that may have been written elsewhere are two tablature arrangements by Arnolt Schlick, published in 1512; although the organist played before Maximilian I on various occasions in the 1490s and 1500s, he was active throughout the German countries. It is true that one of the *Maria zart* settings, the one by Pfabinschwanz, reached the Netherlands in the early sixteenth century (it survives with a Dutchified text in BrusBR II 270).[12] Yet it seems unlikely that the tune itself could have been so widely known there for Obrecht to have chosen it as the model for a mass setting. Since at least one document confirms his presence in the very area where the *Maria zart* song became popular, and, moreover, at the very stage of his career when he is likely to have written the mass, we may reasonably assume that this work, like the lost *Missa Regina celi*, stems from a continued association with Innsbruck musical circles, between September 1503 and September 1504.

At some point in these years Obrecht was also 'perhaps' a singer in the chapel of Pope Julius II. The evidence comes from a document written more than two months after his death, on 30 September 1505, by the papal singer Remigius de Mastaing.[13] In it, Mastaing applies for benefices left vacant by the composer's death, and does so by writing the document *motu proprio*, that is, in the pope's name. To add force to his application, Mastaing invokes an indult that entitles singers of the papal chapel to receive the benefices of deceased fellow members. For this Obrecht should obviously have been a member of the chapel in the first place—and that is precisely what the document appears to confirm. Mastaing places in the pope's mouth a phrase to the effect 'that the said Jacobus, when he lived, was perhaps a *cantor capellanus* and *familiaris* in our [that is,

[10] Undoubtedly the Georg Pfawenschwantz who worked at Constance in 1481–99 (M. Schuler, 'Der Personalstatus der Konstanzer Domkantorei um 1500', *Archiv für Musikwissenschaft*, 21 (1964), 261).

[11] See *NOE* 7, pp. xxxi–xxxii, and Strohm, review of *NOE* 7, in *Notes*, 47 (1990), 554.

[12] Ibid. See also Strohm, *The Rise*, 521–2.

[13] Discovered by Richard Sherr; I am most grateful to Professor Sherr for sharing his material with me in advance of publication.

Julius'] chapel'. Another papal singer, Bonus Radulphi, attempted to obtain Obrecht's benefices with the same strategy, at the instigation of the Master of the Chapel. He appears to have succeeded in the case of the chaplaincy of St Judocus at Antwerp, confirming (despite Mastaing's 'perhaps') that the indult was judged applicable, and hence that Obrecht had been a member of Julius II's chapel.

Since no lists of papal singers have survived for the period between April 1502 and September 1507,[14] there is no way of knowing when Obrecht might have entered the chapel. Doubt is still cast, of course, by the word 'perhaps' (*forsan*) in Mastaing's application, which may mean that Obrecht never actually served as a singer, and was perhaps even prevented from moving to Rome. Yet his formal association had apparently been firm enough to make it possible to obtain benefices on this ground. If the composer was appointed papal singer, then the appointment must have been made after November 1503, when Julius II was elected pope. This leaves as the most probable periods October 1503 to September 1504 (when his whereabouts are unknown), or perhaps the three months after May 1505 (when he was stranded in Ferrara without a position). In the latter case, Obrecht's illness and death might have prevented him from moving to Rome, thus explaining the puzzling 'forsan' in Mastaing's application.

Ferrara, 1504–1505

If the eleven months after Innsbruck remain obscure, we reach firm ground again in September 1504, when Obrecht becomes *maestro di cappella* in the chapel of Duke Ercole d'Este of Ferrara. The appointment must have been like a dream come true: seventeen years had gone by since Obrecht had last been in Ferrara, having spent there some of the happiest months of his life. Now, his quest for the better had ended: Obrecht had found the best. This expressed itself not only in a salary that easily put his northern income in the shade, but above all in the personal appreciation of Duke Ercole, who had been an ardent admirer of his music since the early 1480s.

Ercole had been looking around for new musicians throughout 1504. Josquin had left his service in April, having been *maestro di cappella* for hardly more than a year. A month later, the duke's son Alfonso was sent on a diplomatic mission to France, with an assignment that included

---

[14] Haberl, 'Die römische "schola cantorum"', 248.

hiring singers in Thérouanne, Antwerp, and Bruges who had been spotted there in the previous year by the court singer Bartolomeo de Fiandra.[15] In July reports reached Alfonso that his father was mortally ill, and he rushed back immediately, arriving in Ferrara on 8 August. He seems to have brought none of the singers with him, but it is perhaps no coincidence that Obrecht is first listed as *maestro di cappella* in the very next month. It may be that his and Alfonso's paths crossed somewhere in France or Italy in July–August 1504. Alternatively, if Leichtentritt's claim concerning a journey to Florence is found to be correct, Obrecht may have passed through Ferrara as a traveller. If that was the case, Duke Ercole must have been delighted to see him back after all those years, and would not have hesitated for a moment to offer him the vacant position of *maestro di cappella*. What would support the latter scenario is the absence of any correspondence concerning the appointment—as there is for Josquin, Isaac, and Brumel, who were elsewhere at the time of their negotiations.

It is clear in any case that Obrecht, either through lack of experience or because of sheer eagerness for the position, did not bargain for such high payment as had been demanded in the previous year by Isaac and Josquin.[16] He settled for an annual salary of 100 gold ducats, exactly half that received by Josquin, and 20 ducats less than demanded by Isaac.[17] Yet even this was an astronomical figure by northern standards, equivalent at this time to about 7,500–8,000 Flemish groats. This basic income was almost certainly supplemented with extra funds for travel outside Ferrara, money to buy a horse, a housing allowance, and, in due course, benefices—altogether probably doubling the figure.[18] Working conditions, of course, were extremely favourable. At the court Obrecht no longer needed to spend all his time training and caring for choirboys, nor did he ever again have to work through endless routines of commemoration services and endowments. In some ways his position was honorific, allowing him plenty of time for musical composition, with the assurance that his works would find immediate appreciation with a ruler ardently devoted to music. In short, the climate was ideal for Obrecht to be reborn as a composer, to reopen the rich resources of his musical imagination in another outpouring of creativity: high standards of singing, continuous acquisition of up-

[15] Lockwood, '"Messer Gossino" and Josquin des Prez', 22–3; see also above, n. 2. Alfonso visited King Louis XII of France in Paris, and then went to Brussels and London.

[16] L. Lockwood, 'Josquin at Ferrara: New Documents and Letters', in Lowinsky and Blackburn (eds.), *Josquin des Prez: Proceedings*, 110–14, and the same author's *Ferrara*, 202–7.

[17] Transcriptions of the monthly payments to 'messer Ubreto, compositore de canto', on 2 Oct., 5 Nov., 7 and 24 Dec. are given in Murray, 'New Light', 516. For a reproduction of the payment of 2 Oct., see Van Hoorn, *Jacob Obrecht*, plate facing p. 102.   [18] Lockwood, *Ferrara*, 174–7.

to-date repertory, contacts with musicians working with him in the chapel or passing through the city, and indeed the sheer affluence and splendour of the Ferrarese court, of which he was now the chief musician.

Yet the dream was shattered within five months. On 25 January 1505 Duke Ercole d'Este died, and his successor Alfonso I, who inherited the ducal chapel, dismissed Obrecht almost immediately. The last opportunity for the composer to pay his musical respects to Ercole came on 5 February, when a mass *in canto figurato* was sung during the funeral services.[19] Hereafter his name no longer figures in the court accounts, with the exception of two minor payments in the following week. On 10 February Obrecht is listed as one of the members of the court entourage for whom taxes are paid; two days later, on 12 February, a debt of his is settled with the Ferrarese bankers Jacomo and Baldissera Machiavelli.[20]

It is unclear why Alfonso decided to dismiss Obrecht, whose mere presence at the court could only have enhanced his renown. Nor is it clear why the composer failed to obtain a position elsewhere in the next few months. Surely a man of his reputation, who had held one of the best-paid musical positions in Europe, should have done well in the atmosphere of cut-throat rivalry between the north Italian courts. Certainly it was not for want of trying. In early May, three months after he had lost his position at Ferrara, Obrecht tried his luck in Mantua. We know this from a letter of recommendation written on his behalf by Alfonso's brother Ferrante, and addressed to Marquis Francesco Gonzaga:[21]

Most Illustrious and Honoured Lord: *Messer* Hobreth, formerly master of the chapel of my late father, of blessed memory, the present bearer, is coming to Your Excellency to give you certain of his compositions. Even though he is possessed of such singular virtue that is always to be received warmly by you, as is your custom and habit towards every person of virtue, nevertheless, having requested of me that I might with these lines address myself to Your Excellency, as being a person whom I greatly love, beyond his merits, for his excellent character—it has seemed to me proper for his sake to give you this small notice of him and recommend him to Your Excellency, to whom I also commend myself. Farewell: Ferrara, 2 May 1505. Your Most Illustrious Lordship's Servant, Ferrante d'Este.

The letter raises several questions. Why should a composer whose works were circulating throughout Europe and had recently even been printed by Petrucci, need the recommendation of Ferrante? Why, despite this recommendation, did he fail to obtain a position in Mantua? Did not the

---

[19] Ibid. 208.   [20] Lockwood, 'Josquin at Ferrara', 118.
[21] Transcription and translation in Lockwood, *Ferrara*, 209.

north Italian princes send their agents as far as France and the Low Countries to buy good singers? Then why, if no one less than Obrecht was near at hand, was he unable to find employment?

A possible answer is suggested if we consider what would have obtained him a position immediately—without references, without giving 'certain of his compositions', without even being possessed of 'singular virtue'. There can only be one answer: a brilliant voice. For the Italian courts, even a mere report on the quality of a singer would be sufficient to have him come over, no matter from where, at great expense. That Obrecht lacked this quality is of course speculation, but several pieces seem to fall into place once we assume that this was the case. First, he was paid for a composition in Innsbruck, and may have undertaken a diplomatic journey for Maximilian, but was never appointed there as a singer. Secondly, Ferrarese documents describe him consistently as 'compositore de canto', whereas Josquin, in the same position, had been described equally consistently as 'cantore'.[22] This makes sense: clearly, of all Italian princes, only Ercole d'Este, who genuinely cared about Obrecht's *music*, would have been prepared to appoint him as a court composer rather than singer.[23] Equally clearly, his son Alfonso, who is unlikely to have shared this disposition, would have dismissed the expensive *maestro di cappella* immediately. Finally, Obrecht went to Mantua to present, significantly, 'certain of his compositions', armed with a recommendation in which there is no word on his merits as a singer. The fact that Obrecht asked Ferrante to write the letter in the first place can only mean that he expected little of the decisive test, a voice trial.

The assumption that Obrecht's voice, in his late forties, might have lost its former lustre (if indeed it had ever been a brilliant voice at all) could explain the surprisingly unsuccessful course of events after January 1505. It could also shed revealing light on his unique relationship with Ercole, which ended sadly in that month. With this remarkably enlightened music-lover, it seems, was buried the prospect of a better life. If Obrecht had been a court composer rather than singer in his service, then he would certainly have aimed for a similar position elsewhere. Yet this is precisely what the north Italian courts were not able to offer. Good singers brought direct, audible status; good composers only produced works that could be acquired anyway. In this sense the north Italian courts offered 'the better' only to the virtuosi, the stars. By nature they were not charitable

[22] Compare Murray, 'New Light', 516, and Lockwood, 'Josquin at Ferrara', 118, with ibid. 137.
[23] This might perhaps explain why Obrecht received only half the annual salary earned earlier by Josquin (see above).

institutions that, like St Donatian's in 1500, might help an ill and impoverished musician in times of hardship. The centres were fiercely competitive, and lavished their riches only on those who would add tangibly to their public splendour.

Apart from a possible trip to Mantua in May, Obrecht must have spent his last months in Ferrara. His prosperous life at the court had ended, yet he was not destitute, and he may well have continued to live in the house for which he had earlier received his housing allowance. Nor was he necessarily without work. As a priest Obrecht may well have been active in the Dutch or German communities in Ferrara, particularly since there was a lingering plague epidemic, which would have required him to administer the sacraments of the church to its victims, and to hear their confessions. The Black Death, in the late Middle Ages, no longer had the devastating psychological effect it had caused in the fourteenth century. It was a fact of life: the disease recurred in regular cycles throughout Europe, often lingered for years in a single town, rarely killing more than about ten per cent of the population. Mortality among the clergy had always been high, for obvious reasons. Yet for Obrecht the plague was evidently no reason to leave Ferrara. On the contrary, the increased need for pastoral care may well have persuaded him to stay. And thus it may have been through direct contact with sufferers that he finally became infected himself, probably in July 1505.

Once the symptoms emerged—a blackish pustule at the point of a flea bite followed by swollen lymph nodes and the notorious purple buboes—Obrecht must have been taken into the Ferrarese hospital of plague sufferers, for he was to bequeath nearly 100 ducats' worth of silver to this institution. This, and the fact that he could apparently afford such expensive treatment, suggests that the composer did not die a poor man. Yet money could not buy him any remedy beyond such ineffective treatments as blood-letting, lancing of buboes, nursing, and bed-rest. His days were numbered, and the time had come to prepare his soul for the afterlife. In remission of his sins, 'since he was a pious person', Obrecht donated various silver items to the plague hospital, leaving them for this purpose to the ducal counsellor Antonio di Costabelli. Five years after his death, on 12 March 1510, the city received their equivalent in cash, more than 302 lire (at this time about 7,500–8,000 Flemish groats), from Costabelli (Doc. 50):[24]

From the fabric of the new houses that are to be made above the hospital for

---

[24] I am most grateful to Bonnie Blackburn and Leofranc Holford-Strevens for transcribing and translating this record for me.

those infected by plague, 302 lire [and] 2 soldi in cash (?) for the aforesaid from the magnificent Messer Antonio di Costabelli, ducal counsellor, etc. for the value of six cups, six goblets, and a small gilded confectionery dish without feet, [all] of silver, which weighed in all one hundred and fifty-nine ounces, 159 oz., at 38 soldi per ounce, weighed and valued as such by the master of the mint, as he has so borne witness to me, which silver belonged to the late Messer Jacomo Obreth, formerly singer of our illustrious lord duke, and which since the year 1505 has remained in the possession of the aforesaid magnificent Messer Antonio, then governor and ducal commissary for the plague, after the death of the said Messer Jacomo, who died of the plague in that year in this city of Ferrara, to this end, that the moneys received for the said silver, together with the L. 181. [s.] 16 of which record was made in the account-book q.q.q. in credit to the said fabric on fo. 18, shall be converted to the said fabric of the said new houses . . . by the said Messer Jacomo, and in remission of his sins, since he was a pious person. And of the said silver notice was made in writing in the account-book m.m.m. at fo. 163, L. 302 s. 2 d. –.

Death came in July.[25] Obrecht's demise was not universally bewailed in the way that Ockeghem's had been eight years earlier, yet it did provoke some artistic responses. In August, the Ferrarese humanist poet Gasparo Sardi wrote two versions of an epitaph praising the composer's learning, art, voice, and invention in a fairly stereotyped way:[26]

Epitaph of Hobreht, musician: The musician Hobreht, learned, and second to none in art or invention, is buried in this tomb. *Concerning the same:* The musician Hobreht, most learned [and] second to none in art, voice, or invention, is buried here.

It is likely that Obrecht could afford to pay for a tomb in one of Ferrara's churches (if, as a plague victim, he was not consigned to a common ditch), and quite possibly either of Sardi's epitaphs was inscribed on the tomb-stone (if it was not a purely literary exercise). Yet wherever the composer was buried, his grave has not been identified, nor is it ever likely to be: undoubtedly it was removed at some point in the centuries following his death.

Another artistic response may have come from none other than Josquin

[25] This can be deduced from two applications for Obrecht's benefices by Jodocus Pipe and Johannes Talman, dated 1 Aug. 1505 (discovered by Richard Sherr, to whom I express my thanks for sharing this information). Before 1507 a 'Jacobus Obrechs' was listed under 27 June in the obituary of St Goedele's at Brussels; B. H. Haggh, 'Music, Liturgy, and Ceremony in Brussels, 1350–1500' (Ph.D. diss., University of Illinois, 1988), 640. It is not certain that this is the composer; Obrecht is not known to have had any connections with St Goedele's, yet nothing would argue against a death-date of 27 June.

[26] Transcribed after Van Hoorn, *Obrecht*, plate facing p. 106: 'Ephyt. Hobreht musicus: Musicus hoc Hobreht, doctus, nullique secundus †ingenio atque arte† [cancelled] arte vel ingenio, sarco-phago tegitur. De eodem: Musicus hic Hobreht, doctissimus, arte secundus nulli alio, tegitur, voce vel ingenio.'

des Prez. Willem Elders has argued persuasively that his motet *Absolve quaesumus Domine*, which is written entirely in black notes, may have been intended as a tribute to Obrecht.[27] The latter's name is admittedly not mentioned: at the expected point in the liturgical text ('animam famuli tui N ab omni vinculo delictorum'), the unique source gives only the letter 'N', for *nomen*. Yet the final phrase 'requiescat in pace, amen' contains altogether 97 notes, a number that could be interpreted as a symbolic representation of Obrecht's name (JACOB OBRECHT $= 9 + 1 + 3 + 14 + 2 + 14 + 2 + 17 + 5 + 3 + 8 + 19 = 97$).[28] What adds force to this interpretation is a striking analogy observed by Elders in Josquin's lament for Ockeghem, *Nymphes des bois*, which is similarly written in black notes. This setting ends with the same phrase 'requiescat in pace, amen', and as Jaap van Benthem observed, the number of notes in this final phrase, 64, undoubtedly represents Ockeghem's name (OCKEGHEM $= 14 + 3 + 10 + 5 + 7 + 8 + 5 + 12 = 64$). Since, moreover, the opening of *Absolve quaesumus* seems to allude to the Patrem of Obrecht's *Missa Fortuna desperata*, it is possible that Josquin interpreted Obrecht's death as the consequence of Lady Fortuna's capricious actions; now that his soul was beyond her reach, Josquin implored God the Father to absolve him, 'so that in the glory of the Resurrection he may rise to new life amid Thy Saints and chosen ones'.

Not all Obrecht's colleagues reacted quite so generously. As soon as the news of his death reached the household of Cardinal Galeotto della Rovere, Vice-Chancellor at the Vatican, two of its members immediately tried to secure two benefices he had held. On 1 August 1505, Jodocus Pipe and Johannes Talman submitted applications for the provostship at Torhout (which Obrecht had received in 1500) and the chaplaincy of St Judocus at Antwerp (which had been his since 1494). The same benefices were claimed two months later, on 30 September, by the Vatican singers Remigius de Mastaing and Bonus Radulphi, who asserted in their applications that Obrecht might have been a member of the papal chapel (see above).[29]

---

[27] For this and what follows, see W. Elders, 'Josquin's *Absolve, quaesumus, domine:* A Tribute to Obrecht?', *Tijdschrift van de Vereniging voor Nederlandse Muziekgeschiedenis*, 37 (1987), 14–24.

[28] Obrecht himself spelt his surname certainly as 'Hobrecht', which gives the number 105; cf. *Mille quingentis, Inter preclarissimas virtutes*, and the recently discovered portrait. (This should be taken into account when considering the far-reaching numerological speculations in K. Vellekoop, 'Zusammenhänge zwischen Text und Zahl in der Kompositionsart Jacob Obrechts: Analyse der Motette *Parce Domine*', *Tijdschrift van de Vereniging voor Nederlandse Muziekgeschiedenis*, 20 (1966), 97–119.) It is quite possible, however, that Josquin knew the name without the initial 'H', which was the usual spelling outside the county of Flanders (Wegman, 'Bergen op Zoom', 200).

[29] Richard Sherr has discovered documents showing that the chaplaincy of St Judocus went

This, then, is Obrecht's known legacy: two benefices, six cups, six goblets, and a small gilded confectionery dish without feet, all of silver, and a portrait. There is no will (such as we have for several other fifteenth-century composers), although one may well turn up eventually: it could tell us about his other possessions and their value, any friends and relatives that were still alive (his father had died in 1488, Busnoys in 1492, and Cordier in 1501), and about the perpetual commemoration services that he undoubtedly endowed for the safety of his soul. Of all the things Obrecht left in this world, it was only such services that he could have hoped to last until the present day, and beyond, until the end of time.[30] Everything else was transitory, his music more so than the rest. The international celebrities of his youth—Dufay, Ockeghem, Busnoys—were already figures of the past, superseded by the stars of the day—Josquin, Isaac, Obrecht—who in turn could only be superseded by younger generations, as time would continue to run its relentless course. Just as Obrecht must have witnessed the destruction of old and 'worthless' music, so his works would one day cease to sound, and eventually be discarded altogether. What else, then, could he expect from posterity but its prayers, provided he had made firm financial provisions for them? What other importance could his music, his life, ever have in future—except as they would be weighed on the Day of Judgement? What other expectation was there in the face of death, except—as he so often had set it to music—that 'He shall come again with glory to judge the quick and the dead; of whose kingdom there will be no end'?

If these were his dying thoughts, as the medieval *ars moriendi* recommended them, history so far has turned out to be different. Obrecht is no longer remembered in the way he, like his contemporaries, would have wanted to be remembered: with prayers and Masses in perpetuity. Our concern with the past is not eschatological, not dictated by the expectation of future judgement. We study the past for its own sake, judge it *now*, and aim to do so on its own terms. We retrieve and preserve it, pass it on to the future—that is *our* idea of perpetuity. And thus, ironically, it is Obrecht's music that has outlived any provisions he may have made for his commemoration, and will continue to live. It is his life that generations

---

eventually to Gherardus Ghigels, on 16 Feb. 1506. Ghigels's reception of the chaplaincy is recorded in the accounts of the Church of Our Lady at Antwerp (Piscaer, 'Jacob Obrecht', 13).

[30] For some 15th-c. composers the chain of perpetual remembrance has indeed remained unbroken: Nicholas Sturgeon (d. 1454) and John Plummer (d. 1484) are still commemorated on Obit Sundays in St George's Chapel, Windsor; see John Plummer, *Four Motets*, ed. B. Trowell (Banbury, 1968), 7. For the possibility that Obrecht was commemorated at the church of St Goedele, Brussels, see above, n. 25.

of scholars have gone to great pains to piece together, and will gain colour and depth with every further discovery. In this sense (if in no other) Obrecht and his music have transcended death: they live, because they are part of our experience, and constantly renew themselves as they enter more deeply into that experience. It is the inevitable consequence of that fascinating and intensely rewarding process that this study will soon be outlived by Obrecht's life and music as well, and will then be seen as more revealing of our time than his.

APPENDIX I

DOCUMENTS

Doc. 1 (17 April 1450): SAG 330.24, 1449/50², fo. 10ᵛ

Jan Hobrecht wert vooght van Ghijselin, Gheleynen, ende Betkin, Andries Gheeraerds kinderen, verstorven de patre. Actum xvij aprilis aᵒ l.

Doc. 2 (11 May 1450): SAG 330.24, 1449/50², fo. 20ᵛ

Kenlic etc. dat dit es den staet van goede toebehoerende Ghiselen, Ghelaine, ende Betkine, Andries Gheerarts kinderen bij Marien Laps filia Jacops, zijnen wettichen wive was, den vorscreven weesen toecommen, verschenen, ende verstorven van de vorscreven Andries, haerlieder vader was, daer zij hoir af zijn van den drien deelen van den viven, de gheele versterfte in viven ghedeelt, mids dat vanden andren ij deelen hoir zijn Jan Gheeraerts, der voorscreven weesen broeder, ende Kathelijne Gheeraerts, der weesen sustre, met Janne vander Baten, haren wettichen man. Welc goed Jan Hoebrecht als vooght vander vorscreven weesen upbrynct voor onse heeren scepenen etc. ghelijc dadt verdeelt es ieghen der weesen moedre, broeder, ende suster vornoemt bij ghemeenen maghen ende vrienden, ter weesen profijte. Eerst van xxxvj ghemeten lants, lettel min of meer, ghecocht binnen huwelicke vander weesen vadre ende moedre, gheleghen in diverse percheelen in de parochie van Steelant, Peerboeme, ende Willemskercke, met zulken commer van renten, cheinse, jaerghetijden, dycagen, wateringhe, ende anderssins, alsser jaerlicx uutgaet ende up vallen mach, dat der weesen vader ende moeder in haren handen hilden, ende de moeder noch besittende es. So behoort der weesen moeder toe deen heelt ende haren v kindren dander heelt, ghemeene ende onverdeelt, ende ander kindren heelt houdt de moedre de heelt tharer bijlevinghen. Item hebben de moedre ende haer v kindre ghemeene een huus ende hofstede te Hughersluus, met zulken cheinse alsser uutgheldende x sc. gr. tsiaers. Item hebben zij insghelijcx een huus met stroe ghedect up Meersem binnen Ghend, met iij gr. v miten siaers uutgaende, verhuert viij sc. gr. tsiaers, daer af men sculdich Jacop Gauwe boven betaelinghen noch vij lb. v sc. gr. Item hebben de v kindre te Hughersluus een huus omme af te doene hemlieden ghemeene toebehoorende. Item vander Jan Gheeraerts ende Katelijne Gheeraerts, zijn zustre, met Janne vander Baten, haren man, der weesen broeder ende suster, van vader ende moeder thuwelike gheadt hebben ende elc van hem beeden xx lb. gr., so zijn de drie weesen vander heelt vander

imbringhene van dienen begroodt metten hoveliken ende cateyliken goede ten-
selven sterfhuuse elc toot x lb. gr. Ende bovendien es den voorscreven iij weesen
ghebuert vander selven hoveliken ende catteylijken goede, te wetene Ghiselen
zeker cateylen dien hij temwaerts heeft toot omtrent xij sc. ij den. gr., ende
Ghelainkin ende Betkine te gadre iij lb. x sc. gr. Comt als vorscreven Ghelains
ende Betkins deel xxiij lb. x sc. gr. rustende onder de moedre, versekert also hier
onder verklaert es, ende vorde x lb. gr. dien Ghiselen ghebueren vander begroe-
tinghen vander huwelic goede vorscreven, heeft hij eene stede met ij schueren,
een pesterije metten plecken, ende xj ghemeten zomerbruchten metten pachtlande groot xxvj ghemeten, al inde parochye van Steelant, dies sal hij der moeder
moeten goetdoen xj lb. gr. also zij dies eens zijn, twelcke hij selve midsdien hij
vere tsijnen jaren ende vroetscepen commen es, regeren ende manteneren sal
tsijne proffijte. Item in sculden van baten der moeder ende den v kinderen
toebehoorende dat zij meernen dat ghecruchelike [sic] sculdich zijn an vele di-
versse persoone lxv lb. xij sc. j den. gr. Voort zijn de moeder ende haer
v kinderen jaerlicx sculdich vrouwe Lisbetten van Munte, weduwe Gillis van
Graven, xvij lb. parisis siaers lijfrenten tharen live onbesedt. Item in sculden van
commere die men der moedere ende haren v kinderen heesschende es van divers-
schen persoonen, te wetene van achterstelle van pachtlande, xxij lb. vij sc. iiij
den. gr. Ende daer boven in anderen diverssen sculden van commere lvij lb. ix
den. gr. Ende noch bovendien Janne Ghuus van coepe van zekeren erven daer der
weesen vader voortijts jeghen hem cochte vij lb. iiij sc. gr. naer dinhouden vander
kennesse die daer af es. Ende quame namaels onversiene bate af commere elken
daer afstaende in sinen rechte, ende de moedere heeft belooft hare vornoemde iij
weesen te houdene met huerlieder somme vanden ghereeden ghelde vooren verclaert, onghemindert den principale, ende metten baten ende bladinghen jaerlicx
commende vander weesen ervachtichede ende huusinghen, van etene, drinckene,
cleedinghen, abijten, ende alre sustinanchien, dies hemlieden behouden sal redelic ende tamelic naer huerlieder staet. Ende sal der weesen recht van husen
houden te ghereke van dake ende van weeghe redelic ende tamelic ghelden ende
weensde bonie . . . ende seinsen ende lasten uter weesen goedinghen gaende ende
dien upvallen moghen, al sonder der weesen cost. Twelken metgader der vorscreven somme van xxiij lb. x sc. gr. Ghelaine ende Betkine toebehoerende, de
moedere heeft bekent ende versekert up haer ende up al thare ende vort zijn
borchen ende elc over al Jan Gheeraerts, haer zone, Jan vander Baten, haer
behuwede zone, ende Philips Kempenen. Ende hierup kenden hemlieden tvor-
screven hoyr ende oec principalic de vooght inder name vanden weesen wel
vereffent, verdeelt, ende al wel om steeden jeghen der weesen moeder vander
versterften van Andries Gheeraerts vorscreven. Ende inghelijcx der moeder jeghen hare voorscreven kinderen ende hebben daer af elc andere quite ghescolden.
Ende de vorscreven Jan Hoebrecht wort verlaten vander vorscreven vooghdije
ende de moeder wart vooght van haren voornoemden weesen, ende heeft als
vooght in de name van haren weesen Janne Hoebrecht gheel ende al quite
ghescolden van al den handelinghen die hij vander weesen goede gheadt heeft,
niets ute ghesondert. Actum xj maij a° l.

Doc. 3 (autumn of 1451): SAG 301.42, 1451/2, fo. 25^r

Naer de handelinghe van ghedinghe gheweest etc. tusschen Gheeraert van den
Velde ende Arende Yman alias Van der Meer over hemlieden, ende over de
ghuldebroeders ghemeenlic van den gulde van Sent Andriese dat men nomt
tgulde van den trompetters in Ghend, van een zijde, ende Janne Muelenijser,
guldebroeder vanden zelven gulde, over andere, spruutende uut zekere ghescille
dat de vorscrevene Jan Muelenijsere gheadt ofte ghemaect adde tusschen hem
ende eeneghen anderen guldebroeders van de gulde voren ghenomt, de de vorscrevene guldemeesters tanderen tijden versocht adden te hemlieden waerts te
hebbene volghende haerlieden zeghele ende ordinanchie die zij adden van den
selven gulde van outer tijden . . . (The remainder is missing, but a space of
approximately three times the size of this entry has been left blank to add further
text.)

Doc. 4 (24 November 1452): SAG 301.42, 1452/3, fo. 18^r

Wij scepenen ende raed vander stede van Ghend doen te wetene alle den ghenen
die deze presente brieven sullen sien of horen lesen dat, omme de eerbaerheit,
nutscip, ende proffit vanden vorscrevenen stede, ende ten fyne dat de selve van
nu voortan duechdelic bewaert soude sijn, also zoe wel van node heeft van abelen
ghesellen antierende de trompetten, uut laste vanden drie leden vanden vornoemder stede onthouden hebben ter vorscrevener stede behouf Ghisel de
Keyser, Theeus Nijs, Roel Ghijs, Willem Oebrecht, Loykin Ghijs, ende Jan
Toysbaert, trompetters, haerlieder leven lanc duerende. Ende hebben hemlieden
uuter name vanden selven stede toegheleyt over haerlieder jaerlicxse wedden
elken iij lb. gr. ende twee abijten siaers, te wetene een strijpt ende een pleyn
vanden stede goede, up welke wedden ende abijten de vorscrevene stede te diene
ende de heeren vanden selven stede te bewaerne alsoot behoeren sal. In orcon-
scepe der waeheden [sic] so hebben wij scepenen ende raed als boven deze
presente beseghelt etc.

Doc. 5 (1453/4): SAG 400.17, 1453/4, fo. 386^r

Item ghegheven bij laste van scepenen den vj trompetten van dezer stede, van
datzij waren metten ghedeputeerden van dezer stede ter vorscr. plaatsen [Rissele]
ten schietspele in hoofscheden, xxiiij sc. gr.

Doc. 6 (8 November 1454): SAG 400.18, 1454/5, fo. 30^r

Item ghegheven ten beveelne van scepenen den viij sten dach in november
Willem Hoebrecht over hemzelven ende zijnen andere v ghesellen, trompetten
van dezer stede in hoofscheden, thulpen haerlieder costen van datzij trocken te
Rissele bij onzen gheduchten heere den grave van Charrolois, ter feesten ende
steecspele daer wezende, ij lb. gr.

Doc. 7 (8 July 1456): SAG 400.18, 1455/6, fos. 74^r and 96^r

Item ghegheven ten bevele van scepenen den vj trompetten van dezer stede in hooscheden, doe zij trocken in Hollant bij onzen gheduchten heer ende prince den xiij^{en} dach in hoymaent anno lvj, xx sc. gr.

Doc. 8 (7 March 1457): SAG 400.18, 1456/7, fos. 258^r and 348^r

Item ghegheven bij laste als boven den vj trompetten van dezer stede thulpen haerer costen, datzij trocken te Bruessele om der blijder mare wille van der edeler gheboorte vander dochter van onzen gheduchten heere minen heere den grave van Charrolois, naer tverclaers vander cedulle actum vij^a martij anno lvj [1457 NS], iiij sc. gr.

Doc. 9 (February 1457): LAN B3661, fo. 17^v

A Rolland Ghijs et Ghiselin de Kesere et leurs compaignons, trompettes et clarons de la ville de Gand, que mondit seigneur de Charrollois leur a fait donner pour lour vin, nagaires quilz sont venuz de la ville de Gand pour jouer au baptisement de lenfant de mondit seigneur a Brouxelles en ce present mois de fevrier. En xx escus dor de xlviij gr. la piece, xxiiij lb.

Doc. 10 (April/May 1457): SAG 400.18, 1456/7, fos. 258^v and 348^v

Item ghegheven ten beveelne van scepenen den vj trompetten van dezer stede van datzij bij consente van scepenen vornomt ute gheweest hebben te Brugghe metten Oosterlinghen in hoofscheden naer tverclaers vander cedulle van haeren peerde hueren, vij sc. gr.

Doc. 11 (May 1457): LAN B3661, fo. 39^v

A Rolland Ghijs et Ghiselin de Keyser et leurs compaignons, trompettes de la ville de Gand, que mondit seigneur lez a fait donner pour leur vin, destre venu jouer a Bruges ausdites joustes. En vj florins de rin, vj lb.

Doc. 12 (26 June 1459): SAG 301.45, 1458/9, fo. 125^v

Scepenen vanden keure, ter neerendster bede ende versoucke van hooichen ende moghende prince mijnen heere den hertoghe van Cleve, hebben gheconsenteert dat Pieter Beys, ontfangher ende tresorier vanden stede goede, leenen sal den zesse trompetters ende claroenners die trecken zullen ten dienste van mijnen vorscrevenen heere van Cleve int voyage bij hem anghenomen te doene uuter name van onsen harden gheduchten heer ende prince bij onsen heleghen vadere den paeus van Roeme ter dachvaert te Manto in Lombaerdien, omme hemlieden op te stellene inden selven dienst, de somme van zesse ponden gr., zonder dat die somme hemlieden afghetrocken ende ghediffalkaert sal werden van hueren wedden binnen den tijde dat zij uut sullen wesen, maar sullen haerlieden wijfs die wedden ontfaen telker maend omme hemlieden ende huere kindren daer op te levene binnen de vornoemde reise. Ende den selven trompetters ende claroenners wedercommen ziinde van den vornoemden dienste, so sal de stede de vorscrevene somme afslaen ende diffalkieren van huerlieder wedden, die dan vallen zullen inden dienst vanden stede, int welke de vornoemde trompetters ende claroenners ende elc sonderlinghe huer consent ende beloofte ghedaen hebben. Actum xxvj junij anno lix.

Doc. 13 (1459): SAG 400.19, 1458/9, fo. 358ʳ

Item ghegheven ten bevele van scepenen den zesse trompetten van dezer stede, achtervolghende den scrivene van harde, hoghe, ende moghende prince minen heere den hertoghe van Cleve, thulpen den coepe van hoirlieder peerden, doezij trocken te Mantua met minen vornoemden heere, die daer trat uter name van onzen harde gheduchten heer ende prince, naer tverclaert vander cedulle, vj lb. gr.

Doc. 14 (13 November 1459): Vatican City, Archivio Segreto Vaticano, Reg. Vat. 506, fo. 142ᵛ

Pius etc., universis Christi fidelibus presentes litteras inspecturis salutem etc. Gloriosus et excelsus Dominus, qui sua mundum ineffabilj claritate illuminat, commovet et excitat cunctos Christi fideles ad benefaciendum, ut per opera sua bona eterne beatitudinis retributiones premia ac munera valeant et mereantur reportare. Cum itaque sicut accepimus dilecti filij Gisbertus Cesaris alias de Keyser, Rolandi Gijs, Mattheus Nijs, Ludovicus Gijs, Villhelmus Obrecht, Johannes van Alterer et Arnoldus de Keyser, laici opidi Gandavensis, Tornacensis diocesis, dilecti filij nobilis viri Johannis ducis Clivensis tubicine⟨s⟩, cupientes terrena in celestia et transitoria in eterna felici commertio commutare, pro suarum et progenitorum ac amicorum suorum animarum salute de bonis a Deo sibi collatis, quandam capellam ad honorem et reverentiam ac sub vocabullo [sic] Sancti Andree in ecclesia Sancti Johannis dicti opidi, et in cripta eiusdem ecclesie sitam, construi et edificari fecerint, ipsaque capellania capellano seu capellanis in divinis inibi deservientibus, ampliatione, necnon calicibus, libris et alijs ornamentis ecclesiasticis egeat, atque ipsius capellanie non suppetant facultates, sintque propterea Christi fidelium suffragia plurimum oportuna, nos cupientes ut dicta capellania congruis honoribus frequentetur, ac ornamentis ecclesiasticis decenter et fulciatur, et in suis structuris debite conserventur, inibique in divinis laudabiliter deserviatur, et ut fideles ipsi eo libentius devotionis causa ad illam confluant, ac ad illius conservationem et augmentationem huiusmodi eo promptius manus porrigant adiutrices, quo ex hoc ibidem dono celestis gratie uberius conspexerint se refectos de omnipotentis Dei misericordia ac beatorum Petri et Paulj apostolorum, eius auctoritate confissi, omnibus vere penetentibus et confessis qui in Sancti Andree et Sancti Lazari ac Nativitatis Sancti Johannis Baptiste et Sancti Johannis Evangeliste necnon Penthecostes festivitatibus, et per earumdem festivitatum octava, ac in prima die veneris Quadragesime et feria iijᵃ post festum Resurrectionis Dominice, dictam capellaniam devote visitaverint annuatim, ac ad conservationem et augmentationem predictas manus porrexerint adiutrices, singulis eorum festivitatibus a primis vesperis usque ad secundas vesperas, ac die veneris et feria iij^a supradictis, tres annos et totidem quadragenas de iniunctis eis penitentijs misericorditer relaxamus, presentibus perpetuis futuris temporibus duraturis. Datum Mantue anno Incarnationis Dominice millesimo quadringentesimo quinquagesimo nono idibus novembris, pontificis nostri anno secundo.

Doc. 15 (30 July 1460): SAG 330.28, 1459/60, rolle, fo. 21^r

Jan Hobrecht wart vooght van Willem Hoebrechts kinde bij Lysbette Gheerarts, verstorven de matre. Actum xxx julij a^o lx.

Doc. 16 (30 July 1460): SAG 330.27, 1459/60, fo. 127^r

Kenlic etc. dat dit es den staet van goede toebehoerende Copkin Hoebrecht filius Willems bij Lysbette Gheeraerts, zijnen wettigen wive was, der vornoemder weese toecommen ende verstorven etc. bijden overlijden vander vorscreven Lysbetten, zijnder moeder was, welc goed Jan Oebrecht als vooght vanden vornoemden weesen upbrynct etc., ghelijc dat ten steerfhuse vander vornoemden Lysbette, ziere moeder was, verdeelt, verheffent, ende ghepoint es jeghen Willeme, zijnen vader vornoemt, ter presentie ende bijzijne van ghemeenen maghen etc., thaldermeesten orbueren ende profijten vanden selven weese. Eerst verclaert de vornoemde vooght hoe dat de vornoemde weese heeft hem verstorven bijden overlijden vander voorseiden Lysbette, zijnder moeder was, van harer zijde commende tvierendeel duergaende van xvj gemeten lants, lettel min of meer, heffende iiij gemeten ligghende ende streckende in vele diversche sticken ende percheelen binnen der prochien van Steelant bij Hugherslus in Asseneden ambocht, met zulken bomen ende catheilen alsmer up bevinden mach ende met zulken commere ende laste van dicagen, ghescote, ende anderssins alser jaerelijcx uutgaet etc., verpacht in advenante van ij sc. vj den. gr. siaers elc gemet, der weesen vierendeel van desen lande ligghende ghemeene ende onverdeelt met Janne ende Ghelayne Gheerarts, ghebroeders, ende Catheline Gheerarts, haerlieder zuster, met Cornelis Beelenzone, haer man, der weesen oems ende moye, an welc vierendeel van desen lande der weesen toebehoerende Marije Laps wedewe van Andries Gheerarts, nu Jan Wolfaerts wijf, der weesen grootvrouwe vander moederliker zijde, behoudt deene heeltsceede duergaende tharer bijlevynghe haer leven lanc gheduerende, ende an dander heelft van desen, die de weese hebben moet, behoudt de vornoemde Willem zien vader de heelft te zijnder bijlevynghen oec zijn leven lanc gheduerende, aldus en heeft de vornoemde weese van dese nu ter tijt duergaende maer heffens tprofijt vanden j. gemet lants zonder meer, elke ghehouden inde commer ende last diere jaerelijcx uutgaet ende up vallen mach alzo verre alser elc baten in heft alzoot behoort. Item esser zeker erfachtighede gheleghen ende streckende binnen de vornoemde prochien van Steelant ende in Axelambocht, ghecocht ende ghecreghen met ghemeenen goede binnen den huwelicke vanden vornoemden Willem ende Lysbette Gheerarts, der weese vader ende moeder, dats te weten ij gemeten lants gheleghen onder dander vander vorscreven xvj gemeten lants wijlen ghecocht jeghen Katheline Gheerarts met Cornelyse Beelenzone, haren man vornoemt, ende iij gemeten gheleghen teenen streke in Axelambocht binnen der vrijheden van Hugher sluus, elcx van desen twee percheelen van lande lettel min of meer ombegrepen met zulcken commere alser jaerelicx uutgaet, de vornoemde ij gemeten verpacht ter tijt van nu ij sc. vj den. groten siaers gemeten, ende de vornoemde ander iij gemeten verpacht .x. sc. gr. siaers boven commere, ende van desen ij percheelen van erven ghecocht binnen huwelyc behoort de vornoemde weese als erfachtige proper toe deen heelft, ende Willeme zijnen vader dander heelft, ende anden weese behoudt de selve Willem de heelft te zijnder bijlevynghe zijn leven lanc gheducrende, elken ghehouden inden commere diere jaerelicx uutgaet ende ancleeft, alzo verre alser elc bate in heft alzoot behoort, ende vanden catheilen diemen up al bevinden mach elken hebbende zijn aendeel, etc. Item verclaert de vornoemde vooght dat de vornoemde weese heeft in ghereeden ghelde commende van zijnder heeltsceeden van alder ghereede goede, juweelen, inhaven, ende catteilen, metgaders der scult van baten, bleven, ende vonden ten steerfhuse vander vorscreven Lysbetten, zijnder moeder was, dat de vornoemde Willem, der weesen vader, bij duegdelike prijsyen daer af leden ende gesciet, bij rade, advyse, ende overeendraghene van ghemeenen maghen ende vrienden van der vornoemden weesen, ten alder meesten orbuere etc., vander selver weesen alte male gheaenveerdt ende an hem ghesleghen heeft, ende ditte boven der weesen last van Lysbette, zijnder moeder was, testamente, sepulturen, ende uutfaert met dies daer an cleefde, ende boven allen commeren, costen, ende lasten diemen der vornoemden weesen heeschen mochte ter causen vander versterfte vander vorscreven Lysbetten, zijnder moeder was, danof de vornoemde Willem belooft heeft zijne vornoemde weese vrij, costeloos, ende al scadeloes te houden ende te quyten zuver ende net de somme van iij lb. gr. rustende onder Willem, der weesen vader vornoemt, met welke somme onghemindert der principale, ende metten baten ende bladen jaerelicx commende vanden weesen goede voren verclaerst, de vornoemde Willem belooft heeft zijne vorscreven weese te houden van etene, drynken, cleederen, coussen, scoens, etc., ende voort van alder sustinanchien, etc., ende boven dien te ghelden ende weerene ende te betaelene der weesen porcie ende aendeel vanden commere jaerlicx gaende uuten vorscreven percheelen van goede, zonder der weesen cost oft last, al dewelke metgaders der somme voren verclaert etc., de vornoemde Willem bekent ende verzekert heeft up hem ende up al tzijne, ende voort zijn borghen over hem ende elc over al, Victoer Symoens ende Pieter Clays, sceppere. Verclarynghe dat Lysbette, der weesen moeder, up dat zo ghebeden hadde de doot van Maijen Laps, wedewe Andries Gheerarts, haer moeder, vanden goede dat den steerfhuse vander selver Marien toebehoeren zoude voren uut ghehadt zoude hebben, in recompensatie ende begroetinghe van tghuent dat Janne Gheerarts ende Catteline Gheerarts met Cornelyse Beelenzone, haer man, haer broeder ende zuster wijlen waren, thuwelyc ghegheven was bijder selver Maijen ende Andriese haer man, x lb. gr. eenswechdraghende, ne maer omme dat de vornoemde Lysbette, der weesen moeder, nu overleden es der weerelt, zoe moet de selve weese ter doot vander vornoemden Maijen, zijnder grootvrouwe, up dat hijt ghebiedt hem af staen in de stede vander vornoemden Lysbette, zijnder moeder, omme dan de vornoemde x lb. gr. voren uute te hebbene al eer dander hoyr van Maijen yet deelen zullen ghelijc dat tanderen tijden bij maghen ende vrienden gheordonneert gheweest es, an welken x lb. gr. de vornoemde Willem pretendeert recht thebbene, ende hier af elken staende in zijnen rechte om ter doot vanden vornoemde Maijen te gheschiene alzo verre als recht bewijsen sal. Up dwelke de vooght scalt quyten der weesen vader vander versterften vander weesen moeder etc., ende kenden hem verdeelt etc. wart vooght van zijnen vornoemden kinde. Actum xxxᵃ julij aᵒ lx.

Doc. 17 (5 August 1461): SAG 301.46, 1460/1, fo. 122ᵛ

Kenlic dat Ghiselbrecht de Keysere, Willem Obrecht, Jan van Aeltere, Mathijs Nijs, Lodewijc Ghijs, ende Roelant commen zijn eendrachtelic voor scepenen, lieden sculdich ziinde Michiel Baert de somme van xxvij lb. ellef sc. iiij den. gr. goeden scult, van zes selveren trompetten die hij hemlieden ghelevert ende ghemaect heeft, welke somme zij belooft hebben de vornoemde Michiel te betaelen te vij terminen ende payementen van drie maenden te drie maenden, daeraf deerste payement vallen sal den vierden dach van november naestcommende. Versekert up hemlieden ende up althaer ende elc over al. Actum den vᵗᵉⁿ dach van oughste lxj.

Doc. 18 (20 August 1462): HAR, Grafelijkheidsrekenkamer 5586, chapter 'Pijpers en Herauden'

Item den xxᵉⁿ dach in Augusto bij bevele van mijnen heer, dair Aerst vanden .A. die boidscip of dede, gegeven vij trompetten die bij mijnen heer waeren ten Brielle, toebehorende mijnen genadigen heer van Charloys ende de stede van Gendt, viij post. gulden facit xviij sc. gr.

Doc. 19 (8 August 1464): HAR, Grafelijkheidsrekenkamer 5588, chapter 'Pijpers en Herauden'

Item den viijᵉⁿ dach in Augusto bij bevele van mijnen heer, dair Aerst vander A die boidscip af dede, gegeven vj trompetten die gheen britsen en hadden, ende seiden datse bij mijnen heer van Charrolois wouden, die doe tot Gorinchem was, iij postulatus gulden facit vj sc. ix gr.

Doc. 20 (17 September 1464): SAG 330.30, 1464/5, rolle fo. 6ᵛ

Willem Obrecht ter causen van Beatrisen Jacops, zijnen wive, vliet sghedeels vanden versterfte van Pieter Jacops, zijns wijfs vader was, ende en beghert vanden zelven versterfte bate te heffene noch commer te gheldene naer de wet vanden poort. Actum xvijᵉⁿ dach septembris aᵒ lxiiij.

Doc. 21 (25 April 1465): SAG 301.48, 1464/5, fo. 81^r

Kenlic etc. dat Willem Oebrecht ende Beatricen Jacops, sijn wettich wijf, commen sijn etc., kenden ende lijden dat zij hebben vercocht wel ende redelic Lievin
vanden Speye alsulc deel ende recht van erven, bossche, ende erfelijker rente als
zij hebben ligghende binnen der vrijheit ende prochie van Eecloe, Wackene,
Waerscoote, ende Lembeeke, der voorscrevene Beatricen toecommen ende ver-
stoorven van Lysbetten Smeets, harer moeder was. Desen coop es ghedaen omme
eene sekere somme van penninghen danof hem de voornoemde Willem ende
Beatrice, siin wijf, kenden zijnde vernoucht ende wel betaelt, ende scolden den
voornoemde Lievin daer af wettelic quite. Ende de voornoemde Willem ende sijn
wijf over hemlieden, haerlieder hoyr, ende naercommeren, de voorscrevene par-
cheelen van erven ende goede paysivelic te doen ende laten ghebrukene jeghen
alle de ghenen die hem eenich beledt, ontpasschement of onghebruuc daer af
soude mueghen of willen doen, in wat manieren dat ware, belovende voort den
voorscreven Lievin ter erven te doene vanden voornoemden percheelen van
erven, telker plaetschen daer die gheleghen es, hand ende mont doende, ten coste
vanden selven Lievin tallen tijden alst hem ghelieven sal. Actum xxv aprilis a° lxv.

Doc. 22 (23 February 1467): LAN B2064, fo. 66^v

A Ghijsbrecht de Keysere, Matheus Nijs, Loys Ghijs, Jehan Aelteman, Willem
Obrecht et Adrian de Keysere, trompettes de guerre de mondit seigneur de
Charrolois, la somme de quatre livres ung solz monnaie dicte pour don, que
mondit seigneur de sa grace leur a fait pour une fois au jour de son partenir de
ladicte ville de Gand, pour ce par leur quittance faicte le xxiij jour dudit mois de
fevrier oudit an lxvj [1467 NS] ladit somme de iiij lb. i s.

Doc. 23 (10 February 1468): SAG 301.49, 1467/8, fo. 63^v

Naer de ansprake die Eloy Ghijs als dekin, Mattheus Nijs, Jan van Haeltert, Jan
Smesman, ende Lievin van Merchem als proviserers vanden Gulde van Sent
Andries ende Sent Lazarus inde crocht van Sent Jans kerke binnen Ghend,
daden Ghiselbrechte de Keysere voor scepenen van kuere in Ghend, toghende
dat de selve Ghiselbrecht biden lesten huerlieder voorsaten dekin ende proviserers gheweest vanden voorscreven gulde ghecondampneert hadde gheweest van
meshuze in zekere boeten, naer den huutwisene van zekeren wettichen brieven
den voorscreven gulde tandren tiden verleent bij heeren ende wette, welke boete
hij gheweyghert adde ende te legghene ende te betalene, begheerende mids dien
hem bedwonghen te hebbene ter betalinghe van dien. So waest dat de vornoemde
Ghiselbrecht, naer dat hij gheseit adde dat hem tvornoemde gulde, waer af hij ter
date van desen ghestelt was in sinen rechte, up tselve gulde hem submiteerde
ende bleefs bij onderwisene van scepenen vornoemt vanden vorscreven boeten,
int segghen vanden vorscreven dekin ende proviserers consenterende, int hin-
hauden vanden voorscreven letteren bij heer ende wette ghegheven, ende die
approberende in alzo verren alst in hem es, waer af de vorscreven dekin ende

proviserers begheerden te hebbene acte, die hem gheconsenteerd was bij desen. Actum x^a dach februario lxvij [1468 NS].

Doc. 24 (1 January 1470): BAR, Rekenkamer 1925, fo. 335^r

A Rolant Ghijs, Matheeus Nijs, Loys Ghijs, Jehan de Altere, Aernekin de Keysere et Guillaume Obrecht, trompettes et clarons de la ville de Gand, la somme de dix livres dudit pris, que mondit seigneur a de sa grace donné pour une fois pour semblable estrine; pour ce par leur quictance ladicte somme de vj lb.

Doc. 25 (30 April 1470): SAG 301.50, 1469/70, fo. 99^v

Kenlic etc. dat Willem Oebrecht, trompere, commen es etc., kende dat hij heeft vercocht wel ende redelic Pietren tHaerne, cleedecoeper, eene selveren trompe; desen coop es ghedaen omme iiij sc. ij den. gr., elke onse, draghende in gheele xxix onssen xij½ inghelse, loopt te gadere in ghelde boven betaelt vj lb. xix sc. gr., welke somme de voornoemde Pieter den selven Willem belooft heeft te betaelen met vj gr. de weke, waer af deerste vj gr. vallen sullen in saterdaghe den lesten dach van meye in dit jaer lxx eerstcommende ende also voort alle saterdaghe daer naer volghende vj gr. gheldende toot de voorscreven gheele somme vul betaelt sal sijn. Ende bij dat Pieter vuer weken thenden een liete overlijden sonder vulle betalinghe daer af te doene, so consenteert hij dat de gheele somme of reste van diere al ghevallen sal sijn dwelke hij bekent ende versekert heeft etc. ende voort up sijn huus staende in de Buerchstrate, mijn heere vanden Gruuthuuse ghehuust an deen zijde, ende meester Pieter Boudins an dander. Actum ultima aprilis lxx.

Doc. 26 (11 and 15 November 1471): SAG 400.23, 1471/2, fo. 91^r–v

Item betaelt Willem Hoebrecht van dat hij reed achter de stede metten trompette ende becondichde de blijde tijdinghe vanden gheallyerden vanden Coninc Frenant ende onzen vornoemden harde gheduchten heere ende prinche, den xj^en dach van november anno lxxj, van zijnder rede, xij den. gr. Item Willem Hoebrecht van dat hij reed metten trompette achtre de stede ende becondichde de generale processie ghehouden te zine binnen dezer stede ter causen vander voorscrevener blijder tijdinghe vanden Coninc Frenant van Cecylien ende onzen vornoemden heere. Actum xv^a dach novembris, anno lxxj, xij den. gr.

Doc. 27 (19 February 1472): SAG 301.51, 1471/2, fo. 13^v

Alse van der handelinghe gheweest voor scepenen etc., tusschen Jan Houtrappe, als dekin met ziere gheswornen provisers vanden gulde van Sente Andries ende Sente Lazarus dat men hout Sente Jans in den crocht bij den ghesellen die hem gheneren metter conste van trompen ende pijpene, of een zijde, ende Stoffel Ghijs, gilde broeder int voorseide gulde, of andre, ghespruut ter causen van dat de selve Stoffele, contrarie zekeren ordinantie bij den voorseiden gulde breeder ghemaect ende onderhouden, ende ooc gheconfirmeert bij heere ende wette, tandren tijden dienst ghenomen ende ghedaen heeft met eenen vremden man, die int voorseide gulde niet en es, dair an hij verbuert hadde, naer vertwijsen den selven ordinantie, de boete van xij gr. ende voort gheroert, omme dat hij daeraf ghecalengiert zijnde alsoet behoorde, ende voor hemlieden betrocken, gheseyt hadde omme dat deken ende provisers voorseit hem ghewijst hadden in de vorseide boete, dat zij ghewijst hadden een quaet . . . vonnese, daer an hij verbuert hadde, alzo zij houden, de boete van iij lb. parisis, die zij overghegheven hadden den heeren ende scepenen. Naer versouc kende den vornomden Stoffele bedwonghen thebbene tonderhoudene de voorseide ordinantie ende over te legghen de voorseide boete ende boven dien ghecorrigeert van ad hemlieden in exemple anderen van ghelijken te wachtene. Waer toe de voorseide Stoffel dede verandworden dat hij den voorseiden dienst ghedaen hadde binnen der stede van Thielt, daer haer de voerseide ordinantie niet en bestreckene, dies hij hem wel ghedrouch in scepenen voernomt, want de selve ordinancien niet en behoren breeder noch voorder verstaen te zijne dan binnen der vrihede ende scependomme van der vorseider stede, ende annoppende de woorden: 'Mach wesen'. Als deken ende provisers hem, Stoffele, ghewijst hadden tgund dat voerseit naer dat hij uut onverduldicheden seyde, dat zij hem ghewijst hadden een quaet vonnesse omme de redene voeren ghealligiert, meenende niet te messeghene ende bijdien dede sluten ontsleghen te zijne van de voorseide ansprake, ten welken de voorseide dekin ende proviserers deden repliqueren dat al tghuend dat hij dede allegieren tsijne ontscult hut gheene stede hadde, want hij Stoffele den dienst die hij dede te Thielt ghenomen hadde met eenen vrijen man ende dien daer gheleit ende daer wesende eenen andren onvrijen ghenomen ende met hem den dienst ghedoen presenteerde dat te doen blijckene up dat hijt ontkende, met mer woorden an brede zijden gheallegiert. So waert dat scepenen, naer ghehoort hebbene de voorseide handelinghe, ende gheledt up de jonchede ende clene verstanesse van den voorseiden Christoffele, wijsden den Stoffele te comene in zondaghe naestcommende tSent Jans in den crocht voorseit ter messe van den voorseiden gulde brouders, ende elcx te biddene, dekin ende provisers, up zinen eenen knye dat hij hem over de minne van Gode de voorseide woorde vergheven wilden sonder mer te desen tijt ende onghehouden breedert betalende de de [*sic*] voorseide xij groten. Actum xix sporcle lxxj [1472 NS].

Doc. 28 (2 October 1477): SAG 301.54, 1477/8, fo. 24ʳ

Scepenen vander kuere in Ghend, ghehoort tversouc ghedaen bij Roelant Ghijs, trompette der zelven stede, omme bedwonghen thebbene Pieteren de Gruter als borghe voor mijnen heer van Archy hem te betalen ende over te legghene de somme van twalef pond gr. van dienste bij hem ghedaen als trompette in doorloghe, wijsden inde kennesse bij den vorscreven Pieteren ghedaen vanden vornoemden bortocht te betalen den vorscreven Roelant Ghijs de zelve somme van xij lb. gr. te iij payementen te wetene deen derde te lichtmesse, dander derde te meydaghe, ende tderde derde over de vulle betalinghe talfougst int jaer lxxviij al eerstcommende. Behouden dien eest zoo dat binnen middelen tijde de vornoemde Pieter eeneghe betalinghe betoghen can ghedaen zijnde bijden vorscreven heer

van Archy, oft yement anders van zijn weghe up de vornoemde somme van ij lb.
gr. dat hem die afslach ende payement doen sal ende hem Pieteren staende in zijn
rechte up den zelven heer van Archy also zijn goede raad ghedraghen zal. Actum
ij in october aº lxxvij.

Doc. 29 (21 December 1479): SAG 301.55, 1479/80, fo. 84ᵛ

Kenlic etc. dat Jan Hauttrappe, tromper, kende dat hij vercocht heeft wel ende
dueghdelic Willem vanden Hulse ende Willem Oebrecht, ende Pieter van Lijze,
Arend Ghijs, ende Michiel vanden Hueke, als dekens ende provizerers van Sente
Andries ende Sente Lazarus Gulde van Sente Jans kercke inde crocht binnen
dezer stede, ende datte ten gulde behoef, de somme van xj sc. gr. siaers erflic sour
renten vallende te twee payementen in elc jaer: v sc. vj den. gr. tSente Jansmesse
int jaer xiiijᶜ ende lxxx eerstcommende, ende v sc. vj den. gr. te Kerssavende
naervolghende, ende van dan voort telker Kerssavend ende tSent Jansmesse
achternavolghende v sc. vj den. gr., gheldende eeuwelic ende erflic gheduerende
in zulcken ghelde, etc. Desen coop es ghedaen omme de somme van xj lb. gr., die
de voorscreven vercooper kende ontfanghen hebbende vanden cooper, welcke xj
sc. gr. siaers erflicker rente de voorscreven vercooper bezet heeft up vive van
zijnen huusen staende inde Ghelvestrate, deen neven dander, Pieter vanden
Borch ghehuust an deen zijde, ende Jan Donker an dander zijde, elc huus met
allen zijnen toebehoorten belijt in tgheheele met xx den. gr. siaers erflic daer
uutgaende te landcheinse zonder meer commers. In condicien, hadden de voornoemde dekens ende provisciers naermaels eenich ghebrec van eenechen ghe-
vallenen payementen, dat men dat ghebrec zal moghen verhalen (mits gaders alle
costen daer ancleevend) ande voornoemde panden ende zekere bijpandynghen
ende eyghenvuuren, etc., besprec wezende dat de voornoemde vercoopers de
zelve xj sc.groten siaers elders zal moghen bezetten, ende dus voornoemde panden zal moghen zuveren binnen drie jaeren eerstcommend, mits betalende tver-
loop van rente van tijde metten costen van dien, ende den gulde de rente elcker
bezetten up goet suffissient dewel bezet of beter in Ghend binnen den houden
vesten, dit ende daer af leveren wetteliken coopien zulcke alsser ter dienen ende
toehooren zullen zonder den costen vanden gulde. Ende esmen van desen in
ghebreke van teppioeren vanden drie jaeren, zo consentiert de voornoemde Jan
over hem zelven ende over zijnen naercommers dat dese rente zal blijven staende
up de huusen ende panden vooren verclaerst. Hier over staet als landheer vanden
tween huusen als ontfangher vanden stede erflicke rente, ende vanden anderen
drien huusen, Jan vanden Haghen, als deken vanden neeringhe vanden temmer-
lieden. Actum xxjᵃ Decembris lxxix.

Doc. 30 (29 March 1484): SAG 301.57, 1483/4, fo. 142ᵛ

Meester Jacop Hoobrechts draecht up Willem Hoobrecht, zijnen vader, ij lb. gr.
die hem tachter ende sculdich es Kathelijne, weduwe van Gheleyn Gheeraerts,
die vallen te belokenen paesschen lxxxiiij eerstcommende ter causen van sekeren

percheelen van lande daer af de kennesse ghedaen es voor scepenen van Hugher-sluus. Actum xxix martij lxxxiij voor paeschen [1484 NS].

Doc. 31 (28 July 1484): CBV 1061, fo. 187^r

Datum xxviij^a Jullij anno lxxxiiij^{to} . . . Domini hodie dominum Jacobum Obreth de Bergis in magistrum puerorum seu choralium, loco domini Johannis Hemart antiqui magistri coralium, retinuerunt.

Doc. 32 (9 September 1484): CBV 1061, fo. 192^r

Datum .ix. septembris. Capitulo generali in crastinum Nativitatis Beate Marie Virginis existente, lecta fuit ordinatio facta tam super regimen spirituali quam temporali puerorum chori, ad longum descripta in uno registro actorum capituli anno m^o.cccc.lviij^o, die vicesimasecunda mensis septembris. Et conclusione ac mandato capituli data fuit copia humana regiminis magistro corum [sic] novissime instituto, ut secundum contenta et declarata in eadem ordinacione, ipse magister diligenter regat et instruat ipsos pueros etc. et reddat compotum de hijs quod recipiet pervenientes ex muneribus et generositatibus fiendis ipsis pueris et annis singulis, et non sit deffectus.

Doc. 33 (17 June 1485): CBV 1061, fo. 216^v

Domino Johannj Crassequaule et alij longo de Duaco, tenoriste parvis vicarijs, in capitulo ad mandatum dominorum convocatis per magni ministri organum expositum, et dictum fuit nisi domum magistri infantium singulis diebus visitaverint, et in cantu plus quam pro presenti sciant addiscendo profecerint, exmittendum eosdem et eorum quenlibet licentiant et suis solitis salarijs privant.

Doc. 34 (27 July 1485): CBV 1061, fo. 223^v

Fiant lintheamina pro parvis pueris chorij, dicatque magnus minister eorum magistro quod acuratius quam pro prius non fecit eorum regiminj et statui superintendat, quia prurigine inficiuntur, quod alias non est visum.

Doc. 35 (2 September 1485): CBV 1061, fo. 229^r

Super stipendijs suis, que ab officio parvorum vicariorum recipere debet, puerorum chorj magister xij coronas communes, ut ex ipsis in nundinis Antwerpiensis sibj necessaria emere possit, exsolvj voluerunt domini mej illas, namque defalcabit termino solutionis cedente.

Doc. 36 (21 October 1485): CBV 1061, fo. 237^r

Magister infantium chori recedat, et audiantur ante eius recessum compota et rationes, et compota magistro officij [parvorum] vicariorum reddat.

Doc. 37 (24 October 1485): CBV 1061, fo. 237^r

Magistro infantium chori loquatur dominus Johannes Jorlandi, magister parvorum vicariorum, et conveniat cum eo de libris cantus quos composuisse asseritur, illosque emat in defalcando pecuniam quam ecclesie tenetur.

Doc. 38 (27 February–2 March 1488): SAG 400.29, 1487/8, fo. 392^v

Item Willem Hobrecht, trompet, van dat hij gheweest heeft met brieven ande wet van Denremonde, ende van danen te Mechelen; trac wech den xxvijsten dach van sporch ende quam weder den tweesten dach van maerte, comt van v daghe te perde, te ij sc. gr. sdaechs, x sc. gr.

Doc. 39 (3 April 1488): SAG 400.29, 1487/8, fo. 361^v

Item Willem Obrecht, trompet, van dat hij heeft gheweest met brieven an Christoffel Claess te Nerghem, comt van eenen daghe te voet, actum iij^a aprillis lxxxvij [1488 NS], naer paeschen, xij den. gr.

Doc. 40 (13–15 April 1488): SAG 400.29, 1487/8, fo. 401^r

Item Willem Hobrecht, trompet, van dat hij heeft gheweest met brieven ande wet van Bruessele; trac wech den xiijsten dach van aprille ende quam weder den xvsten dach van der zelver maend, comt van iij daghe te perde, te ij sc. gr. sdaechs, vj sc. gr.

Doc. 41 (after 15 August 1488): SAG 400.30, 1488/9, fo. 27^r

Item vander versteerften van Willem Hobrecht, trompet, vanden gheheelen goede, dat deelde her Jacop Hobrecht priestre, ende dit gheappointiert bij scepenen xxiiij sc. gr., afghetrocken voor den ainbringhere, ende yssuers, boden, xviij gr., blijft net, xxij sc. vij den. gr.

Doc. 42 (after 1 October 1488): RAG K5224, 1488/9, fo. 2^v

Ontfanghen van dootghelde vanden gulde brouders ende zusteren boven den dienste . . . Item Willem Oobrecht bij meester Jacop vanden Velde, x sc. par.

Doc. 43 *Mille quingentis* (after November 1488). Edition based on unique textual source, SegC s.s., fos. 81^v–83^r

> 1   Mille quingentis verum bis sex minus annis
> Virgine progeniti lapsis ab origine Christi,
> Sicilides flerunt Muse, dum Fata tulerunt
> Hobrecht Guillermum, magna probitate decorum,
>
> 5   Cecilie ad festum, qui Ceciliam peragravit
> Oram; idem Orpheicum Musis Jacobum generavit,
> Ergo dulce melos succentorum chorus alme
> Concine ut ad celos sit vecta anima et data palme.

Variants

The voices are labelled here after Petrucci (RISM 1504¹), as follows: **S** (Superius), **A** (Altus), and **B** (Bassus).

3 Sicilides] Scicilides **S**   4 decorum decorum **S**   5 qui] q̄ (= qui *or* que) **S**: que **AB**
6 Oram idem] *om.* **B**   7 *om.* **AB**   dulce] et lux perpetua *add.* **S** *from text of cantus firmus, musically imitated at this point*   8 et] *om.* **S**   palme] amen *add.* **S**

Commentary (by Leofranc Holford-Strevens)

The poem is written in hexameters, a classical metre, but with structural rhyme, a medieval device: vv. 1–4 exhibit rhyme between caesura and line-end within each verse (e.g. quingent*is* ~ ann*is*), that in v. 3 being disyllabic: vv. 5–8 consist of two couplets, the verses in each being linked by rhyme at the caesura (fest*um* ~ Orpheic*um*) and line-end (e.g. peragr*avit* ~ gener*avit*). The two end-line rhymes are disyllabic, as is the caesural rhyme in vv. 7–8: the difference in quantity (*mĕlos* ~ *cēlos*), though respected in the scansion, is ignored in the rhyme as commonly in medieval verse. Language and versification, though not flawless, have classical aspirations: in style the poem is far superior to the prose of *Inter preclarissimas*.

 1. Metre would require the supplement *mille ⟨et⟩*, the *e* of *mille* being elided in the verse, though not necessarily in the setting; but the mistake may well be authorial.

 3–6. The phrase *Sicelides* [correctly spelt thus] *Musae* begins the fourth eclogue of Vergil's *Bucolics*—the so-called 'Messianic eclogue' supposed in the Middle Ages to foretell the birth of Christ, hence well known to anyone with even a smattering of education. For Vergil the Sicilian Muses are those of pastoral poetry, but since that has nothing to do with Willem Obrecht we should interpret the phrase literally as implying a Sicilian connection; had the author simply required an ornamental epithet for *Muse* scanning – ‿ ‿ – he ought to have used *Pierides*.

 5. *que* (**AB**) makes St Cecilia travel through Sicily; although the conflation of saint and island in Old French *Cecile*—reflected here and in Doc. 26—might have led to such a connection, it forms no part of her legend. This difficulty, and the need to link Willem with the island, commend the reading *qui*, a possible interpretation of q̄ (**S**) in this MS, e.g. fo. 14ʳ Qui tollis, **CT**; confusion between *qui* and *que* due to similarity of abbreviation is frequent, and in the present verse the proximity of the feminine *Cecilie* could easily induce the misreading.

However, once we read *qui*, we can no longer begin a new sentence at *Cecilie ad festum*, for the correlation *qui peragravit, idem generavit* is unwarrantably emphatic: 'The man who travelled was the same man who begot', as if that might not have been expected; nor can we understand 'Willem begot Jacob while travelling', for the verb ought then to be *peragrabat*, and *idem* would still be uncalled-for unless the combination of travelling and begetting were somehow remarkable. Consequently *idem* must mark a new beginning, with its idiomatic function of stating an additional fact about the person or thing under discussion; *Cecilie ad festum* can no longer modify *generavit* (as it could if we read *que*), nor can it modify *peragravit*, for one could not travel through so large an island as Sicily on a single day, but must be taken with *fata tulerunt*, so that Willem Obrecht, who had travelled Sicily, died on St Cecilia's day, the connection between death and travel being the name *Cecilia*. Musically v. 4 is the last line of the *prima pars*, but parallels for a break in mid-sentence between *partes* are found, as Bonnie Blackburn points out, in Josquin's *Planxit autem David* and the five-part *Beati quorum remissae* attributed to Josquin (see Osthoff, *Josquin Desprez*, ii. 106–7 and 129–30).

5–6. *Ceciliam peragravit oram* is open to two objections: (i) *Ceciliam* (= *Siciliam*) must be taken as an adjective; (ii) *oram*, though followed by a pause, enjambs across the rhyme. As to (i), the assimilation of the place-name *Sicilia* to the personal name *Caecilia* might have caused the author to construct *Cecilia* adjectivally, on the analogy of *lex Caecilia* for a law introduced by a Caecilius; this is perhaps more plausible than emending *Ceciliam* to *Cecilie*—hypothetically corrupted by a scribe who could not be bothered to read ahead— at the cost of impairing word-play on *Cecilia*, less elegant without a change of case, while still not meeting objection (ii). The enjambment across the rhyme of a disyllable elided before a strong pause cannot be justified either by enjambments in unrhymed classical hexameters or by any emphasis upon the word in question. However, the author may have recalled Vergil, *Aeneid* 1. 2–3, 'Laviniaque (*var.* Lavinaque, Lavinia) venit | litora', with an adjective in *-ius* qualifying an enjambed substantive meaning 'shore' and separated from it by the verb.

Examination of the microfilm clearly shows *oram* S *ora* A (om. B); one might entertain the conjecture *ore*, 'Jacob, Orphic in his voice', or even *ore . . . Orpheico*, 'Jacob with the Orphic voice',[1] supposing that *ore* was corrupted by a persistence-error after *Ceciliam* and *Orpheico*, having lost its construction, adjusted to the case of *Jacobum*, but any corruption must have taken place in a single copy of the verses, before they were entered under the three voices; palaeographically less plausible is the accusative *os* in apposition to the object, 'Jacob, the mouth of Orpheus'. Furthermore, although with any of these emendations the difficulties noted in the previous paragraph would be overcome, the author should not be judged by the standards of recognized poets. It may be safer to retain the transmitted reading.

6. *Orpheicum* for *Orphicum* is unclassical, but see the fourteenth-century motet *Apollinis / Zodiacum /* IN OMNEM TERRAM, triplum, v. 17 'Orpheÿco potus fonte' (whence *Alma polis / Axe poli*, triplum, v. 21 'Orpheico fonte poti'), and Busnoys's *In hydraulis*, v. 20 'Vale, vale, instar Orpheicum'.[2]

Jacŏbum exhibits the characteristic medieval adjustment of quantities in loanwords: in Hebrew, Greek, and indeed in late-antique Latin the vowel is long, but the short vowel entails the normal Dutch stress on *Ja-*.

8. *data palme*. Literally, the soul is to be given to the palm; such poetic inversions are well attested, on the model of Vergil, *Aeneid* 3. 61 *dare classibus Austros*. The author may also have had in mind *leto datus* 'killed', 'dead'.

Doc. 44 *Inter preclarissimas virtutes* (?1490s). Edition based on unique source, SegC s.s., fos. 78ᵛ–81ʳ

¹Inter preclarissimas virtutes tuas ingentesque animi dotes, pietas, iuxta apostolum 'ad omnia valens', magnopere illustrans. ²Quo fit ut animum semper promptum benivolumque exibeas ad hoc ut, †pluribus misteria cum peregrinos ac

---

[1] i.e. 'Jacob who sings like Orpheus', cf. the name Chrysostomos ('Golden-Mouthed') given to the orator Dio of Prusa (AD *c.*40–after 112) and Patriarch John of Constantinople (AD *c.*347–407) on account of their eloquence.

[2] Previous authors have divided *Orphei cum* 'for Orpheus with (the Muses)', *Orphei* being the Greek dative Ὀρφεῖ as in v. 57 of the Messianic eclogue; but (i) this encumbers the verse with a self-contained second foot, (ii) *cum Musis* makes no reasonable sense if attached to either *idem* or *Jacobum*, and with *Orphei* ('He also begot Jacob for Orpheus and the Muses') is no improvement on *Orpheicum*. Moreover, whereas changing the word-division of our manuscripts in an ancient text originally written without it is simple *interpretatio*, in a text of more recent origin it is as much *emendatio* as changing the letters.

pauperes distincte†, tua musica manu sublevetur. ³Laudat te enim cleri largitas, tua namque excellens magnificentia multo magis excellit iustos promovens. ⁴Gloriosa apud Deum condicio tua. ⁵Pauperes nutris, virtuosos ditas, ecclesiam fabricas, humiles elevas, ex quibus odor bonus commendaris. ⁶'Estote fortes in bello'.

⁷Eya, propter tuam paternitatem talem ac tantam in meis semper carminibus iubilans, non quas debeo sed quales possum laudes resono, presensque pagina rudi armonie stilo confecta, ad Dei laudem tuamque consolationem, humiliter offero. ⁸Nam quid aliud nunc pro servitio impendere possum, nescio. ⁹Pecuniis non indiges, sensu ac prudentia abundas, prosperitate et letitia consolaris, tranquillitate et pace letaris, inter dignitatum cultores laudaris. ¹⁰'Estote fortes in bello'.

¹¹Igitur hoc presens carmen musicale et me Jacobum Hobrecht, humillimum servorum tuorum, benignus accipe et pro tuo libito. ¹²Manda et rege feliciter et longevus.

Variants

All voices except superius (S) labelled as in source (small letters in margin): C (Contratenor), T (Tenor), B (Bassus).

1 valens] vales SCB   illustrans] illustraris B   2 ad hoc . . . misteria] *om.* CB   cum] tum S   distincte] instincti S   manu] *om.* S   sublevetur . . . largitas] *om.* B   3 tua . . . excellens] *om.* S   promovens] promoves SCB   5 ecclesiam fabricas] *om.* CB   humiles elevas] *om.* S   7 eya] ca S   talem ac tantam] tantam ac talem B   quales] quale B   presensque] presens quorum C: presens quoque B   tuamque] que S   humiliter] *om.* B   8 nunc] *om.* B: nunc nunc C   9 abundas] *om.* S: abundes C: abundaris B   prosperitate] *om.* B   consolaris] consola S   tranquillitate . . . letaris] *om.* S   11 humillimum . . . tuorum] *om.* SC

Commentary

1. Albert Smijers has noted the reference to 1 Tim. 4: 8: 'nam corporalis exercitatio ad modicum utilis est, pietas autem ad omnia utilis est' (Vulgate; 'Twee onbekende motetteksten', 131).

2. The manuscript reading *pluribus misteria cum/tum peregrinos ac pauperes instincti/distincte* makes no apparent sense, and is evidently corrupt. The first two words are transmitted only in the top voice and could be explained as a misreading of *pluribus misteris* (recte *misteriis*; Smijers, ibid.). Assuming an ablative absolute, *instincti/distincte* would have to be emended to *instinctis*, *distinctis*, or even Smijers's *institutis* ('having instigated/embellished/set up many services'). The phrase *cum peregrinos ac pauperes* is likewise puzzling. Rather than emending this reading, unanimously transmitted in all three voices, to *cum peregrinis ac pauperibus*, it seems preferable to take *cum/tum* as *quum*, and to connect it to a verb. *Peregrinos ac pauperes* then being the object, one may either assume a missing verb implying their appointment (for instance: *cum ⟨accepisti⟩ peregrinos ac pauperes*), or perhaps emend *instincti/distincte* into one. Although the passage cannot be emended without considerable guesswork, its general sense is surely that the addressee's generosity towards strangers and the poor is of particular benefit to music.

5. 2 Cor. 2: 15–16: 'quia Christi bonus odor sumus Deo in his qui salvi fiunt et in his qui pereunt' (Vulgate). I am indebted to Dr Mark Edwards (New College, Oxford) for pointing out this reference to me.

7. Smijers emended to *praesentemque paginam . . . confectam*, yet the object of *offero* is surely *laudes*, *pagina* (ablative) being the medium through which these are presented.

11. The tenor joins the other voices in stating the motet text only at this line; up to this point it states the cantus-firmus text 'estote fortes in bello'.

Doc. 45 (between 10 March and 9 June 1492): Bruges, Bisdom, Kerkfabriek Sint-Donaas, 1491/2, fo. 17ᵛ

Item solutum domino Johanni Grac pro scriptura unius misse nove composite per magistrum Jacobum Hobrecht, xx s.

Doc. 46 (13 November 1492): SAG 301.62, 1492/3, fo. 23ʳ

Zegher de Leenheere es commen voor scepenen vander kuere in Ghend, kende ende lijde dat hij vercocht heeft wel ende redelic meester Jacoppe Hoobrecht filius Willems, presbyter, deen heeltscheede duergaende van eenen huuse ende stede staende beneden den Zantberghe inde Talboomstrate, eene loove zijnde, Pauwels Blijc ghehuust ter eende zijde ende al hoirs van Pieter den Buelen ter andere, met ghelijcker portie duergaende met allen den plaetsen, aysementen, vrijheden, ende anderen ghelaghen diere an alle zijden toebehooren ende an-cleven moghen, van vooren tot achter, bijden gheheel huus belast met viij sc. x den. gr. tsiaers eerffelic, te weeten de ij lb. [*recte* sc.] x den. gr. landcheyns den Heelighen Gheest in Sent Jans kerck, ende dandere vj sc. gr. de Freemery van Sinte Lysbetten zonder meer commers. Desen coop es ghedaen omme de somme van xxiiij sc. gr., die de vercooper hueren vanden voornoemde meester meester [*sic*] Jacop zijnen cooper kennen upgheghevene hebbende, ende scelt hem mids dien danof quicte. Dies en zal de voornoemde meester Jacop de voorscreven zijne ghecochte heelft van huuse, noch deel van dien, moghen transporteren, up-draghen noch vercoopen inden handen van eeneghen cloosters, gulden, nee-renghen, of ander van dode hand, in eenegher wijs. Actum den xiij novembris a° xcij.

Doc. 47 (13 November 1492): SAG 330.39, 1492/3, fo. 13ʳ

Meester Jacop Hobbrecht, presbyter, wonende tAndwoorpen, als gheel hoyr bedeghen van zulcken versterften van goede als daer Willem Hoobrecht, trompet, ziin vader was, uute verstorven es, es commen voor scepenen van ghedeele in Ghendt, kende ende verclaersde dat hij van alden goede, negheen uutghesteken noch gesondert, der versterfte vanden voorscreven Willem anclevende, jeghen Beatrijsen Jacops, wijlen hauderigghe bleven achter den vornomden Willem ende alsnu twijf van Zegher den Leenheere, wel verpaert, verheffent, verdeelt, en verscheeden es, ende zinen rechten deele van al dien themwaerts ende ghe-andveert heeft. Kennende hem ooc bijder voornomder Beatrijsen metten voor-nomden Zegher, hueren man, te vullen ghedaen ende gecontenteert wesende van zulcke penninghe als zoe ende de voorscreven Willem tziinen overlijdene onder hemlieden rustende hadden, hem toebehoorende ende up tijdt voorleden toecommende ende verstorven bijden aflivichede van Lysbetten Gheeraerts, tvoorseits Willems eerste wijf, ziinder moeder was. Sceldende mids desen den voorscreven Zegher ende Beatrijsen ziinen wive van tguent dat hij hemlieden ten occasione vander voorscreven versterfte penninghe oft anderssens generalic oft specialic emmermeer zoude moghen of weten te te [*sic*] heeschene wel ende wettelic quyte zonder meer reprochen of verclaers, nu ende teeuwelicken daghen. Actum den xiij[en] in november, a° xcij.

Doc. 48 (1498/9): BAR 32552, fo. 72[r]

Betaelt Meester Jacop Obrecht, priestere-canter van Sint Donaes kerke in Brugghe, voor hem ende zijnen medeghezellen de somme van xx lb. grooten ter causen van Love ende Salve daghelijcx alle avonde ghezonghen thebbene ter heeren vander glorieuser Maghet Marien binnen der voorsc. kerken van Sint Donaes, daer inne begrepen tluuden, oorghelen ende luminaris, ende dit van [*space left blank*], xx lb.

Doc. 49 (1499/1500): BAR 32553, fo. 73[r]

Heer Jacop Obrecht, priestre ende canter van Sint Donaes kerke in Brugghe, voor hem ende zijne medeghezellen de somme van xx lb. gr. ter causen vanden Love ende Salve daghelijcx alle avonde ghezonghen thebbene ter heeren vander glorieuser Maghet Marien binnen der voorsc. kerke, daer inne begrepen tluuden, oorghelen, ende luminaris, ende dit van eenen jare, xx lb. [*Marginal note:*] Bij ziner quictancie. Nietmin zij angaande dezen Salve ghesproken met mine heeren van Sinte Donaes, ofte met voorscreven zancmeestre, omme middele te vindene dat de zanghers die ten zelven Salve behoren commene dat bet hayeren dan zij toot noch toe ghedaen hebben. Want zomen verstaet, zo es de zelve zancmeestre ghehouden met hem thebbene boven zinen kinderen in elc Salve vier ghezellen sanghers ende de best zinghende vander kerke die hij elc behoort te ghevene eenen grooten telker werfste. Ende nu den dicxsten tijd zo ne commen daer maer boven de twee ofte drie, waer bij daer ghetidelicke groote confusie ghesciet, zo dat beter ware, om de eere vander kerke ende vander stede (mids dat ten Salve ghemeenelicke commen alle edele ende vreemde lieden die hemlieden binnen deser stede vinden), tzelve Salve niet ghesonghen dan ghezonghen. Ende dinct commissarissen om huerlieden advis hier up dat goet ware, ghemerct dat elc zangher behoort thebbene eenen groten ende de zancmeester dobble met zinen kinderen, datmen ordeneerde vanden stede weghe eenen notablen persoon ten salarisse van tien scellingen groten tsiaers, die elke zanghere die ten zelven Salve quame ter vier eer de Ymmene ofte Sequencie ghesonghen ware, ende gheen andre up zinen eed, een teeken weerdich zijnde eenen groten, de welk zij telker maend bringhen zouden in handen vanden tresorier die hemlieden die aflossen ende betalen zoude rem. Dit nietmin remitterende ter discrecie van mine voorsc. heeren vanden kerke ende vanden wet, om hier up bij hemlieden beter middele ende expedient ghevonde te zine in dient moghelic zij.

Doc. 50 (12 March 1510): Accounts of the city of Ferrara; after photograph in Van Hoorn, *Jacob Obrecht*, plate facing p. 104

Da la fabrica deli novi alogiamenti, che se hano a fare suso il polixeneto deli amorbati, L. trecento due, s. due, et per la dicta dal mag^{co} Messer Antonio di Costabelli, ducale Cons^{ro}, etc., contanti (?) per la valuta de tazze sei, bichieri sei, et una confetiera picola dorata senza pede, dargento, che pesorno in tuto onze cento cinquanta nove onze 159 a s. 38 per oncia pexate et extimate cossi per il mistro dala cecha come cossi mi ha atestato, liquali argenti forno del q. Messer Jacomo Obreth, gia cantore del Illmo Signore Duca nostro, et che restorno sino dal anno 1505 aprovo (?) il p^{to} mag^{co} Messer Antonio, tunc gubernator et ducale commissario sopra la peste, doppoi la morte del dicto Messer Jacomo, qual morite de peste dicto anno in questa cita de Ferraria, a questo fine che li dinari del ritrato de dicti argenti, insieme cum le L. 181.16 delequal ne e facto scriptura in m. q.q.q. in credito al dicta fabrica c. 18, se habino a convertire in la dicta fabrica deli dicti novi alogiamenti . . . per el dicto Messer Jacomo, et in remissione deli suoi peccati, per essere persona pia. Et de dicti argenti ne fue facto memoria in scriptura del men. m.m.m., c. 163, L. ccc ij s. ij d.

APPENDIX II
RHYTHMIC DENSITY IN THE MASSES OF JACOB OBRECHT

'Today's musicians and singers no longer follow the rules of our learned fore-bears. Nowadays they use only ₵, and of proportions only sesquialtera', Giovanni Spataro complained in 1529.[1] As far as Jacob Obrecht is concerned, the good old days to which Spataro alluded ended in the years around 1490. Four masses copied by about 1491–3, *Fortuna desperata*, *Je ne demande*, *N'aray-je jamais*, and *Rose playsante*, are written entirely in ₵. The same is true of the undated but presumably late three-voice masses *De tous biens playne*, *Fors seulement*, and *Je ne seray plus*. All other mature masses (with the obvious exceptions of *Caput* and *L'homme armé*) use O in at most three sections, and are otherwise written in ₵.

The shift to ₵ as the predominant or unique mensuration in masses and motets from the 1490s seems to have been widespread in continental Europe. As a historical development it was as momentous as the general shift from major prolation to perfect *tempus* rhythm around 1430.[2] In Obrecht's work the shift to ₵ coincides with several other changes: the disappearance of head-motifs, the avoidance of non-schematic types of cantus-firmus treatment, and the creation of the mature style. It also runs parallel with another important development, the progressive increase in rhythmic density. This phenomenon is not unique to the work of Obrecht but underlies all mensural polyphony from the thirteenth to seventeenth centuries. It reflects a persistent tendency in this period for tempi to slow down, that is, for later works to presuppose slower inherent speeds than earlier ones. The study of rhythmic density offers important insights into Obrecht's historical position in long-term mensural developments. It provides a possible explanation for the disappearance of O in the 1490s, and may give important clues to the chronology of his masses.

Rhythmic density in fifteenth-century music can be studied with the method of average note-value.[3] This method involves the adding up of all note-values in a given piece, and dividing the total by the number of notes, thus arriving at the average value (V). In practice, it seems best to count the top two voices only,[4]

[1] Blackburn, Lowinsky, and Miller, *A Correspondence of Renaissance Musicians*, 336 and 345.
[2] Besseler, *Bourdon und Fauxbourdon*, 109–24.
[3] For this and what follows, see R. C. Wegman, 'Concerning Tempo in the English Polyphonic Mass, *c*.1420–70', *Acta musicologica*, 61 (1989), 40–65.
[4] Unless either or both of these voices is stating cantus firmus (as in *Malheur me bat*, *Sub tuum*

since these are least subject to stylistic change. The unit of value is the semibreve (S); an imperfect breve is thus counted as 2 S, a minim as 0.5 S, and a dotted semiminim as 0.375 S. If a mass section has an average note-value V = 0.75 S, this means that semibreves and minims are used in approximately equal proportion. A section with an average value of 1.5 S uses notes generally twice as large, and therefore needs twice the speed to produce a similar sound (1.5 ÷ 0.75 = 2). The central idea behind this is that it makes no difference whether one sings large notes quickly or small notes slowly: rhythmic density is held in a direct balance with tempo. Changes in density, consequently, are likely to reflect changes in speed. Musical evidence bears this out. In fifteenth-century music there is always a shift to larger values when the mensuration changes from O to the faster ¢. An example is Obrecht's *Missa Petrus apostolus*, where V(O) = 0.675 and V(¢) = 0.757. The stroke in the sign ¢ prescribes a tempo increase. The synchronous change in rhythmic density suggests that the semibreve speed in ¢ is approximately 0.757 ÷ 0.675 = 1.121 times faster than that in O.

The study of rhythmic density in a number of repertories has indicated a standard pattern of development: in both O and ¢ tempi tended to slow down, and they did so in consistent ways. This can be indicated graphically, as in Fig. 3. The horizontal axis represents V(O), the vertical axis V(¢). Each point on the graph represents one mass by Obrecht; the position of each point is determined by the average note-values in O and ¢. *Petrus apostolus*, for instance, is represented by the point of intersection between the value 0.675 on the horizontal axis and 0.757 on the vertical axis (see arrow). In this way all masses by Obrecht that employ O and ¢ (or its equivalent, O2) have been indicated in the graph. Two groups of masses, 1 and 2, indicated with the symbols ● and ■, can be distinguished. They differ in the way ¢ relates to O; the average relationships are indicated in the graph by straight lines.[5] Three masses, *Gracioulx et biaulx*, *Sub tuum presidium*, and *Maria zart*, are unclassifiable; they are indicated with the symbol □. Since the average note-values are smallest in the bottom left-hand corner, the implied tempi are slowest there. On the assumption that tempi gradually slowed down, the relative order of composition within each group should be approximately top right to bottom left.

There is considerable evidence to support that assumption. In clearly defined repertories, later works usually employ smaller note-values. In cases where developments of rhythmic density can be studied in combination with dating evidence, it is always by assuming a *decrease* in tempo that the two types of evidence appear to correlate.[6] This is illustrated in Fig. 4. It charts, in the same way as Fig. 3, the

---

presidium, Caput, Fors seulement, and *Je ne seray*), in which case the two highest freely composed voices have to be taken.

[5] The line of Group 1 represents the statistically 'best-fitting' equation V(¢) = 1.196 V(O) − 0.057, that of Group 2 V(¢) = 0.858 V(O) + 0.269. The correlation coefficient R for Group 1 is 0.831, for Group 2 0.989.

[6] Attempts to date 15th-c. compositions on the basis of rhythmic density have been made by C. Hamm, *A Chronology of the Works of Guillaume Dufay Based on a Study of Mensural Practice* (Princeton, NJ, 1964), and R. C. Wegman, review of M. R. Maniates, *The Combinative Chanson: An Anthology* (Madison, Wis., 1989), in *Music & Letters*, 72 (1991), 510–13. For an example in

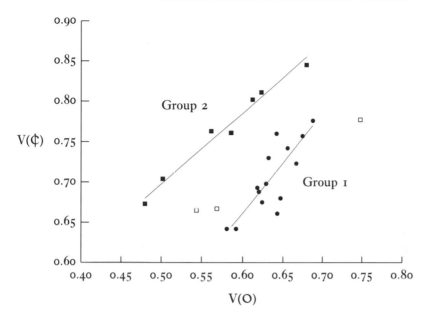

FIG. 3. Scatter diagram of rhythmic density in the masses of Jacob Obrecht (Groups 1 and 2), based on the average note-value in O and ¢

average note-values of three distinct repertories: thirty English masses from the period 1430–75 (O), thirty-five motets from the Eton Choirbook, *c*.1475–1500 (●), and twenty-four Obrecht masses, *c*.1475–1505 (□).[7] The two groups from the period 1475–1505 are significantly further bottom left than the group from the period 1430–75. Even within the latter group, a top-right to bottom-left development is suggested. For instance, only three English masses survive in sources pre-dating 1445, and all three appear in the extreme top right-hand corner; the masses on the other side, bordering on the Eton repertory, do not appear in sources pre-dating *c*.1465.[8] In Obrecht's mass *œuvre*, too, the top-right to bottom-left development broadly parallels the available dating evidence (see below).

The relationship between ¢ and O cannot be studied outside the period covered in Fig. 4: before 1430 perfect and imperfect *tempus* (with minor prolation) were rarely conceived in different speeds, and after 1500 perfect *tempus*

17th-c. music, see A. Curtis, 'La Poppea Impasticciata or, Who Wrote the Music to *L'Incoronazione* (1643)?', *Journal of the American Musicological Society*, 42 (1989), 28–30.

[7] For the values of the English masses, see Wegman, 'Concerning Tempo', 49; the values of the Eton repertory will be published in another context.

[8] Three masses in the top right-hand side appear in the early sources AostaS D19, TrentC 87, and TrentC 92, finished by about 1445 (Dunstable's *Rex seculorum* and *Da gaudiorum premia*, and Benet's *Sine nomine*). The masses on the other extreme (various *Sine nomines*, mostly anonymous, but one by John Plummer) do not appear in sources copied before the late 1460s.

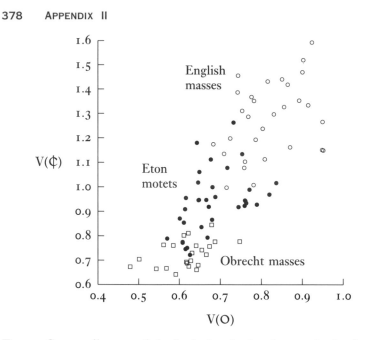

FIG. 4. Scatter diagram of rhythmic density in ninety polyphonic compositions from the period *c*.1430–1500

became virtually obsolete. On these grounds one could call the years 1430–1500 a distinct mensural period. This 'O–₵' period saw a complete halving of the average note-values, and thus presumably a comparable slowing down of tempo (as is evident from Fig. 4). The two extremes in this respect are Obrecht's *Missa Si dedero* (1490s) and the anonymous *Missa Salve sancta parens* (?1430s). In both mensurations the two masses relate to one another in an approximate 2 : 1 ratio.[9] This slowing-down process must have been a complex development, and its details are still to be established. The available evidence does, however, suggest a tentative pattern of evolution. In the short term, rhythmic density tended to increase at a faster rate in ₵ than in O. As a result, the two mensurations gradually moved towards a point where they would end up having the same implied speeds (as can be seen clearly in Fig. 4). Composers could of course 'redefine' the relative speed of ₵ at any time. Even then, however, the new speed would be bound in a fixed relationship with that of O, and slow down together with it (as in Obrecht's Group 2). The speed in ₵, in this sense, can be seen as a variable derivative from that in O.

Possibly it is for this reason that when dates are available, they tend to correlate better with the rhythmic density in O than that in ₵. This is true also of Obrecht's mass *œuvre*. For instance, V(O) is larger than 0.64 only in the masses

[9] V(O) is 1.593 in *Salve sancta parens* and 0.673 in *Si dedero* (a ratio of 2.37 : 1). The figures for V(₵) are 0.924 and 0.480, respectively (a ratio of 1.93 : 1).

datable before about 1488 (with the possible exception of *Plurimorum carminum II*). V(O) is smaller than 0.59 only in the most mature masses, datable in the early 1490s (see Table 4). With ₵ the picture is not nearly as consistent. The reason for this is simple: ₵ can relate to O in two different ways. Hence a single figure for V(₵) tells us little unless we also know the figure for V(O). Considered together, however, the two figures tell a great deal. If the pattern of development outlined above is correct, they would suggest an approximate order of composition.[10]

Table 4 is arranged in this order.[11] It is immediately apparent from the table that the arrangement lacks chronological precision. For instance, although the early masses *Petrus apostolus*, *Beata viscera*, *O lumen ecclesie*, and *Sicut spina rosam* do indeed appear at the top (numbers 1–4), the internal order of this group is different from the order suggested by stylistic evidence. And although the masses of the critical phase follow shortly on this group (5–6, 11, and 13), their internal order is different as well, and they are, moreover, intermingled with masses that appear to be slightly later, perhaps from about 1488–9 (7–10 and 12). On the other hand, the two mature masses that existed by 1491–3 are indeed close together (21–2). Although they could theoretically belong to Group 1 (there being no values for O), their direct associates in structure and style are clearly part of Group 2, and are, moreover, close enough in rhythmic density to suggest chronological proximity (19–20). Earlier mature masses are mainly where one would have expected them (12, 14–16, 18); only *Grecorum*, *Pfauenschwanz*, and *Je ne demande* seem far out of place (7–8, 23). Three ₵-only masses are left unclassified, as it is hard to tell whether they belong to Group 1 or 2 (26–8): they could be placed either between numbers 8 and 14 (which would be consistent with their early mature style) or between 23 and 25.

So it is primarily in its general trend that Table 4 appears to be in agreement with the development of Obrecht's style. This trend, the gradual slowing down of tempo, can be seen as the continuation of a long-term development, stretching back to the 1430s. The masses of Jacob Obrecht represent the final stage of that development. In the works of composers born after about 1480 one finds O only by rare exception: ₵ is the chief mensuration, triple metre usually being notated through a proportional relationship with ₵ (usually ₵3). In fact, the notion of tempo change as such was abandoned (the move from ₵ to ₵3 theoretically involves no change of the *tempus* speed). It is only after this major change that the theory of a single, fixed unit of time (*tactus*) could be developed: the semibreve

[10] The order can only be approximate since the figures are statistical averages. In all masses there is some amount of variation in rhythmic density between sections; the standard error indicated by this variation is usually about 5%, but in a few cases it can run up to 15–20%.

[11] *Vecy la danse barbary* is not included in the table, since neither of the top two voices survives. It should be stressed that while the figures themselves constitute objective empirical evidence, the division into groups, and the arrangement proposed in Table 4, are interpretations of that evidence, based on the high internal correlation of the groups, and the knowledge that tempi generally tended to slow down. The relative positions of masses in which the figure for V(O) is based on only one or two sections (with the consequent possibility of 'random' variation; see previous note), have been determined mainly according to V(₵).

TABLE 4. *Rhythmic density in the masses of Jacob Obrecht*
(values for O2 in square brackets)

Masses	O	no. of sections	¢ Group 1	Group 2	no. of sections
1 *Sicut spina rosam*	0.688	5	0.776		10
2 *O lumen ecclesie*	0.680	8		0.845	6
3 *Petrus apostolus*	0.675	5	0.757		4
4 *Beata viscera*	0.642	5	0.760		5
5 *De Sancto Donatiano*	0.656	6	0.742		6
6 *Adieu mes amours*	0.667	5	0.723		3
7 *Grecorum*	0.632	1	0.730		8
8 *Pfauenschwanz*	0.629	2	0.698		7
9 *Ave regina celorum*	0.618	5	0.693		6
10 *De Sancto Johanne*	0.620	6	[0.688]		4
11 *De Sancto Martino*	0.647	5	0.680		6
12 *Plurimorum carminum I*	0.623	1		0.811	10
13 *Salve diva parens*	0.612	6		0.802	7
14 *Caput*	0.624	6	0.675		6
15 *Plurimorum carminum II*	0.643	1	0.661		10
16 *L'homme armé*	0.592	6	[0.642]		4
17 *Scaramella* (CT only)	0.581	3	0.642		8
18 *N'aray-je jamais*	—	—	0.625		13
19 *Malheur me bat*	0.562	1		0.763	9
20 *Libenter gloriabor*	0.586	1		0.761	7
21 *Rose playsante*	—	—		0.753	10
22 *Fortuna desperata*	—	—		0.749	10
23 *Je ne demande*	—	—		0.735	13
24 *Cela sans plus*	0.502	3		0.704	10
25 *Si dedero*	0.480	1		0.673	9

¢-only (Group 1 or 2)

26 *Fors seulement*	—	—	0.708		14
27 *De tous biens playne*	—	—	0.700		14
28 *Je ne seray plus*	—	—	0.673		15

Unclassifiable

29 *Sub tuum presidium*	0.748	5	0.777		5
30 *Maria zart*	0.569	2	0.667		7
31 *Gracioulx et biaulx*	0.554	3	0.665		13

speeds of O and ₵ had merged into one. The *tactus* theory, therefore, is by definition not applicable to the 'O–₵' period.

The study of rhythmic density indicates two possible causes for the disappearance of O. First, as pointed out above, the slowing-down process moved inexorably towards a point where ₵ and O would effectively have the same speed. The absence of significant mensural contrast took away the need to maintain such contrast in the notation. Secondly, as implied speeds halved in the period 1430–1500, perfect *tempus* units expanded to twice their original duration, just as perfect *modus* units had gradually expanded in the fourteenth century. In the 1420s, for instance, perfect *tempus* (with average note-values exceeding 1 S) was almost identical in implied speed to perfect *modus* in Machaut's Mass of Our Lady (which has average note-values in the region of 2.5 S). Perfect *modus*, meanwhile, had expanded and would increasingly be regarded as a rhythmic superstructure, governing groups of tempo units rather than individual beats. Around 1500, O came close to reaching the same status, and needed in turn to be replaced by a 'quick' triple metre. The logical step was to move down one further level, and to replace perfect *tempus* by perfect prolation. This seems particularly likely as the minim had almost become the counting-unit in O: in Obrecht's masses as well as in the Eton Choirbook, V(O) approaches 0.5 S (= 1 M). By notating perfect prolation one could maintain this level of rhythmic density, while winning back a quick triple mensuration. This happened in England, where perfect prolation became prominent in the years after Eton (Fayrfax, Ludford, and contemporaries). This step was not made on the Continent, however, possibly because perfect prolation was too closely associated there with augmentation (the English had rarely used the mensuration in this sense after the 1430s). The 'replacement' was rather ₵3: this sign provided the rhythmic contrast with ₵ that O was no longer able to give.[12] Long-term corollaries of these developments are the gradual disappearance of alteration, imperfection, and ligatures, and the downward extension of the notation system by creating lower levels of division (invariably duple). With the general move to ₵, and the abandonment of triple organization on the levels of *modus*, *tempus*, and prolation, the foundation was laid for the binary, additive system of notation developed in the sixteenth and seventeenth centuries.

The cause of these developments can be identified as the slowing down of tempo. This phenomenon, which can be observed in virtually all mensural polyphony from the thirteenth to seventeenth centuries, remains as yet unexplained. Slowing-down processes have been demonstrated in the musics of other cultures, particularly the Middle and Far East.[13] The basic pattern there, however, was different. The process usually involved orally transmitted tunes, which grew more and more ornate in the course of centuries—added ornaments becoming melodically essential, and being ornamented in turn. The fundamental difference in mensural polyphony was of course the role of notation. Compositions,

---

[12] This is also implied in Spataro's comment quoted above. Signs like ⸮ were regarded as synonymous with ₵3 (this is the case already in Obrecht's masses).

[13] I am indebted to Professor Rembrandt Wolpert for pointing this out to me.

once written down, are fixed in their rhythmic appearance. The slowing-down process, therefore, could affect the speed of an individual work only marginally. It was rather in the chronological *succession* of works that tempi decreased significantly.

Yet the role of the notation system does suggest a possible explanation. A written copy of a musical composition is not the record of an actual performance, but of a mentally conceived sound. In writing out the copy, a composer makes mental estimates of the tempi of such mensurations as O and ₡, and these estimates, as we have seen, are reflected in rhythmic densities that remain remarkably consistent across different sections in the same mensuration. Yet this consistency, however remarkable, does not necessarily mean absolute accuracy. If the mentally conceived speeds tend to be slightly slower than their 'real' counterparts, then there will be at least a statistical tendency for a composer to use smaller note-values. And as the new composition enters the repertory, its marginally slower implied speeds will tend to become slower actual speeds, which in turn might be 'underestimated' in new compositions, and so on. Stated in these crude terms, of course, the process would be too directly and neatly cyclic. The repertory in circulation, at any point, would have reflected the 'tempo estimates' of several different composers over a number of years. Hence the standard speeds for O and ₡ could never have been more than averages, of implied speeds in several works that must have fluctuated within certain metronomic margins. The hypothetical tendency of which we speak, therefore, should have been one for new compositions to be under rather than above the average, and thus for the average itself to come down in the long run.

There is empirical evidence to support this hypothesis. Tests carried out by Manfred Clynes and Janice Walker have revealed 'that in a musical piece the experience of thought rhythm, alone, for most musicians is consistently slightly slower than when it executes the movement it thinks'.[14] That is to say, a musician who mentally executes a particular composition will consistently tend to do so *more slowly* than when he actually performs the same work in sound. As far as fifteenth-century composers are concerned, their intuitive estimates of the 'right' speeds for a new piece in O and ₡ would obviously have been conditioned by the repertory they sang every day. Yet the results of Clynes and Walker suggest that these estimates would have tended, if anything, to be marginally slower than those in that repertory. The crucial role of notation was that this 'underestimation' immediately became a fixed and permanent feature of the new work. Just as tempo differences *within* compositions are expressed with remarkable consistency in the rhythmic density, so the unintentional tempo differences *between* compositions should be at least statistically detectable, certainly in the long run.

In this respect Fig. 4 speaks volumes. The historical tendency for tempi to become slower was so consistent and regular that even close contemporaries who

---

[14] M. Clynes and J. Walker, 'Neurobiologic Functions of Rhythm, Time, and Pulse in Music', in M. Clynes (ed.), *Music, Mind, and Brain: The Neuropsychology of Music* (New York and London, 1982), 188–91. Clynes and Walker conducted their tests with eight musicians, each of whom was asked to tap the rhythm of a mental execution of an existing composition (five trials), and to perform the same composition on a solo instrument (likewise five trials).

composed in quite different styles and who could have known very little of each other's music (e.g. Obrecht and the Eton composers) still operated in roughly the same 'tempo region'. This strongly suggests that tempi were indeed perceived everywhere as fixed and stable, and that only the continuous production of new repertory brought them down, so that by 1500 they were about half those of around 1420.

This means that the mensural notation system was inherently unstable, subject to imperceptible but continuous 'inflation'. Major changes of mensural practice can be seen as attempts to adjust to that inflation at critical points. These adjustments eventually changed the nature of musical notation as such. The 'O–₵' period is defined by two adjustments occurring in the 1430s and 1490s. The disappearance of O in the music of Obrecht and his contemporaries was probably a symptom of a deeper phenomenon: O began to lose its distinctive nature by about 1490, and hence there was little musical point in maintaining the mensuration. As the tempi of O and ₵ gradually merged in one speed, that speed was perceived as universal and given the name *tactus*. All the mensuration signs of the past were reinterpreted in terms of this new concept, in the notoriously Procrustean *tactus* tables of the sixteenth century. These latter developments, of course, belong to an age in the history of mensural notation that Obrecht did not live to see. Yet his mature masses reach the threshold of that age, and make us understand how and why it evolved from the mensural period in which he lived.

BIBLIOGRAPHY

I. Collected Editions of Obrecht's Works

Werken, ed. J. Wolf (30 vols.; Amsterdam and Leipzig, 1908–21; repr. Farnborough, 1968).

Opera omnia editio altera, ed. A. Smijers and M. van Crevel (9 vols.; Amsterdam, 1954–64).

New Obrecht Edition (*NOE*), gen. ed. C. J. Maas (Utrecht, 1983–   ):

NOE 1. *Missa Adieu mes amours / Missa Ave regina celorum*, ed. B. Hudson (1983).

NOE 2: *Missa Beata viscera / Missa Caput*, ed. T. Noblitt (1984).

NOE 3: *Missa De Sancto Donatiano / Missa De Sancto Martino*, ed. B. Hudson (1984).

NOE 4: *Missa De tous biens playne / Missa Fors seulement / Missa Fortuna desperata*, ed. B. Hudson (1986).

NOE 5: *Missa Grecorum / Missa Je ne demande*, ed. T. Noblitt (1985).

NOE 6: *Missa L'homme armé / Missa Libenter gloriabor*, ed. T. Noblitt (1986).

NOE 7: *Missa Malheur me bat / Missa Maria zart*, ed. B. Hudson (1987).

NOE 8: *Missa O lumen ecclesie / Missa Petrus apostolus*, ed. B. Hudson (1988).

NOE 9: *Missa Pfauenschwanz / Missa Rose playsante*, ed. T. Noblitt (1989).

NOE 10: *Missa Plurimorum carminum I / Missa Plurimorum carminum II*, ed. T. Noblitt (1991).

NOE 11: *Missa Salve diva parens / Missa Scaramella / Missa Sicut spina rosam*, ed. B. Hudson (1990).

NOE 12: *Missa Si dedero / Missa Sub tuum presidium / Missa Veci la danse Barbari*, ed. T. Noblitt (1992).

NOE 13: *Missa Cela sans plus / Missa Gracuuly et biaulx*, ed. M. Staehelin.

NOE 14: *Missa Je ne seray plus / Missa N'aray-je jamais*, ed. T. R. Ward.

NOE 15: *Motets I*, ed. C. J. Maas.

NOE 16: *Motets II*, ed. C. J. Maas.

NOE 17: *Secular works and textless compositions*, ed. L. Kessels and E. Jas.

II. General Literature

ANGLÈS, H., 'Un manuscrit inconnu avec polyphonie du XVᵉ siècle, conservé à la cathédrale de Ségovie', *Acta musicologica*, 8 (1936), 6–17.

Antiphonale Sarisburiense, ed. W. H. Frere (repr., Farnborough, 1966).

ANTONOWYTSCH, M., 'Renaissance-Tendenzen in den Fortuna-desperata-Messen von Josquin und Obrecht', *Musikforschung*, 9 (1956), 1–26.

BANK, J. A., 'Uit het verleden van de Nederlandse kerkmuziek', *Sint Gregorius-blad*, 1939, 1–6.

BENT, M., 'Diatonic *ficta*', *Early Music History*, 4 (1984), 1–48.

BERGER, K., *Musica Ficta: Theories of Accidental Inflections in Vocal Polyphony from Marchetto da Padova to Gioseffo Zarlino* (Cambridge, 1987).

BESSELER, H., 'Musik des Mittelalters in der Hamburger Musikhalle', *Zeitschrift für Musikwissenschaft*, 7 (1924–5), 42–54.

—— 'Von Dufay bis Josquin, ein Literaturbericht', *Zeitschrift für Musikwissenschaft*, 11 (1928–9), 1–22.

—— *Bourdon und Fauxbourdon: Studien zum Ursprung der niederländischen Musik* (2nd rev. edn., Leipzig, 1974).

—— and GÜLKE, P., *Schriftbild der mehrstimmigen Musik* (Musikgeschichte in Bildern, 3/5; Leipzig, 1973).

BEUKERS, M., '"For the Honour of the City": Utrecht City Minstrels between 1377 and 1528', *Tijdschrift van de Vereniging voor Nederlandse Muziekgeschiedenis*, 41 (1991), 3–25.

BLACKBURN, B. J., 'Two "Carnival Songs" Unmasked: A Commentary on MS Florence Magl. XIX. 121', *Musica disciplina*, 35 (1981), 121–78.

—— 'On Compositional Process in the Fifteenth Century', *Journal of the American Musicological Society*, 40 (1987), 210–84.

——, LOWINSKY, E. E., and MILLER, C. A., *A Correspondence of Renaissance Musicians* (Oxford, 1991).

BLOXAM, M. J., 'A Survey of Late Medieval Service Books from the Low Countries: Implications for Sacred Polyphony, 1460–1520' (Ph.D. diss., Yale University, 1987).

—— 'Sacred Polyphony and Local Traditions of Liturgy and Plainsong: Reflections on Music by Jacob Obrecht', in T. F. Kelly (ed.), *Plainsong in the Age of Polyphony* (Cambridge, 1992), 140–77.

—— 'Plainsong and Polyphony for the Blessed Virgin: Notes on Two Masses by Jacob Obrecht', *Journal of Musicology*, in press.

BOUWS, J., 'Jeronimus de Clibano van 's-Hertogenbosch (±1460–1503), zangmeester in Brugge en Antwerpen', *Vlaamsch jaarboek voor muziekgeschiedenis*, 2/3 (1940–1), 75–80.

BOWERS, R., 'Obligation, Agency, and *Laissez-faire*: The Promotion of Polyphonic Composition for the Church in Fifteenth-Century England', in I. Fenlon (ed.), *Music in Medieval and Early Modern Europe: Patronage, Sources and Texts* (Cambridge, 1981), 1–19.

BRIDGMAN, N., 'The Age of Ockeghem and Josquin', in *New Oxford History of Music*, iii (Oxford, 1960), 239–302.

BRIQUET, C.-M., *Les Filigranes: Dictionnaire historique des marques du papier* (Geneva, 1907).

BROEKHUIJSEN, C., 'Obrecht in Missa?' (MA thesis, University of Amsterdam, 1983).

BROM, G., *Archivalia in Italië belangrijk voor de geschiedenis van Nederland*, i/2 (The Hague, 1909).

BUKOFZER, M., '*Caput*: A Liturgico-Musical Study', in *Studies in Medieval and Renaissance Music* (New York, 1954), 217–310.

BURCHARD, J., *Liber Notarum*, ed. E. Celani (Rerum italicarum scriptores, 32/1; Città di Castello, 1906).

BUSNOYS, A., *Collected Works, Part 2: The Latin-Texted Works*, ed. R. Taruskin (Masters and Monuments of the Renaissance, 5/2; New York, 1990).

BUSSE BERGER, A. M., 'The Origin and Early History of Proportion Signs', *Journal of the American Musicological Society*, 41 (1988), 403–33.

——*Mensuration and Proportion Signs: Origins and Evolution* (Oxford, 1993).

CARAPEZZA, P. E., '*Regina angelorum in musica picta*: Walter Frye e il "Maître au Feuillage Brodé"', *Rivista italiana di musicologia*, 10 (1975), 134–54.

CLYNES, M., and WALKER, J., 'Neurobiologic Functions of Rhythm, Time, and Pulse in Music', in M. Clynes (ed.), *Music, Mind, and Brain: The Neuropsychology of Music* (New York and London, 1982), 171–216.

COHEN, J., *The Six Anonymous L'homme armé Masses in Naples, Biblioteca Nazionale, MS VI E 40* (Musicological Studies and Documents, 21; American Institute of Musicology, 1968).

CRETIN, G., *Déploration de Guillaume Cretin sur le trépas de Jean Okeghem*, ed. Er. Thoinan (Paris, 1864).

CREVEL, M. VAN, 'Verwante sequensmodulaties bij Obrecht, Josquin en Coclico', *Tijdschrift der Vereeniging voor Nederlandsche Muziekgeschiedenis*, 16 (1946), 107–24.

CURTIS, A., '*La Poppea Impasticciata* or, Who Wrote the Music to *L'Incoronazione* (1643)?', *Journal of the American Musicological Society*, 42 (1989), 23–54.

D'ACCONE, F. A., 'A Late 15th-Century Sienese Sacred Repertory: MS K.I.2 of the Biblioteca Comunale, Siena', *Musica disciplina*, 37 (1983), 121–70.

DAHLHAUS, C., *Foundations of Music History*, trans. J. B. Robinson (Cambridge, 1983).

D'ALESSI, G., 'Maestri e cantori fiamminghi nella Cappella Musicale del Duomo di Treviso, 1411–1531', *Tijdschrift der Vereeniging voor Nederlandsche Muziekgeschiedenis*, 15 (1939), 147–65.

DECAVELE, J. (ed.), *Gent: Apologie van een rebelse stad* (Antwerp, 1989).

DE KEYZER, B., 'Jacob Obrecht en zijn vader Willem: De Gentse relaties', *Mens en Melodie*, 8 (1953), 317–19.

DE POTTER, F., *Gent, van den oudsten tijd tot heden* (Ghent, 1882).

DE SCHREVEL, A. C., *Histoire du Séminaire de Bruges* (Bruges, 1895).

DE SMET, J.-J. (ed.), *Corpus chronicorum Flandriae*, iii (Brussels, 1856).

DE SMIDT, F., *Krypte en koor van de voormalige Sint-Janskerk te Gent* (Ghent, 1959).

DE VOLKAERSBEKE, K., *Les Églises de Gand* (Ghent, 1857).

DE VOS, D., 'Een belangrijk portret van Jacob Obrecht ontdekt: Een werk uit de nalatenschap van het atelier van Hans Memling?', *Jaarboek 1989–90 Stad Brugge, Stedelijke Musea* (Bruges, 1991), 192–209.

DEWITTE, A., 'Boek- en bibliotheekwezen in de Brugse Sint-Donaaskerk XIIIe–XVe eeuw', in *Sint-Donaas en de voormalige Brugse Katedraal* (Bruges, 1978), 61–95.

DUBRULLE, H., *Bullaire de la province de Reims sous le pontificat de Pie II* (Lille, 1905).

DUNNING, A., *Die Staatsmotette 1480–1555* (Utrecht, 1970).

ELDERS, W., *Studien zur Symbolik in der Musik der alten Niederländer* (Utrecht, 1969).

—— 'Josquin's *Absolve, quaesumus, domine*: A Tribute to Obrecht?', *Tijdschrift van de Vereniging voor Nederlandse Muziekgeschiedenis*, 37 (1987), 14–24.

—— 'The Performance of Cantus Firmi in Josquin's Masses based on Secular Monophonic Song', *Early Music*, 17 (1989), 330–41.

—— 'Guillaume Dufay's Concept of Faux-Bourdon', *Revue belge de musicologie*, 43 (1989), 173–95.

ERASMUS, *Omnia opera* (Basle, 1540).

—— *Opus Epistolarum Des. Erasmi Roterodami*, ed. P. S. Allen, i (Oxford, 1906).

FALLOWS, D., *Dufay* (London, 1982).

—— review of Strohm, *Music in Late Medieval Bruges*, and Lockwood, *Music in Renaissance Ferrara*, *Early Music History*, 6 (1986), 279–303.

—— review of Picker, *Johannes Ockeghem and Jacob Obrecht: A Guide to Research*, *Music & Letters*, 70 (1989), 247–9.

FÉTIS, F.-J., *Biographie universelle des musiciens* (Paris, 1860–5).

FINSCHER, L., 'Obrecht, Jacob', *MGG* 9, cols. 1814–22.

FORNEY, K. K., 'Music, Ritual and Patronage at the Church of Our Lady, Antwerp', *Early Music History*, 7 (1987), 1–57.

FRIS, V., *Histoire de Gand* (Brussels, 1913).

GACHARD, M. (ed.), *Collection des voyages des souverains des Pays-Bas*, i (Brussels, 1876).

GLAREANUS, H., *Dodekachordon* (Basle, 1542).

—— *Dodecachordon*, trans. C. A. Miller (Musicological Studies and Documents, 6; American Institute of Musicology, 1965).

GOMBOSI, O., *Jacob Obrecht: Eine stilkritische Studie* (Leipzig, 1925).

HABERL, F. X., 'Die römische "schola cantorum" und die päpstlichen Kapellsänger bis zur Mitte des 16. Jahrhunderts', *Vierteljahrsschrift für Musikwissenschaft*, 3 (1887), 189–296.

HAGGH, B. H., 'Music, Liturgy, and Ceremony in Brussels, 1350–1500' (Ph.D. diss., University of Illinois, 1988).

—— 'New Documents from the Low Countries', paper read at the meeting of the Capital Chapter of the American Musicological Society, Washington, DC, 20 January 1990.

HAINS, S. E., 'Missa De Sancto Johanne Baptista' (MA thesis, Smith College, 1974).

HAMM, C., *A Chronology of the Works of Guillaume Dufay Based on a Study of Mensural Practice* (Princeton, NJ, 1964).

HAMMERSTEIN, R., *Die Musik der Engel: Untersuchungen zur Musikanschauung des Mittelalters* (Munich, 1962).

HARRISON, F. LL., *Music in Medieval Britain* (London, 1958).

Het Spel van de V vroede ende van de V dwaeze Maegden, ed. M. Hoebeke (The Hague, 1979).

HEWITT, H., 'A Study in Proportions', in *Essays on Music in Honor of Archibald Thompson Davison* (Cambridge, Mass., 1957), 69–81.

HIGGINS, P., '*In hydraulis* Revisited: New Light on the Career of Antoine Busnois', *Journal of the American Musicological Society*, 39 (1986), 36–86.

—— 'Tracing the Careers of Late Medieval Composers: The Case of Philippe Basiron of Bourges', *Acta musicologica*, 62 (1990), 1–28.

—— 'Musical Politics in Late Medieval Poitiers: A Tale of Two Choirmasters', paper read at the Eighteenth Medieval and Renaissance Music Conference, Royal Holloway and Bedford New College, London, 6–9 July 1990.

HINTZEN, J. D., *De kruistochtplannen van Philips den Goede* (Rotterdam, 1918).

HOORN, L. G. VAN, *Jacob Obrecht* (The Hague, 1968).

HUDSON, B., 'Two Ferrarese Masses by Jacob Obrecht', *Journal of Musicology*, 4 (1985–6), 276–302.

—— 'Obrecht's Tribute to Ockeghem', *Tijdschrift van de Vereniging voor Nederlandse Muziekgeschiedenis*, 37 (1987), 3–13.

—— 'On the Texting of Obrecht's Masses', *Musica disciplina*, 42 (1988), 101–27.

HYMA, A., *The Youth of Erasmus* (Ann Arbor, Mich., 1930).

Important Old Master Paintings: New York, Friday, January 15, 1993, auction catalogue, Sotheby's (New York, 1993).

ISAAC, H., *Messen*, ed. M. Staehelin (Musikalische Denkmäler, 8/ii; Mainz, 1973).

Johannes Ockeghem en zijn tijd, exhibition catalogue (Dendermonde, 1970).

JOSEPHSON, N. S., 'Formal Symmetry in the High Renaissance', *Tijdschrift van de Vereniging voor Nederlandse Muziekgeschiedenis*, 41 (1991), 105–33.

—— (ed.), *Early Sixteenth-Century Sacred Music from the Papal Chapel* (CMM 95; Neuhausen-Stuttgart, 1982).

JUST, M., *Der Mensuralkodex Mus. ms. 40021 der Staatsbibliothek Preußischer Kulturbesitz Berlin: Untersuchungen zum Repertoire einer deutschen Quelle des 15. Jahrhunderts* (Tutzing, 1975).

KEIL, H., *Grammatici latini*, vi (Leipzig, 1864).

KENNEY, S., 'Four Settings of "Ave Regina Coelorum"', in A. Vander Linden (ed.), *Liber amicorum Charles van den Borren*, (Antwerp, 1964), 98–104.

KEUSSEN, H., *Die Matrikel der Universität Köln*, i (Bonn, 1928).

KOOIMAN, E., 'The Biography of Jacob Barbireau (1455–1491) Reviewed', *Tijdschrift van de Vereniging voor Nederlandse Muziekgeschiedenis*, 38 (1988), 36–58.

KYRIAZIS, M., *Die Cantus firmus-Technik in den Messen Obrechts* (Inaug.-Diss., Universität Bern, 1952).

LEICHTENTRITT, H., *Music, History, and Ideas* (Cambridge, Mass., 1938).

LESZCZYŃSKA, A., 'Kadencja w Fakturze Motetów Jacoba Obrechta', *Muzyka*, 33/2 (1988), 41–51.

LINGBEEK-SCHALEKAMP, C., *Overheid en muziek in Holland tot 1672* (Poortugaal, 1985).

LLORENS, J., *Capellae Sixtinae Codices musicis notis instructi sive manu scripti sive praelo expressi* (Studi e testi, 102; Vatican City, 1960).

LOCKWOOD, L., 'A Note on Obrecht's Mass "Sub tuum presidium"', *Revue belge de musicologie*, 14 (1960), 30–9.

—— 'Music at Ferrara in the Period of Ercole I d'Este', *Studi musicali*, 1 (1972), 101–31.

—— '"Messer Gossino" and Josquin des Prez', in R. L. Marshall (ed.), *Studies in Renaissance and Baroque Music in Honor of Arthur Mendel* (Kassel, 1974), 15–24.

—— 'Josquin at Ferrara: New Documents and Letters', in Lowinsky and Blackburn (eds.), *Josquin des Prez: Proceedings*, 103–37.

—— *Music in Renaissance Ferrara, 1400–1505* (Oxford, 1984).

LOWINSKY, E. E., 'Secret Chromatic Art *Re-examined*', in B. S. Brook, E. O. D. Downes, and S. van Solkema (eds.), *Perspectives in Musicology* (New York, 1972), 91–135.

—— and B. J. BLACKBURN (eds.), *Josquin des Prez: Proceedings of the International Josquin Festival-Conference* (London, 1976).

MAAS, C. J., 'Towards a New Obrecht Edition: A Preliminary Worklist', *Tijdschrift van de Vereniging voor Nederlandse Muziekgeschiedenis*, 26 (1976), 84–108.

MARGOLIN, J.-C., *Érasme et la musique* (Paris, 1965).

MARIX, J., *Histoire de la musique et des musiciens de la cour de Bourgogne sous le règne de Philippe le Bon (1420–1467)* (Strasburg, 1939).

MEIER, B., *Studien zur Meßkomposition Jacob Obrechts* (Inaug.-Diss., Albert-Ludwigs-Universität, Freiburg im Breisgau, 1952).

—— 'Zyklische Gesamtstruktur und Tonalität in den Messen Jacob Obrechts', *Archiv für Musikwissenschaft*, 10 (1953), 289–310.

—— *Die Tonarten der klassischen Vokalpolyphonie* (Utrecht, 1974).

MURRAY, B., 'New Light on Jacob Obrecht's Development—A Biographical Study', *Musical Quarterly*, 43 (1957), 500–16.

—— 'Jacob Obrecht's Connection with the Church of Our Lady in Antwerp', *Revue belge de musicologie*, 11 (1957), 125–33.

NAGLE, M. E., 'The Structural Role of the Cantus Firmus in the Motets of Jacob Obrecht' (Ph.D. diss., University of Michigan, 1972).

NARDI, P., 'Relations with Authority', in H. De Ridder-Symoens (ed.), *A History of the University in Europe* i (Cambridge, 1992), 77–107.

NICHOLAS, D., *The Domestic Life of a Medieval City: Women, Children, and the Family in Fourteenth-Century Ghent* (Lincoln, Nebr., and London, 1985).

NIEUWENHUIZEN, J. VAN DEN, 'De koralen, de zangers en de zangmeesters van de Antwerpse O.-L.-Vrouwekerk tijdens de 15e eeuw', in *Gouden jubileum gedenkboek van de viering van 50 jaar heropgericht knapenkoor van de Onze-Lieve-Vrouwekatedraal te Antwerpen* (Antwerp, 1978), 29–72.

NOBLITT, T., 'Die Datierung der Handschrift Mus. ms. 3154 der Staatsbibliothek München', *Musikforschung*, 27 (1974), 36–56.

—— 'Problems of Transmission in Obrecht's *Missa Je ne demande*', *Musical Quarterly*, 63 (1977), 211–33.

—— 'Obrecht's *Missa Sine nomine* and its Recently Discovered Model', *Musical Quarterly*, 68 (1982), 102–27.

—— 'Chromatic Cross-Relations and Editorial *Musica ficta* in Masses of Obrecht', *Tijdschrift van de Vereniging voor Nederlandse Muziekgeschiedenis*, 32 (1982), 30–44.

NOLET, W., and BOEREN, P. C., *Kerkelijke instellingen in de Middeleeuwen* (Amsterdam, 1951).

NOWOTNY, R., *Mensur, Cantus Firmus, Satz in den Caput-Messen von Dufay, Ockeghem und Obrecht* (Inaug.-Diss., Munich, 1970).

OCKEGHEM, J., *Collected Works*, ed. D. Plamenac (American Musicological Society, 1959–66).

OPMEER, P., *Opus chronographicum orbis universi a mundi exordio usque ad Annum M.DC.XI. continens historiam, icones et elogia summorum pontificium, imperato rum, regum ac virorum illustrium, in duos tomos divisum* (Antwerp, 1611).

OSTHOFF, H., *Josquin Desprez* (Tutzing, 1962–5).

PERKINS, L. L., 'Musical Patronage at the Royal Court of France under Charles VII and Louis XI (1422–83)', *Journal of the American Musicological Society*, 37 (1984), 507–66.

—— 'The L'Homme Armé Masses of Busnoys and Okeghem: A Comparison', *Journal of Musicology*, 3 (1984), 363–96.

PICKER, M., 'Josquiniana in Some Manuscripts at Piacenza', in Lowinsky and Blackburn, *Josquin des Prez: Proceedings*, 247–60.

—— *Johannes Ockeghem and Jacob Obrecht: A Guide to Research* (Garland Composer Research Manuals, 13; New York and London, 1988).

PIETZSCH, G., *Fürsten und fürstliche Musiker im mittelalterlichen Köln* (Beiträge zur rheinischen Musikgeschichte, 66; Cologne, 1966).

—— *Archivalische Forschungen zur Geschichte der Musik an den Höfen der Grafen und Herzöge von Kleve-Jülich-Berg (Ravensberg) bis zum Erlöschen der Linie Jülich-Kleve im Jahre 1609* (Beiträge zur rheinischen Musikgeschichte, 88; Cologne, 1971).

PINCHART, A., *Archives des arts, sciences et lettres: Documents inédits*, i/3 (Ghent, 1881).

PIRRO, A., 'Jean Cornuel, vicaire à Cambrai', *Revue de musicologie*, 7 (1926), 190–203.

—— 'Obrecht à Cambrai', *Tijdschrift van de Vereeniging voor Nederlandsche Muziekgeschiedenis*, 12 (1927), 78–80.

—— *Histoire de la musique de la fin du XIVe siècle à la fin du XVIe* (Paris, 1940).

PIRROTTA, N., 'Music and Cultural Tendencies in 15th–Century Italy', *Journal of the American Musicological Society*, 19 (1966), 127–61.

PISCAER, A., 'Jacob Obrecht', *Sinte Geertruydsbronne: Driemaandelijks tijdschrift gewijd aan de geschiedenis en volkskunde van West-Brabant en omgeving*, 15 (1938), 1–15.

—— 'Jacob Obrecht: geboortedatum en andere bijzonderheden', *Mens en Melodie*, 7 (1952), 329–33.

PLANCHART, A. E., 'Fifteenth-Century Masses: Notes on Performance and Chronology', *Studi musicali*, 10 (1981), 3–29.

—— 'Parts with Words and without Words: The Evidence for Multiple Texts in Fifteenth-Century Masses', in S. Boorman (ed.), *Studies in the Performance of Late Mediaeval Music* (Cambridge, 1983), 227–51.

—— 'Guillaume Du Fay's Benefices and his Relationship to the Court of Burgundy', *Early Music History*, 8 (1988), 117–71.

PLUMMER, J., *Four Motets*, ed. B. Trowell (Banbury, 1968).

POLK, K., 'Flemish Wind Bands in the Late Middle Ages: A Study of Improvisatory Instrumental Practices' (Ph.D. diss., University of California, Berkeley, 1968).

—— *German Instrumental Music of the Late Middle Ages: Players, Patrons and Performance Practice* (Cambridge, 1992).

PONTIERI, E., 'Sulle mancate nozze tra Federico d'Aragona e Maria di Borgogna (1474–1476)', *Per la storia del regno di Ferrante I d'Aragona re di Napoli* (2nd edn.; Naples, 1969), 161–208

PREVENIER, W., and BLOCKMANS, W., *The Burgundian Netherlands* (Cambridge, 1986).

PRIZER, W. F., 'Music and Ceremonial in the Low Countries: Philip the Fair and the Order of the Golden Fleece', *Early Music History*, 5 (1985), 113–53.

REESE, G., *Music in the Renaissance* (rev. edn., New York, 1959).

ROSS, R. D., 'Toward a Theory of Tonal Coherence: The Motets of Jacob Obrecht', *Musical Quarterly*, 69 (1981), 143–64.

SALOP, A., 'The Masses of Jacob Obrecht (1450–1505): Structure and Style' (Ph.D. diss., Indiana University, 1959).

—— 'Jacob Obrecht and the Early Development of Harmonic Polyphony', *Journal of the American Musicological Society*, 17 (1964), 288–309.

SCHULER, M., 'Der Personalstatus der Konstanzer Domkantorei um 1500', *Archiv für Musikwissenschaft*, 21 (1964), 255–86.

SCHWEIGER, H., 'Archivalische Notizen zur Hofkantorei Maximilians I.', *Zeitschrift für Musikwissenschaft*, 14 (1932), 363–74.

SCOTT, M., *The History of Dress Series: Late Gothic Europe, 1400–1500* (London, 1980).

SLIM, H. C., *The Prodigal Son at the Whores'—Music, Art, and Drama* (Distinguished Faculty Lecture, 1975–6, University of California, Irvine).

SLOOTMANS, C., *Jan metten Lippen: Zijn familie en zijn stad; een geschiedenis der Bergen-op-Zoomsche heeren van Glymes* (Rotterdam, 1945).

SMIJERS, A., 'Twee onbekende motetteksten van Jacob Hobrecht', *Tijdschrift der Vereeniging voor Nederlandsche Muziekgeschiedenis*, 16 (1941), 133–4.

—— 'De Missa Carminum van Jacob Hobrecht', *Tijdschrift voor Muziekweten-schap*, 17 (1951), 192–4.

SMITS VAN WAESBERGHE, J., *Herbeni Traiectensis De natura cantus ac miraculis vocis* (Beiträge zur rheinischen Musikgeschichte, 22; Cologne, 1957).

SPARKS, E. H., *Cantus Firmus in Mass and Motet, 1420–1520* (Berkeley and Los Angeles, 1963).

—— 'Obrecht, Jacob', *The New Grove Dictionary of Music and Musicians*, xiii. 477–85.

STAEHELIN, M., 'Möglichkeiten und praktische Anwendung der Verfasserbestim-mung an anonymen Kompositionen der Josquin-Zeit', *Tijdschrift van de Ver-eniging voor Nederlandse Muziekgeschiedenis*, 23 (1973), 79–91.

—— 'Obrechtiana', *Tijdschrift van de Vereniging voor Nederlandse Muziekgeschie-denis*, 25/1 (1975), 1–37.

STROHM, R., *Music in Late Medieval Bruges* (Oxford, 1985; rev. edn., Oxford, 1990).

—— review of *NOE* 7, *Notes*, 47 (1990), 552–4.

—— 'The Close of the Middle Ages', in J. W. McKinnon (ed.), *Man & Music: Antiquity and the Middle Ages* (Basingstoke and London, 1990).

—— *The Rise of European Music, 1380–1500* (Cambridge, 1993).

STRUNK, O., 'Origins of the "L'homme armé" Mass', in *Essays on Music in the Western World* (New York, 1974), 68–9.

TARUSKIN, R., 'Antoine Busnoys and the *L'Homme Armé* Tradition', *Journal of the American Musicological Society*, 39 (1986), 255–93.

THIBAULT, G., 'L'Oratoire du château de Montreuil-Bellay: Ses anges musi-ciens — son motet polyphonique', in *Memorie e contributi alla musica dal Medioevo all'età moderna offerti a F. Ghisi nel settantesimo compleanno (1901–1971)* (*Quadrivium*, 12; Bologna, 1971), i. 209–23.

THOMAS, B., *The New Historicism and Other Old-Fashioned Topics* (Princeton, NJ, 1991).

TINCTORIS, J., *Opera theoretica*, ed. A. Seay (Corpus scriptorum de musica, 22; American Institute of Musicology, 1975 and 1978).

TODD, R. L., 'Retrograde, Inversion, Retrograde-Inversion, and Related Tech-niques in the Masses of Jacobus Obrecht', *Musical Quarterly*, 64 (1978), 50–78.

URSPRUNG, O., 'Alte griechische Einflüsse und neuer gräzistischer Einschlag in der mittelalterlichen Musik', *Zeitschrift für Musikwissenschaft*, 12 (1929–30), 193–219.

VANDER LINDEN, H., *Itinéraires de Marie de Bourgogne et de Maximilien d'Autriche (1477–1482)* (Brussels, 1934).

VANDER STRAETEN, E., *La Musique aux Pays-Bas avant le XIXe siècle* (Brussels, 1867–88).

VAN WERVEKE, H., *De Gentse stadsrekeningen in de middeleeuwen* (Brussels, 1934).

VAUGHAN, R., *Philip the Good: The Apogee of Burgundy* (London, 1970).

—— *Charles the Bold: The Last Valois Duke of Burgundy* (London, 1973).

VEESER, H. A. (ed.), *The New Historicism* (New York and London, 1989).

VELLEKOOP, K., 'Zusammenhänge zwischen Text und Zahl in der Kompositionsart Jacob Obrechts: Analyse der Motette *Parce Domine*', *Tijdschrift van de Vereniging voor Nederlandse Muziekgeschiedenis*, 20 (1966), 97–119.

VENTE, M. A. (ed.), *Bouwstenen voor een geschiedenis der toonkunst in de Nederlanden*, iii (Amsterdam, 1980).

VERSTRAETEN, F., *De Gentse Sint-Jacobsparochie* (Ghent, 1976).

VLAM, C. C., and VENTE, M. A. (eds.), *Bouwstenen voor een geschiedenis der toonkunst in de Nederlanden*, i (Utrecht, 1965), ii (Amsterdam, 1971).

WARD, T. R., 'Another Mass by Obrecht?', *Tijdschrift van de Vereniging voor Nederlandse Muziekgeschiedenis*, 27 (1977), 102–8.

WATHEY, A. B., 'Isoperiodic Technique in "Cantus Firmus" Organisation, *c*.1400–*c*.1475' (Research Paper, St Edmund Hall, Oxford, 1979).

WAURIN, J. de, *Recueil des croniques et anchiennes istories de la Grant Bretaigne, a present nomme Engleterre*, ed. W. Hardy, v (London, 1891).

WEERBECKE, G. van, *Missa Princesse d'amourettes*, ed. W. Elders (Exempla musica neerlandica, 8; Utrecht, 1974).

WEGMAN, R. C., 'Music and Musicians at the Guild of Our Lady at Bergen op Zoom, *c*.1470–1510', *Early Music History*, 9 (1989), 175–249.

—— 'Concerning Tempo in the English Polyphonic Mass, *c*.1420–70', *Acta musicologica*, 61 (1989), 40–65.

—— 'Another "Imitation" of Busnoys' *Missa L'Homme armé*—And Some Observations on *Imitatio* in Renaissance Music', *Journal of the Royal Musical Association*, 114 (1989), 189–202.

—— 'Another Mass by Busnoys?', *Music & Letters*, 71 (1990), 1–19.

—— Letter to the Editor, *Music & Letters*, 71 (1990), 633–5.

—— 'Petrus de Domarto's *Missa Spiritus almus* and the Early History of the Four-Voice Mass in the Fifteenth Century', *Early Music History*, 10 (1990), 235–303.

—— 'The Anonymous Mass *D'ung aultre amer*: A Late Fifteenth-Century Experiment', *Musical Quarterly*, 75 (1991), 566–94.

—— review of M. R. Maniates, *The Combinative Chanson: An Anthology* (Madison, Wis., 1989), *Music & Letters*, 72 (1991), 510–13.

—— 'Het "Jacob Hobrecht" portret: Enkele biografische observaties', *Musica Antiqua*, 8 (1991), 152–4.

WHITE, H., *The Content of the Form: Narrative Discourse and Historical Representation* (Baltimore and London, 1987).

WILS, J., *Matricule de l'Université de Louvain*, ii (Brussels, 1946).

WINTERNITZ, E., 'On Angel Concerts in the 15th Century: A Critical Approach to Realism and Symbolism in Sacred Painting', *Musical Quarterly*, 49 (1963), 450–63.

WOLFF, H. C., *Die Musik der alten Niederländer (15. und 16. Jahrhundert)* (Leipzig, 1956).

WOODLEY, R., 'Tinctoris's Italian Translation of the Golden Fleece Statutes: A Text and a (Possible) Context', *Early Music History*, 8 (1988), 173–244.

WRIGHT, C., 'Musiciens à la cathédrale de Cambrai', *Revue de musicologie*, 62 (1976), 204–28.

——'Performance Practices at the Cathedral of Cambrai 1475–1550', *Musical Quarterly*, 64 (1978), 295–328.

ZILVERBERG, S. B. J., *David van Bourgondië: Bisschop van Terwaan en van Utrecht (± 1427–1496)* (Groningen, 1951).

Index of Compositions by Obrecht

Page numbers in *italics* refer to illustrations.

GENERAL INDEX

Page numbers in *italics* refer to illustrations.